RATIONAL PSYCHOLOGY

HISTORY OF PSYCHOLOGY SERIES

GENERAL INTRODUCTION

The historically interesting works reprinted in this series helped to prepare the way for the science of psychology. Most of these books are long forgotten, but their relevance to the field is unmistakable. Many of the writings on mental and moral philosophy, published before the dawn of scientific procedures, have much to commend them to present-day scholars. These books serve as groundwork for a fuller account of the background from which the field emerged, and they should be attractive to students who seek in the past for hints of the future direction that certain types of research can take. Each work will have an Introduction stating the provenance and significance of the book and will add appropriate biographical information.

ROBERT I. WATSON
General Editor

University of New Hampshire

RATIONAL PSYCHOLOGY

(1849)

BY LAURENS PERSEUS HICKOK

A FACSIMILE REPRODUCTION
WITH AN INTRODUCTION
BY ERNEST HARMS

SCHOLARS' FACSIMILES & REPRINTS
DELMAR, NEW YORK
1973

RATIONAL PSYCHOLOGY

A FACSIMILE RE-EDITION PUBLISHED BY·

SCHOLARS' FACSIMILES & REPRINTS, INC.,

P.O. BOX 344, DELMAR, NEW YORK 12054

© 1973 SCHOLARS' FACSIMILES & REPRINTS, INC.

PRINTED IN THE UNITED STATES OF AMERICA

Library of Congress Cataloging in Publication Data

Hickok, Laurens Perseus, 1789-1888.
Rational psychology (1849).

(History of psychology series)
1. Psychology. I. Title.
BF111.H6   1973   150   72-13798
ISBN 0-8201-1117-1

INTRODUCTION

LAURENS PERSEUS HICKOK (1798-1888), once president of Union College, Schenectady, New York, and author of the first major textbook on psychology—in addition to six other books—is one of the forgotten great men in American scientific history. In the *Dictionary of American Biography*, Ernest Sutherland Bates designated him as "unquestionably the ablest American dialectician of his day" and "his *Rational Psychology* is the first profound treatment of epistemology that has come from any American pen since Jonathan Edwards." Morris Cohen has called him "easily the foremost figure in American philosophy between the time of Jonathan Edwards and the period of the Civil War." A. A. Roback, in his *History of American Psychology*, has drawn the quintessence: "There was a modern ring to many of his expressions and it is he who probably for the first time employed such terms as 'introspection,' 'psychographic,' and 'conditioned' in the psychological sense; and if posterity has not given him his due, it is through no fault of his own." This re-edition of his masterwork will help to make good this default, and not only for Hickok's sake, but also because he seems to have sown seeds which may prove to be still of considerable importance for the future of American psychology.

L. P. Hickok was born in Bethel, Connecticut, in 1798, the son of a well-to-do farmer. Quite alert and active from his youth, he opened, while still in high school, a small tutoring school. At the age of 20 he entered Union College, from which he was graduated in 1820. The years around the beginning of the nineteenth century were the busiest for Eliphalet Nott, who served as president of Union College for more than sixty years. Nott's approach was to unify general theological Christian concepts and synchronize them into the same academic and speculative frame with the teaching of physical and other basic sciences. These ideas seem to have seeded new concepts in Hickok's mind.

We have no information about why, upon returning to his home town, he announced his intention to become a minister. He studied privately with two local theologians and became ordained in Kent, Connecticut, in 1824. After five years he moved to Litchfield, where he seems to have been a successful pastor until 1836. There are reports of his temper-

v

mental nature. But at the same time we read of his success as a clergy-man. He seems already at the time to have achieved fame as a speaker, being rather frequently called upon to address various public gather-ings. This seems to have been the main reason he was called as pro-fessor of theology to Western Reserve College in 1836, and from there to Auburn Theological Seminary in 1844. At the time he had already reached a status of prominence as demonstrated by the honorary D.D. degree conferred upon him by Hamilton College.

At his installation in the chair of Christian Theology at Auburn, Hickok gave an address which evidenced the originality of his thought. He had selected as his topic "Theology as a Science." It seems this was the fruit of Nott's inspiration to depart from a merely descriptive and clerically didactic theology and instead to try to apply scientific prin-ciples as developed by natural sciences of his day to the field of theology. The essence of his presentation was that a real science of theology could be established only if laws and principles were applied to the perceived facts. This meant that statements contained in religious documents ought to be collated and systematized. We find here a sentence which seems unique in the history of theology: "Theology as a science requires this combination of facts within their principles," denoting as principles "Ritual, Doctrine, and Spirituality."

However, this attempt at scientification of theology could not have made it possible for him to accept theology to a degree that he could have attempted to teach it. This scientification alone, however, did not seem to satisfy the searching of his mind. He was continually driven by a profound urge to deepen and detail basic scientific orientation. In 1845, we see him proceeding in a slow and very definite development aiming at further clarification. In 1846 Hickok spoke at Hamilton Col-lege on "Intellectual Development in Its Spontaneity and Its Liberty." Here he speculated in philosophical areas far from theological and theistic determinations. He moved here in the biological geneticism of man. As the seed originated the plant, so the mind is the inner germ of man. All that man is and becomes originates from his inner disposition. He must unfold his intellectual capabilities. There is a necessary syste-matic development. All intellectual development must be based upon liberty and can only be attained where liberty for it can be established. Such establishment is the first principle of mental cultivation. Hickok no longer spoke as a theologian, but as a philosopher involved in thorough research into the problems of the motivations of human existence. Indeed, Hickok must at that time have been deeply involved in the preparation of *Rational Psychology*.

During the next two years, Hickok presented two addresses which show very clearly the formation of a specific scientific point of view. In 1847 he spoke at Middlebury College about the "Idea of Humanity." He moved on from biological and individual genesis to the aspect of genesis and fate of humanity. Humanity, as he styled it—today we would say "society"—is endowed not only with its own wants but primarily with its perceptions which cause its social actions and their consummations. The spiritual laws are the guides for the human family to its own perfection. Clearly, it was sociological thinking that was presented here.

The next year, 1848, Hickok returned with an address aimed at the theologians of his alma mater, Union College. His topic was "The Complete Christian." His thesis was "the perfect christification of human life," which he simply wanted.to be called the Christian life. Five major aspects of operation with which such a life ought to concern itself are enumerated: the intellectual, the sentimental, the esthetical, the ethical, and finally the truly religious. We are indeed presented here with a rather complete covering of the total human behavioral spectrum, viewed specifically from a psychological point of view. Hickok presented himself here as a perfect representative of the psychological horizon of human existence.

The concept and contents of this address appeared to be very much in accord with Eliphalet Nott's thinking. Because of this it may be easy to understand that in the same year Nott started a correspondence with Hickok pertaining to his return to Union College. We do not know how much Nott knew of Hickok's preparation of his *Rational Psychology*. It must at that time have been near completion and perhaps already in print. But we have a certain right to assume that Hickok must have mentioned or discussed his first major publication with his former teacher. We are told that the correspondence between the two men regarding Hickok's appointment to the staff of Union College lasted for three years. In 1852 Laurens P. Hickok finally assumed the position as professor of Mental and Moral Philosophy and a vice president of Union College.

Rational Psychology appeared in 1849, published by Derby, Miller and Co. at Auburn. Hickok titled himself "Professor of Christian Theology in the Theological Seminary at Auburn." The first edition com-

viii

prised xi and 717 pages. The subtitle clearly and simply expressed the book's intention: "The Subjective Idea and Objective Law of All Intelligence." In an attempt to phrase it in present scientific language one might say that it tries to offer the empirical contents of our world of experience and its description and evaluation by intellectual means. One could in our scientific language designate it as speculative psychology.

From the beginning, Hickok left no doubt as to his scientific position. The first sentence of the book reads: "Psychology is the Science of the Mind." And this is followed by the statement that "Empirical Psychology attains the facts of mind and arranges them into a system." The Rational Psychology "starts out rationale of experience itself in the necessary and universal principles which must be conditional for all facts of a possible experience." This sets the course for what Hickok justifiably designated as an Ontology of Psychology. However, first we are guided through what he called the "groundwork of psychology." This is a chapter of definitions and terminology. We have to familiarize ourselves with a set of concepts rather different from our present terminology. We learn to know Hickok's concept of truth and true science and his meanings of inductive and transcendental science. Then we are presented with what Hickok considers the special psychological faculties. We are dealing here with senses, understanding, and reason. This makes it evident that we are offered here a set system. This is one of the threefold psychological concepts reigning everywhere during the nineteenth century. The composition of the book in its main contents is a minute and detailed presentation of this system of threefold faculties.

The major part of the book is the section entitled "The Sense." Today we would speak of the senses and would designate chapter one as being on sense perception. Hickok divided his sense perception into external and internal. The latter, in turn, is divided into organ sensations, emotions, and imaginations. After the first stock-taking, considerable space is given to a discussion of judgment as the major regulatory tool of cognition.

There are few authors in the philosophical or psychological literature who have attempted a rigorous, systematic presentation similar to Hickok's. "Subjective Idea and Objective Law" are his basic principles. He follows them rigorously throughout the work. Accordingly he started out with a description of the "sense in its subjective idea." Space and time are the basic modes of appearance of the perceived phenomenon. Motion creates the variety of forms in which they occur. Hickok calls primitive intuition, the way space and time are experienced, as pure form. In this way they are the basic conditions of the human mind. Through this theoretical concept Hickok places himself somehow between Kant and Aristotle. He denies the Kantian "Ding-an Sich" on the one hand and Aristotelian absolutism on the other. He replaced them with a psychologically perceivable intuition. As further operational modes he assimilates categories in the Kantian style. However, there is another rather un-Kantian factor basic to the human mind. It is the ability of coordinating which he designates as the "self-sameness" of experiencing. Today we might call it the unity of self-consciousness. For Hickok it is experienced by primitive intuiton. It is also the factor by which Hickok believes he overcomes the limitation of the Kantian metaphysic. What he described up to this point as the mechanism of human consciousness, Hickok designated as the subjective faculties of the sense.

Next Hickok is led to the presentation of what he called "the idea of the empirical intuition." In accordance with his phenomenological position, he denies a speculative approach for empirical experience by way of abstraction. Instead he tries a descriptive approach which he called anticipation. He deduces his concepts from the Greek concept of *prolepsis* which operates on the basis of "distinction." In developing his system of categories, Hickok applied an adjusted kind of Hegelian dialectic. He sets, for instance, non-appearance against appearance, attempting in this way to define reality. There is an extraordinary kind of psychological sequence developed. For instance, the concept of discrimination results from the insight into the concept of particularity which in turn leads to that of different quality. Continuing in this way his system of concepts, we meet heterogeneous versus homogeneous, intensive versus extensive, or protensive diversity versus unity, plurality versus totality, intensivity versus extensivity, and solidity versus variety. Almost nothing like this has ever been attempted in the history of psychology. But we may compare these categories of speculation with J. P. Guilford's categories of thinking offered a few years ago. At the end of this chapter Hickok offers a final summing-up which ought to be specially noted: "Sensation must be discriminated in observation and thereby given distinct quality as the matter—and this distinct quality must be constructed in attention, and thereby given definite quantity as the form of the phenomenon" (p. 265).

In this way Hickok considered the tools given for the actual observation and establishment of the world as we observe it. In his own language he expressed it "as subject to our sense." For this scientific confirmation, however, there has to be added their establishment by "objective law." This means the laws according to which our sense perception operates.

Again we have here to follow Hickok's synthetic manner of presentation which is basic to his approach. First he defined the concept of science in general and then the specific, inductive kind.

As the most basic law of all, Hickok established what he calls "the Colligation of Facts." It means that all phenomena of the reality of our experience must in some way be interrelated. Without such an interaction, existence as it is and as it appears, would not be possible. The world does not appear disintegrated but as a whole.

The detailed presentation of the objective laws starts with the elaboration of the distinction between the quantitative and qualitative. After going through the categorical law setting, presented above in great detail, Hickok turns to the obscurity, deceptive appearance, and relativity of lawful perception. We find astonishing insight into facts which, decades later, experimental psychology made the object of observation and research.

One of his basic terms, "consilience," introduced here, has been dropped from newer theoretical scientific discussions. However Hickok gave it considerable attention. It means specific kinds of "scientific crutches" like hypotheses which he believed ought to be intensively applied in rational psychology. He wishes to determine clearly and specifically that which the approach to formulated laws can offer as secure results. Finally he introduced what today we might call the philosophical and typological implications in the approach to truth and reality. Whether one approaches the ascertained facts from a materialistic, idealistic, or Pyrrhonistic point-of-view will basically change the "objective law" picture we will receive.

The next part of the book is devoted to the second major function of *Rational Psychology*, that of Understanding. Hickok proceeded again according to the principles of composition he has laid down in the beginning. He first presents the subjective idea, the actual substance of understanding, and then the objective law aspect, which governs our understanding. The actual position of understanding is first presented. This is his concept: "Sense perception gives us the phenomena only as individual facts. Understanding through thinking shows us the interconnections of phenomena as they function around us as reality." The most basic a priori elements of understanding again are space and time. They require the most detailed analysis of the specificity of their functioning. Space, we are told, is the all-prevailing, immense, and absolute permanence. The problems of time are perpetuity, succession, and simultaneousness. The essential elements in experience for space are substance and accidence; for time, source and event. In such a way all elements of the categorical system mentioned above are treated similarly.

The concept of understanding, as Hickok has presented it here, allows us to speak of the universality of nature. It offers a sound basis for a concept of a universe which is a whole and which is able to accept into itself all experiences which can fall into the frame of our consciousness. Basic principles for this aspect are 1) substance as ground and source, 2) cause as conditioning change, and 3) reciprocity as concomitance which is coincidental.

The basic factors representing the *objective laws* regarding understanding concentrate on location. From the whole of space and time come the particular conditioning of certain space locations and timely specifications of a certain moment. Tackled realistically, the immediate experience of space calls in the first place for an understanding of human visional perspection and of all the problems and implications which go with it. Only this can free us from the subjectivity of our own experience. This means the momentary follow-up of viewed phenomena. We are induced to the search for scientific coordinates for the understanding of the appearance of the phenomena as regards space and time. Such personal establishment and insight into the ordered sequence of factors of time prove to be evident postulates of orientation and security in the flow of our constantly changing existence.

The final part of the volume offers a psychological discussion of the concept of Reason. Hickok designates it as "the last and highest faculty of man." What the senses perceive and understanding judges is here made into a demonstratable science. First we are presented with what Hickok understands under the subjective idea of reason. Basically reason means the demonstration of the absolute. The concept of the absolute itself is the basic reality of the human self or personality which can only be conceived as space and timeless. Personality is viewed as having three fundamental qualities: pure spontaneity, pure autonomy, and pure liberty. Only by the aid of reason are we enabled to comprehend an absolute personality without which the concept of human existence would be impossible.

The completion of the volume consists of the presentation of Reason in its objective laws. For a proper comprehension of human existence we need a personality concept which we can separate into a real and an absolute one. We need to be able to separate the material animal sphere of existence and the ethical world of man. The latter connects him with the theistic world. We have to designate the real world as the world of human existence with its appetite, complacency, and play-impulses. There are five factors of the realistic human personality to deal with. They are the aesthetical, the mathematical, the philosophical, the psychological, and the ethical. The ethical impulses stand above all others because they establish the individual as a personality in the community. As the ultimate concept Hickok tried to establish that of an absolute personality. It is based upon the idea of our being able to comprehend the total operation of man's total nature. This is not only his physical one but also includes his ethical world. It means a demonstrative science of a universal humanity combined with the universality of nature. This is the final aspect of Hickok's *Rational Psychology*.

We have offered here an interpretive overview of the book's main contents; firstly to facilitate the reading of the volume. There are a large number of unfamiliar and reinterpreted terms which are apt to make the study of the volume rather difficult. Although its stringent architecture is a helpful guide, the language and uncommon manner of interpretation will be made easier if the reader is given a mental survey map of the author's train of thought. For most psychologists the book will seem to be a speculative philosophy and phenomenology. Its psychological investigation is not based, as is the style of the late nineteenth century, upon inductive reasoning or experimentation. We must not forget that Hickok's work is not psychology of our age; it must therefore be accepted with considerable reservations. We must keep in mind that the book appeared just before the middle of the nineteenth century when theology made its last attempts to throttle the scientific mind by theological authority. Hickok was not only aware of these events but was also an ardent crusader for progressive change of the basic scientific position even in regard to the didactic of theology. In viewing this transition Hickok realized that the acknowledgment of psychology as a science which could replace theology gave a justification to this field and a speculative interpretation of it had to be worked out. Hickok tried to offer this justification and speculative interpretation in his *Rational Psychology*. Such speculative confirmation of the basic concepts and problems of the empirical psychic realities of man's range of experiencing was, to him, essential for any scientific occupation with psychology. If we look from this viewpoint into the minds of the vanguards of experimental psychology, for instance Gustav Theodor Fechner (1801-1887), we will find an almost desperate insecurity in regard to this problem. Fechner today is called an oddity and a poet. But if we turn to the giant of early psychological experimentation, Hermann von Helmholtz (1821-1894), we not only find him confessing in his major work, *Psychological Optik* (1856-66), the total absence of the proper establishment of scientific principles for psychology, but even, in his last years, seriously struggling with this problem. From a wider, historical point of view, it was a fortunate mistake that psychology chose physiology for a scientific background and did not start until the turn of the century to try to develop an autonomic scientific basis in a transition from physiology. The few who tried earlier or at the same time, like Hickok, to establish a speculative or phenomenological psychology, as for instance the ingenuous German psychologist Friedrich Eduard Beneke (1798-1854), suffered the same fate of having been thoroughly forgotten and having to be rediscovered in our times.

Hickok is actually one of a few, in the historical development of psychology, who saw this transitional problem quite clearly. He went ahead fearlessly and tried to solve it. In our didactic language one might speak of a philosophy of psychology or of its propaedeutic. In this pedagogical sense a *rational psychology* was still valid in the academic areas of Germany at the start of the century. Before a student was allowed to go ahead with his specialized study he had to take "orientation courses" such as philosophy and logic, theory of science, and occasionally an introductory course in psychology. This represented, in a wider range, what was on Hickok's mind in composing *Rational Psychology*.

Historians have found it difficult to place Hickok in any traditional lines. To relate him to Jonathan Edwards (1703-1758), as has been tried, leads far afield. Some have tried to tie him to the German tradition of idealism, pointing at Hegel. However, this also fails. De facto, he represents a most unusual position by himself. But one can see in him a definite representation of a functional psychological tendency which becomes internationally common after the middle of the century, of which he is actually a forerunner. It is the three-way divided tendency, viewing the human psyche as functioning on the basis of thinking, feeling, and will with a coordinating ego of self in the background. Most European psychologies, not only the German, but also for instance that of the Dane, Harald Hoeffding, were conceived in this way. One can point to John Dewey in this country and his psychology of 1887 which comprised three elements. Hickok applied this three fold aspect in various directions, as for instance in the division of sense, understanding, and reason. This entire concept has been almost completely abandoned in our present American psychology.

Hickok apparently was very conscious of the uniqueness of his attempt. There is ample evidence of his having been well informed by reading of the history of philosophy and psychology. We find him very aware of being the inventor of a unique terminology and of transforming the meaning of terms used by others to his own interpretation and meaning. We mentioned above A. A. Roback's brief treatment of Hickok in his *History of American Psychology* where he points to the fact that there are a number of terms existing in present-day psychology, the invention of which can be traced to Hickok. One could easily multiply by three the number Roback mentions. One could further point to a number of concepts, later applied intensively, like "Gestalt" and "Totality." However, such traces would lead far beyond the frame of this introduction. Similar factors also play a secondary role in the concept of this book. The major issue for Hickok was a total and complete coverage of what a rational basis of psychology meant. In his later books this aspect apparently became increasingly the essential problem and task. We meet here a strict and very consequent execution of a speculative organization coined into a theoretical system. Such a speculative order of things was Hickok's main desire. Once again we should point to the basic pattern of presenting the subject matter of a specific field phenomenologically only to have this complemented with the objective laws deductible for the same area. Such a systematic presentation continues through the entire work and represents the most specific of Hickok's entire scientific makeup. This remarkable manner of presentation could not be emphasized enough. There are few books in the history of psychology which offer such an extraordinarily well organized presentation.

When Hickok came to Union College in 1852, his major contribution to his new task was *Rational Psychology*. This book created a considerable sensation. There was a small group of philosophers who hailed its importance but there was a much larger group, especially clergymen, who attacked it intensively. Two or three reprints of the first edition must have appeared between 1849 and 1854. Hickok apparently intended to use *Rational Psychology* as his major teaching tool. However, it seems that the book was not well received by the students of Union College. Its acceptance as a textbook was hampered by its length and intensive speculative elaboration. In 1861 a revised edition appeared which was 200 pages shorter. When one examines this new edition, one finds much of the detailed elaboration cut out in favor of a streamlining for college use. It is simplified in many respects: long explanations are shortened, extensive explanations are dropped. Hickok compromised with the learning ability of the Union College student. Comparing the two texts we cannot help but feel that the first edition, reprinted here, has by far more of an original brillance of speculation which has been greatly diminished in the later textbook edition. The text edition underwent two more reprintings but remained unchanged.

After this new text edition appeared, a strong wave of attacks arose against it in the theological periodicals of he United States. *The Bilbiotheca Sacra* (April 1859), *The Princeton Review* (October 1861), and the *American Theological Review* (July 1861) carried the brunt of these attacks. There were accusations of heresy, pantheism, disrespect of the church and clerical professions, illogicality, and similar negativism, even though Hickok had clearly spoken against pantheism and had denied the unreligious character of his concepts. One of the most negative attackers was Edwin Hall who had been a professor of theology at Hickok's former college of Auburn. He even distributed pamphlets against him with accusations of pantheism. Hickok replied in a tempered way with lengthy, repetitious statements made previously and adjusted to the adverse criticisms. But nowhere was there any indication that these attacks influenced or caused any changes in his position.

After Hickok joined Union College, according to the College Report of January 1853, he immediately revised and intensified the instruction in metaphysics, as in those days the philosophical and psychological disciplines were called. After acting for a few years as vice president he became acting president of the college, which at that time was the largest academic institution in the United States. Reports tell of the controversial temperaments of the blunt and "realistic administrator" and the hot-headed and seriously ailing president, Eliphalet Nott. Hickok in his sobriety and realism kept things going. In spite of this load of practical work he continued to develop his total scientific concept by writing one volume after another.

In 1853 he authored a book entitled *A System of Moral Science*. It shows not only his originality but also his attempt to serve the practical needs of teaching.

In the first sentence Hickok emphasized that "it is the purpose of the book to bind by law all facts into an orderly system" and that in this "moral science that had to find its principles within the spiritual part of man's being." He finally felt it necessary to emphasize that he wanted to present "a textbook for college study for his own use in instruction."

Since our purpose remains to familiarize ourselves with the personality of the author of *Rational Psycholgy* this book on moral behavior which immediately follows *Rational Psychology* seems to reveal more than does anything else. For Hickok moral science was not a set of rules of a categorical character. Nor was it a moral epithet derived from religious settings. Moral science was conceived by him as a behavioral system on an ego-psychological basis. There is, of course, the theoretical scientific frame of ethical concepts, but for him in the center stands the teaching of a system of self-formulated duties which represent the duties toward mankind. They start with personal duties of self-control: "Not doing harm to oneself, and exercising control over body and spirit." Self-culture follows as a growing in stature, knowledge and wisdom." There is further the set of duties toward others, such as kindness and respect. Finally there is the duty toward nature and lastly toward God. The entire basis of this moral science is the intensive development of the ethical qualities of the individual. Upon these fundamentals—in a wider psychological frame—can be built a set of concepts of various forms and degrees of authority, civil and social behavior pattern as well as authority relationships toward the divine and the family. This unusual concept of a set of inner rules for human existence—his main thesis—is emphasized as being executed by man's rationality. It is the rationality which he had made it his task to present in his *Rational Psychology*. Factually this rationality is for him the sum of human existence. One gets the proper aspect of the central role of his *Rational Psychology* if one sees it as the background for all his wider concepts about the entire human existence as it is presented in this volume on human ethical behavior.

Already in *Rational Psychology* Hickok has mentioned the aspect of an empirical point of view in psychology (p. 17), presenting so to speak phenomenologically, the psychological sphere of empirical experiences of man. In 1854, a year after the appearance of *A System of Moral Science*, he presented his *Empirical Psychology*, with the subtitle "The Human Mind as given in Consciousness." The book itself complements *Rational Psychology*. He not only carries out this complementing task but also presents a new unique pattern of psychology characteristic of him. He emphasizes that this *Empirical Psychology* has a rather descriptive character and not a philosophical one. He designates it as a "psychography" and not as psychology. He rejects any determination from the physical or physiological point of view. Although he mentions and is aware of the experimental aspect which became basic for psychology in its later development, he did not realize the importance of experimentalism. He did not see any need for its application for mediating the psychological facts and their teaching. He emphasized distinctly that empirical psychology can rely educationally upon verbal statement and definition. As methods of learning and assimilation of the empirical psychological facts, he emphasized for the student to develop the "habit" of "introspection." Hickok realized with amazing clarity, in regard to scientific methodology, a method which for a hundred years, had been viewed as an invalid scientific method of psychology. Hickok's *Empirical Psychology* is in this respect as unique as his *Rational Psychology*. It is one of the few attempts of a psychological textbook based upon introspection as an academic method. In his *Empirical Psychology* Hickok presents a long introduction on what he considers the introspective method to be and how it ought to be applied. This chapter is unique in American psychology. Today, of course, Hickok's "introspection" would be considered self-observation and checking of psychological experiences. For instance, he discusses not only the different ways of phenomenological description, but also the variety of interrelationships between the observed phenomena. From this introspective point of view he develops a kind of categorical scheme about the relationship of the phenomenologically established facts. Finally, the variety of problems of classification, harmonization, and systematization are carefully treated. What today's reader may miss in the scientific justification of *Rational Psychology* is presented here now and is explained accordingly. One could call this *Empirical Psychology* the key to a more modern understanding of *Rational Psychology*.

In the way in which present psychological concepts proceed, one would expect that this *Empirical Psychology* would have been written before the *Rational Psychology*. In the genesis of Hickok's development, however, in the way in which he was coming to psychology from theology, it must be understood that the rational establishment of a scientific approach to the psychological world of experience had to come first. However, the first page of *Rational Psychology* evidences that the concepts of *Empirical Psychology* and probably to a considerable degree the contents itself was already in his mind when he began writing *Rational Psychology*.

There can be no doubt that such an *Empirical Psychology* was the primary topic as a teaching subject at Union College. Empiricism was the basic scientific concept and most essential to the new interest in natural science as it was advanced and nurtured at Union, especially after Hickok's arrival. Actually he had probably to experiment himself with this empiricism in his approach to teaching psychology. There are several editions of *Empirical Psychology* which show his attempts to become more and more adjusted to this actual new teaching task. There is, for instance, an 1859 edition subtitled "for the use of colleges and academies." A later edition (1887) was issued in collaboration with Hickok's nephew Julius H. Seelye, president of Amherst College. It is subtitled "Science of the Mind from Experience." It shows a completely new coinage according to the status of empirical conception in the sense of natural science of those days. It is clearly expressed here that empirical psychology as an empirical science was to be considered the "door which leads to the rational point of view." *Rational Psychology* had lost its primary role.

However, in regard to Hickok's own personal growth and development his *Rational Psychology* remained his intimate personal standpoint which was that of a speculative rational approach. Four years after the first edition of *Empirical Psychology*, Appleton & Co. published Hickok's *Rational Cosmology* (1858). From the scientific point of view common at that time, this should simply have been a philosophy of science. It sums up the theoretical essentials of the major scientific fields. From Hickok's viewpoint, however, it became a "cosmology," rather unempirical and predominantly a speculative review of the current status of the theories of the sciences. This work was the most rejected and severely attacked of all of Hickok's books. It ran against the tendency of factual empiricism and was criticized for being written from an unobjective, ultraconservative point-of-view passing over scientific insight and newly formulated concepts.

After this unpleasant experience, Hickok refrained from publication for a decade and a half. There were also the years during which he carried a heavy load as acting president of Union College. Reports from the history of the college tell of the severity of this task, and his struggles with adversaries. However, we also here how greatly he was liked by his students.

After serving as president of Union for only two years (1866-68), Hickok retired and moved to Amherst into the company of his nephew and collaborator. In retirement he returned to his writing. In 1872 he produced two volumes: *Creator and Creation* (Boston: Lee & Shepard) and *Humanity Immortal* (Boston: Lee & Shepard). In 1875 his last book, *Logic of Reason*, was published by Lee & Shepard. If one wishes to characterize these books which have a similar theoretical basis, one ought to classify them as rational metaphysics. However, they fall into line with Hickok's earlier works as reflecting basic rationalistic concepts. All of Hickok's works appear like a symphony, intonated with the great and powerful accord of his *Rational Psychology*.

ERNEST HARMS

New York City

LAURENS PERSEUS HICKOK
(1798–1888)
Philosopher, Presbyterian clergyman
Courtesy Schaffer Library, Union College

RATIONAL PSYCHOLOGY:

OR

THE SUBJECTIVE IDEA AND THE OBJECTIVE LAW OF ALL INTELLIGENCE,

BY

LAURENS P. HICKOK, D. D.

PROFESSOR OF CHRISTIAN THEOLOGY IN THE THEOLOGICAL SEMINARY OF AUBURN.

AUBURN:
DERBY, MILLER & COMPANY.
1849.

H. OLIPHANT, PRINTER, AUBURN.

PREFACE.

"It is neither necessary nor possible that all men should be PHILOSOPHERS." A spontaneous intelligence begins in childhood, and is altogether absorbed in the experience of the varied phenomena of the senses. In this respect, most men perpetuate their childhood through life and never rise above a spontaneous intelligence. They perceive that which appears in the light of the common consciousness, and deduce more or less practical conclusions from experience; but a few minds only of a generation turn themselves back upon consciousness itself, and reflect upon what and how experience must be, and make the conditioning principles of all intelligence the subject of patient and profound investigation. The capability to rise into the higher light of a purely philosophical consciousness, and become familiar with *a priori** principles and transcendental demonstrations, depends so entirely upon the free energizing of the spiritual and the self-controlling of the rational in man, that it becomes a vain hope to find but few in an age to whom such a position is attainable, and for whom such exercises in pure thought possess any interest. No one, who would explain the process or present the results of his investigation in this field, should expect the

---

* There has been occasion to use this Latin phrase so frequently, that for typographical convenience it has been printed as one English word.

multitude to give any attention to his communication ; yet the ready sympathy of all who are engaged in these common studies, and the reciprocations of a deep and serene interest in every kindred spirit, may give confidence to any one who has his message to deliver, that if he will but give it utterance in clear voice he shall in such " fit audience find though few."

A perfect philosophy must be universally comprehensive. False principles and wrong processes necessitate an *erroneous* philosophy ; while partial principles and processes of demonstration, though not false, must yet give a *defective* philosophy. If we use no element other than truth, and thus avoid a false system ; still, until we have comprehended all its truth, we have not attained to the perfected system of science. It would, doubtless, be an arrogant assumption for any one, at the present age, to affirm that from his stand-point all truth may be discovered and a full encyclopedia of science may from thence be ensphered. Each thinker attains a portion only of all truth, and as it is viewed from his position ; and it can only be from the collected attainments of many, that we gradually mount to higher stations and reach to more comprehensive conclusions. Not the man, but thinking humanity, is the true philosopher. The tributary streams of ages go to make up the full flow of philosophic thinking, and at length this may pour itself into what yet, to finite intelligence, shall ever be a shoreless ocean.

The preparation and publication of this work has been under the full influence of these considerations. It is not expected that it will be of any interest to the many ; sufficient quite, if it reach and occupy the minds of the few, and propagate its reciprocations of free thought through the growing number of such as *can* and *do* familiarize themselves in purely rational demonstrations. Nor has it been deemed that there is here a perfected and universally comprehensive philosophy ; though it is believed that the true direction is here taken, and it is also hoped that some progress has been gained, towards the ultimate attainment of that position from which the complete science of all sciences. if ever to be consummated, must at length be perfected. It is intended only as a contribution to the common current of rational philosophic speculation, and is silently cast into the stream of thought to flow on with it if found to be congenial, or to be thrown ashore if it prove only as a foreign cumbering drift upon its surface.

THEOLOGICAL SEMINARY, }
AUBURN, Dec. 1848. }

ERRATA.

74th Page, 12th line from top, for *affected* read *effected*.
100th "   17th   "   "   for *subjective* read *objective*.
225th "   11th   "   "   for *void thought* read *void of thought*.
241st "   13th   "   "   for *impracticality* read *impracticability*.
365th "   10th   "   "   for interrogation read period.
409th "   14th   "   "   for *coacervum* read *coacervation*.
574th "   last line, for *allusions* read *illusions*.
637th "   12th line from top, for *mist* read *midst*.
 "   "   3d line from bottom, for *is* read *it*.
688th "   4th   "   "   for *alluvial* read *diluvial*.

CONTENTS.

INTRODUCTION.

PSYCHOLOGY is the Science of Mind. *Empirical* Psychology attains the facts of mind and arranges them in a system. The elements are solely the facts given in experience, and the criterion of their reality is the clear testimony of consciousness. When, between any number of minds there is an alledged contradiction of consciousness, the umpire is found in the general consciousness of mankind. What this general consciousness is, may be attained in various ways; from the languages, laws, manners and customs, proverbial sayings, literature and history of the race; and a fair appeal and decision here must be final, for any fact excluded thereby must be *altcrum genus*, and should also be excluded from the philosophical system. Such an appeal to general consciousness may properly be termed the tribunal of Common Sense.

Rational Psychology is a very different process for attaining to a Science of Mind, and lies originally in a very different field from experience, although it ulti-

2

mately brings all its attainments within an experience. As this is the specific subject designed for present investigation, it is important as preliminary thereto, that we attain a clear apprehension of what it is ; and it may also be of advantage to examine some of the ends to which it may be applied, and thus beforehand see some of the uses to which it may be made subservient.

I. *An explanation of what Rational Psychology is.*

In this science, we pass from the facts of experience wholly out beyond it, and seek for the *rationale* of experience itself in the necessary and universal principles which must be conditional for all facts of a possible experience. We seek to determine how it is possible for an experience to be, from those apriori conditions which render all the functions of an intellectual agency themselves intelligible. In the conclusions of this science it becomes competent for us to affirm, not as from mere experience we may, that this *is*—but, from these necessary and universal principles, that this *must be.* The intellect is itself investigated and known through the apriori principles which must necessarily control all its agency, and thereby the being of intelligence is expounded in its constituent functions and laws of operation.

An illustration of what such a Science of Mind is, may be given by a reference to other things as subjects of rational comprehension. Whatever may be placed in the double aspect of its empirical facts and its conditional principles, may be used for such a purpose. Thus Astronomy has its sublime and astonishing facts, gathered through a long period of patient and careful observation. Experience has been competent to attain the appearances and movements of the heavenly bodies; the sattelites of some of the planets, and their relations to their primaries; the apparent changes of figure and place in some, and the occasional transits or occultations of others. The general relations of different portions of our solar system have in this way been found; the sun put in its place at the center, the planets put in their places in their orbits around it, with the direction, distance, and time of periodical revolution accurately determined. A complete diagram of the solar system may thus be made from the results of experience alone, and all that belongs to *formal* Astronomy be finished. In this process, through experience, we are competent to affirm, *so the solar system is.* But if now on the other hand beyond experience, we may somehow attain to the conception of an invisible force, operating through the system directly as the quantity of matter and inversely as the squares of the distance, we shall be competent to take this as an apriori principle, determining experience itself, and quite independently of all observation may affirm, *so the solar system must be.*

Again, I take a body of a triangular form, and by accurate mensuration find that any two of its sides are together greater than the third side. Another triangular body, of different size and proportion of its sides, is also accurately measured, and the same fact is again found. The mensuration of the first did not help to the attainment of the fact in the last, but an experiment only ascertained that so it *is*. Repeated experiments may have been made of a vast number of triangular forms, isoceles, right-angled, and scalene, and of them all, at last, I may make the same affirmation, this is; but from experience I am not warranted to include any thing else than so it is, and in so many cases as the experiment has reached. When, however, I construct for myself a triangle in pure space, and intuitively perceive the relations of its sides, I do not need any experiment, but can make this intuition valid universally, and affirm for all possible triangles, so the facts *must be.*

Thus with any artificial construction. The building is not the promiscuous mass of its materials, but these arranged according to plan and system. An Empiric may take a model and copy after it by careful mensuration; but the scientific architect projects the whole structure from apriori principles, and sees the whole from the first, in the pure laws of its combination. So the fabricator of plaster-busts takes the features of some face by an actual impression, and then fitting his moulds to the original shape, he casts the pliant mortar therein and there comes forth the exact counterpart. But the perfect Ideal, as the creation of genius, is an existence prior to all experience, and

which no experience can give.   The artist perseveringly works on after it, chipping off progressively the
interposing refuse from the marble, and at length the
objective being of his archetype stands before us—a
Venus or an Apollo.

Such everywhere is the distinction between an empirical and a rational process.   In the one we have
the facts as they appear; in the other, we have the
conditioning principle which determines their appearance, and which makes our experience of them possible.   And now, the human mind, as an intelligent and
free agent, may as readily as any other subject, admit
of an investigation under each of these aspects.   Facts
as given in experience, and those arranged in an orderly system as they appear in consciousness, constitute Psychology in that important division which we
have denominated *Empirical:* and those apriori conditions which give the necessary and universal laws
to experience, and by which intelligence itself is alone
made intelligible, are the elements for a higher Psychological Science which we term *Rational.*   So far as
this science is made to proceed, it will give an exposition of the human mind not merely in the facts of
experience, but in the more adequate and comprehensive manner, according to the necessary laws of its being and action as a free intelligence.   It will, moreover, afford a position from which we may overlook the
whole field of possible human science, and determine
a complete circumscription to our experience; demon-

strating what is possible, and the validity of that which is real. In it is the science of all sciences, inasmuch as it gives an exposition of Intelligence itself.

Such, also, is truly a *transcendental* philosophy inasmuch as it *transcends* experience, and goes up to those necessary sources from which all possible experience must originate; but not transcendental in that sense in which the name has become a derision and reproach by the perversion of those who have assumed it and dishonored it, and with whom it has been a transcending of all light and meaning, and going off into a region of mere dreams and shadows. A true transcendental philosophy dwells perpetually in the purest light, and sustains itself by the soundest demonstrations; nor is it practicable, by any other method of investigation, to draw a clear line between empiricism and science, assumption and demonstration, facts which appear to be and principles which must be.

Pure Mathematics, and in a somewhat more limited field pure Physics also, proceed in the firm and sure steps of a demonstrated science, because they go out utterly beyond all appearance, and attain their elements from a region transcending all that experience can reach. They deal with the necessary and the universal, and hence, as resting upon that which must control all experience and make it possible, it can never occur that any facts in experience should come in contradiction to them. Nor can any thing assumed to be philosophy and attempting to pass itself off as sci-

ence, and least of all psychological science, take the
high road of a sound and valid demonstration, except
it shall both start from and lay its course by, the stern
demand and rigid rule of apriori principles. True science must be both supported and directed by those
ultimate truths, which are self-affirmed in their own
light, and which both must be, and must everywhere
and evermore be. An empirical system may defend
itself and maintain its integrity against all that shall
assail it from within ; but where the skeptic resolutely
goes out beyond those assumptions which are conditional for it, and calls in question the stability of its
very foundation, it is utterly helpless. Thus, the telescope brings distant objects within the reach of observation, and thereby vastly enlarges the sphere of vision.
By its aid we may go on in the addition of one newly
discovered phenomenon to another in the broad fields
of space, and enlarge the system embraced in experimental astronomy to the maximum of power which
may be attained for our glasses. We need have no
other solicitude for the validity of our system as empirical, save only in the assurance of a correct observation. If any doubts spring up within the facts of our
science, we can repeat the observation at pleasure
and dispel them. But when, at length, we encounter
the skeptic who will not shut himself up within our
conditioning assumption of the validity of telescopic
observation, and seriously questions the correctness of
this whole manner of appearances, and of seeing new

objects through magnifying glasses, most surely we shall avail nothing in attempting to cure this skepticism by multiplying our experiments and making such objects to appear through the telescope, nor even by forcing the skeptic to the consciousness that he sees them there himself. He is assailing the system from a point utterly beyond all the facts of observation, and with fatal effect disturbing the integrity of astronomical science in its very foundation, and must needs be met in the very point of his doubts and forced to the conviction that the laws of telescopic vision are valid. And surely this cannot be done by looking through the telescope, nor even by taking it to pieces and subjecting all its parts to careful inspection. We shall be obliged to attain those optical principles which are apriori conditional for all making of telescopes, and thus know how telescopic vision is possible in its own conditioning laws, and determine what *must be* by a rational demonstration, and in this process only can we force such an assailing skepticism from its position.

As is the telescope an instrument for the eye, so is the eye, and all the organism of sense, an instrument for the intellect. While we are solicitous about the facts as they appear in the sense merely, we shall find no difficulty in building up our empirical system and maintaining the validity of our philosophy. Yea, if we wish to take the mind itself in pieces and examine its varied phenomena, and put all together again according to observed connections and relationships, an empirical psychology may be thus readily attained, and a system of mental science completed. But when we meet with a skepticism which plants its objections back of all experience, and doubts altogether about this whole matter of appearance in the senses, then are we doing absolutely nothing for science except as we also go back of experience, and by a rigid transcendental demonstration determine from the conditioning principles of all intelligence how experience in the senses is possible to be; and then, by this, also demonstrate in the facts their validity, inasmuch as they are found actually to be, what from their conditioning laws it has already been seen that they must be. There is a skepticism which resolutely and perseveringly questions all validity of experience, and doubts the whole testimony of consciousness relatively to the reality of all being; yea, that founds upon an alledged contradiction of reason and consciousness, the demonstration for the necessity of absolute and universal skepticism; and while to such, all experience must be a mere *seeming to be*, with no reality, this can certainly never be cured by any repetition of appearances merely as they seem to be. A solid basis for science is here attainable by no other possible process than through the apriori investigations and conclusions of a Rational Psychology. The want is both seen and felt, that something not of experience should be given, by which to demonstrate the validity of experience; nor will thinking minds be long deeply interested in any

speculations which do not attempt, at least, to go up
to the original and conditioning sources of all knowledge.

The history of philosophy furnishes here ample instruction. Those investigations only which have
sought to rise to their conditioning principles, in reference to the subject in hand, have laid a very strong
grasp upon the philosophical mind, and fixed the attention of thinking men for any long period. More especially is this true in reference to all philosophy which
subjects the human mind to examination, and gives
its theory for expounding man's intellectual and moral
agency. If the whole be left to repose upon the mere
affirmations of common sense, and thus the whole science be circumscribed by the limits of general experience in consciousness, it cannot meet this philosophical want, and will not hold the interest of philosophical minds. The point of all dangerous skepticism is
wholly out of and beyond the experience in which
common sense originates, and if this is not at all sought
for, and the effort, at least, made to reach this point
and demolish the skepticism, the influence of the work
must be limited to those minds which have not yet
seen the difficulty, and felt the need of an apriori demonstration. Thus, whatever the subject under examination may be, the skepticism which endangers it
as a philosophy will ever lie at its foundation, and
can only be met by going back of its facts and giving
validity to its conditioning principles ; and such studies

as are directed to such apriori principles will alone possess any philosophical interest.

This is the very spirit of the far-famed Socratic method of philosophizing, and in this lies its influence and its interest. By a series of skillful interrogatories, Socrates forced the disciple back to the elementary principles of the subject under discussion, and made him to seek some conditioning truth, clear in its own light, and on which all subsequent deductions might be seen to be safely dependent. The scholar was in this way made cautious and docile, and the sophist was driven to expose his own ignorance, amid all his shallow pretensions. Plato, the most illustrious of his disciples, and the world's great teacher in philosophy, still more thoroughly pursued science up to her primitive sources. The Intellectual Idea was taken as the archetype and *in*forming essence, and only in this could facts be made intelligible, and by this only could nature be interpreted. Aristotle, in succession, no less rigidly forced philosophy upward to the science of first principles. His investigations regarded the modes in which nature manifests herself in facts and phenomena, rather than the inherent laws and forces which condition her development; yet it is only through these conditioning laws that any portion of nature can be adequately expounded. He sought rather to reduce science to its logical elements, and to find here the conditioning sources of all correct concluding in judgments. These sages of antiquity have held their power over the philosophic thinking of ages and their voice has penetrated through more than twenty centuries and is still distinct to teach all who have ears to hear.

The dialectical conflicts of the school-men, long exercised the minds of men in the most subtle and often empty speculations, and ultimately exhausted all the resources of syllogistic disputation, and wearied the world with its abstract terms and dry logical distinctions. Descartes sought to bring back philosophy again to the study of things in their first principles. The germ of his system lies in the following extract: "It is absurd to suppose that which thinks not to be in the very time in which it thinks. And hence this cognition—*I think, therefore I am*—is the first and most certain which may occur to any one philosophizing in order." Thought, as the essence of spirit, and extension as the essence of matter, make up the universe of being, and as opposites and incommunicable in their own nature, are brought and held together in communion through the doctrine of "divine assistance." Spinoza identified thought and extension in a higher substance, and made all modes of spiritual and material being only a manifested development of this higher existence. Leibnitz sublimated all being into indivisible atoms, and as thus indistinguishable by any outer, they must be distinguished each from each by an inner peculiarity, and which, analagous to mind, is a faculty of representing. Every atom with its inner representation-force was thus a monad, and when representing in unconsciousness, is matter; when partially conscious, is animal; when in full self-consciousness, is human soul; and the Absolute Monad arranges all the representations through a "pre-established harmony."

Lord Bacon, also, as the great modern expounder of Inductive Philosophy, urges to the investigation of nature not in scattered and isolated facts, but in their inherent laws which bind them together in systematic unity. An intellectual analysis into fact and law, matter and form, must be made through all subjects of science, and thus nature must be dissolved, not chemically by fire, but intellectually as by a divine fire. And Locke, again, turned his inquiry to primitive sources that he might accurately circumscribe the entire field of human knowledge. While he has laid the foundation for only a very partial philosophy in the rejection of all apriori knowledge, yet from the force and clearness of his investigation of sensation and experience, he has for more than a century and a half, held sway over much the larger portion of the philosophic mind of Britain and America. Out of this system have arisen the idealism of Berkely, the vibration theory of Hartley, the materialism of Diderot and Helvetius, the universal skepticism of Hume, and, for the counteraction of the last, the common sense basis for all philosophy as assumed by Reid and most of the Scotch Metaphysicians.

And once more only, it may emphatically be said

that for more than half a century the deep and strong current of German thought has been impelled and directed in its course by the profound critical investigations of Kant, relative to the origin and validity of all knowledge. He says, " up to this time it has been received that all our cognition must regulate itself according to the objects; yet all attempts to make out something apriori by means of conceptions concerning such, whereby our cognitions would be extended, have proved under this supposition abortive. Let it be once therefore tried whether we do not succeed better in the problems of metaphysics, when we admit that the objects must regulate themselves according to our cognitions." This reversed order of investigation is the peculiarity of the Critical Philosophy, and is analagous to that charge in the stand-point for all investigation which occurred in astronomy, when the sun was put in the center of the system and the observer carried around it, instead of the spectator being himself at rest and the sun revolving. And we need to add merely this remark, that in general, whether as disciples or opponents of Kant, the thinking mind in Germany and of those who have been aroused by German speculations, have found the interest of the investigations to lie in the deep and earnest search after apriori principles.

The interest excited by the works of Cousin, Coleridge, Whewell and Morell's History of Modern Philosophy furnish additional evidence of the sway which any bold thinker attains, when he resolutely and forcibly pushes forward the apriori elements and primitive principles of all science. Nor is this fact at all discredited by the querulous complaints and captious reproaches from such as find the ground of these speculations too high for the attention they have to give to them, since there is at least the interest to seem to have formed a judgment about that which they have not as yet at all comprehended.

The prevailing system of metaphysics must necesarily strongly affect all contemporary physical investigation, and very much mould all natural science after its own forms. All philosophy must strike its roots in the reason, and its first principles must be found or assumed from beyond the empirical, and entirely within the transcendental. The physical can find no law of exposition save in the metaphysical. It is in this field that the foundations of all systematic philosophy must be laid, and if these are assumptions solely, their conclusions, whether salutary or dangerous, can neither be sustained nor refuted by other assumptions. Assumption and counter-assumption may forever stand, the one over against the other, and there shall be no force in either to demolish its opposite. We must be able to go over into its metaphysical region, and secure here a legitimate possession, or we can never give to our assumed science authority in its own right to eject the intruding skeptic, nor forbid that he should any where at pleasure erect his fortifications in hostility. An empirical system, standing upon assumptions as its first principles, can at the best only maintain itself in possession while its original right remains unquestioned. When the title-deeds are contested in the grounds of their valid authority, it cannot avail to produce any of the declarations and statements within them, but we must confirm their legitimacy by something beyond the instrument itself, and hold possession from the evidence that they reach back and take hold on the original powers of sovereignty. The most incorrigible skepticism may remain utterly undisturbed in any philosophy, except as it is competent to give to its first principles a sound and clear apriori demonstration.

And here we would remark, that it enters into the very essence of Rational Psychology, to make this apriori investigation of the human intellect; to attain the *idea* of intelligence, from the apriori conditions which make an intellectual agency possible, and thereby determine how, if there be intelligence, it *must* be both in function and operation; and then find the facts which shall evince that such intellectual agency is not only possible as idea in void thought, but is also actual as valid being in reality. Such an attainment in psychological science, may open the way to the determination of the validity of all science, inasmuch as in this process we attain the very laws of human intelligence itself, and may therefore use our position for determining the valid being of the objects given through such an intellectual agency. And this introduces another preliminary topic for examination, to which we will now turn our attention.

II. *The ends to which the conclusions of Rational Psychology may be rendered subservient.*

Rational Psychology is itself a science, and complete in its own department. It gives the mind, through all its functions of intellectual agency, in the conditioning laws which control all its operations and interpret all its processes of knowledge; and when thus completed it has filled its own measure and answered its own end. But interesting as is this Science of the Mind, and worthy to be pursued for its own sake, and competent to give satisfaction even when resting within its own conclusions, yet is there the opportunity of starting from its results, and making its conclusions subservient to farther advances. It may be rendered directly instrumental in the solution of some of the most interesting and difficult problems within the whole compass of the sciences. Indeed, through no other process is it practicable to obtain a position, from whence some of the highest points in philosophy may be brought within the range of direct examination.

There are many questions, involving the highest speculative and practical interests of mankind, which stand precisely in this condition, that they receive a ready assent in the common conviction, and control the universal conduct of the world; and yet when this

3

universal assent is carefully examined, and the effort is made to trace the conviction up to its original ground, it is found to rest wholly upon assumption. All attempts to elucidate the correctness and to settle the validity of such convictions, are soon found to be utterly impracticable except through some process of an apriori and rational investigation. All experimental processes must fail, for the point of difficulty lies beyond experiment, even in that which is conditional that there may be any experience. The attempt to forestall all such inquiry by affirming that such convictions are themselves ultimate facts, and not possible to be made any clearer by any efforts towards a higher investigation, inasmuch as these convictions are themselves the highest point of possible attainment, cannot afford any satisfaction to philosophy, since it is really but affirming that all philosophy and science are impossibilities, and all knowledge is but a resting in the appearances given in the sense. All that can be done is to say that so it appears, and as appearance gives this conviction which is our ultimate fact, we affirm that so it *is ;* and here we must stop short in all attempts to rise to any higher position where we may farther affirm so it *must be.* When any one speculatively doubts the validity of these convictions in experience, or even assumes to have proved them to be fallacious, there is nothing that can at all be answered, except still to urge this fact of universal conviction, including the skeptic himself, and there rest as having reached the ultimate point of human attainment, and leave the skeptic to his doubts if he must still be so philosophical, and so little under the dominion of common sense, as to have them.   The empirical philosopher and the reasoning skeptic, it is quite manifest may here stand the one over against the other in perpetual contradiction, hopeless of all reconciliation and agreement.   Their respective positions perpetuate the everlasting conflict of two counter-assumptions; one, that the convictions of common sense are ultimate; the other, that reason goes beyond all experience, or at least goes against it and falsifies its convictions.   On his own premises each may maintain his own conclusions, and yet neither can go back to the assumption of his antagonist, and obtain a final triumph by demolishing it.

And now, some of these very questions may be brought within the scope of a clear examination, from the position to which a Rational Psychology reaches. Having gained its own end, and given the human intellect as determined in a demonstrated science, it may be used for the farther purpose of settling the conflicts of those counter-assumptions; nor will it be practicable to make any thing else subservient to such a desirable issue.   And it may subserve the double purpose of illustrating the great importance of a strictly transcendental philosophy, and by overlooking the field in general, give a better preparation for our future exploration thereof, if we here make a particular and somewhat extended reference to some of the more important of these questions, in the exact order in which they stand related to the conclusions of a Rational Psychology.

1. The objects given in sense are out of, and in some cases at a distance from, the knowing agent. This is especially true of the objects given by the sense of smell, of hearing, and of sight. One will suffice for the illustration of all, and as the better adapted to a clear exemplification we will take the object as given in vision. The problem which philosophy has felt herself called upon to solve is this: How may the intellect know that which is out of, and at a distance from, itself? The general admission has been that in some way the object must affect the sensible organ by impulse. An impression is thereby made upon, or an affection produced within the organism, which by its nervous susceptibility perpetuates the affection and communicates it to the brain, and through the brain the affection is carried up to the point of its communication with the intelligent spirit, and there in the secret penetralium of the spirit's dwelling-place a junction is formed between the invading impulse and the receiving intellect, the mind thereby attains its knowledge of the object, and the process of perception is completed. But, inasmuch as nothing can act except where it is, and when it is; and the object is not where the point of the mind's receiving agency is, but sometimes at a great distance therefrom; it follows that there must at this point of perception be some

representative of the distant object. This representative is what is directly perceived, and by it the distant object is made known. Such a theory, modified in minor particulars by different philosophers, induced the necessary conclusion that all knowledge of an outer world is mediate, through representatives of its objects, and never direct as an immediate perception of the objects themselves.

In the investigations to which this theory of a representative perception of objects was subjected, many perplexing queries arose, and different philosophers answered them, each in his own way as he best could. What is this representative of the outer object, a spiritual or a material being? Is it an image of the object as excerpt and detached from it? or originated in the brain? or in the intellect? or in some media between the object and the organ? Does the representative at all exist when the mind is unconscious of the perception? May it not be a direct creation and infused into the mind by divine agency? Yea, may not these representatives be in the Deity, and identical with the divine essence, and that thus, according to the theory of Malebranche, "we see all things in God?" But however these connected queries may have been answered, the general doctrine of perception remained, that not the object but some representative thereof was immediately given to the sense. From this a two-fold skepticism naturally arose, one or the other face being presented according to the side on which the theory was carried out to its issue.

On one side, this theory of mediate perception gave occasion for a skepticism in reference to the reality of all external objects. How can the correctness of our perceptions be at all determined? If we say the representative is like the object, it can be only a mere assumption, inasmuch as no comparison can be instituted between them, for the representative only is given; and if by any means the object could be attained for a comparison, then would the representative and all comparison with it be wholly superfluous. Yea, inasmuch as the representatives are all that the intellect possesses, how is it possible that we may know that any thing other than the representatives really exist? That the objects at all are, must be wholly a gratuitous conclusion. Berkely's argument is still more stringently drawn. All that can be known is through the mediate representations of sensation; and all that can come within consciousness is the sensation itself; and this sensation as wholly mental can have no likeness to any material objective being. To suppose that mental sensations and material objects can resemble each other would confound mind and matter together. The conclusion, in his own language necessarily follows: "The existence of a body out of a mind perceiving it is not only impossible and a contradiction in terms, but were it possible and even real, it were impossible that the mind should ever know it."

This conclusion of Bishop Berkely was not at all the offspring of a religious skepticism. By giving up

the knowledge of an outer material world and holding
on to the knowledge of an inner mental world, he assumed that the skepticism in religion, which follows
so readily and in his view so necessarily from the theory of a representative perception, was wholly avoided.
He considered the belief of an external world, on the
ground of the common assumption that sensation,
which is wholly mental, can be a representative of objective realities, which are wholly material, to be the
chief source not only of all error in philosophy, but
also of all heresy in religion.   By excluding all knowledge of matter he thought to save the knowledge of
the soul, and thereby a firm ground for the doctrines
and duties and immortal hopes of religion.   And thus
it was that on this side, the doctrine of mediate perception terminated in *Idealism*, which denies all knowledge of the reality of objective being, save as it exists
in the sensations of the mind itself.

On the other side, this theory produced to its issue
attains to a skepticism still more startling.   This representative, coming from the outer object, and acting
upon the nicely arranged organism of the sense, puts
in motion the animal spirits, or gives vibration to the
nervous and cerebral filaments, and thereby propogates
its peculiar motions and manifestations onward to the
sensorium, in which the sensation becomes perfected
in a complete perception.   But, inasmuch as no motion extending throughout any material organization
may at all propogate its movement beyond what is

material in the organic sphere, so there can be no possible projection of any representation of the object, through such motion, out of the organism and into some supposed spiritual receptacle, which as without parts must be utterly incompetent to receive or transmit any representation by impulse. The representative of the outer object can never be carried beyond the sphere of the material organization, and therefore all perception by means of this representation must be completed somewhere within the material organization itself. All perception is perfected in the subtle, refined, yet still material organism. An impinging force from without communicates its impulse to the material arrangements within, and in the peculiar modification thus given to these organic particles, there originate perceptions, feelings, and thoughts. Various explanations may be made in reference to the manner how, but all spiritual agency is excluded, from the necessity that impulses and motions must be wholly material. "Consciousness itself," says Hobbes, "is the agitation of our internal organism, determined by the unknown motions of a supposed outer world." Thought is the product of sublimated and skillfully arranged particles of matter put in motion by the representative of some outer object. To reverse the process, and begin with the completed perception tracing it backwards, will also arrive at the same conclusion after the manner of Diderot and the school of the French Encyclopediasts. Every cognition when carried back in its ultimate analysis must resolve itself into some sensible representation; that which produced this representation in the sense must have come within the organization from some external impression or affection; and thus all which may ever be in possession of the intellect, and which is not wholly a chimera, must be able to again be attached to its own original archetype. Thus philosophy is compelled to reject every thing as possibly bringing its reality to our knowledge, which has not its direct reference to something external and material. The result on this side, by any process of carrying the theory to its conclusion, is *Materialism;* the doubting of all reality except that of material being.

But a more incorrigible skepticism still results from this theory when comprehensively examined and entrepidly prosecuted to its legitimate conclusions. It is the testimony in the convictions of universal consciousness that we perceive immediately the external objects themselves. Every man is convinced that it is the object, and not some representative of it, which he perceives. The knowledge that the object is out of myself, and other than myself, and thus a reality not subjective merely, is the testimony of common sense every where. All minds, that of philosophers as well as common people, are shut up to the testimony of consciousness for a direct and immediate perception of the outward object. The skeptic himself admits, yea, insists upon this, and founds upon it the necessary conclusions of his skepticism, rendered the more invincible thereby from the contradiction which follows.

For when the unexamined convictions of consciousness, as direct for the immediate perception of an outer world, are brought to the test of philosophical investigation, the demonstration comes out full, sound, and clear, that all such immediate knowledge is impossible. The very sensation through which the knowledge is given is wholly mental, and at the most can be determined as only representative of the object, and not that it is that object itself. It is not possible to affirm beyond the immediateness of the sensation ; and all that can directly be known is, that the mind has such sensations, and this it may deem to be a perception of an outward object, but the reason attains the irrefragible conclusion that the sensation only, and not the object as external, can be immediately in the consciousness. A demonstration of reason, thus, concludes directly against the testimony of universal consciousness. And now, where are we as intelligent beings ? Consciousness contradicts reason ; the reason belies consciousness. They are each independent sources of human knowledge ; unhesitating conviction must follow a clear decision of either ; and yet here they openly and flatly contradict each other. The nature of man as intelligent, stands out a self-contradiction. From the very light which is within us, we are made to conclude that light itself to be darkness, and thus all ground for knowledge in any way is self-annihilated. The truth of our intellectual nature is itself falsehood, and there remains nothing other than to doubt universally. This is the dreadful, but from the philosophy of representation in sensation, the unavoidable conclusion of David Hume; and here we come out to a necessary *Universal Skepticism.*

Reid, more especially to counteract the last, but equally as defensive against all the above forms of skepticism, introduces here his theory based on the assumptions of *common sense.* Rejecting all notion of any representation in perception, and imputing all such conclusions to the wandering and delusive speculations of philosophy, he takes the universal decision of common consciousness on this subject—that we immediately know the outer material world in the perceptions of sensation—to be the truth ; and forestalls all contradiction, by denying all validity to any speculations which attempt to reach back beyond such decision of universal consciousness. Wiser than all philosophy ; higher than all speculations of the reason ; farther back than any demonstrations can be allowed as valid ; this decision of common sense is the first thing given, the ultimate truth in which all philosophy must begin, and on which all demonstration must be dependent, and which is never to be disputed. He thus saves himself from all skepticism as above, in any of its forms, by denying their fundamental assumption of a mediate perception, and assuming that the human intellect was so made as to see the outer world immediately.

Here, then, are two counter-assumptions standing one over against the other, nor can one demolish or be demolished by the other. One assumes that sensation can be none other than a representative of the object in perception; the other assumes that sensation gives the outer object immediately; and here they both stand on their ultimate positions. Neither can attempt to go back of their assumed ultimate truths, neither will admit that the assumptions of the other are clear in their own light and self-affirmed; and thus neither may fortify his own position nor assail the opposite, and each can stand upon his own ground and defy all the logical and metaphysical artillery of his antagonist.

We are ready now to say, that one end to which the results attained in Rational Psychology may be made effectually subservient, is the complete termination of this drawn-battle, and the settlement of all these questions, on the basis of an apriori demonstrated science. If we can attain the law of all perception in sensation, and in that interpret nature as she actually gives phenomena to our knowledge, we have in this secured to ourselves the capacity to examine these counter-assumptions in a higher light than their own, and the competency, therefore, to decide which, or whether either be true. In their foundation-assumptions we may pronounce a judgment upon both Idealism and Materialism, and by reconciling all apparent contradictions in our original sources of knowledge, we may also subvert the universal Pyrrhonism of David Hume. We shall also be able to give a far other interpretation of experience than that it is an ultimate fact, resolvable only into the original formation of the human mind. We shall find the law which creative power and wisdom followed in giving to the human mind the faculty of perception, or of knowledge through sensation. These results are wholly inaccessible through any other pathway than that which is prepared in the investigations of a rational psychology.

2. There is a more important end in the destruction of a still deeper skepticism to which the results of this science may be applied, and which will be disclosed in the following remarks:

The sense is a medium for perception in which are given the qualities of an outer, and the exercises of an inner world. Colors, sounds, tastes, &c., are revealed in consciousness through sensation; and thinking, feeling, choosing, &c., are also revealed in consciousness through an inner sense. All these accidents of an outer world of matter and an inner world of mind, as given in perception, may be demonstrated as realities from the results of rational psychology in its determination of the laws of perception. Thus far, we shall have demolished the forms of skepticism above noticed as idealism, materialism, and absolute skepticism. But, while much is attained for science in demonstrating the validity of our perceptions, there are still more important regions beyond, yet insecurely held in possession by philosophy. We have thus the reality of the thinking, but not the thinker; the reality of color, but not the thing colored. The accidents are known, but not that in which the accidents inhere. All qualities as given in sense stand disconnected, and cannot by perception alone be put together in their existence, as the common properties of one and the same subject. I perceive a redness, a fragrance, a silky smoothness, but I do not perceive through sense that in which they all inhere, as one thing—the rose—so that I can say I perceive the rose as a thing in itself, and then moreover perceive that the rose is red, fragrant, smooth, &c. I perceive in the inner sense that there is a thinking, feeling, and choosing; but I do not perceive the mind, and then perceive this one mind to think, feel and choose. It is only through a discursive judgment that I can connect them in one common subject; and the sense does not *judge*, it only *perceives*. It may be made valid for real *qualities* and *events*, but it can never attain *substances* and *causes*.

And now, it is by these notions of substance and cause that we can extend our knowledge at all beyond the mere isolated qualities as they appear in sense. We put the several qualities, not merely into one group as in the same place, but into one substance as existing in the same thing; and also the events, not merely as successive in a time, but as originating in one cause as the same source. And when we thus

connect qualities and events as *perceived*, in their notions of substance and cause as *understood;* we may
then greatly extend our knowledge in several ways.
Had we the faculty of perception through sense alone,
we could merely attain the *predicates of qualities*, as less
and more, like and unlike, outer and inner, antecedent
and consequent, &c., and which stand only in the conjunctions of space and time; but by the faculty of the
understanding which connects qualities as existing in
things, we attain these qualities as the *predicates of
substances*, and thereby a great enlargement of judgments is effected.

Thus, in my notion of substance in which the qualities inhere, I have the conception of *body;* and by
simple reflection upon this conception I can say that
all bodies must have extension, figure, position, divisibility, impenetrability, &c., as *primary* qualities. And
in the same way, in my notion of cause, I have the
conception of an *agent*, and by merely reflecting upon
this conception I may say that all agents must have
force, activity, passivity, &c., as their primary attributes. And in this I have not mere predicates of qualities, but predicates of things. And then, moreover, I
may add to such *things*, all the qualities which the perceptions of the sense can attain, as their *secondary*
qualities. Thus of some body—gold—in addition to
the primary qualities common to all bodies, I may say
from the perceptions of sense, that it is yellow, fusible,
malleable, soluble in aqua regia, &c.; and of some

agent—the sun—that it has not only the primary attributes common to all agents, but also that it imparts light and heat, melts wax, hardens clay, converts liquids into vapor, &c. In this way I may enlarge my knowledge of things as far as I may extend my perceptions, and know not merely appearances as perceived, but things as understood. And much farther still; I may say that like substances have like qualities; and that like causes produce like effects; and may then classify nature through all her genera, species, and varieties; and also by an induction of similar facts conspiring to one end, may deduce general laws, and thus extend my conclusions not only to embrace what I have perceived, but all that it is possible should be perceived in nature.

Here is the basis of Inductive Science. I assume this uniformity in the substances and causes of the universe, and thus conceive of nature as bound in harmony by universal laws, and have then no difficulty in concluding from what is, to what will be; and from what I have perceived, to what perception could any where give in any experience. I may take some hypothesis, and using this for the time as if it were the true law of nature, I go out to examine and question nature through all her works. If I find her answers quite contradictory to my hypothesis, I throw it away as worthless and false; but if I find her answers in conformity with my hypothesis, it is hypothesis no longer, but a veritable law of nature, by which she is henceforth to be interpreted through all her secret chambers. I may, again, be observing the casual facts of nature as they arise promiscuously around me, and with the conviction that there is some law of order though wholly as yet undiscovered, there may from some conspiring incidents perhaps, a thought sudden as inspiration flash upon my mind, in which the whole complexity of facts is put at once in clear and systematic unity. So Harvey, amid the promiscuous facts of anatomical dissection, notices the valves which open and close within the different chambers of the heart, and as the concurring facts appear, that these valves are so arranged that they may admit the blood coming *from* the veins, and then with every pulsation send it through the lungs and onward *to* the arteries ; instantaneously, the fact of the circulation of the blood in the animal system, and the law for it, are clearly apprehended. So, also, the falling apple might, as is sometimes said it did, suggest to Newton's wakeful thought the universal action of gravitation. That force of attraction which brought the apple to the earth, manifestly reaches much higher than to the bough from which it fell; why not then to the height of the air, and hold to the earth its surrounding atmosphere ? Why not to the moon, and control her changes ? Yea, why not act from the sun through all the system, and hold each planet in its orbit ? A careful induction confirms the supposition, and determines the ratio of the force, and at once the law of

4

gravitation is assumed to pervade the universe. The revolutions of the farthest planet and the wandering of the most eccentric comet are subjected to its control.

But here, the grand inquiry essential for all knowledge, both in the particular things of experience and the general judgments of induction, is to be made and answered. How shall these notions of substance and cause be verified? It is not sufficient that the perception has been plain, nor that we have been careful to secure a broad induction of facts before we have defined the particular thing, or deduced the general law. Such considerations are important merely in reference to the *modus operandi*, and the determination of the correctness of the process. We need to go back of the process, and examine the conditioning principle. How do we attain the validity of subśtance and cause? How do we determine their uniformity? By what right do we assume that Nature has universal laws? That in a large induction of facts such an order has been found, will not be ground sufficient to conclude, therefore, this order is invariable and universal—experience has been thus hitherto, therefore it will be such evermore. Experience itself is based upon the connections of substances and causes, inasmuch as without them, all perception is only of the isolated and fleeting qualities and events with nothing to connect such in a unity of nature; and here we have not only assumed them for connecting qualities into things, but also have assumed their uniformity for connecting things in a general law of nature. Have we, then, a firm ground on which to stand, when we thus attempt to go out beyond the province of the sense? The grand question is, how come we by the notions of substances and causes? and especially, how come we by their perpetual order of connection? The results of reflection; the truth of experience; the validity of all thinking in judgments; and the entire superstructure of inductive science; all rest entirely upon the answer which may be given to such a comprehensive inquiry. If we can find a firm foundation on which to rest an affirmative in this matter, then is a science of experience and of nature possible; if not, the most that is within our reach is probability and belief, and the whole region of Natural Philosophy is open to the skeptic.

But from the philosophy of sensation, according to the system of Locke, no such foundation can be attained. Sensation is the medium for attaining qualities; and by comparing, abstracting, or combining these, we may attain such predicates as greater and less, even and odd, likeness and unlikeness, &c., in which the subject must always be the quality according to its modifications; but certainly, no such modification of the quality can attain to a subject for it, and put the quality in a judgment as the predicate of such subject. The substance and cause are not at all given in the sensation, and cannot possibly come within the

light of consciousness; and it would be wholly an
illusion to suppose that because in our thinking we
have the notions of substance and cause *with* the qualities perceived by sense, therefore they have been
given *in* the qualities as perceived, and taken by an
abstraction *out of* them. They are no modifications
of, nor abstractions from, the qualities and events as
perceived through sensation; but are themselves the
conditional grounds for all qualities and sources for
all events, and are wholly out of and beyond all that
can be made to appear in our consciousness. And
yet, taking this illusion as a reality, and assuming
thence that substances and causes are given in sensation and taken by abstraction from it, this philosophy is
forced to convict itself of the further absurdity, that
what is given in sensation may be taken as a universal
law reaching beyond what has been perceived, and determining how that must be which has not been perceived; inasmuch as it assumes a universal uniformity of their qualities and effects, in the like substances
and causes.

Hume, resting upon the basis of the philosophy of
sensation, saw this inconsequence very clearly, and
established a skepticism thereon utterly impregnable to any attacks from this philosophy. All that
can be known is given in sensation ; and this is
solely " impressions," or the less distinct " ideas,"
which are the copies of the impressions in reflection.
These " impressions," which include all our primary

sensations, and in which we have all the qualities of an outer world and all the exercises of the mental world, may follow consecutively, and in these sequences we may determine an antecedent and consequent, but the mere sequence is all that is given.   No reflection upon the sequence can attain to any causal *nexus* which necessitates this order of antecedents and consequents.   Such sequences *are* and *have been* together, but in this there is no possible ground for the conclusion that they *will be*, much less that they *must be* together hereafter.   This efficiency, as necessary connection, is not in the "impression" as attained in sensation, and hence no reflection can attain to causation as the "idea," or copy thereof.

This most acute of all skeptics both saw and admitted the fact, that the human mind in some way attained the seeming conviction that this connection was a necessary one; and yet, as manifestly such could not be given in sensation, and therefore could not be knowledge, he quite ingeniously and as philosophically as the system of sensation will admit, attempts to account for such conviction.   It is solely the result of habit, from the frequent repetition of the impression of the sequences.   We become accustomed to such an order of sequences, and the repetition at length makes so vivid an impression that it becomes a settled "belief" that it is necessary and universal.   But the philosopher who has investigated the grounds of this belief, plainly sees that it is wholly destitute of all validity. It is a mere persuasion induced by habit only, and from the very sources of all knowledge in sensation this must be utterly excluded. Skepticism may here take up its position unmolested at the very basis of all reasoning from effect to cause, and in the very foundations of the Inductive Philosophy. It is not possible that we should know nature to have any laws in her successions; we can at the most have only persuasion and belief, and the philosopher sees that this is all induced solely by a mere repetition of a particular order of sequences.

Precisely the same philosophizing in reference to substance induces the skepticism of any permanency in the being, as above, of any necessity in the order of events. The substance is as impossible to be given in sensation as is the cause. We have such qualities grouped together, and it may in the same way be explained, that inasmuch as we have so often seen them together, we come at length to the conviction that they are necessarily together, and that there is some common permanent substance in which they inhere. The philosopher knows that there are only the qualities of redness, fragrance, softness, &c. together in the sensation, and that the substance which we call a rose, is nothing but the grouping of the mere qualities in the sense. These qualities of matter and the exercises of mind, as given in perception, are perpetually arising and departing in the sense, and have no other ground of connection than "a divine constitution."

The qualities appear, perpetuated in certain groups; and the exercises appear, prolonged through certain series; but sense can give no permanent substratum, and all knowledge that there is a permanent body, or a perduring agent, is alike impossible. All reasoning from the perpetuity of any classifications in nature, or any characteristics in mind, are wholly based upon the credulity of what we have been accustomed to perceive, or the assumption of an arbitrary divine constitution.

Here, then, we have the disclosure of a difficulty more formidable than that which, in a representative perception, eventuated in the skepticisms of Idealism, Materialism, and absolute Pyrrhonism. We cannot think qualities into things, nor exercises and events into agents, except through the notion of substance in which the qualities inhere, and of cause on which the events depend; nor can we determine any order of classification or succession for these qualities and events, except through the uniformity of substances and causes. All is but a rhapsody of separate fleeting appearances in our perception, until we have somehow connected these in their substances and causes into things; and then classified these things and their changes under those permanent laws which give system to nature, and make of all that may appear in perception a universe. And yet the whole philosophy of sensation cannot give these substances and causes, and their uniformity; but can only give this that they may be believed or assumed, yet cannot be known. In our thinking, we use them as necessary conditions for bringing our conceptions into the order of a consistent experience; but our use is founded upon credulity or assumption, and the skeptic may doubt all its conclusions at pleasure. We cannot think at all without such notions; they are the very connectives of conceptions into judgments; but they are illusions or assumptions, and hence we can never demonstrate that our thinking in judgments by them is valid. Every judgment thus formed has the fatal defect at its root, that it has sprung from a delusion.

And now, surely nothing can avail here, that only attempts to sharpen the senses, or exactly to apprehend appearances. These notions of substance and cause can never be made to appear. No possible functions of the sense can reach them. Unless we can transcend all knowledge from sensation, and attain to these notions as wholly new conceptions in reflection, and verify them in the higher functions of an understanding as having a valid reality of being, we cannot exclude the skeptic from any portion of the field of natural science. Yea, we can have no title as science to any possible attainments in natural philosophy, inasmuch as our whole pretended tenure of this large and fair domain is an illegal assumption. This, then, is a farther use to which we may, perhaps, in the end find the results of Rational Psychology to be subservient. If we can come to the knowledge of the understanding in its conditioning laws of operation, and determine to the intellect, in its process of thinking in judgments, an equal validity as before in its process of perception ; then may we from such results demonstrate also the validity of their being for the objects of the understanding, as before for the objects of the sense. And such verification of the being of substances and causes, and their uniformity as universal laws in the connections of nature, will be an annihilation of all skepticism in this entire department of science. And most surely such a consummation is hopeless, in any other manner than through an apriori or transcendental method of investigation.

3. A more serious difficulty than any which we have yet encountered remains still behind, and needs to be obviated. The following order of thought will bring this difficulty to light, and disclose the use which may be made of the results in Rational Psychology for its removal.

In the circumscription of all knowledge to that which is given in sensation and the modifications which may be made thereof in reflection, the necessary and universal connections of cause and effect are left to rest wholly upon assumption. Hume is manifestly consistent with the fundamental principle of the philosophy of sensation, in denying to human knowledge any thing in cause and effect beyond simple antecedent and consequent. No science can be based upon the universal laws of nature, for it is impossible from this philosophy to go any farther than probability when it is assumed that nature has any universal laws. Hume recognizes the fact that the human mind does, in some way, attain the conviction that the events in nature have a necessary connection, and that the order of this connection is uniform and invariable. This conviction is far from knowledge, and is at bottom only credulity, growing out of the frequent repetition of the sequences in our experience, and therefore a belief from habit merely; yet does it become complete and controling, and impossible to be counteracted by any thing but the most irrefragible demonstration.

Hume's argument against the possibility of proof for a miracle as an interruption of the order of nature, the necessary connection of which has such complete conviction in the human mind, is really unanswerable upon any empirical grounds. There must ever be a stronger conviction against the miracle than there can be persuasion for it. The supposed interposition of a God out of nature, who for good reasons interrupts the order of nature, is wholly gratuitous on the ground of this philosophy, inasmuch as all argumentation from the connections of cause and effect must be wholly inadequate to conclude upon the existence of such a being. The conviction that a God at all, is, can at the most rise no higher, and be deduced from nothing other, than the conviction that nature is uniform in her sequences; and then, to assume a Deity whose existence might make a miracle possible can surely have

little weight with the philosopher, who very distinctly
sees that both the Deity and the miracle must rest
upon contradictory data; the existence of the Deity
upon an argument from the invariable and unbroken
order of causation, and the miracle itself a fact which
is a direct subversion of this invariable order. Such
skepticism in reference to all pretences that miracles
have been wrought is utterly incorrigible, except
through some other discipline than that which may
be administered by any empirical philosophy. The
skepticism is legitimate from the premises; the sophistry has been on the side of such as have kept the
philosophy and yet attempted to answer the skeptic.

But this skepticism in regard to miracles, and to the
being of a God who might work miracles, sustained
by the controling conviction that the order of nature
is uniform, and yet the conviction so controling demonstrably only a credulous illusion, becomes a demonstrated pantheism or a demonstrated atheism, in
several processes of argumentation from the partial
premises of different philosophies. The philosophy of
sensation has ever tended directly on towards universal materialism, and ultimately through fatalism to
blank atheism. With Locke, there was the distinct
and clear admission, that while sensation was *passive*
in the reception of objects from without, yet was there
an *active* principle for reflection within; and that these
active faculties constructed a multitude of complex
and abstract ideas out of the materials furnished by

the senses. And yet, inasmuch as reflection could have nothing to do beyond merely elaborating that which was given in the senses, it must necessarily have confined its whole work to that which was wholly within the real forms of space and time. Its tendency to Materialism and Fatalism may be correctly traced in England through Hartley, Priestly, Darwin, and others. But in France, the more marked issue appears. Condillac so modified reflection as to make it the mere self-consciousness of the feeling given in sensation; and then shows that every faculty—attention, memory, comparison, judgment, and even the will and all our emotions—may be accounted for as modified and "transformed sensations." The passage from this was easy and sure to a complete material mechanism in all the phenomena of our inner being, until it attained its compound of Materialism, Fatalism, and Atheism in the conclusions of d'Holbach, D'Alembert, and the French Encyclopedia, where man appears as only a combination of material organizations; his intellectual being the mere development of necessitated sensations; his morality the impulse of self-gratification; his immortality going out in the dissolution of his bodily organism; and his God the mere personification of nature in her blind operations, which a diseased fancy and a superstitious fear had elevated to universal dominion.

On the other hand, the philosophy of rationalism has tended towards absolute Idealism, and ultimately to Fatalism and Atheism in the opposite direction. With Kant, in his speculative philosophy, there is reality given in sensation, and here is truly all the *material* of knowledge ; but this can come into our cognition in no other manner than according to the *formal* conditions of our subjective being. All, therefore, that we can know is the phenomenal only, and as these phenomena are connected and generalized into a Soul, a Universe, and a Deity, they are but the modifications of the material given in sense reflected through the regulative forms of the subjective understanding and the reason. We can not demonstrate that there is any objective being as the correlative of our formal thought, nor can we demonstrate that there is not such objective valid reality. Ontology, in reference to the Soul, Nature and God, must be left to opinion and faith, and can never become science. Phenomena are, as valid realities ; but what they are in themselves, and only as our formal faculties represent them in our own subjective apprehension, no philosophy can possibly determine. The way was thus open for Fichte to deny the reality which had been assumed here for the phenomenal, and to show that the phenomenal was as truly a reflection from the forms of our subjective being, as in Kant's philosophy had been proved for the Soul, Nature, and the Deity. Thus, instead of admitting with Kant, the being of our formal subjective intellect and the reality of the objective phenomenal matter, Fichte contends that the last is mere opinion and can not be demonstrated science, and that thus only our formal subjective being is that with which we must begin, and on which all philosophy must rest. And now, by the mere process of thought, the way is to be shown from this subjective being alone, out to all our ideas of the universal and the absolute. The subjective, as self or Ego, by thinking, attains to that which limits itself by the laws of its own being, and wholly prevents the action from going out uninterruptedly and losing itself in the infinite; and such necessary limitations in our activity we take cognizance of, objectify in our consciousness, and deem them to be the phenomena of an outer world. Another step is then taken, by recalling our activity from these limitations in our thinking which we have made to be outward phenomena, and thus in reflection we come to apprehend our own activity and attain the contents of our consciousness, and here determine that the mind itself is the whole sphere of its operations, and that its activity can do no more than to objectify its own limitation in its own laws, and then come back and find itself as the subject of its own acts and the object of its own consciousness. All possible theoretic or speculative knowledge is thus wholly subjective, and embraced within the sphere of the Ego only. All that man is competent to do is to know himself. And yet, the thinking may proceed with this seeming objective, and attain to a seeming objective world; and by developing our own subject, we attain to all the ideas of a Universe and a Deity. We thus make the objects we find in our thinking, and all is purely ideal, our own subjective being excepted.

One step more was necessary to the absolute idealism of the process, and that step is taken by Hegel. This assumption of the being of a self, or subjective Ego, by Fichte, is affirmed in Hegel's Philosophy to be wholly gratuitous. It all originates in the spontaneity of thought, and we are not permitted by any data that can give science, to assume any being back of thought. The being of THOUGHT alone, it is permitted to us to use as our starting point; and on this all science must rest, and from this all philosophy must be developed. With Hegel, thought is the only reality; and the self-development of spontaneous logical thinking the only philosophy, and the only process to a possible science. Thought must begin with the absence of all things as opposed to the thought of the being of any thing, and thus all being begins in non-being. Did not non-being stand as the opposite of being, it were impossible that being should be thought. Existence is thus the conjunction of being and of nothing in the thought. Neither can exist but as in the existence of the opposite, and thus existence is truly the antithesis or indifference of the two. And precisely thus with any specific existence. Quality can not be thought, except as substance is also given as its opposite. Both substance and quality, separate and alone, are impossible to be thought as being; *reality* is thus the indifferentism, or the "contradiction" of the two opposite poles, substance and quality. And by the same process perpetuated is originated all of nature, of life, of intelligence, and the absolute; and this is carried out through all philosophy, all natural theology, and is used to explain all that is peculiar in Christianity. The ideal having been thus considered as identical with the real; all that is necessary is to assume the being of thought and its laws of development, and then the logical process of thinking evolves the self, the universe, and the Deity. The whole is necessitated in the law of the logical process, and created by it. It has an ideal being, and yet in it is all the real being which it is possible that we should know. Man, Nature, and God are the necessitated and yet wholly ideal creations of spontaneous thought. Nor is this process ever finished; but as the law of thinking goes on in humanity, the development of thought is thus ever progressing, and the Deity as the absolute can be existent only in the advancing consciousness of the race, and thus an ever unfolding and never perfected being. The whole objective element of philosophy, of theology, and of Christianity is thus annihilated and lost, and nothing remains but the pure ideal as the product of thinking within its law. The phenomenal in experience, the dynamical in philosophy, the inspired and the miraculous in religion, all vanish into empty thought; and all the sublimities of nature and its God are the mere personifications of a void subjective consciousness. "Thus the extremes of sensationalism and idealism meet at length. The one says that God is the universe, the other that the universe is God. Diderot and Strauss can here shake hands, and alike rejoice in the impious purpose of sinking the personality of the Deity into an abstraction, which the holy can not love, and which the wicked need not fear."

A philosophy exclusively based upon either the objective or the subjective is necessarily partial in its very beginning, and must eventuate, when carried to its legitimate issue, in one-sided and therefore erroneous conclusions. The philosophical speculation on either side must follow some law of order, and if it be the law impressed upon the objective in its development of cause and effect, it must ultimately absorb all things within the workings of a mechanical necessity ; and if it be the law which directs the subjective development of thought, it must in the end involve all things within the rigid conclusions of a logical fatality. A comprehensive survey of both, readily determines what must be the landing place of each.

Let the *objective* be the starting point, and the observed facts in their law of experience must give direction to all investigation. In following out such investigations, physical science will be greatly promoted ; the laws of cause and effect in astronomy, chemistry, physiology, geology, &c., will be followed out to their furthest traces in human observation; and practical utility and social expediency will be the ground-springs

5

of human action. But such a philosophy has at length only to open the eyes and look around from its position to determine its own interests, and it must find itself fast bound within the chain of a fixed causation, and shut up within the prison of nature hopeless of all deliverance. Without some salient point in nature, from which, *saltu mortali*, we may fairly project our philosophy beyond nature, then must our whole being perforce content itself to abide within nature, and take the destiny of nature; and the man must recognize himself, and all that is about him, as separate links in the same indefinite chain of coming and departing events, each in its destined place fulfilling its own mission, and all constituting a progressive series of necessitated successions which is both unalterable and interminable. We can know nothing beyond nature, we must conclude that there is nothing beyond nature to be known.

And here, let it be most gravely enquired, if there be not some long-standing and far-famed theories in metaphysics among us, which must infallibly terminate in the above conclusions, whenever they shall be resolutely pushed onward to their consequences. A philosophy which includes in the same category of causation the changes in matter and the originations in mind, though it may use the qualifying terms of a *natural* and *moral* necessity, but which still do not mark any discrimination in the *connections* but only in the *things* connected, must unavoidably find itself within the charmed circle out of which there can be no escaping. It is not possible that such a theory can vindicate for the human soul in its immortality, nor for the Deity in his eternity, the possession of any attributes which may rise above, or reach beyond, the interminable conditions in the linked series of a fixed causation. An assumed God of nature must be but nature still, evermore stretching the chain onward.

Let, on the other hand, the *subjective* be the starting-point, and the logical order of thinking in judgments must be the law for our whole process of philosophizing. And here, doubtless great progress will be made in intellectual science ; and the most abstract thoughts, and fine-spun distinctions, and broadest generalizations, and most subtle analyses, will be distinctly siezed by the human understanding, and carried out to the most profound demonstrations. But such a philosophy, again, has only to lift its eyes from its minute and critical examination of the goings-on of subjective thought within, and look out upon the bearings of its course, and it must find itself plunging into an abyss of abstractions empty and bottomless; from which there is no escape until itself, the soul, nature, and God are all lost together in an Idealism which ultimately vanishes in nihility. So long as anything remains, the laws of thought must be there, and they are as rigid in their consecutive developments, as the fixed ongoings in the successions of nature, and must bind the soul and the Deity within the same logical necessities. But even these exist only from sufferance, and must be as truly ideal as the thoughts induced by them; and thus both law and logical process of thought, together with all of nature and the absolute to which they had attained, await only that sweeping abstraction which abolishes the whole ideal vision forever.

Nor will it in the end, at all avail to bring philosophy to a secure landing-place, that seeing the errors from starting exclusively with either the objective or the subjective, we attempt to remove the one-sidedness of the process by *identifying* the two. Schelling has most elaborately and profoundly attempted this. He would rest philosophy neither on the subjective nor on the objective, but upon that which is the source in our thoughts out of which both proceed. He would abstract both the objective and the subjective, and begin by gazing in an " Intellectual Intuition" directly upon an essence in which objective being and subjective thought are identical.

This absolute identity of subject and object is the primal self-existent ONE, in whose development all that is subject and all that is object subsequently is evolved. It is not an existing thing as an infinite substance possessing thought and extension, like Spinozas' starting point from the substratum in which both the objective and subjective inhere; but it is existence itself as antithetic to both objective and sub-

jective existence, in which neither the objective nor the
subjective are, but into both of which the existence
itself is ultimately to be produced. Beginning thus
with simple absolute being, the law of self-development as mere "*reflective force*" sees its own inner
essence, and thus objectifies all of itself. These, as
finite reflections of itself, become thus finite objects ; and
in this the philosophy of *nature* is at once here embodied. The second movement is a "*subsuming-force*," by
which the objectified existence is now taken in and
expounded by that of which it is the reflection, and is
thus an awaking into self-consciousness as having
both subject and object; and in this the philosophy
of *mind* is given. The combination and completion
of these two movements, which admits of a re-union
of object and subject in consciousness, is a "*reason-
force*," and gives the absolute ; not bare existence as
potentially at the beginning of the process, but developed, realized, self-conscious being, including all being
both objective and subjective ; and this at once gives
the whole philosophy of *Deity*. These three, NATURE,
MIND, GOD, thus unfolded, may be separately taken,
and all that they contain be evolved by a similar process. This Schelling has done by a most comprehensive process of mental evolution, and in this way
he would unfold the whole possible chart of all philosophy. But once make this philosophy to awake
from its dream of a perpetually unfolding of the absolute, and set itself to the ascertaining of its own posi-

tion, and it must perforce find that it has ensphered itself and all things else in an all-embracing transcendental pantheism. In this assumed absolute identity, thought and being are essentially one; the process of development is the course of logical thinking, and which creates the beings identical with the thoughts; hence the complete development in the reason-force would be both the sum of universal human reason and the being of the absolute reason—i. e. the reason of all men in the aggregated and completed development is God, and God is, only as this evolved reason of all humanity is.

May we then betake ourselves to a process of *Eclecticism*, in this variety and great contrariety of philosophical thinking and its results? Such a method of building up a system anticipates that there is truth in all philosophizing, though more or less partial, distorted and obscured; and the process is to sift the truth from the error, and with this pure residuum of all systems build up the only and altogether true. Undoubtedly it may be yielded to such a theory, that few philosophical systems are wholly of error; and that all truth is consistent with each portion of truth; and that the only and altogether true system of philosophy must be competent to find a place for all philosophical truth within itself; and also, that if all the truth of all philosophical systems were discriminated from the errors of all, and this in combination with all other truth was bound up harmoniously in one system, it would be the true comprehensive philosophy. But how go on with this sifting process, and detect all pure truth and take it from all other systems? Certainly in no other manner than by first taking a stand-point upon some system, which in its law of construction is comprehensive of all so far as they are true, and which at once vindicates its own right to be by embracing the truth of all, and thus demolishing them in building up itself. It is not to be permitted that it should be some arbitrary patch-work, selecting assumed truths here and there, but a law of construction that claims all of right, because it can bring them all legitimately within its colligation. Eclecticism must thus begin its work of taking truths from other systems, by bringing along with it its comprehensive law which shall vindicate its title to what it takes, and not by arrogantly plundering what it pleases. But it may at once be affirmed, that the conditioning of all things upon an absolute cause which goes out into effects of necessity, and thus that nature is as necessary to a Deity as a Deity is to nature, and which is the conclusion of Cousin's Eclecticism, cannot be universally accepted as the true system. It is as really fatalistic and pantheistic, as any which it has assumed to supplant.

There is a movement in *two other* directions which it may be of importance here to notice. Despairing altogether of reaching to any thing supernatural on the one side, or above the logical forms of the understanding on the other side, there is an entire suppression of all speculation in the way of finding the being of a God as supernatural, and who possesses an objective reality. The light shines upon nature and in human consciousness so far as experience and deductions and analogies from experience may go, and so far as the apriori laws of an understanding judging according to cause and effect may reach; but upon all beyond a darkness broods impervious to any ray of light; and here, standing between the light of nature and logic on one side and the darkness of the supernatural and absolutely real on the other, are two classes taking the two directions above referred to, viz: the *Mystic;* and the falsely called *Rationalist.*

The *Mystic*, from the inner prompting and working of his own immortal spirit, verily believes that there is life and conscious real being within this mysterious region of the supernatural. He distrusts and renounces all proffered help from philosophy, and leaves that to work out its problems in physics, and weave its syllogisms in dialectics. He will neither think nor reason any farther. He depends wholly upon some inward illumination, and rests confidingly upon some impulsive *feeling* which is to convey to him an immediate knowledge of the mysterious spirit-world. This may be a philosophical mysticism as with Jacobi; where the faith-principle is attempted to be rationally accounted for, and all its results subjected to a philosophical, rigid, and exceedingly elegant and ingenious analysis; or it may be the fanatical impulses of Peter the Hermit, and Ignatius Loyola; or the credulous admissions of Fox's light within; or the enthusiastic raptures of Jacob Bœhme. The immediate organ of knowledge is some inner emotion and feeling with which the intellect can have little to do, and whose process of revealing is as mysterious as the things revealed. Without questioning how the revelation is to come, or testing the inspiration when it is given, the Mystic turns himself reverently towards the darkness, and in silent contemplation waits in confiding expectation for the message to be given, or the vision to appear. The excited working of his own inner being transfers its products to this dim region of the supernatural, and at once an inner sympathy becomes an objective reality, and the spirit-land is the scene of such communings as abound in the credulous experiences of Immanuel Swedenborg. Nor are these illusions mere chimeras. They are a real reflection from the inner spiritual being, and come of that which is living and immortal in the soul. As possessing objective significancy, they are meaningless and valueless; but subjectively interpreted, they present a very important lesson for philosophy to read and expound. While, thus, there may be realities and indices of outward truth in our subjective emotions and feelings, yet can we never rely upon such inner inspiration for any revelations from the supernatural world. When divine inspiration is truly given, it will not leave its vindication to mere credulity, but will stamp upon itself the šeal of such an accredited authority, that reason will itself respond in perfect acquiescence.

The *pseudo-Rationalist* pursues a different course. He rises quite above the philosophy of sensation and empiricism, and is clearly aware of the empty and dead material mechanism in which that must terminate. He admits apriori truth, and contends strenuously for the authority and validity of rational investigation, and the soundness of the demonstrations thereby affected. In this process, the intellectual functions of judgment and forms of all thinking are correctly attained; and the laws of nature, as universal and necessary, are fairly expounded. Nature is no longer viewed in the mere husk and dead covering of the phenomenal, but the living powers are apprehended working beneath, and ever unfolding new forms of sublimity and beauty. The correlation in the laws of thought and the laws of nature's development is determined, and the objective and subjective seen to run onward in parallel lines, and with equal steps, in apparently interminable progression. In all this there is science, order, harmony, beauty. Life and gladness are on every hand, and where there is seeming disorder or distress, it touches sensibilities and awakens sympathies, the luxury of whose gushing emotions we could not afford to lose. But this is the "ultima thule" of philosophical attainment. The living powers of nature, the sublime disclosures of reason, the pleasures of taste, and the brilliant creations of genius, together with the transcendental attainments in philosophy, are themes of never-dying interest; but the supernatural world, under the moral government of a personal and holy God, and all the inspired Revelations concerning it, and the divine plan of preparing sinners for it, or the purposes of penal retribution in it, are wholly gratuitous assumptions, utterly unphilosophical and indemonstrable. No possible science can reach beyond the parallel laws of the subjective and the objective; an absolute Personality, beyond nature and beyond humanity, is utterly unattainable and inconceivable; and hence all divine inspiration, and revelation, and miraculous interventions, are wholly incredible. All the inspiration there can be is a higher impartation of the universal reason in some favored Sage, who thus becomes the Seer and Prophet of his generation, and whose oracles may live in the religious veneration of posterity until the rising reason of the race has grown beyond them, and then humanity demands its new Prophet, and may expect its needed revelations.

The stand-point of this *partial Transcendentalism* is wholly within nature. It transcends the phenomenal in sensation, truly and philosophically, and such is its deservedly great praise; but to it the supernatural is darkness. Not a darkness as the mere absence of light, but of all being; the darkness of an utter negation. Nature and humanity run on their interminable parallels for such a philosopher, and if aught be beyond them, it must be an absolute void.   It is, therefore, to him, the part of wisdom to suppress the aspirations of the free and immortal within us, for they must be the working of only a delusive hope or an instinctive fear, and the sure precursors of superstition and fanaticism. He discards all reason as organ for the supernatural, and yet calls himself a Rationalist! He shuts himself up hopelessly within the circumscriptions of nature and humanity, and yet calls himself a Transcendentalist! He has so far transcended the mere phenomenal in sense, that he can give unity to physical nature and to human nature, but he acknowledges no faculty for transcending the conditioned development of nature in these correlative laws of operation; and hence, when he turns towards the supernatural, he believes himself to have positively seen a negation and actually known a void, and then confidently avers that the whole region of the supernatural is utter emptiness. And now, having thus turned his back to the sun, he attempts the solution of the mysteries in the motions and shapes of his own shadow. The world without is truly the counterpart of the intellectual world within; the objective is the correlative of the subjective; and hence he is perpetually finding analogies and correspondencies. Their correlation reveals perpetual harmony, beauty, and truth; and so far there is science. But the spiritual, the free, the immortal personality within has no correlation with nature, but only with the supernatural. Between this and nature there is perpetual contrast, and the attempt which this philosophy must make to subject the former to the latter, instead of analogy and correspondence, must induce only contradictions and absurdities. The self-active and the self-conscious can not be made to run parallel with the conditioned and necessitated, without introducing perpetual deformity and discord.

And precisely in this is the ready explanation of what so perpetually appears in all the writings of this modern transcendental school. In its partiality and incompleteness, it must often give unequal representations; the *correlation* in the intellectual subjective and the objective will give truth, the *contrast* in the free and spiritual subjective and the objective must give absurdity. Hence we have at one time, so much life, vigor, clearness and depth of originality, that we stand admiring and delighted; at another time, the whole is equivocal, ambiguous, and so obscure in its profundity, that one man deems it the veracious though mysterious responses of an oracle, and another the ravings of a lunatic; again, we have representations so grotesque and ludicrous, that we can-not choose but smile; and then, so profane and irreverent a blending of the natural and the spiritual, the human and the divine, that we ought indignantly to frown. The human, which it can know, is so often represented in the phraseology of the divine, which it assumes not to know, that the whole speech becomes utterly impertinent, and often shockingly blasphemous. The position is wholly within nature, and it is denied that there may be any projection of the intellect beyond nature, and thus if any thing be said of the supernatural it must refer to the laws of the natural, and if any attributes of Divinity are mentioned they must apply to some of the aggregates of humanity. And hence, that mixture of the meaning and the meaningless, the expressed and the inexpressible, which so abounds through the speculations and teachings of this philosophy. Here and there gleams of light so bright and pure break out from masses of mist and clouds, as to seem almost like flashes of inspiration; and then come shadowy thoughts so strange and wild, as to seem rather the ravings of madness.

It is quite probable that this spurious transcendentalism is just now increasing in the midst of us. It avails itself of the influence of a peculiar phraseology, the assumption of a superior philosophical spirit, a manifest heartiness and earnest sincerity, and a strong claim to originality and independence. But most of all its advantages is the waning confidence in that wide-spread Empiricism which has so long prevailed, and the strong and craving need that is felt for a more spiritual philosophy. On this account, it is presenting special attractions to many of the youth in our seminaries and colleges, who are just beginning to think systematically. In the greenness of their speculations,

there is great liability to strike root in this soft soil
rather than in the firm ground of a solid demonstration,
while yet the mind has not ripened to sufficient maturity to appreciate the hazard of assuming hasty positions,
before it can see very far, very steadily, or very clearly.
But with all the interest which this philosophy would
seek to inspire for the inner life of nature, and the reverence it would cherish for the higher destinies of humanity, it still terminates wholly within the conditions
of those laws, which bind the thinking in logical sequences, and outward events in necessitated successions. The Universe, the Soul, and the Deity, are all
circumscribed within the iron chain of a fixed order of
progress. The chain, though endless, is yet one.
From the first, if any first can be, no link is independent of the others, but one exists for all and all for each,
and all proper personality is impossible. The Deity
is the inner force and law, which is operating as logical
thought in humanity and as causation in physical nature; and by an intestine necessity works out the perpetual development, orderly, incessantly, irresistibly;
yet wholly destitute alike of feeling, of foresight, and
of freedom. Hence those glowing and sometimes truly
sublime representations of the deep, mysterious, silent
and eternal working of this power within and around
us. All things working on, and together working out
their own destiny; and the changeless law pervading
the whole is the God of the whole, and there is no God
beyond and above this.

And now, verily, it can but little subserve the good cause, to meet this highest form of Infidelity with ridicule, hard names and reproachful epithets. The system is the product of severe and earnest thought, and has much of pure and high truth embraced within it. It will never permit itself to be laughed out of countenance, nor can it be beaten down by denunciation. Nature *has* fixed connections and established laws, and her inner causality *is* working out for herself an orderly and progressive development. It is a great attainment for any philosophy to have followed up the road of truth and science thus far, and to have settled the laws of nature's development upon the basis of a rational demonstration. It is the only way in which the errors originating in the limited philosophy of sensation can be met and redressed. But, while it is to its credit, that it goes thus far, yet it is itself but an incomplete and partial philosophy, and terminates in greater difficulties and deeper errors than those which it has removed. The evil is not in what this system embraces, but from what it excludes. What we need is a hardy and complete philosophy which will not stop within nature's Temple and worship only amid the products of her agency and under the authority of her laws and principles. We need from within nature, whence our knowledge must begin, some point for firm footing so high that we may overlook, and truly cast our vision beyond nature, and find an absolute and free Being who has given existence to, and who controls nature.

The mind must be disciplined and the intellectual vision purified and exercised until it may clearly discern a sharp outline, discriminating liberty in personality from physical causation not only, but from instinctive impulses, and constitutional inclinations, and undirected spontaneity, and unhindered agency in one direction. A personality must be found, with a capability to originate objective and substantial being from within himself; and to put forth his creations as other than, and quite distinct from, his own being; and who both in existence and agency shall be wholly unconditioned by any higher causation; and whose line of operation shall be determined by nothing from within his works, but wholly from an imperative out of and independent of his work, and apriori given in his own absolute being. This is essential to the idea of a personal, underived, and independent Deity; and except as we cognize the actual existence of the Person given in this archetypal idea, we can possibly worship none other than an " unknown God."

It is not sufficient that we leap to the conclusion, as is mostly done in all our popular treatises on Natural Theology, and thus attain only the *assumption* of the existence of such a Being—because such will very well relieve the want which we feel in our speculations to find a permanent resting place to our regressus in the tracing up of the series of conditioned effects from conditioning causes, and whence also we may begin to trace down the flowing stream of events as independent of

6

any higher source—inasmuch as in this manner we can possibly attain to no higher than an hypothetical Deity. Our want is satisfied by such an hypothesis, and the being of nature is explained by such a supposition; but that there is actually such a God, is in this way, wholly supposititious and indemonstrable. The true idea of a God is first to be attained, viz. a being who may originate universal nature from himself, and not be himself a component or an included element, but who, though originating nature, in his personality still stands forth beyond and independent of it, and at his pleasure operates upon and within it; and then this idea realized in this, that having in an apriori demonstration determined how it is possible thus to comprehend nature, we should look at nature and find there the correlative and thus the demonstrative of this idea in actual existence. The Being whom we seek to know is transcendental in the highest degree. He transcends all appearance in sensation, inasmuch as he can never be made a content of the sense and constructed into an object in consciousness. He also transcends all the notions of substance and cause in the understanding, inasmuch as while they only connect qualities and events in nature, he himself is the author of those substances and causes, and thus comprehends in his own being the very substance in its causality of all the phenomena of nature, and is thus wholly out of and beyond all the things given in the judgments of our understanding. The only faculty competent to reach and know the objective existence of such a Being must rise higher than merely to *construct* within limits in space and time, as does the intellect in sense; and higher than merely to *connect* such constructions in a nature of things, as does the intellect in the understanding; even that which can *comprehend* nature itself in an origination from liberty, and a consummation in the final ends of a free and absolute Personality; and which can possibly belong only to the functions of the pure reason. God is not phenomenon, nor substance and cause connecting phenomena: He is beyond all this, for this is nature only and is God's creature. He thus as truly transcends the understanding as he does the sense, and can not possibly become objectively known but by the higher faculty of the reason. All philosophy is most absurdly denominated Rationalism, which makes its ultimate conclusions to be in nature, and denies that there is any thing which may be known as the supernatural. It is a Rationalism discarding the very organ and faculty of reason itself.

And here it becomes highly important to note, that some of the strongest entrenchments of skepticism both in philosophy and religion—some of the most elaborate defences of all Infidelity—are now in process of erection upon this high ground. Whether named Liberalism, Neologism, Rationalism, or Transcendentalism; its foundation is here, and the superstructure is going up on this basis. And true philosophy has not accomplished her work and fulfilled the end of her mission, until she has utterly and forever demolished this entire foundation. It were a reproach to philosophy and theology to delay the final conquest of all this region, which from the days of Moses by the gift of divine authority, and from the days of Plato by the right of original discovery, has been the domain of truth, religion, and science; and which only by a lawless usurpation has seemed to have passed into the hands of aliens. Every mind which has worked its way up to these heights of human thought, well knows that in this pure region there is a broad and fair inheritance for philosophy, and which it is incumbent on her to explore, to possess, and to cultivate. If some who have been there, growing giddy from the height or dazzled by excess of the brightness, have taken wrong positions and run false lines, their errors are surely not to be redressed by ridicule nor railing from those who stand below, but effectually in nothing short of girding up the loins, and ascending to the same heights, and making so accurate a survey as shall give the right to subvert their false positions and abolish their wrong landmarks. Error any where, when brought within the grasp of truth, is easily crushed, but never can the hand of truth be laid upon those errors in high places, except as some shall go up in her name, and take a final stand upon this last and highest point where science and skepticism may grapple in conflict.

And certainly, the only possible method of finding such a position is from the final results of a Rational Psychology, which having given the laws of intelligence in the functions of the sense and the understanding, now completes its work in the attainment of the conditional laws of the faculty of the reason; and by knowing the reason in its law, may thus lay the foundation for demonstrating the valid being of the Soul in its liberty, and of God in his absolute Personality, which can possibly be objects for the faculty of the reason alone. A true and comprehensive Rational Psychology is a necessary preliminary to all demonstrations in Ontology, and the subversion of skepticism by giving a position which commands the whole ground of its fundamental assumptions.

From all the foregoing considerations it is now manifest that Rational Psychology may subserve the purposes of science in three distinct departments, by affording a position from which skepticism in relation to the valid being of the objects given in each, may be met and counteracted. We have thus three distinct fields for our investigation, and in each of which lie some of the most important questions fundamental for all science. We need to determine the conditioning principles of *perception in sensation ;* as the basis of an argument for demonstrating that the objects, given in the sense as single qualities and exercises, are valid realities. We need, moreover, to determine the conditioning principles of all *judgments in the under-*

standing; as the ground for demonstrating that the real objects given in sense, and connected in substances and causes and thus becoming a nature of things, are also valid realities. And then, lastly, we need to determine the conditioning principles of all *comprehension of a nature of things in the faculty of the reason;* as the ground for a demonstration that the Soul in its liberty, and that the Deity in his personality, are valid existences. The *Psychology* terminates in the science of the faculties of the sense, the understanding, and the reason; and when this is made the basis of a further demonstration for the valid being of the objects thus given, the science becomes *Ontology.*

In this may be seen an outline of the work which is here proposed to be accomplished. The course lies in the direction towards the highest attainments of thought to which the human mind may elevate itself. So far forth as our positions shall be taken in those apriori demonstrations, which are given in the necessary and universal laws of intelligence, we may compel the convictions of even skepticism itself, and settle the rights and substantiate the claims of science to all her possessions. This is not the place to affirm the competency to put these topics in the clear light of an apriori demonstration; but we are about to make the attempt, in all humility and with some sense of the magnitude and difficulty of the task, to explore how far we may find ground, and how firm it may be, for putting up our intellectual buildings, and securing a completed structure of human science. Is the human mind shut up to *faith* on all subjects? or are there some paths which lead to *science*? So far as the present attempt can avail, the sequel must determine to which alternative we are left.

4. There is another use to which Rational Psychology may be rendered subservient, and which, perhaps, as a connected part of this work, may at some future time receive our attention, viz: *the attainment of a complete method of all possible science.* A perfect classification of science, by which each department should be located relatively to the whole, and securing a completely organized system of all possible philosophy, would be of no small consequence to philosophy itself. Such a method will be practicable, when the science of Rational Psychology shall have been completed. The intellect is the organ of all knowledge, and all that can be attained must be given through the exercise of the various intellectual functions, and the law for their operation must of course give the rule for the acquisition of science. The several laws, by which the functions of our intellectual faculties are regulated, must together determine an ordered method of all human knowledge. The entire circumscription of the field for all possible human science is given in the laws of the intellect itself, and all the divisions and subdivisions of this field are before us, when we have discriminated the functions and laws of operation in our own intellectual being.

An accurate map of all possible science is but a counter-part of that intelligence in which all science originates. A method so ordered would be no random collection of separate cognitions, nor an arbitrary aggregate of separate sciences; but the laws of intellectual agency will determine each to its place, and give sure indication, that when all the laws have been consulted, then all distinguishable science will have been included, and that in this the system is completed. The particular items embraced and the different objects known, may be multiplied and diversified indefinitely, but the field in which they must lie, the category within which they must fall, will be given, and this will be all that a perfect method of science demands.

It may also be affirmed that the compass of all future knowledge is thus given. Unless new intellectual faculties are given, we must henceforth know within the same intellectual laws as now we know. A residence in the future " spiritual body" may much modify all our perceptions and judgments, and in the passing away of the qualities and connections of the material world, nature may be dissolved; but our laws of thought must remain identical as our being. And especially the agency of reason in the liberty of our personality, which has here been so much clogged, and which will there be emancipated from all bondage in the case of the holy, may then go out under the ethical laws of its own imperatives in free, glad and perfect obedience. Thus, when rolling cycles shall have been passed by a glorified soul in pure and holy employment, it must still be acting within the laws of its own intellectual being, and though perhaps but just entering yet upon broader and brighter scenes of existence which stretch ever onward, the laws of its agency must perpetually accompany it; and thus even now may we determine, not the objects it shall know, but the boundaries and divisions of that intellectual field in which they must lie, and in the circumscription of which, the free activities of the blessed spirit must move—

"While life and thought and being last,
And immortality endures."

BOOK I.

GROUNDWORK

OF

RATIONAL PSYCHOLOGY.

~~~~~~~~~~~~~

THE process of demonstration in Rational Psychology must be carried forward upon a Groundwork previously laid, the soundness and validity of which must be clearly apprehended; and this must be made to underlie the whole work and give stability to each step and soundness to the ultimate conclusion, when the process of demonstration shall have been accurately effected. By striking out our course over such previously ascertained valid groundwork, we shall not only carry along with us the confidence that our progress is in a safe and sure way, but may by it, also, at the out-set, order our general plan of procedure and give an outline for the method of attaining our completed Psychological System. In this *First Book*, the business before us will be to lay down such valid Groundwork, over which we may then make our process of demonstration to take its safe course; and then by this, also, to make an exposition of our General Method. This will demand clear discernment and acute discrimination, but the entire book may be brought within a comparatively narrow compass.

SECTION I.

THAT which is determinative of true and valid science, and by which all skepticism may be excluded, may be put as a safe and sufficient Groundwork for the demonstration of a Rational Psychology. We need to attain a universal criterion of true science, and to make this underlie and regulate our whole process. Without such a criterion we must proceed at random and in the dark, and if by chance we might thus stumble upon the treasure we are seeking, yet, inasmuch as we could never verify its genuineness nor determine and appropriate the grounds where it was, we should never be able to avail ourselves of our good fortune.

It was an old question—and who knows when the time shall come that the inquirer will patiently wait for the answer—*What is truth?* Suppose the claim to be sometime made, that *this is a truth;* by what test may such a claim be vindicated? The most obvious course might seem to be, to find some universal peculiarity as essential to all truth, both the known and the unknown, and by the application of this general test to determine each particular claim. But precisely in this point of universal applicability lies the whole difficulty. The truth in any thing is that which separates and distinguishes it from all other things, and thus that which is *its* truth cannot be *the* truth in any thing beside. Truth particularizes its objects, and therefore a general criterion of truth is an absurdity. To ask then intelligibly, what is truth? must be to inquire, what particular thing is true? and not, what universal belongs to truth?

We should be led away very far from our proper work, therefore, if we permitted ourselves to go off in a vain search for some universal characteristic which was to determine all truth in particular. It is not truth as a universal that we at all need, and we have very much facilitated our progress when we have learned to exclude all efforts for that which is not to be attained, and which is not needed. We inquire, not what belongs to all truth; but does truth belong to this particular? The inquiry is rather for true knowledge, than for a knowledge of universal truth. And here we have only a particular in view, viz: knowledge, as distinct from delusion, or opinion, or belief. What discriminates science from all other conceptions?—*What is true science?* The answer to this inquiry involves no absurdity, yet is not the answer very obvious, nor indeed of very ready attainment.

Science is exclusive of all that depends upon testimony. All testimony, whether from a human or divine source, eventuates only in faith. There may be an assurance of faith, but not demonstration as science, from testimony.

Experience in clear consciousness is spoken of as knowledge. And within experience consciousness must stand as the ultimate test of knowledge. If we suppose any man to take his position within experience, and there assume that a decision of consciousness may be questioned, and should attempt to affirm his doubts of the validity of the things given in experience, his very affirmation of his doubts would convict himself of absurdity. He can affirm the fact of his doubting upon no other ground than his consciousness of it and if consciousness is valid for the experience of doubting, it may certainly be equally valid for any other fact in experience. An empirical skepticism on such grounds would preclude the possibility of affirming its own existence.

If, again, it were alleged by two persons, that their conscious experiences contradicted each other, the appeal would lie to consciousness still, but in a broader sense, viz : to the general consciousness of the race of mankind. When by any means it may have been determined what the general consciousness of mankind has been in the same fact of experience ; this must be conclusive, for an alleged contradiction of consciousness to that of the race of mankind must convict of other than a human experience, and exclude from the jurisdiction of common sense.

But, suppose the man take his position beyond experience, and assume that the conclusions of reason overthrow the decisions of consciousness and thus subvert the ultimate grounds of all experience; then, surely, we need some other position on which to stand than our consciousness, or the common consciousness of the race. Berkely admitted the appearance in consciousness, but denied the objective validity. The rod straight in one experience, plunged half its length in water becomes a bent stick in another experience. The skepticism goes beyond experience and denies that the foundations on which all experience rests are solid. And Hume, still farther, affirmed the convictions of consciousness, and admitted the decisions of common sense; but since reason fairly contradicted this, and yet both consciousness and reason were independent and original sources of knowledge, their plain contradiction destroyed all confidence in either, and universal doubt was inevitable, inasmuch as uncontradicted knowledge was from any quarter impossible.

While therefore, we are wont to speak of the decisions of consciousness in experience as knowledge, and so long as we keep within experience this is sufficient, yet if we are forced to the defence of the foundations of experience, we have the very decisions of consciousness itself to investigate and sustain; and an apriori demonstration here is a confirmation of consciousness and a verification of knowledge itself; and for such original demonstration it is meet that we appropriate the term *science* in its philosophical acceptation. Sufficient testimony induces *faith;* experience in consciousness is *knowledge;* and when this is confirmed by an appeal to universal consciousness we have that knowledge which rests upon *common sense.* When we go back of the simple experience of single facts in consciousness, and find the conditional principle which expounds the facts and is the law which binds them in systematic unity, we have then *science* properly so called. If this law be found as a general deduction from many particulars, and which is assumed because it will expound the facts so far as applied, it is *inductive science;* and rests only upon a generalization of experience under the universal assumption, that similar substances in their causality ever give uniformly similar qualities and changes; but which can never carry its positive affirmations any farther than the experience reaches, and is hence to be termed science in the qualified acceptation of *empirical science.* But when this conditional principle has been found apriori, and established as the law which in itself is necessary and universal for the facts to be possible, we have then science in its highest philosophical acceptation, and which is distinguished as *metaphysical*—or, as the same thing—*transcendental science.*

While then it is admitted, that consciousness is a sufficient test for what is simply termed knowledge;

7

and, that common sense is a confirmation of this knowledge, on the ground of universal consciousness; it is still necessary that we attain a criterion for science, as a higher philosophical knowledge, and this in both its inductive and metaphysical or transcendental import. Such a criterion, we now proceed to attain; and the conception of what it is, we will expound as concisely and clearly as is practicable.

To KNOW, in all cases, implies both *the knowing* and *the known;* and thus both a subjective and an objective. The subjective part is the knowing; and so far as subjective only, it involves the intellectual agency and the product of this agency as the completed conception or thought. For our present purpose we may wholly dismiss the consideration of the intellectual agency, and regard only the conception, as completed product or *subjective thought.* The objective part is the known; and so for as objective only, it involves the content or matter as essence, and the mode as form. We may dismiss attention to the content, and retain the form as mode, and we shall in this have *objective form.* All knowledge thus involves a subjective thought and a correlative objective form. If now, with Plato, we call the subjective thought, *Idea;* and with Bacon, call the objective form, *Law;* we shall then say, that in all knowledge, the subjective idea and the objective law must stand to each other in correlation. The criterion of all knowledge, and which when applied makes the result to be science, is therefore this;

the determined accordance of the subjective Idea and the objective Law.

Inasmuch as all intelligent progress in our anticipated investigation depends upon a clear conception and use of this criterion of all science, it is important that we more fully illustrate it both in its inductive and its transcendental application. No statement, however carefully the language may have been chosen to avoid ambiguity, can give to this conception so much perspicuity as an adducing of some plain examples.

Take the process of invention for any machine, as a watch. The intellectual agency subjectively combines particular conceptions in reference to some definite result, as the notation of time, according to intellectually apprehended conditioning principles, until the whole combination at length stands out in its unity as one completed thought. Inasmuch as this is wholly subjective, it is no knowledge of a watch, but solely the conception of how a watch is possible, and is thus subjective idea only. We will now suppose the objective matter of a watch, as it appears in our perception. The component parts, with their shapes, colors, points of contact, polish and peculiarity of substance, are seen; but thus far it is appearance only, and not any knowledge of the machine as a measurer of time any more than to have perceived so many pebbles in contact. But when beyond this appearance of the matter, the intellectual apprehension detects the formative principle which conditioned the entire arrangement, and determined for each part its figure and its place, the combination is then put into systematic form, and a law is in the mass of materials giving to the whole a specific unity. It is then only that the matter which appears is known as a watch. Here is objective law. And now comes the criterion of science. When the subjective idea of the watch, as above, may be referred to the objective law of the watch, as perceived, and their complete accordance as correlates thus determined, we not only know the watch, but we intelligently apprehend this knowledge. We know our own knowing, and this is *science*.

It may not be of any importance for a criterion which order shall be taken in the attaining of the idea and the law. The subjective idea may be first, and the watch manufactured after it as the archetype ; or the subjective law may be first apprehended, and then wholly abstracted from the appearance as mere thought only. The only difference is that the first *creates* the science, and the second *learns* it. But for both there is science, because it is competent for both to determine an accordance between the subjective idea and the objective law.

This illustration might be extended by a reference to any portion of nature, or to universal nature as a whole. We may assume any phenomenon, and take our theory for explaining why it is thus and not otherwise. In this hypothesis we shall have the subjective idea ; but such, even if it were perfectly self-con-

sistent, is mere empty thought and not knowledge.
So also I may perceive growing plants and animals;
the phenomenon of crystalization, magnetism, electricity, combustion, &c.; but this is mere appearance
in consciousness—material content without form.
When, however, I apprehend in these phenomena an
*in*forming principle of development, which determines
their mode of being; I have therein an objective law,
by which I know them in their own specific unity.
And now, if it is competent for me to go further,
and take my subjective hypothesis as idea, and apply
it to this objective law as found in the actual phenomena, and determine the according correlation of
idea and law, then I have a science of all these phenomena. And so, lastly, I may have the thought of
a force, directly as the quantity and inversely as the
square of the distance, in all matter, and may thus
conceive how it is possible that matter may be combined into worlds, and worlds into systems, and all systems into a universe; yet such is subjective idea only.
But when I perceive worlds and systems wheeling in
space as material appearance, and intellectually apprehend the power of gravity holding all things in the
one combination of universal nature; I then have an
objective law, and know nature as *in*formed by it.
And when I can take the idea and the law as distinct and determine their correlation, I can expound,
and have thus a *science* of nature.

Here, then, is an illustration of our conception of

the criterion of science. And yet thus far, it is a criterion for inductive or empirical science only. The idea for a possible watch, or world, or universal nature, is not apriori except in the particular case. We cannot say the idea must universally and necessarily be such, nor that the objective law could not have been otherwise; but only, that such subjective idea determines the objective combination to be possible, and that such objective law being as it is, the combination could not have been otherwise. Such laws of nature must give such combinations for our experience; but how determine that such laws *must be*? or, that they *are*, in any one instance beyond what an actual experience has confirmed? How subject physical laws to an apriori science? As yet, the illustration applies only to a science, which cannot carry its demonstrations beyond the field of actual experience.

As a criterion for a transcendental science, the idea must be wholly attained through an apriori process. It must be seen as that which necessarily and universally must be; and which is therefore to control all experience, neither springing out from it nor depending upon it, and thus making for science an altogether metaphysical basis. We may take the following illustrations.

The idea of a line is that of a point produced in space; that of a circle is the circumvolution of a line about the point in one end; of a sphere, the revolution of a circle about its diameter; of a cylinder, the revolution of a parallelogram about one of its sides; of a cone, the revolution of a right angled triangle about one of the sides containing the right angle; &c. The idea in the above cases is wholly apriori. Experience can never give the idea in its exactness and completeness, while all experience must be conformed to it. But while the idea in each case is strictly necessary and universal, yet it is mere subjective thought and not objective knowledge. It determines only how a line, or other mathematical figure is possible. Nor is the perception of a material line, as appearance in consciousness, any knowledge of a line; except as there is the intellectual apprehension of the form conditioning the matter, and thus giving the law which determines the appearance to be what it is. And thus of the circle, or any other regular figure. And now comes the criterion of my knowledge of the line, or the circle, &c. If I can take the idea of the figure, and determine its correlation with the law of its actual construction, I thereby verify my knowledge, which is properly science. And inasmuch as this idea is independent of all experience, and this law is universally necessary in all experience, so that no line circle, &c., can be without this inherent, *informing* law; it thus follows, that my science is not at all inductive and empirical, but metaphysical and transcendental.

The same illustration, of the criterion of an apriori science, is given in any determined combination or computation of numbers. The subjective idea of such combination is apriori, and yet merely the void thought of the possible only. But an actual computation is no knowledge, except as the rule is seen to control and give form to the process, and thus becomes the objective law of the combination; and then, when this apriori idea and this universally necessary law in the combination are determined as standing in accordance, the result becomes an apriori science. All experience must be controlled by it, nor can it be admitted that nature may give any thing which is contradictory to it.

These illustrations must suffice for a clear conception of a universal criterion of science, and of the distinction between such as is empirical and such as is transcendental.

If then, we may be able to set all the processes of intellectual agency in this apriori light, and attain a transcendental idea according to which only can any intellectual functions operate intelligently, we shall thus come philosophically to know the knower; and shall possess a science of intelligence itself through all its departments, by a determination of the complete accordance of this apriori subjective idea with the law which we shall detect through all our actual intellectual being. The criterion for our results, as valid science, is this accordance of subjective idea and objective law; and, that we may make it rational or transcendental science, we must attain the idea, not from any deductions or assumptions in experience, but as that which is apriori seen to be universally necessary to a possible experience. For such investigation the human mind is competent. The intellect can make its own functions and operations the objects of its investigation, and determine the apriori principles necessary to such agency. Man can intelligently expound his own intelligence, and philosophically interpret his own philosophy; and in this consists the science of all sciences, viz : a rational exposition of our psychological being and agency.

When we have attained in this way an attested science of intelligence itself, we shall find ourselves in a position for correcting or confirming our perceptions and judgments. As the astronomer may not only use his telescope, but may also subject it to the laws which must condition all optical appearance, and may thus adjust and correct it intelligently and confirm the validity of his observations by it ; so, in this science, may all our intellectual operations be overlooked, and the validity of the objects known be verified. While we may thus discriminate the objects perceived from mere illusion, hallucination, and *clairvoyance ;* so also may we silence the skepticism of the idealist, the materialist, and the universal pyrrhonist; and more important still, may subvert the credulity of the mystic on the one side, and the unbelief of the rationalist on the other. The importance of such an investigation thoroughly made can not well be over estimated, and especially in view of what is so emphatically and with probable truth affirmed by a learned friend in his Introduction to "PLATO AGAINST THE ATHEISTS," that "the next battle ground of Infidelity will not be the Scriptures. What faith there may remain will be summoned to defend the very being of a God, the great truth, involving every other moral and religious truth —the primal truth—*that* HE IS, *and that he is the rewarder of all who diligently seek him.*"

A true, complete, and sound transcendental philosophy was, perhaps, never more to be desired, though the name was never so sadly perverted and vilified. Like the Hebrew champion, it has been blinded and bound and made to grind in the prison-house of the uncircumcised; but in its recovered strength it may terribly avenge itself, when placed between the pillars of that profane temple in which it has been exposed to mockery. So far as the demonstrations of a Rational Psychology may be made to reach will the possession be legalized to science. The whole domain of philosophy may be thereby utterly and forever freed from the intrusions of skepticism, but except as we hold these title-deeds in our hands, shall we be unable to sue out a summary process of ejectment against any determined trespasser.

The groundwork for such a process of philosophizing is laid in this determinate criterion of all transcendental science. If our work can be made to stand upon an apriori idea as subjective conformed to an ascertained law in the facts as objective, we shall possess a valid science of Rational Psychology. But, in addition, such an ascertained groundwork will determine for us our General Method.

SECTION II.

GENERAL METHOD FOR RATIONAL PSYCHOLOGY.

By attaining the different intellectual faculties and their functions of operation in all ways of knowing, and beforehand seeing how the way to an apriori demonstration may be made to lie over this groundwork of an apriori idea conformed to an objective law, we shall at once determine what our General Method must be.

Mind is an agent, spontaneous in its activity, and puts forth its agency in three distinct capacities, the sentient, the intellectual and the voluntary. The products of these specific capacities of action may be termed respectively, sensations, cognitions, and volitions: the capacities themselves are the Sensibility, the Intellect, and the Will. The mind as one agent is competent for action in these three capacities. Rational Psychology is conversant with all these capacities, but is more particularly concerned with the functions of the Intellect, and with the others as conditional for this, rather than giving to them a direct attention.

The Intellect is inclusive of the entire capacity for

knowing, and is the source for all cognitions attainable through the functions of whatever faculty. The cognitions differ, not numerically merely, but also in kind, as they are the products of the Intellect through different faculties. These different faculties are, THE SENSE, THE UNDERSTANDING, and THE REASON. What these are respectively as distinguished from each other, and what their relations and dependencies, will better appear in the progress of our investigation. It is of importance here only to note, that their distinction is fundamental, and any confounding of one with the others must necessarily induce, not obscurity merely, but errors, contradictions, and absurdities. These three faculties include all the powers of human intelligence, and fill our entire capacity for intellectual action; nor may we attain the conceptions of any other form of intellectual agency for any being. So far as human conception can reach, we have exhausted the entire subject of psychological investigation in reference to all possible forms of knowledge, when we have attained the functions, and their law of operation respectively, of the Sense, the Understanding, and the Reason.

Inasmuch as our design is not the mere attainment of the cognitions given in any or all of these faculties, and which would stand only as simple appearance in consciousness; but much farther than this, viz. the law for the process itself, and thereby an interpretation of the intellectual agency, and not merely a consciousness of the products of this agency; it becomes necessary that we attain the subjective idea of each distinct faculty, and also the objective law of each, and the determination that they stand to each other as correlatives. The appearance in consciousness may be termed knowledge; but it is only the philosophical interpretation of the process by which this knowledge as appearance in consciousness is attained, that can properly be termed *science*. And, moreover, since it is not from experience that we seek to attain our subjective idea—which could only attain to the affirmation that so our form of cognition is; or, that so in future it must be, on the hypothetical assumption that all experience must be uniform; and in this way merely an inductive science, which is incompetent to exclude skepticism from its very foundation—but we seek this subjective idea as transcendental, and conditional for any experience in knowing, and such as that according to it only is the process of intellectual agency at all possible, and thereby attaining to a rational and apriori science which may expel all skepticism from both foundation and superstructure; it becomes necessary that we attain to a position which transcends all experience, and in that pure region intelligently and demonstrably possess ourselves of the conditioning idea, determinative of how a knowledge in the sense, and in the understanding, and in the reason, respectively, is possible to be, and, therefore, if such knowledge ever actually is, how it must be.

But, farther, inasmuch as such subjective apriori

idea is but a mere void thought, and only determinative of how it is possible a knowledge may be in either one of the faculties, of the sense, the understanding, and the reason; it becomes necessary that we go farther, in the case of each faculty, and attain, in the actual facts of such different kinds of cognitions, a manifest law running through the facts and binding them up in systematic order; and then also determine that this law in the facts, is the exact correlative of that apriori idea, which it had already been found must regulate all possible experience in knowing.

Our work thus necessarily divides itself into *three parts*—the Faculty of the Sense; of the Understanding; and of the Reason. We must attain the apriori subjective Idea for each, and also the objective actual **Law** of each; and in each case determine the correlation of the idea and the law respectively. In this we shall have reduced each faculty of knowledge to an apriori philosophical science, according to the universal criterion for all science; and in this Rational Psychology will be completed. Moreover, in these conclusions of Rational Psychology, we shall find the data for demonstrating the valid being of the objects given through these intellectual faculties; and thus in each department we may add also the outlines of an *Ontological Demonstration.*

BOOK II.

THE PROCESS

OF

RATIONAL PSYCHOLOGY.

PART I.

THE SENSE.

DEFINITIONS AND SPECIFIC METHOD.

In *the Sense* I include our whole faculty for bringing any object within the distinct light of consciousness, and making it there immediately to appear; and such cognitions, as appearance in consciousness, constitute knowledge in the sense. The intellectual agency, which takes up these appearances in consciousness as distinct objects of knowledge, I term *apprehension*. When the apprehension is that of appearance having position and figure in space, it is of the *external sense;* when the apprehension is that of appearance determinative of the inner state and agency of the mind itself, and thus that the states and acts of the mind become its own objects in consciousness, it is of the *internal sense*. The completed process in the functions of the sense is *perception*, viz: the *taking* of the appearance as object given in consciousness *through* some medium. The appearance, as object perceived, is called *phenomenon*. The states and acts of the mind apprehended in the internal sense, as truly as the objects apprehended in the external sense, and which have position or shape in space, are phenomena ; since they all *appear* in consciousness and are thus perceived. We as truly perceive a thought or an emotion, as we do a color or a sound. The phenomenon has its *matter* and its *form*. The *matter* is the content which is given from somewhere in the sensibility ; and the *form* is that modification of the matter which permits that it may be classified, or ordered in particular relationships with other phenomena.

The capacity for receiving the content, as matter for a phenomenon, is *sensibility*. The affection induced by the reception of the content in the sensibility is *sensation*. In this we include the affection particularly which *precedes* perception, and is conditional for it. The eye, or the ear, as organ of sensibility, may be affected by a content from somewhere given, as by the rays of light or the undulations of the air, and this impression or affection is it precisely, which we mean by sensation, and which is the condition for the intellectual apprehension and perception. There is, also, an affection of the inner state which may *succeed* the perception, and for which the perception is conditional. The perceived landscape, or music, &c. may affect the inner state agreeably or otherwise, and such affection, if called a sensation, should be distinguished from the result of an organic affection. We might call the organic sensibility the *Sensorium*, and the sensibility of the inner state the *Sensory;* and the products or affections in the first, *sensations;* and those in the last, *emotions;* and the distinction would be sufficiently marked. But in the case of knowledge through sense, we have occasion only for a reference to that which *precedes* perception, and shall not need here, therefore, to recognize any such distinction.

The faculty for giving form to the matter in the sensation is the *Imagination*. It is the faculty which conjoins and defines—the constructing faculty—and is a peculiar intellectual process, which may hereafter in our work be better disclosed. It is sufficient here to say, that while this is essentially the same operation that gives form to the material already in sensation, and that which constructs form in pure space; i. e. it is the same agency which gives roundness to the ring or the wheel in sensation, as that which constructs the roundness of a mathematical circle in pure space; yet is the term *Imagination* more appropriately applied to the latter than the former. The last is purely the work of the intellect, and thus wholly from imagination; the first has been conditioned in its in-

8

tellectual agency by the content in sensation. They may be distinguished as an act of *attention*, and an act of *imagination*.

An object which is void of all content in sensation, and has only its limits constructed in space or time, is termed *pure*; while such object as has a content in the sense is termed *empirical*. Thus, any mathematical diagram is *pure* object; and any color, or weight, or sound, &c. is *empirical* object. *Intuition* is an immediate beholding; and is *pure intuition* when the beholding is in reference to a pure object, and *empirical intuition* when the beholding is in reference to an empirical object. Thus, the immediate beholding of three times three points in space ⋮ ⋮ to be nine, is a pure intuition; but the immediate beholding of three times three balls, or counters, to be nine balls or counters, is an empirical intuition. Inasmuch as the whole field in which the objects are given in the sense is to be examined, we shall have occasion to make a *Division* in this part of our work, and attain the subjective idea of the process in the sense in the construction and apprehension of *pure* objects, and also of *empirical* objects.

That we may the more clearly apprehend the meaning of, and the necessity for, an apriori investigation, the following further preliminary considerations are important in this place.

A *Judgment* is a determined relationship between two or more cognitions or conceptions. Thus, in a line, I perceive a straightness or a curvature; and I affirm, as determined of the cognition of the line and that of straightness or curvature, a relation between them as of subject and predicate in the judgment the line is straight, or, the line is curved. There are other forms of judgment, but the above is here sufficiently precise. In the formation of judgments the intellectual process is in two ways, each giving its own specific kind of judgments, and which from the process is termed an *Analytical Judgment*, or a *Synthetical Judgment*. An Analytical Judgment takes the cognition or conception as in the consciousness, and by an analysis of it attains other cognitions or conceptions, which are determined in their relationship to the first and predicated of it. Thus of the line; I need only an analysis of it, and I shall find as already in it, extension, divisibility, &c., and may affirm the relationship in an analytical judgment—the line is extended; is divisible, &c. The process is here so simple and direct as to need no farther explanation. The validity of such judgments is determined in the very process of the analysis. We do not in this process add anything to our knowledge, for we already have in the given cognition all that we ultimately predicate of it in our judgment, and can only say that the process has made our cognition more distinct, but not more extended.

A Synthetical Judgment attains, in some way, an entirely new cognition, and adds this in its determined

relationship to the given one, and thus truly extends
the cognition over more than its original ground.
Thus the cognition of color as phenomenon may
not only be analyzed, and affirmed that it has position,
figure, divisibility, &c., but that which no analysis
could get out from it, a further experience may get
and add to it, viz : that it may be changed in intensity, in position, in figure; may be in motion, may be
blended with other colors, may vanish away, &c.
Here, beyond what is given in the simple cognition of
the phenomenon, and thus beyond what any analysis
of the color can give, by various experiments we have
new phenomena in a determined relationship to the
original color, and we affirm in the synthetical judgment—the color is changed; is moved; is blended;
&c. Now the process, in this case, explains at once
the manner of attaining the new cognition and determining its relationship to the old, and the correctness
of the judgment depends upon the validity of the experience. The original perception of the color, and
the subsequent perception of its change, or motion,
&c., both rest upon the same basis in experience; and
it is as valid to affirm that the color changes or moves,
from the subsequent experience, as that the color itself is, from the original experience. The knowledge
is verified in consciousness. But, here, suppose the
skepticism to arise, that the appearance in the consciousness may be delusive; and suppose the argument to be urged, that as the *matter* given to the sen-

sibility is not the *form* which is apprehended in the intellect, therefore, by a conclusion on one side, there can be only a mere intellectual form; or, by a conclusion on the other side, there can be only the material content; or, from this alleged contradiction between consciousness and the deductions of reason, we can only doubt whether either the matter or the form exists; we must at once see that the ground on which we had made our synthetical judgments has fallen away, and our experience is itself to be verified, if we would annihilate this three-fold skepticism. We are not yet competent to affirm anything about our phenomenon of color, and its changes, motions, and blendings, until we have examined experience itself, and become competent to determine its validity in its conditioning laws.

The validity of our experience is, in this, made to rest upon the judgment—that the definite phenomenon intellectually apprehended in the consciousness, is identical with the material content received in the sensibility—or, in fewer words—that the intellect apprehends what the sensibility has received—and unless the validity of such a judgment can be demonstrated, the skepticism may remain. To leave this to an assumption is to betray the whole science of perception. But such a judgment is wholly synthetical. By no analysis of the apprehension can we attain the sensation, and by no analysis of the sensation can we attain the apprehension. Neither is given in the other, and no analysis of either or both can conclude in such a judgment. As a synthetical judgment also, it is quite beyond all experience to determine the relationship of these two conceptions, that of the apprehended phenomenal form, and that of the received material content; inasmuch as they are conditional for perception, and cannot therefore be given in perception. We are, therefore, forced to attain some transcendental position if we would attempt to determine in a judgment what relation the form in the intellectual apprehension has to the material content in the sensibility. And both in the faculty of the understanding and of the reason, as well as here in the faculty of the sense, we shall find our whole difficulty to lie in synthetical judgments, viz: the determination of the relationship of the two conceptions, one of which is predicate of the other in the judgment. The only relief possible is some apriori position, from which may be carried forward a transcendental demonstration.

An *apriori* Cognition may be discriminated from all others in this; that it is not a dependent nor a consequent, not a product nor a remnant; but possesses in itself Necessity and Universality. It must so be, and this everywhere and evermore.

And here we are ready to give the *Specific Method* of our process of Rational Psychology for the faculty of the Sense. We isolate this from all the other functions of knowledge, and must in our *first Chapter*, from an apriori position, attain the *subjective Idea* of how perception in sense is possible; and, as this must include both the form in the apprehension and the content in the sensation, so there must be the *two Divisions* of the Idea in the pure Intuition, and the Idea in the empirical Intuition. In a *second Chapter*, we must attain an *objective Law* in the facts of perception, and determine the correlation of this Idea and Law. We may then give the outline of an *Ontological Demonstration.*

CHAPTER I.

THE SENSE IN ITS SUBJECTIVE IDEA.

FIRST DIVISION.

THE IDEA IN THE PURE INTUITION.

SECTION I.

THE ATTAINMENT OF AN APRIORI POSITION.

ALL human knowledge begins in experience. Except phenomena are given in the sense, and the intellect quickened into activity in perception, it can exert neither the faculty of the understanding nor the reason, but the human mind remains a void and no cognition is possible. We must begin our intellectual action in sensation. But experience can include the real and the limited only, while there are cognitions of the strictly necessary and universal; and thus is it manifest that our intellectual agency, which begins in the perceptions of the sense, is not confined to experience merely. All Mathematical Axioms, at least, are apriori cognitions, independent of power, not deducible from any data in experience, but including all possible experience, and in their own light seen to be necessary and universal. That a straight line is the shortest which can join any two points; that no two straight lines can enclose a space; that any two sides of a triangle must together be greater than a third side, &c., are cognitions not possible to be given in experience, for no experience comprehends them while they include all possible experience. They are no product of power, for they condition all power in their own necessity of being; they are no deduction from facts, for they are inclusive of universal facts. We shall in our progress find wide regions of apriori truth, as independent of the experience given in sensation as mathematical axioms, and which the human mind may possess as cognitions; and thus the fact is plain, that while the intellect begins its agency in the functions of the sense, it yet subsequently attains cognitions which are altogether beyond every possible empirical apprehension.

And, here, our first care is to lay open a plain passage from the phenomenal to the transcendental, and attain a position upon such apriori cognitions as shall subserve our main design in a Rational Psychology, and by such a process as shall admit of clear and satisfactory examination at every step; and thus, having taken our position out from experience, we may proceed to the philosophical investigation of how experience must be.

The Intellect may not take a leap in the dark out of the world of sense in which its agency begins into the pure region of apriori cognitions, but must be competent to expound to itself and to others how it has reached its starting point in a transcendental philosophy. A surreptitious passage is, also, equally as inadmissible as a blind and presumptuous leap to the necessary and the universal. Dogmatism may arbitrarily assume, or sophistry may wrap itself in specious fallacies stealthily to take, the ground on which is to be built a rational philosophy, but in no such way shall we establish a title for science, or dispossess the skeptic of the territory he has usurped. We must be able first to trace our pathway out from, and be competent to return again to, the familiar region of the phenomenal, and to determine its bearings and distances from the purely intellectual. We shall thus readily determine, that though subsequently attained by us, yet is the necessary and the universal the truly primitive region. In the process of our intellectual acquirement the empirical is first, but in the order of conditioned relations the empirical is last. In this point of view the distinction made between a *logical* and a *chronological* order is significant. As logical condition the necessary and the universal are before the conditioned and the partial; the possible before the actual, the intellectual before the phenomenal. Just as in the work of nature the germ precedes the plant; the embryon is before the adult; the cause antecedent to the effect. Yet as in nature, empirically apprehended, we are forced to reverse the process, so is it also in Empirical Psychology. In learning nature in experience we do not first find ourselves at the original sources of her secret operations, but quite upon the outside of all her products. We can not look on and watch the progress of her mysterious developments, as the work goes onward from the central salient point to its consummation; but we must retrace, as we may, what has been done by following back the print of her footsteps. Thus, in the intellectual operations, we first find the phenomenal as already given, and then go back to the intellectual; we have first the fact, and then we search out the principle; first the knowledge, then the scientific conditions by which it was possible we should know. Thus the first is last, and the last is first. With the phenomenal in possession it is incumbent first, to find our way out to the purely intellectual, and having attained the transcendental position, there note that though chronologically last found, yet that logically it was first, and necessarily conditional for the phenomenal from whence we started.

Commencing with the phenomenal, the process will be to make an abstraction of all that has come into consciousness through sensation, and thereby find that which was prior to, and conditional for, the perception. When the matter shall be taken away, the real form will remain; and when that which gave reality to the form is taken away, the possible or pure form only is left.

1. *The pure form for all phenomena of an external sense.*—Whatever object we may apprehend in an experience—a house, tree, mountain, &c.—it is for the sense; and as phenomenal, an assemblage of single qualities only. We now take any such object—a house—and proceed to make abstraction of the several phenomena which any organs of sense have given in the perception. Color has appeared, and we now exclude it; smoothness or roughness, hard or soft, weight or resistance, as they have been given, we now take away; and so also of sounds, odors, tastes, or any qualities of any possible function of the sense, we now remove; and thus make a complete abstraction of all content which the entire sensibility may have received. We shall have still remaining the *void place* which had been occupied by the qualities now abstracted. This remains for the intellect alone, and is as nothing in the experience; but for the intellect it remains immovable and indestructible. It remains in defiance of all further attempts to a more complete abstraction in that place. It is the real *form* of that object from which the *matter* has now been utterly taken away. While this real form is no longer cognition in experience, the intellect truly possesses it, and clearly cognizes that it was conditional for the phenomenon as object, and that without it the matter could not have had place and figure, and that the place was prior to

the matter which appeared in it, and is now when the matter is gone.

But, although we have taken away all content of sense, and can not go further and take away the place, still have we not taken away all product of the intellect. There is a defined and limited place, a constructed form which has real outline and shape, and we may intellectually proceed further in this direction with our abstraction, and take away that which limits and defines this void place, and thus annihilate that in which its unity and wholeness exists. We have then a void which is limitless, undefined, unconstructed, unconjoined into any total, and which is simply a pure intuition of what is possible for form and content. And this we may call *pure* form, in distinction from *real* form limited in the intellect, as real *form* was distinguished from real *phenomenon* in perception. This is *pure Space* as given in the intuition; and to distinguish such intuition from the immediate beholding of the relations of pure diagrams in space, and which is pure intuition, we will call this intuition of pure space itself the *primitive Intuition*. Pure space, therefore, as given in the primitive intuition, is pure form for any possible phenomenon. It is impossible that we should carry our abstraction any further, in any direction. Pure space, as unconjoined in the unity of any form, is given in the primitive intuition, and is a cognition necessary and universal. Though now obtained from experience, and in chrono-

logical order subsequent to experience, yet is it no deduction from experience, nor at all given by experience; but it is wholly independent of all experience,
prior to it, and without which it were impossible that
any experience of outer object should be. It is wholly
a transcendental cognition, and yet far more valid and
sure in its own light to the intuition, than any perception of phenomenon in the sense can be. Here, then,
upon the valid cognition of pure Space in the primitive
intuition, we may safely take up one of our transcendental positions.

2. *The pure form for all the phenomena of an internal sense.*—In the light of consciousness we discriminate between one mental state, or mental exercise and another, and thereby distinguish all the different products of our entire mental faculties. We thus
determine in consciousness the inner phenomena of
thoughts, emotions, purposes, &c. All these are quite
a different kind of phenomena, as intellectually apprehended, from such as appear externally in space, and
require some other than the form which may be found
in the primitive intuition of space for their condition.
What their pure form is, it is now the design to determine.

As before, we begin with the phenomenal already
in possession and proceed to an entire abstraction of
it, and thus attain what is apriori conditional for it.
We will take any of these inner phenomena, as they
come and depart in the changes of our internal state—

say, a train of thought as passing in the mind. **As** one arises and departs for the introduction of **another,** the apprehension of them must be successive, and **thus** together they form a series. If, then, we abstract the phenomenal, as the states and exercises of the intellect in thinking, and thereby utterly exclude the thoughts **in** the train, there will remain the succession in the instants in which they passed, and which must be a *void period* that had been occupied by the passing thoughts now abstracted. This abides for the intellect alone, and resists all efforts that it should be taken away. There is nothing phenomenal remaining in it, and yet it remains incapable of annihilation. It is a *real form* for the content of the thought which once filled it, but which has now been taken quite out of it, and left it indestructible. We have now attained it, in the chronological order, after the possession of the phenomenon, but yet it is manifest that it was conditional for the phenomenon and was prior to it, for without it there could have been no succession in which the series of the thoughts could have transpired.

We shall attain the cognition of void period in the same way if we take any passing phenomena of the external sense. These outer phenomena as apprehended by the intellect affect the internal state, and as the perception of one outer phenomenon passes and another arises, the inner sense is determined as successive in its affections, and the phenomena must thus fill a period in the inner sense as truly as a place in the external sense. If, then, we make an entire abstraction of the outer phenomena, and with them the perception as affecting the inner state, we shall have the successions in the instants in which they occurred, and which as limited by their beginning and terminating is a void period, as the *real form* in the internal sense. And as before, this remains indestructible though the phenomena have vanished, and which must have been prior to the phenomena, or there could have been no period for their succession.

But, though we have taken away all content as phenomenal, and cannot proceed any farther to take away the successions in the period, yet have we still a product of the intellect that may farther admit of abstraction. The void period has its limits of beginning and ending as constructed in an intellectual agency, and these may now be utterly abolished, and that which gave unity and totality to the definite period as lying within beginning and terminating instants will then fall away. We have then an emptiness of all phenomena, and of all conjunction and limitation of instants, and only a diversity of instants remains as possibility for any period to be constructed, and to be filled with some phenomenal content. This, therefore, in distinction from the *real* form where the void period had its limits, may be termed the *pure* form for all possible phenomena of an internal sense. It is *pure Time* as given in the intuition, inasmuch as it is immediately beheld as conditional for all possible period, prior to any period being actually limited, and necessarily continuing though all bounded period be taken away. To distinguish such intuition of pure time from the immediate beholding of the relations of pure periods as real form, we will call it, as in the same position above in reference to pure space, the *primitive Intuition.*

Now, inasmuch as all phenomena must be given in an external or an internal sense ; and pure space is the pure form for all possible phenomena of an external sense which must have place, and pure time is the pure form for all possible phenomena of an internal sense which must have period ; we have in pure space and time the pure forms for all possible phenomena. And as we have taken pure space as one transcendental position, we may now also take pure time as another, satisfied that they are both given in an apriori cognition, and that they give to us the possibility for all the real forms in which the intellect can order any appearance in the sense.

Now, it is altogether true, that the faculty of the sense cannot overlook and in an apriori manner examine itself, and go back and take up positions out of itself ; and if we had no other faculty than that of perception in sensation, and the capability of abstracting comparing and combining what had been given in sensation, most certainly we could attain no transcendental positions. It would be like asking the eye to see itself, or the touch to feel itself ; thus demanding

9

that experience should bring itself within its own circumscription and by subjecting itself to its own action literally experience itself. But certainly we encounter no such absurdity when we assume a faculty higher than that of the sense, and which is competent to make the very conditions of sense its objects of cognition; and that the possession of such higher faculty is not mere assumption, beside the demonstration which will be given in its proper place, we have already sufficient evidence in the above results. If all cognition must be of that only which is first given in the sensation, then certainly the primitive intuition of pure space and time must be an impossibility. When we have taken away the content of sense we should have no possible cognition left. Space and time would be not only void, but it would be a void of space and of time; and the intuition that pure space and time were prior to the content put within them, and conditional for the possibility that such content should appear, would be preposterous. It would be making the sense cognize that which is prior to, and conditional for, its own action. Pure space and time are never an appearance in sense, nor at all a part of what is given in sense, and the fact that we cognize them at all is the evidence of a higher faculty than sense, and especially that we cognize them to be necessarily and universally conditional for all perception in sense.

We are making no assumptions merely, and standing upon no mere chimeras, when we take up our position, in the primitive intuition, upon the apriori cognitions of pure space and time. That they are the pure forms for all possible phenomena, that they are apriori to, and conditional for, all phenomena, is seen in their necessity and universality.

SECTION II.

SPACE AND TIME VIEWED IN REFERENCE TO PHENOMENA AND TO EACH OTHER.

THAT we may the better familiarize ourselves with apriori cognitions, and accustom the mind to the transcendental positions now taken, and thus be better prepared to prosecute our investigations of the sense in its idea, we will dwell a while upon the pure forms of space and time, and consider them relatively to phenomena, and also in their reference to each other.

In reference to *phenomena*, it should be noted,

1. *That space and time are no part of the phenomena which appear in them.*—Phenomena have their extension and succession ; but the extension which appears in the phenomenon does not make space, nor do the successions which appear in the passing phenomena make time. Space already is, in order that phenomenal extension may be ; and time already is, in order that alteration and succession of the phenomena may be. Phenomena appear extended or successive in space and time, but they give nothing from

themselves to space and time, nor do they take any thing to themselves from space and time. The phenomenon can embody within itself nothing of the being of space or time; neither make itself out of them, nor absorb into itself any thing from them. The phenomena remove, but space does not remove with them; they arise and vanish, but nothing of time comes and goes with them. No possible modification of the phenomena can include within it or draw after it any modification of space and time. They are utterly distinct from each other, and neither inherents nor adherents one with the other.

2. *Phenomena are conditioned upon, but not caused by, the cognitions of space and time.*—Phenomena must come within, but can not be produced by space and time. Were there only space and time, it were impossible that from these any phenomenon should originate. But while not the products of space and time, it is impossible that phenomena should be except as there are space and time. They must have place and period or they could not appear, and place and period cannot be except as pure space and time are first given in the primitive intuition. Phenomena, thus, are possible only upon the condition that pure space and time are first given; but when pure space and time are first given, they cannot originate phenomena.

3. *Space and time have a necessity of being independently of all phenomena.*—That the three angles of a

triangle are together equal to two right angles is a necessary and universal truth, but yet not independent. Provided the triangle be, then this truth is necessary, and as universal as the being of triangles, but wholly dependent upon the existence of the triangle. The truth is wholly grounded in the being of the triangle. If the triangle be not, then the three angles are not, and of course an equality to two right angles is not. But not thus with space and time. They must be, not only in order that phenomena may be, but independently of their being, and the same whether phenomena be given in them or not. We cannot say of any thing that is in space and time, that provided this is, then space and time are; but it is manifest that they stand in their own necessity of being, whether any phenomena be or be not, be conceived to be or be not conceived.

4. *Space and time have no significancy in reference to other cognitions than such as are phenomenal.*—As the pure forms for all that may occupy place and period space and time have a significancy; but as they are only pure forms they can have significancy in nothing which is not relative to a possible content that may appear in them. The phenomenon cannot occupy space and time except as appearance in some of the real forms of space and time, and the pure form has meaning only in reference to such real form. Neither in the external nor the internal sense can any object be given which is not phenomenal, and which

must not appear under some of the possible forms in pure space and time. But if there be cognitions which are not phenomenal, and thus do not come within the possible forms of space and time, to such cognitions space and time can have no significancy. If the reason, as organ for cognizing the supernatural, may attain the pure ideas of liberty, personality, right, Deity, &c., such cognitions have no reference to space and time, and coming within none of the forms and conditions thereof, cannot secure that space and time should have any meaning in reference to them. These cognitions themselves cannot become phenomenal and stand within any form as figure or period, but only their products. To an intellect that should cognise substance in its causality directly, and not through the phenomena as qualities, the forms of space and time would be wholly impertinent. Their whole meaning and significancy have reference to phenomena, and they can possess no relevancy except to a possible sensible experience.

Of space and time in reference to *each other*, the following things may be noted.

1. *Their measure respectively.*—Space has *three dimensions*. Let a point in space be produced in three directions, such that the lines shall be to each other, respectively, one at right angles to both of the remaining lines, and this diagram will be the index of all the possible measures of space. The point produced in one direction only gives extension, or *length;* the

point produced in the second direction at right angles to the first gives, in reference to this first, expansion, or *breadth;* and produced in the third direction at right angles to the two, and in reference to them both, gives solidity, or *thickness;* and which, accordingly as the base is made of one or the other of the two lines, is in reference to the base *height* or *depth.* No other dimensions can be given in space than length, breadth, and thickness.

Time has but *one dimension.* From any point as an instant of time succession may go on in a series, but its progress can be only in one direction, and all measure of time must be a progressus or regressus up and down the same series. One instant can therefore be determined as only antecedent or subsequent to all other instants, and must stand at such a distance before or after any given instant, and the period can only be time *how long.*

2. *Significancy in reference to each other.*—Space in reference to time has *no significancy.* Time is the pure form for phenomena as given in the internal sense only, and in these there can be only succession. The inner phenomenon may endure in time, but can have neither length, breadth nor thickness in space. A thought, or other mental phenomenon, may fill a period, but cannot have superficial or solid content; it may have duration, but not shape; it may be before or after another, but not above or below it, nor with any outer or inner side. The inner sense can be determined

within none of the forms of space, and thus its pure
form which is time, cannot admit that space in reference to it should have any meaning.

Time in reference to space *has significancy.* Space
is pure form for the external sense, and as the intellectual apprehension of the outer phenomenon must
modify the inner state, in this way the outer object
can be brought within the form of time. Time, thus,
may have meaning in reference to space. While I
cannot say that time is in space, I can say of space
that all its parts are in one time; and that all space
perdures through time. This significancy between
space and time as only one way, and not reciprocally,
is very remarkable; but the fact is readily expounded
when we know that outer objects come also into the
internal sense, while inner objects can never appear
in the external sense.

3. *In reference to their division by their own parts.*—
Space cannot be so divided as to bisect itself by *any*
of its parts. No part of space can be a diameter to
all space, and thus divide all space into two portions
as above and beneath each other, or as on this and that
side of each other. All portions of space must yet
be wholly within space, and thus no part can bisect
the whole.

Time cannot be so divided but it bisects itself by
all its parts. The instant determines what portion of
all time precedes, and what portion of all succeeds it,
and thus divides all time into *a parte ante* and *a parte*

post. And what is true of any instant is true of all instants, and thus all portions of time must completely bisect the whole of time.

4. *In reference to the collocation of their own parts.*—Space has its parts *every way conterminous.* All portions of space terminate on all sides in space, and thus all spaces are limited by space in all directions.

Time has its portions conjoined *only as successive.* Every portion of time stands in a series of all time, and no portion can be limited by other portions except as before and after. Space has spaces on all sides, time has periods only as before and after; hence, spaces are conterminous, and times consecutive.

5. *Space and time are in themselves every way immutable.*—Space as a whole is inclusive of all places, and time as a whole is inclusive of all periods. Thus no *external* change can be effected in either, for there is no place out of space, and no period out of time in which a change might occur. To remove externally would demand a void of space and of time out of the whole, into which the whole might be removed. And equally as immutable must both be *internally;* for every portion of space must keep its position relatively to all other portions, and every portion of time must keep its period relatively to all other portions. Space does not move, but things move in space; and time does not flow, but things succeed each other in their changes in time. To remove one portion of space or of time from its position internally would de-

mand a void of space and of time within themselves, through which the portions to change their positions might pass. Both from without and from within must space and time be wholly immutable.

6. *In both space and time the lesser portion always pre-supposes a larger.*—The pure form of space and time as given in the primitive intuition is limitless, and altogether diverse, as having no conjunction in unity. When, therefore, any portion of either is made a portion as a definite and distinct whole in itself, it is by conjoining and limiting what was before diverse and without limit. That which is not included within the limits of the figure or period must still be limitless, and excluded from the limited, and thus the pure form as intuition must always include the real form as construction. We can not add constructed portions of space and time together that the aggregate may include all of space and time, but the primitive intuition has its pure form still beyond any possible aggregation of definite portions. The limited can not be except as first the limitless is given; and this limited, however comprehensive, must still be within the limitless, and the construction of the place or period within the unconstructed. The pure form always stretches away in the primitive intuition beyond any real form that may be taken.

7. *The concurrence of both space and time is conditional for all determination of motion.*—All conception of motion is an absurdity, and thus an impossibility,

except as both space and time have given each their
real form to the conception. Without space there can
be no change of place, and thus no conception of motion; and without time, there can be no conception of
the same phenomenon in two different places, and thus
no conception of motion. The same phenomenon in
two places demands succession, and that must be determined in the form of time; and the two places occupied by the same phenomenon in two successive periods demands a permanent, and that must be determined in the form of space. Thus my hand can not
reach both my head and my knee except as at successive periods, and I can not determine succession
but in the form of time; and the two places of my
head and my knee, successively reached by the same
hand, can not be determined in their diversity of position except by the permanent distance which separates them, and this permanent distance can be determined only in the form of space. But when both
space and time concur in their forms, the determination of motion is readily secured. The occupying of
a permanent position during two periods determines
rest, and the occupying of two positions during two
periods determines motion from one to the other. In
the alteration of place there has concurred an alteration of period, and thus a motion through contiguous
points of space has its concurring instants of successive time, and the conception is consistent and intelligible.

A conception of another kind of motion may be, **viz**: the arising or evanishing in the same place; but this conception demands the same principle for its being made intelligible. The form of time, as above, must be applied to determine the succession in period; and the permanency, which is to determine the diversity of position, is in the degrees of intensity in the sensation which lie between the two positions. Thus at one period there may be twenty degrees of light, and at another ten degrees in the same place. The form of time determines the successions of the two periods; the permanency of intensity in the sensibility, estimated from zero upwards, and thus separating twenty degrees from ten degrees by a permanent amount of intensity through which the light had successively vanished, is of the same significance as a permanent space between two places through which the motion had proceeded, and explains the motion of waxing and waning on the same principles as locomotion.

8. *The quantity in the motion, space, and time, are proportionals, but the determination in neither can be absolute.*—A *moment* of motion, an *instant* of time, and a *point* of space must all concur in the conception of a determinate quantity of either motion, space, or time. No motion can be except through contiguous portions of space and in successive periods of time: and no determined time can be except as a movement relative to some permanent; and that the time be other than subjective merely, the permanent must be outward in

space; and no determined space can be except through motion in successive time. And while all must concur in the determination of the quantity in either, they will stand, the two in any way with the remaining one, reciprocally, in the following peculiarity of ratio, viz : the motion given, the space and time are in direct proportion; the time given, the space and motion are direct proportionals; the space given, the time and the motion are inverse proportionals. Thus the greater or the less quantity of time, the greater or the less quantity also of space with the same motion; the greater or less quantity of space, the greater or less quantity also of motion with the same time; and the greater the time, the less the motion, and the less the time the greater the motion, in the same space.

But, while these proportionals perpetually subsist between the determined quantities of motion space and time, yet can not the absolute and independent quantity in either be determined. When any two are given, the third is readily attained; but in all cases the quantity given and that attained, are still only relative and never absolute. No absolute measure of either motion, space, or time, is possible. All attempts to attain an independent measure of either involves the absurdity of a υσ̓τερον προτερον. We assume one quantity, in the supposition that a second is stationary, and find the third as only proportional to the first, and are thus ever in the vicious circle out of which we can never leap to find an absolute first as condition for the

last. Motion has no meaning except in reference to
some permanent changing its place; space has no significancy except in reference to something which may
have position; and time has no significancy except in
reference to something that may have period; and not
any thing can give its own motion, place, and period,
but only in reference to some other thing. Thus the
motion, the space passed over, and the time in passing,
of the hands of a chronometer, must have reference to
the motion, space, and time of the diurnal revolution
of the earth, and are only measures of either compared
with the same in the earth's diurnal revolution, and
could be no measure for the revolution of Saturn, or
any other planet on its axis, in either motion, space,
or time. An apriori determination of either is impossible; and yet *that* this is impossible, and *why* this is
impossible, are both apriori cognitions, and transcen-
dentally attained.

What has now been noted of the pure forms of
space and time in reference to phenomena, and relatively to each other, may here be sufficient for accus-
toming the mind to such apriori conceptions, and elu-
cidating the necessity and universality which inherently belong to them, and to all demonstrations by them.
Inasmuch as they are above all experience, they do
not partake of the conditions and limitations which
belong to experience, and to all knowledge in experience, but they truly condition experience itself, and
determine that all possible experience must regulate

itself by them. In our further progress we shall attain
to a more familiar acquaintance with these pure forms
in the primitive intuition, and their employment in a
transcendental science; and shall also attain to the
conception and use of many other apriori truths, as
elementary and conditional for a complete Rational
Psychology. We may now proceed directly in our
process for attaining the apriori subjective idea of the
sense in the pure intuition.

SECTION III.

THE PROCESS OF AN APRIORI CONSTRUCTION OF REAL FORM IN PURE SPACE AND TIME.

SPACE and time as pure form are given in the primitive intuition. They are immediately beheld, and
this irrespective of any content in the sensibility, and
are thus *pure* Intuition; and as prior to any real forms,
and only conditional for all possible forms of figure and
period, they are *primitive* Intuition. As pure form in
the primitive intuition, they are wholly limitless, and
void of any conjunction in unity, having themselves no
figure nor period, and having within themselves no
figure nor period, but only a pure diversity in which
any possible conjunction of definite figures and periods
may, in some way, be effected. We now begin our
work from this transcendental position, and our first
business is to determine the process by which a

conjunction may be effected, and real forms be constructed in pure space and time.

Although we have come from the phenomenal in sense out to this pure condition for all that may be phenomena, by abstracting all that has been given in the sensibility and the intellectual agency, yet can abstraction be of no further avail. We now seek, not the process of attaining a real form by beginning with some phenomenon, and taking away its content in the sensibility thereby leaving its void form in the intellect, which would be but an empirical process; but we begin at the other extreme of the process, and seek to construct our real forms from the formless and limitless space and time as given in the primitive intuition, and in this apriori process determine how a construction of real forms in space and time is possible; and thereby for what is, a determination apriori how it must have been, and for all that is to be, how only it is possible that it should be.

And here, with space and time as given in the primitive intuition, where all is mere diversity without any conjunction in unity, and therefore wholly limitless and indefinite—where all possible position, shape and period may be, but where no fixed position, defined figure, and limited period yet is—it is manifest that nothing can appear as real form in any intellectual apprehension, except as in some way this real form be constructed as product within this primitive intuition. As utterly void of all construction and product, pure space and time must ever so remain, except as invaded by some constructing agency, which shall conjoin what is diverse, and limit what is indefinite, and thereby produce real bounded and united forms within the void intuition. Pure space and time are not agents that may collect themselves into definite and discriminate portions of each, and affix precise limits within themselves, by which their parts may possess outline and each become one whole figure in space or period in time. Some agency *ab extra* must make such conjunctions, and give such limits. But the primitive intuition is no agent for constructing, producing, and limiting; this is a mere immediate beholding of what is, and no producer of it. Thus, as no constructed real form is in pure space and time, the primitive intuition can never of itself attain such real form. The intellectual agency as imagination, or form constructer, which Coleridge calls the *eisemplastic power*, from εισ ενπλαττειν to shape into one, must introduce itself within the void, and produce its real forms for its own subjective apprehension. The pure forms of space and time can never take real form within themselves, and which may be apprehended as definite figure and period, except through such intellectual construction.

We will, therefore, look minutely to this entire process of an intellectual construction of real forms in pure space and time, inasmuch as in this will be found the subjective idea of the sense in the pure intuition. In this section we will give this agency in its *results*

10

only, and reserve for consideration in future sections the more profound and difficult work of attaining the *apriori principles* of the process.

1. *The construction of real forms in pure space.*— Let there be an intellectual agency given, which may come within the field of the primitive intuition in pure space, and exert its constructive faculty therein, and let us notice what must be its results. In the spontaneity of its own functions it moves through the void in pure space, constantly within the intuition, and is thus perpetually and directly beheld in all its progress. In the as yet uncollected diversity in pure space, this agency is in the field of the primitive intuition, and at that point in the diversity of pure space a position is taken. The void is no longer empty. A point is made to stand definitely and precisely in the intuition, and is a limit as beginning or starting-point in the process. As this agency moves onward there are perpetually new positions attained, and new points made to stand out prominently and precisely in the intuition. So far as this agency goes in its spontaneity, it has brought the diverse points through which it passed into a conjunction, and made its own pathway precise and plain by collecting into itself the points as continuous contiguity. Here, then, is a definite real form as product of the intellectual agency. There is the limit or starting-point, as beginning; the perpetuated product in the continuous points all conjoined in the progressive movement; and there

is the limit, as terminating point of this agency ; and here first arises in the intuition a completed product, and a definite real form—the mathematical *line*—appears. Pure space is no longer void diversity as given in the *primitive* intuition, but a conjunction of the diversity has been effected, and a line as one whole in its unity is cognized. This is wholly a product of the productive imagination and has subjective reality only, hence as void of all empirical content it is *pure* object, and is cognized in *pure intuition ;* but, as being *real* form produced in pure space, there is more than mere *pure* form in the *primitive intuition.*

And now, nothing hinders, that such an intellectual agency may be possible in its going forth to the construction of all possible forms in pure space. Right lines, and lines which shall be joined in their terminations in all possible relative directions, and thus holding between them all possible angles, and which may enclose all possible rectilinear figures, may be constructed. Curved lines, and of all possible circularity and modification of curvature, and meeting in the construction of all possible curvilinear angles and figures, and the blending of right and curved lines in all possible modifications of mutual relationship in angle and shape, may be produced from all possible positions in pure space. All the real forms possible in pure space are thus of practicable production in a pure intuition. In the particular is given the universal, and it is an apriori cognition, that as one pure object may be thus constructed, so it is competent that all the real forms which pure space may receive can in the same way be constructed. And as such construction may be, so also it is an apriori cognition that, if at all, thus they *must* be constructed. The primitive intuition can give the diversity in its unconjoined manifoldness only; and if any conjunction, in the unity of a definite real form as pure object, be effected, it must be through the constructing agency of some eisemplastic or form-producing faculty. The pure object must be given to the pure intuition, by some intellectual agency constructing it within the field of its immediate beholding. We have in this way the process of an intellectual agency, or productive imagination, which results in an apriori possibility for all real forms in pure space.

2. *The construction of real forms in pure time.*—Time as pure form in the primitive intuition, is like pure space utterly unconjoined and indefinite. It is conditional for all possible periods, but as yet no definite and limited period has been given within it. The intuition cannot construct, but only immediately behold what may be constructed. The same intellectual agent as productive imagination, but in a somewhat modified view of the agency, must construct the real form as pure period within the primitive intuition. As time is the pure form for the internal sense, and all determination of succession in time rests upon the determination of changes in the inner state, so all

construction of period must demand that the inner state be, in some way, continuously modified in its affection. And that this modified affection, as change of the inner state may be determined, it must be made to stand in a relationship in the intuition to some permanent. Mere movement cannot determine succession, but only movement in reference to somewhat that is permanent; and as the period to be constructed is pure, so the permanent must be in the pure intuition also. And now, all the above requisites may be attained in the following way, and are wholly impracticable in any other manner.

Let the intellectual agency be conceived as moving along a pure line in space. This line is itself a permanent in the intuition, and every point in the line is a permanent, and as the intellectual agency passes along the line within the immediate field of the intuition, the movement as change of place gives continuous modification to the inner state, and this succession of affection in the internal sense is the determination that a time is passing. The *movement* is that which is here alone regarded, and not the *line* as product of the movement. This intellectual agency is commenced at a given point in the line, and at that given point the affection in the inner state begins, and as the movement passes onward the inner state is continuously modified, until at length the movement terminates in another point in the line and the modification in the inner state ceases. At each contiguous point in

the line there has been a coincident modification of
the inner state, as the intellectual movement passed
along through it in the intuition, and in each modification of the inner state an instant of time has passed,
and thus successively from the commencement to the
termination of the moving agency, and thereby a definite period has been constructed, in which the passing instants have been conjoined in unity and limited
on each side as a complete whole.

This is more than pure form in the primitive intuition of time, since a real conjunction of the diverse instants has been effected and a completed limit set to
it, and thus a real form produced; but inasmuch as
there is no content of the sensibility, it is *pure object*
only, and existing merely in the subjective intuition.
And here, it is plain, that nothing hinders the construction of all possible periods that may be in time,
of all possible varieties of duration. The primitive
intuition gives the pure form of time in its indefiniteness, and the productive imagination may move on in
any extension of a line, and give its modifications to
the inner state, and thereby its definite succession of
instants, and in this way its pure periods as real forms
in time to any possible degree that such pure periods
can be in time. And as all possible periods *may* be
so constructed, so also it is an apriori cognition that
if any is constructed at all it *must* be in this manner.
The primitive intuition cannot construct, but an agency must move within it, and conjoin what is diverse

in its manifoldness into one completed product, and which may thus be intuitively seen in its definiteness, and its distinctness from all other constructed periods.

With pure space and time in the primitive intuition open to an intellectual constructing agency, all possible figures in space and periods in time may become pure objects in the subjective intuition. And this is the only possible method of attaining real forms from the primitive intuition. I can have no line in pure space, except as by my constructive agency I *draw* the line; and no other figure in pure space, except as through the same agency I *describe* that figure; nor can I have any period in pure time, except as through an intellectual agency I successively affect my inner state, and in the conjunction of the instants *construct* the period. In this manner may all possible real forms in pure space and time be given in a pure intuition, but in no other manner can any real form be effected. We have thus a conditioning principle, apriori determined, that all possible pure objects in space and time *must be constructed by an intellectual agency.*

Let it here be noted that pure space and time in the primitive intuition offer nothing to invite, to guide or to hinder an intellectual constructing agency. In the spontaneity of the productive imagination, all possible real forms *may* be thus given. This *result* being attained it is demanded that its process be subjected to a much deeper analysis, and in which many points of

difficult explanation must be carefully examined.   To
this we proceed in the next section.

SECTION IV.

THE APRIORI ELEMENTS OF ALL POSSIBLE FORMS IN PURE SPACE AND TIME.

ARISTOTLE generalized the multiplicity of our conceptions of things, as *objective*, upward to their highest
sources.   In this way he sought to attain the most
comprehensive predicates which may be used in forming judgments.   He looked to things as represented
in the thought, and to words as the symbols of thought,
and referred these words to the objective being of
things.   Words are in themselves expressive, precisely, of the thing represented in the thought.   To
the same mind the thing represented in the thought
must ever be the same, and the word as symbol for
it must ever possess the same meaning.   So far then
as the simple representation in the thought and the
word as the symbol for it reaches, there can be no occasion for any error.   The representation of any particular tree, or house, or other object, is simply the
thought of that which has been apprehended in consciousness, and of course conformable thereto, and
not liable to error.   The word is the symbol for such
representation and as incapable of error as the repre-

sentation itself. Both representative and symbol, thought and word, are for the same thing to the same mind.

But in reference to the *being* of the thing thought and expressed by the word as its symbol, this word is wholly indifferent for either truth or error, and can express neither except as joined with other words in the form of some judgment. It neither affirms nor denies the being of the thing, but merely symbolizes its representation, until there is an affirmative or negative judgment, and here first arises truth or error. The judgment affirms or denies correctly or incorrectly in relation to the thing represented in the word. And in this manner all logical demonstration must rest upon the determination of the judgment under the principle of contradiction, viz : the being of the thing *is*, or *is not*, as the judgment affirms or denies.

Words, as symbols of thoughts representing *particular* things, can be the elements of only particular judgments, and can thus express only particular truths ; but on the other hand, words of more *general* signification will give occasion for more comprehensive judgments, embracing more general truths. Hence the interest in attaining the most comprehensive terms, and generalizing our representations to their highest predicaments. Such a generalization of things including many particulars within them, gave the opportunity for arranging the particular under the general, and they were hence called CATEGORIES. Of these

Aristotle attained ten, and subsequently added five more as *post predicaments*. But, while thus the interest inducing such a generalization appears, and the results are carefully given, yet does Aristotle give us no reason for so many, and no more. He doubtless had no system for attaining the categories, which by being exhausted might determine when all had been found, or some mention would have been made of it, important as such a criterion of the completeness of the work would be.

Kant attains the highest predicates in a very different manner. Instead of generalizing our representations of objective being as symbolized in language, and thus attaining the most comprehensive terms for general judgments, he goes directly to the *subjective* faculty of the judgment, and by analyzing the entire use of the understanding in its functions of thinking in judgments, he attains the highest conceptions that may thus be given, and thereby limits all capacity of thinking in judgments within the regulative application of these primitive conceptions. They give the highest forms for the most comprehensive judgments, to which the functions of the understanding itself can reach ; and of course, no content of a judgment in the real being of things, objectively, can reach beyond the form in which it must subjectively be presented. His design is not to detect the falsehood nor to establish the truth of our judgments in reference to the *being* of the things which the judgment includes, by an application of the principle of logical contradiction, but in attaining the apriori forms subjectively in the understanding, to determine the *possibility* for all thinking in judgments whatsoever.   He would inquire, not as Aristotle, through logical symbols of the representations of objective being, what is true? but, from the apriori forms in the subjective faculty of judgment itself, what can we know?

This method has the clear advantage of a completely exhaustive process, inasmuch as a thorough analysis of the functions of judgment must attain all the primitive conceptions by which all the apriori possible forms of judgments are regulated, and give to them an exact classification according to the respective forms of judgments constituted under them.   If the analysis be complete the categories must thereby be all attained, and correctly arranged; and also avoid this, which must occur in the method of Aristotle, that the general terms embraced in the category will be promiscuously of such as belong both to the intuition and to the judgment.   Accordingly, having given space and time to the primitive intuition, Kant attains the four categories of the Quantity, the Quality, the Relation, and the Mode, and each having their three respective predicates as primitive conceptions belonging to them, and all of which are given in the faculty of the judgment, thus making twelve categorical conceptions as conditional regulative principles for the functions of the understanding.

But the real defects in both of these methods is in their too great exclusiveness, each on opposite sides. Aristotle is so far *objective*, and looking to the *matter* as given in the judgment, that the system is naturally carried by its successive philosophers out wholly on this side, and made to merge all knowledge finally in the material; while Kant is so far *subjective*, and looking to the *form* in the judgment, that the system is readily carried out wholly to that side, and ultimately placing all knowledge in the ideal. This perpetual reproach to all metaphysical investigation, the ever-lasting antagonism between materialism and idealism, and thus constantly inducing, and indeed requiring in the interest of philosophy itself, the presence of skepticism, needs most carefully to be avoided, and the truth on both sides to be so intelligently apprehended, and in this way also so harmoniously blended in the metaphysical system, that it shall not permit it ever to fall over on either side. The matter cannot be known without form, nor can the form be known but as conditional for possible content; and thus nothing in the conception of the one may be exclusive of that which is necessary in the conception of the other. If we would apprehend objective being, we must know it in its form; and if we would attain the subjective form, we must know it as having possible material content; and thus that which must be ever in accordance with both cannot admit that it should be forced to an exclusion of either.

Should we then find substantially the same primitive conceptions as those of Kant, which we doubtless must, inasmuch as what is really attained as subjective form must also be conditional for objective being, and be found in an analysis of the faculty of judgment—yet, if we can so attain them as to keep wholly in view their objective as well as subjective aspect, and this also in a manner that shall secure as thorough apriori completeness as his, this will doubtless be attended with many advantages.

This will be our design in the method pursued. Not a promiscuous and random generalization of terms for objective being; nor yet a specific analysis of our subjective faculty of judgment; but in the light of an apriori cognition, we shall determine what is conditional for both the objective and the subjective, the matter and the form, in all possible knowledge of the phenomenal. We shall in this way find that there are *three* entirely distinct *modes of intellectual agency* demanded for the completion of the giving and determining of the phenomenal in an experience, and that these three are all that can be employed in such work; and that each of the three agencies have also *three elementary principles* conditional for carrying the process onward to the completed result, and that each agency can have only these three elementary principles. The sequel will show that this gives a more precise and restricted meaning to the faculty of the understanding than that which is taken in the system of

Kant; and also, that instead of giving to the sense the capacity of being a mere " receptivity" of a content for perception, we include within it an intellectual agency competent to complete the perception. This intellectual agency, which is competent to apprehend the phenomenon in the sense and in this to effect a completed perception, being separated from what Kant has included altogether in the understanding, will be a limitation of that faculty to a narrower field. This fact, with the reason for it of embracing both the objective and subjective aspects of all cognition, and the advantage of always having these in the same view, will be readily apprehended by the intelligent reader, and need not to be made a matter of further reference.

We shall have in the faculty of the sense, *two* distinct intellectual operations to investigate, one coming within this first Division for attaining to pure objects, and the other within the second Division for empirical objects; the first answering to Kant's Category of Quantity; and the second to his Category of Quality. We shall then have, in the faculty of the understanding, in a Second Part of our work, another distinct intellectual operation before us, answering to Kant's Category of Relation. There will then remain, in the faculty of the reason, in a Third Part of our work an intellectual operation to be investigated quite peculiar, and referring wholly to the supernatural, as all the former have to the natural, and which covers the ground that Kant has excluded from all speculative philosophy and put within the peculiar region o f what, with him, is the practical reason. These will be called *Apriori Intellectual Operations*, rather than the technical term of *Categories*, and we here begin with the first in order.

We have already examined the general process for the possibility of real form in pure space and time, and found that as the primitive intuition does not construct, an intellectual agency must construct the pure object. This is done by conjoining that which was before diverse and unlimited in the primitive intuition, and bringing it by this agency into a completed and defined pure object. Thus all figures in space and all periods in time may be constructed. This, then, is the intellectual operation to be here further considered, that we may attain the apriori elements which enter into the process. It is properly a *constructing* agency, and as this is effected by conjoining what before was unconjoined or diverse, it is the work of CONJUNCTION that we are to examine, and see what are the elements conditional for it. What are the elements in *the operation of conjunction*?

1. In the primitive intuition of pure space and time nothing is conjoined, and thus no product can be cognized because nothing is produced. Such possible product is the result of a constructive agency, and this must be effected by *conjunction*. And now, what must be *the first element in the apriori operation of*

conjunction? This may be determined by an immediate beholding in pure space and time.

The intellectual agency in conjunction must not merely *move* within the primitive intuition. If there were only a mere passing in pure space and time no result could remain, for no line as its pathway would be left by the movement. It would be a mere passing through the void intuition, leaving it still to be void, when the movement had wholly transpired. It must, then, be an agency which can take up and collect within itself, this diversity in the primitive intuition as it passes along through it. One point in pure space assumed as a position, and made the starting-point or commencing limit of the movement, must not be left as it was before it had been so assumed, but must be conjoined to the point next assumed as position, and this also to another, and thus onwards to the point which becomes the terminating limit of the intellectual movement. If I take up any number of diverse objects one by one, and throw away the first when I take the next, no possible accumulation can result, because no product can be thus generated. Merely to repeat one, one, one, would not be to count; but that any number should be generated in the process, the first one must be retained and conjoined with the succeeding one, and thus conjoined they are no longer diverse as one, one, but the first is produced into the second making them together to be two, and this product of two is then produced into the next one, making all together to be three, and thus onward through all the progressing agency until it terminates. So in the diversity given in pure space and time, the agency must collect and conjoin within itself in its own movement the diverse points in space or instants in time, and in this conjunction only can there be a product as a line or a succession. The agency *collects within itself* what it takes up in passing, and thus only is it *intelligent* agency.

And now, as this *may* be to any degree possible in pure space and time, and for any possible amount and modification of figure and period, so also thus it *must* be for any and every figure or period that shall become product therein. Such a conjunction of what is diverse in the primitive intuition is a universal necessity for all possible product in space and time, and is hence an apriori cognition. All possible experience must be regulated by it, and conform to it. But this conjoining process is a strictly *uniting* process— it *unifies* the diverse as given in the primitive intuition, and thus pure space and time remain no longer a diversity but a unity where this intellectual agency has passed, and only where it has passed. In the passing it has collected into itself and thereby *united* what it has taken up, and all this is done in the immediate intuition and is thus directly beheld. It needs no demonstration, it is already intuition. The first element, therefore, in all processes of conjunction

11

and thus in all products as real forms in space and time, as found by an apriori cognition, is *Unity*.

2. As this conjoining process goes on constructing the diversity in unity, that which it has taken up and gathered within itself, being no longer diverse but conjoined, becomes a collection or synthesis, i. e. a *diversity in unity*—and which is the precise conception of a *multiplicity*. A number of diverse points in space, merely as they stand in their diversity, may be said to be *many* (multi), inasmuch as it is possible they may be conjoined; but it is by their conjunction, or *implication* one in another, as the product of an intellectual agency, that we come to the cognition that it is other than *many*, it is the many *united*, (multi impliciti.) As the least that is possible in the conception of unity is that of one conjoined to one, (unus plus,) which is plurality; and this admits of any possible increase (unus plus, duo plus, tres plus, &c.), and is still plurality; this expresses the conception more completely than multiplicity. It is so many and *more;* and thus though a unity yet an incomplete process with still the agency going on in its work of conjunction. Such, it is apriori seen, must be true in all construction of real forms in pure space and time. The agency must commence with a position as a starting point, and move to another position conjoining it to the first, and in this is *unity;* and as it is one and more, (unus plus) and as yet indeterminate how much more, inasmuch as the uniting process is

not yet completed, it must be a *plurality*. **All con-**
junction must stand thus in the pure intuition, **as a**
begun but incomplete product so long as the **agency**
is in progress, and thus having within itself **the ele-**
ment of *Plurality*.

3. The unity in a plurality, though an apriori **con-**
dition for all real form in pure space and time, **yet is**
not all that is conditional. The diversity in the primitive intuition is not thereby a unit, though in **unity.**
The terminating limit is not yet given, and **thus it**
cannot be said yet what the completed real form **shall**
be. It is in the process of construction, but all **possi-**
ble form yet beyond what has been constructed **still**
remains in the primitive intuition, and thus open **to**
the constructing intellectual agency, and thereby **for-**
bidding that we should say more than that there **is**
the unity in a plurality. There must come the **ter-**
mination of the agency, and the intellect must **cease**
to collect any more of the diversity into itself, **and**
thereby affix a terminating limit to the conjunction,
and thus define what has been united on all sides,
and then first arises a completed pure object as **entire**
product in space and time. This unity in the **plural-**
ity completed, becomes then a whole, cutting itself **off**
from all that is not included within its own circumscription, and standing out in the pure intuition **as a**
real form, definite in its own constructed totality. **All**
real form must possess a *total* of the plurality in **unity,**
and thus a third apriori element is *Totality*.

It is now manifest that while no real form in space and time can possess less than the elements of *unity, plurality,* and *totality* ; so likewise can no pure object possess more than these three apriori elements. The whole process of construction, for either figure in space or period in time, as the intellectual agency enters upon it and goes on to its completion, can demand nothing less nor more, than that it take up the diverse, and give unity in a plurality which shall ultimately possess totality. Here, therefore, are all the possible elements of all possible conjunction in pure space and time.

Now of all possible real form thus constructed in pure space and time, whether it be that of figure or period, we may say that it possesses a *Quantity.* Quantity is thus the general term which is to express all possible real form in pure space and time ; and of all possible quantity there may be apriori predicated of it, that it must possess unity, plurality, and totality. It cannot possibly be made intelligible, except all the three apriori predicates, as above, belong to it. The apriori intellectual operation of conjunction in its elements is the same as Kant's category of quantity, attained by analyzing the faculty of judgment through the forms subjectively of universal, particular, and individual judgments. In the process above pursued, we may see not only that our faculty of judgment *has* so many forms, giving so many primitive conceptions : but *why* it has, viz : that an apriori cognition in pure space and time, through a direct intuition, determines that all possible intellectual construction of quantity *must* have so many and no more elements.   It is not possible that any intellect should give quantity in pure space and time in any other process or through any other elementary conditions.   All possible experience of shapes in space and successions in time must conform thereto, and so far from attaining them by an analysis of any of our Intellectual functions, we determine them to be universally necessary for all intellectual construction of objects in consciousness.

We have in the above, attained all that is necessary in the determination of the *process* of conjunction, and of the *result* in a definite and completed form as quantity.   But a work equally as necessary and quite as abstruse yet remains to be accomplished, viz: What is conditional for the intellectual *agency* that it may be competent to such a conjoining operation ?   Except as this inquiry shall receive a satisfactory answer, we have brought the subject of Rational Psychology through but half its difficult way to the attainment of the sense in its subjective idea, as necessary to be acquired under the first division of the intuition.   This, then, will form the subject of another section, the determination apriori of what is necessary *in the intellect*, in order that it may operate such results in the product of a completed pure quantity.

SECTION V.

THE UNITY OF SELF-CONSCIOUSNESS.

THE Unity found as a first element in the apriori operation of conjunction, and which is conditional for the production of all quantity, is itself also a produ t. The collecting into itself the diverse points and instants in pure space and time, as its agency passes over the primitive intuition, is the peculiar work of the intellect, and such collection into itself becomes a conjunction in unity, whereby a quantity is first generated in the intuition. Such unity can be no product of the primitive intuition, but only of a constructing agency which performs its work within it, thereby giving real form within pure space and time. But what is conditional in this intellectual *agency itself*, that it may be competent to such a work of conjoining a diversity in unity?

It is manifest that if such agency were in itself diverse, and its movement a repetition of single and disjoined acts, that it could make no collection, and effect no conjunction, and thus could produce no unity in the primitive intuition. An agency which was as manifold as the diverse points and instants in pure space and time, and thus only an act in its own point or instant, would possess no capacity for passing over from one point or instant to another, and collecting them continuously into a quantity. The agency must, therefore, itself possess a higher unity than that which it produces in pure space and time; and it is only this possession of the higher unity that can make the unity in the conjunction as product to be possible. And now, the demand is, that we attain as an apriori cognition, what is conditional for this *higher unity* of the intellectual agency.

1. *It must be competent to more than the simple act.* —In order to any conjunction in unity there must be perpetuated movement; but the simple act can effect no movement. If it were a constant repetition of itself, it would still result in no movement. It would be merely an act in one point, and a repetition of the act in another point, and thus only an alternating agency and not a moving agency. It would be simply origination and extinction in the same point, and this repeated in any diversity of points could not conjoin them. The oscillations of any number of pendulums in diverse spaces occurring in alternation, can not conjoin those spaces, inasmuch as the agency arises and finishes in its own space, and does not pass on to collect into itself that which is diverse from its own. As simple act, however perpetually repeated and in whatever diversity, cannot be a movement through the diversity, it can not, therefore, produce any conjunction in unity. In order to this it must be a perpetuated agency, and though successive in the diverse

points and instants yet itself in unity through the whole operation. In this manner only can the agency conjoin that which is diverse through which it passes, and construct a real form as product of its movement, and leave it as a result within a pure intuition. **We** will call this apriori condition—*The Unity of the conjoining agency.*

2. *There must be more than the unity of conjoining agency.*—An agency in unity throughout, moving through the diverse points and instants in pure space and time, and performing its work in conjoining the diverse points and instants in unity, could not yet accomplish anything towards giving its products as real forms to the apprehension, when the operation went on in darkness. A mere blind movement could make no product to appear, and hence its whole work would yet be as nothing. The perpetuated movement must be itself in the light, and the whole process of conjunction go on in the light, and thereby its product be put altogether in the light, or the whole movement of the agency must be in vain, and its results hidden from all possibility of a revelation.

And here we must determine what Consciousness is to subserve, in this apriori process towards the apprehension of the pure object; for this light of which we are here speaking is the very thing we mean by consciousness. This has certainly been very variously described, doubtless very differently conceived, and not seldom very much misconceived. If we will allow the conception to fashion itself under the analogies of an inward illumination rather than as an agent, or any faculty of an agent, or any act of such faculty, we shall come the nearest to the reality. When the spontaneous agency of the intellect, as productive imagination, has conjoined the diversity in the primitive intution in unity, and thereby constructed the pure object as its product, no farther *action* is necessary to be supposed. The whole process of the construction, and the completed product, all stand out in the mind's own light, and such illumination will be available to reveal what has been done, and to show the product. The pure object is put within this light, and thus the mind possesses it in its own illumination, and this is the same as to say that the object stands in consciousness. Not as an act, but as a light ; not as a maker—for that is the province of the intellectual agency—but rather as a revealer : after such analogies shall we doubtless best conceive of consciousness, and which may thus be termed " the light of all our seeing." In this conception, the difficulty of cognizing consciousness and determining precisely and affirmatively what it is becomes very obvious. It may be competent to evince for itself *that* it is, while it is not competent that it should give any representation of itself determining *what* it is. All the intellectual constructions as products appear in consciousness, but we have no circumscribing agency and light out of consciousness, by which consciousness may itself be made to appear. It is that inward illumination in which all that is therein constructed may appear, while itself is a light too pure and transparent to admit that it should be seen.

And further, with this conception of consciousness, it is also apriori manifest that it must possess unity. Were the conjoining operation to be at this point or instant in one light of a consciousness, and in a diverse point or instant in another light of a consciousness, the former manifestation would be separate from the latter, and no perpetuated appearance of pure object could be effected. There would be a separate revealing for each moment of the constructing agency, and in this way only a flashing and extinction of light which would be a diverse consciousness for each point or instant of space and time, and in this conception, no continuity of process nor perpetuity of appearance would be possible. The light of consciousness in which the conjunction is effected must be throughout in unity or neither the construction nor the apprehension can be completed.

And here, let us go back to our first apriori position in the primitive intuition. When we made abstraction of all that had been given in the sensibility, and thus left the real form of the phenomenon; and then made abstraction of the real form as definite figure or period, and thus left the pure form of space and time in their limitless and unconstructed diversity; we did not extinguish any light in which either the phenomenon or the real form had appeared. That light still remains and gives us the limitless diversity of pure space and time which no abstraction can remove. It is now, it is true, wholly subjective, and exists in the primitive intuition only, and so far has significancy only for that mind within which the primitive intuition is; but it is there as a light revealing a pure form, in which nothing is needed but new constructions to be given, and real forms and phenomenal content again appear. This light of the primitive intuition is essentially one in its own unity, for it has the limitless diversity of space and time beneath it, and all agency that may operate to conjoin, and all products that may be conjoined in pure space and time, must be illuminated and revealed thereby. That original faculty of the primitive intuition, which is when all that has been given to it has been taken from it—which must apriori have been in order to that experience of the phenomenal which was abstracted from it—that, essentially, is in the subjective being, as conditional for the possibility of apprehending any thing which the productive imagination may construct, or the affection in the sensibility may present, for phenomena. This one illumination, which as primitive intuition gives pure space and time, as pure intuition gives all real forms constructed, and as empirical intuition gives all that is phenomenal, is the one constant and perpetual light of consciousness revealing all that in any way is put within it. And this self-sameness of light, in which all that may be constructed must appear, we will term—*the Unity of consciousness.*

3. *There must be more than the unity of the conjoining agency and the unity of consciousness.*—Were the agency to be in unity, and the consciousness also in unity, yet if the agency and the consciousness were diverse, the product constructed by the intellect could not appear in the consciousness. The agency might conjoin, but it would be in darkness; and the consciousness might stand in its own light, but it would possess nothing that might appear. The intellect would act with its back to the mirror, the mirror would be incompetent to envisage the products for itself in the plane of its own surface. Both the agency constructing and the consciousness revealing must be in unity, and thus what the intellect constructs that also the consciousness reveals in the same subject.

And this unity of intellectual action and conscious revealing is not only necessary as condition apriori that the construction and the revelation may be given in one subject, but also necessary that there should be any intellectual construction at all. The primitive intuition of pure space and time must give all diversity in which the conjunction of real forms can be effected; and therefore, to the productive imagination, it were impossible that any pure object should be attained except as constructed in that diversity which is in unity with itself, inasmuch as other than this, there can be no *pure* form within which it might construct the *real* form. The same light of an intuition, which gives the diverse points and instants in the pure space and time, must also give the constructing agency through all its process of conjoining and also give its product as completed pure object.

And here, this one subject, in which is the unity of both constructing agency and revealing consciousness, may be termed *the self;* and thus this unity of agency and envisagement will be a unity in the self, and may be termed—*the Unity of self-consciousness.*

In order to the possibility of a conjunction in unity of that which is diverse in the primitive intuition of pure space and time, and thus in order to any possible apprehension of quantity, the unity of self-consciousness is necessary ; and in which is comprehended the unity of the agency, the unity of the consciousness, and the unity of both in the same subject as a self. It might here be competent, perhaps, to push the apriori analysis of conjunction into another department higher up, and investigate what is the pure form as diversity in the primitive intuition, and what thus would give an apriori *scheme,* as it were, for the regulation of the intellect, as productive imagination, in constructing its diagrams as pure objects in space and time, and thereby the more effectually determine what the imagination must be in its primitive sources ; but for all the purposes of attaining to the sense in its subjective idea in the pure intuition, the diversity given in the points and instants of pure space and time as wholly unconjoined and limitless, and yet which may be conjoined and limited in all possible figures and periods, is in itself sufficient; for it enables us to give an apriori examination of the whole process of conjunction, both in what is conditional in the result itself as quantity, and in the constructing and revealing agency as self-consciousness.

It should further, as a caution, be here added, that not the intellectual agency is self, nor the revealing consciousness is self, but their unity is *in that* which we here term the self. We are not here in a condition to investigate any thing at all relatively to a common subject for the agency and the light in which the constructed product appears. This belongs wholly to the next part in the faculty of the understanding. This much only is it here necessary to determine, that for the possibility of all conjunction as giving a quantity in space and time, the agency conjoining and the consciousness revealing must stand together in unity, and which we term the unity of self-consciousness, though we do not here determine any thing about this *self*, as common subject for the imagination and the intuition, the constructing agency and the envisaging consciousness.

From the progress we have now made, and the position to which we have here attained, in the conditional apriori cognition of self-consciousness, it is competent to answer several queries, and settle some important doubtful matters, in reference to the process of perception ; and which, except for such an apriori investigation, must hereafter be as they have heretofore been inexplicable mysteries. We will here indicate the questions and their solution in a cursory manner.

Thus, it is quite explicable why the constructed product should become *an object*.—The constructing agency has put limits, and thus given definite outline, to what is now a precise quantity in pure space and time, and thus space and time are no longer void, unconjoined, and limitless ; but possess a completed form as figure or period, and this directly within the intuition as having its unity in a self. This definite form is thus thrown face to face, directly before the self in its intuition, and is thus an *object* to the apprehension, (obvius jaciens.) The object, as *pure*, is in the imagination only, and thus wholly subjective and that which *seems ;* but, still a real form for any possible content that might be given in the sensibility, and when filled by such content as its matter, becomes phenomenon as perceived object, and which then *appears.*

And further, it may be manifest how this is *my* object.—The constructing agency and the light in which it is revealed have their unity in *my* self, and hence both the conjunction and the envisaging are *mine ;* and as in this process the product is given and apprehended as object, it becomes both an object *to me* inasmuch as it is thrown before me, and *my* object inasmuch as it is *my* construction and *my* presentation. I *myself* can have no pure object which I do not by *my* productive imagination construct, and which also I do not construct in *my* consciousness; and both because I myself construct, and I myself envisage, it becomes that I myself have a pure object.

It is also manifest why pure objects in space and time must be wholly *incommunicable*.—The primitive intuition is wholly subjective; the conjoining and the envisaging are both also wholly subjective; and thus the pure object is object only in my subject. The line I draw, the circle or other figure I describe, the period which I limit, become pure objects only to me, and cannot themselves be communicated to any other subject. The communication can only be by symbols, and inducing that the agency and light in unity in a diverse self, should construct and reveal similar pure objects, in his subjective apprehension. The possibility of the communing in my pure objects by another subject would demand that this diverse subject should be competent to envisage the *self* in which is my imagination and my consciousness united; and then, such *other* self could " search my heart, and try my reins." As if two mirrors were self-conscious, they could only subjectively envisage without the possibility of communication among themselves, but the self which might envisage them, could well see all that was in them.

We may further learn why the self *cannot become*

object to itself.—Only that which may be constructed in the primitive intuition of pure space and time can become object. The agency as process of conjoining may go on within the primitive intuition, and the pure product as quantity constructed may also stand out in the consciousness; but the self in which the conjoining agency and revealing consciousness have their unity must of course lie back of the primitive intuition, and cannot be brought by any construction within any of the conjunctions that its diverse points and instants may receive. The pure forms of space and time are conditional for all real forms that may be constructed within them, and this can be only of figure and period, but the self cannot be subjected to such conditions, and cannot therefore become object. That the self should become object would demand that we should see *through*, and not merely that which is *in*, the mirror.

It may also be disclosed, here, how we may come to the conviction *that* a self is, while we cannot yet determine at all *what* the self is.— *What* the self is we cannot here at all determine, inasmuch as all the agency for knowing which we have yet attained is simply that of conjoining in unity and attaining to the forms for phenomena, while the self cannot be phenomenon nor be constructed in the shapes of space or the successions of time.

But the conviction *that* a self is originates fairly in this, that the unity of constructing agency and revealing consciousness is conditional for all possible pure objects. Our agency, as intellectual, must be in perpetuated unity; our revealings in consciousness, must be in a unity of consciousness; and both intellect and consciousness must be in unity; and thus a higher subject as self must be, though we are not yet prepared to say any thing about it, for a merely conjoining agency can do nothing with it.

Finally, it may be explained in what way *we awake in self-consciousness.*—The spontaneous agency (no matter here whether we include the content in the sensibility or not for our present purpose as an example,) constructs its product in space and time, and this becomes an object in consciousness. This is distinct from the constructing agency, (and more especially so when the matter in the sensibility is given,) and both it and the process of its construction are in the immediate intuition, and thus in the light of consciousness they are diverse from each other. The agency and the consciousness are referred in their unity to one self, which is the *unity* of self-consciousness, but the object cannot be so referred; that is other than self; and this discrimination between what is from *self*, and what is from *not-self*, is the *finding of myself.* In proportion as such discrimination is absent, in infancy, in syncope, delirium, somnambulism, or high mental excitement and passionate absorption, the man has lost himself; is beside himself; not self-conscious.

We have now attained the Idea of the Sense in the

pure Intuition. It is quite competent to state how a pure sense may be which may give pure objects in a consciousness. A primitive intuition must have pure space and time in its limitless diversity, as pure form for all possible real form which may be given in space and time. An intellectual agency, as productive imagination, must construct these real forms by conjoining the diverse in pure space and time; the process to which result must possess the three elements of a *unity*, inducing a *plurality*, and which is completed in a *totality;* thus giving a definite *quantity* as product. But in order to the possibility for such conjoining agency there must be the unity of the agency, the unity of the consciousness, and the unity of both agency and consciousness in the same self, which is *the unity of self-consciousness.* In this way a pure object in space and time may be determined as *my object.* The whole may be concisely expressed in the following apriori formula, viz: *All possible pure object must be conjoined by the intellect in the primitive intuition, under the unity of self-consciousness.*

All this is an idea of the faculty of the sense as wholly pure from all content in the sensibility, and thus wholly *subjective;* and the pure objects are given incommunicably to any other subject than that in which is the agency and the consciousness. It remains, in order to the completed idea of the sense, that we attain the Idea in the *empirical Intuition,* which will now introduce the *Second Division.*

SECOND DIVISION.

THE IDEA IN THE EMPIRICAL INTUITION.

SECTION I.

THE ATTAINMENT OF AN APRIORI POSITION THROUGH A PROLEPSIS.

ALL intuition is an immediate beholding. In the *primitive* intuition we immediately behold space and time as pure form. In the *pure* intuition we immediately behold any definite figures or periods constructed in pure space and time. When a content in the sensibility gives the matter for some phenomenon as quality, and this is brought directly within the light of consciousness, this also we immediately behold; but inasmuch as this is empirical and not pure object, so the distinction is made for it by calling it *empirical* intuition. In all perception of objects in the sense this content in the sensibility is given, and as the *matter* of the phenomenon, its apriori investigation is as necessary to a complete idea of the sense as the process of its construction into form. This, therefore, is the design of the present Division, to attain the subjective Idea of the Sense in the *empirical Intuition.*

The first requisition is that we attain a determinate transcendental position from which an apriori examination may be had, and in which all our conclusions shall carry with them the demonstrations of universality and necessity. We should wholly fail of attaining such a position through a process of abstraction, as before for the pure forms of space and time. An abstraction of all content from the sensibility would be a void of all matter for phenomenon, and thus the nihility of all empirical intuition. An empty organism of sense gives no condition for any intellectual operation, as does the pure forms of space and time in the primitive intuition for the construction of pure figure and period. We are then forced to some other method of attaining a position back of all experience, from whence to attain those conditional principles which make the experience of perceived phenomena possible.

That there should be some content in the sensibility in order to sensation, and thus a condition given for empirical intuition, is at once seen to be a universal necessity. An anticipation of such content in general, as condition for any and all perception of phenomena, and in the conception of which an occasion may be given for determining what intellectual operation is necessary universally for bringing such anticipated content under an empirical intuition, will give to us our determined apriori position. Such a general anticipation of content in the sensibility, as conditional for all possible empirical intuition, will put us at once above all experience in the sense, and give to us an occasion for investigating the whole ground of possibility for bringing such content within the light of consciousness, and thereby making it to be a perceived definite phenomenon. We shall in this be restricted to no partial organism of the sensibility, but whether there be five or fifty sources of organic sensation, and each of these organs be competent to receive content of a thousand-fold variety, still the same conditional principles for bringing any and all under an empirical intuition must be universally necessary. We start from this general anticipation of content, and in it determine what is universally necessary that it may be possible to appear as phenomenon in consciousness, and in this we attain an apriori subjective idea of the entire process of empirical intuition. The position is attained not by an *abstraction* but by an *anticipation*. Such an anticipation was by the old Greek philosophers termed a Prolepsis (πρoληψɩs) and we here use it as inclusive of mere matter in general for all possible phenomena.

It will be necessary to determine how it is possible to bring this content in general into phenomena *distinct* one from another, and also how to order this distinct matter into *definite forms*, so that one phenomenon may be both distinct from all others, and definite in its own being, as appearing in the consciousness. We shall thus have the conditions of two separate processes of an intellectual agency to investigate, viz: that of *distinguishing* the content, and that of *constructing* the distinguished matter into a definite form. We shall in this have the subjective Idea of all perception of phenomena, both as distinct in matter and definite in form; and this is inclusive of the entire intellectual operation which is apriori conditional for all possibility of complete empirical intuition, or, as the same thing, clear perception of phenomena in the sense. The idea of *the operation of* CONJUNCTION has already been attained in the bringing of pure space and time into definite figure and period, and it remains, here, that we investigate the conditional principles of *the operation of* DISTINCTION; and then that we show how the conditions apriori of conjunction, already attained in pure intuition, apply also to empirical intuition, or the perceiving of phenomena.

SECTION II.

THE APRIORI ELEMENTS OF ALL POSSIBLE ANTICIPATION OF APPEARANCE IN THE SENSE.

SENSIBILITY is the capacity of being affected by the presence of some matter which as a content is from somewhere given to it. The affection is a sensation, and answers to the content by which it has been induced. It may thus be manifold in its diversity, according to the diversity in all possible content which may be given to the sensibility. As many diverse *organs* as may be given for the functions of the sense, so great must be the possible diversity of the *kind* of content that may be received; and as diverse as the matter given inducing in each organ its diversity of affection, as sensation, so much may be the possible diversity of the *varieties* of content that may be received. Thus, the eye as organ, may receive one kind of content, and the ear as diverse organ another kind, &c. and thus the *kinds* be diversified through all possible organs. The eye again may receive its content of all possible diversities, inducing all possible diversity in its sensation, and the ear and all other possible organs in the same manner, and thus there may be a diversity of *varieties* in the sensation through all possible content. The diverse organs will give diverse kinds, and the diverse affections in the same organ, and this through all possible organs will give the diverse varieties possible. All possible diversity of sensation may thus be given in an apriori prolepsis of all possible content in the sense.

The prolepsis in the sense is that of a universal anticipation of content in all possible kinds and varieties; inclusive not only of that which conditions our human perception, but of all possible perception of phenomena in any sense. And of this universal prolepsis of content we now apriori determine that it may have all possible diversity of kind and variety. In this universal apriori anticipation of content all is, therefore, diverse, undiscriminated, undistinguished. The sensibility may give all possible diversity of content in all the kinds and varieties of sensation, but the sensation completed is all that the functions of the organic sensibility can accomplish. The sensibility distinguishes nothing, but only gives content in its diversity which must be distinguished by an intellectual agency. Were there no other functions than those in the sensibility, nothing could be determined in its own distinct appearance, but all must remain in the chaotic confusion of undiscriminated universal sensation. An intellectual agency must first brood over the chaos, or no one kind or variety can come out in its distinctness in the consciousness. An agency is demanded which may distinguish amid the kinds and varieties in the sensation. The intellectual agency in distinguishing must perform a different work from that already examined in constructing, and this process of distinguishing needs now to be as carefully investigated as has before been effected for the process of constructing definite forms in pure space and time. In construction, the work performed was that of a conjoining in unity ; in distinction, the work performed is a discriminating in an individuality. The one attains forms in conjunction, the other attains appearances in distinction ; one produces its object by collecting the diversity into it, the other finds its object by excluding all diversity from it. This *Operation of Distinction* is that which we now proceed to examine, that we may attain all the apriori elements which must be found within it.

1. Our universal prolepsis is inclusive of all possible content in a sensibility, whether of an outer or an inner sense, and of all possible kinds and varieties; and as thus wholly undiscriminated, it demands that what is to be a precise appearance in the consciousness, should be completely distinguished in its sensation from all others. Content must first be given to the sensibility, and by discriminating and excluding all diversity from it, that is found in its own distinct phenomenal being in the consciousness. A void sensibility can offer nothing to be distinguished, and the sensibility has itself no function for producing content within itself, and thus from somewhere other than itself must the content come. The intellectual agency as distinguishing operation has first to be supplied with sensation, which must be induced by some content affecting the sensibility; and the apprehending of this involves a discriminating it from non-sensation, and thus a determining that the sensibility is not void. The distinction here is between content and a void, sensation and no sensation; and this intellectual taking up of some content is henceforth in the process an exclusion of all non-content from the apprehending agency, and the determination that some of all possible diversity of sensation appears in the consciousness.

There is something as opposed to nothing which appears, and in this distinction of appearance from non-appearance in the consciousness is first attained the conception of a phenomenal *reality*. Some matter now stands in the consciousness, which has been found by the agency that discriminates sensation from non-sensation; and this is the first element in the operation of distinction, viz : *Reality*.

2. It must be manifest that a completed work of distinction is not given in this, that some content as opposed to no sensation appears. It may be any one of all possible realities in appearance, and in order to its precise determination in the consciousness, it must be competent to deny of this that which may be in all other appearances beside this. That it is real appearance is a determined distinction from non-appearance only, and it needs farther to be determined as distinction from all other possible appearances. The intellectual agency must, therefore, proceed in its distinguishing work and exclude from this appearance all other possible appearances, and thus affirm for it the absence of all other reality than that which is its own. To effect such farther distinction, all other diversity must be cut off from this reality, and stand over against this as other than, and the contrary of, this. All other reality excluded from this determines their distinction from this, and thereby particularizes this in the discrimination of all others apart from this. This denying of that which is in any other possible

reality to be in this present apprehended reality excludes all other reality, and makes this a discriminated *particular*. We have, therefore, in this further
process of distinction, added to the element of reality,
this second element of *Particularity*.

3. That we have distinguished the real from the
non-real, and also the particular from the universal,
has not yet completed the work of distinction. We
may be able to affirm of any real appearance that it
is not any other appearance, and this will be but negative determination. To say of some appearance,
this is not color, nor sound, nor taste, &c., and in reference to variety, this is not redness, nor greenness,
nor whiteness, &c., and so also of the internal phenomena, this is not thought, nor volition, nor grief,
nor joy, &c.; and to carry this discrimination so far
as to deny all other and thus particularize this, would
still only be to affirm what it is not. It discriminates
and thus determines negatively, but finds nothing positively. It is preparatory to a completed distinction,
but is not the consummation of the work. The distinguishing agency must now advance to an individu-
alizing of this particular reality in its own appearance. It must affirm more than what it is not, even
what it is; more than what is excluded from it, even
that which is included in it. That must positively
be found in it which is not in any other reality, and
thus it must separate itself positively, and not merely
negatively from all reality but itself, that it may ap-

pear in consciousness having its own *peculiar* phenomenal variety. This will add to the elements of reality and particularity, the third element of *Peculiarity*.

It is, moreover, apriori manifest, that not only must all complete distinction include the elements of reality, particularity, and peculiarity, inasmuch as nothing can be distinctly apprehended except as a reality which is particular from all others and peculiar in ititself; but that also no operation of distinction can have more than these three elements, for when the appearance is apprehended in its reality, particularity and peculiarity it is completely discriminated, and no work of distinguishing can be carried forward any further. The operation of distinction is always complete in this, that it finds a reality, particularized from all others, and peculiar in itself, and thus a precise appearance is given in the consciousness. This operation of distinction, as an intellectual work bringing the diverse sensation into a precise appearance in consciousness, may properly be termed *Observation*. The completed result as precise appearance in consciousness is *Quality*. All sensation as distinguished in a complete observation becomes quality, and may be of different *kinds* ; as colors, weights, sounds, &c. : and also of different *varieties* ; as red, green, yellow, &c. : and also differ as *inner appearance* ; as thought, feeling, volition, &c. All quality is educed from sensation, the sensation being taken up by the intellectual agency, and in its distinguishing operation found thereby to be a reality, particularized from all others, and peculiar in its own phenomenal being.

We have, in the attainment of these apriori elements of distinction, kept the *result* of the process in view rather than the process itself, and have thus noted what has been *found* by it in the universal content anticipated as prolepsis, as before in the constructing process of conjunction what was *produced* by it in pure space and time; and we attain thus, not merely what our subjective faculty of judgment may accomplish, but what must be effected by all possible faculties objectively, in order to the precise discrimination of any quality in the consciousness. Had we analyzed our faculty of judgment as function for determining quality, we should have found for *Affirmative* judgments, the subjective conception of *reality* of affirmation; and for *Negative* judgments, the subjective conception of *negation* of all reality except in one affirmation; and for *Infinite* judgments, the subjective conception of the *limitation* between the one affirmation and the infinite number of negatives opposed to it; and should thus have exhausted all the primitive subjective conceptions for the determination of quality in our judgments. This would have been the method of Kant, and given his category of quality, including the primitive conceptions of reality, negation, and limitation. But this would have been the subjective side only, and available only for *our* ideal form of judgments, and thus determining what *our* human faculty of judgment was competent to effect. But when we look at a universal anticipation of all possible content for sensibility on the *objective* side, we find that the distinction between sensation and non-sensation is not mere *reality* of affirmation, but affirmation of a *reality;* and that the excluding of all possible sensation as other than the real sensation gives to the reality a *particularity* as object, and not merely a *negation* as functional form; and that the positive determination in the reality of that which separates it from what is in other reality, gives to it *peculiarity* as object, and not simply the functional form of *limitation* between an affirmative judgment and the infinite judgments that may stand opposed to it. We have thus hereby attained the elements of all possible distinction on the objective side, and can affirm that universally and from necessity all possible distinguishable quality must possess reality, particularity, and peculiarity. The operation of Distinction in all possible sensation must find these apriori elements, so many and no more.

It must also be here noted that some things are apriori conditional in order that a distinguishing *agency* may be, as we before found apriori conditions for the possibility of a conjoining agency. We need here merely to notice them cursorily, as what was given above more fully will be mainly applicable to the agency discriminating as well as the agency construct-

ing. There must be the Unity of discriminating agency, or the diversity in sensation could not be distinguished, inasmuch as what was taken up at one apprehension would else be lost at another. There must
be a Unity of the sensibility also, or one kind of sensation would belong to one subject, and another kind
to another. And both distinguishing agency, and sensibility must be in Unity of consciousness, or the content to be discriminated could not be put in the same
consciousness as the distinguishing operation. And,
lastly, all must be in the higher unity of the same subject, that both the sensation, the distinction. and the
consciousness, may belong to the same self, and thus
what the self has in sensation, the same self distinguishes, and the consciousness in which all appear is
also in the same self; and which may be termed as
before, the *Unity of self-consciousness.*

We may thus affirm, as an apriori cognition, *that all*
possible quality must be discriminated in the elements of
all Distinction viz : *reality, particularity and peculiarity.*
This would give the idea of the sense in its *matter* for
a phenomenon, as a prolepsis of all possible content
in sensation; but thus far the matter is only *distin-*
guished, not *conjoined* into form, which last must be
effected in order that it may come within an empirical
intuition; we will then now attain the process for
apriori giving *form* to the content as distinguished,
and thus complete the Idea in the empirical Intuition.

SECTION III.

THE DETERMINATION OF WHAT DIVERSITY THERE MUST APRIORI BE IN ALL QUALITY.

VOID sensibility can possess no sensation. It is no matter of consideration here whether the sensibility be itself more or less sensitive. There may, doubtless, be a readiness to become affected, in different sensibilities, through widely different degrees. It may be that in us men, there is far less capability of being affected by a content in our sensibility, than would be in beings whose perfection of sensibility was the highest possible. Perhaps an organ of sense sufficiently perfected might be so affected by the content given in magnetic or electric influences, or in chemical elective affinities, or even in the light itself, that it should give to the discriminating agency of the intellect sensations which might be precisely distinguished, and thereby unriddle all those mysteries which are now mere hypothesis and theory, and make them to be plain facts in perception. Nor is it of any moment here to determine how comprehensive a sensibility may possibly be. It may be conceived that new organs of sense should be indefinitely added to our five or six, and that the field of perception should thus be indefinitely augmented. But whether the

13

sensibility be more or less perfect in sensitiveness, or
more or less comprehensive in varied organs for receiving content as matter for sensation, this is universally true, that all sensibility of all possible perfection
and compass must have its content from somewhere
given to it, in order that any affection as sensation
should be given in it. No quality can appear, except
as its matter to be distinguished has somehow been
given in a sensibility.

And now, all quality as thus anticipated may admit of a diversity in two different directions of consideration. The *matter* as content in the sensibility,
and as thus inducing sensation, may be diverse. It
may be given through different organs of sense and
thus be diverse in *kind*, it may give different sensations in the same organ, and thus be diverse in *variety*.
Colors, sounds, smells, thoughts, feelings, &c. are all
diverse in *kind;* and thus with all possible organs
and faculties of an outward or inward sensibility.
Red and blue ; bitter and sweet ; warm and smooth ;
joy, grief, hope ; conception, recollection, &c., &c., are
all diverse in *variety;* and thus through all the difference of sensation that may be given within the same
organs and faculties of an external or internal sense.
In all this diversity as appearing in the matter, there
is difference as contrariety in the *reality itself,* and the
diverse may therefore be termed that of the *heterogeneous.* This diversity as heterogeneous in quality has
already been sufficiently explained in the consideration

of the operation of Distinction in its primary elements. All such diversity possible is ordered in the appearance through a process of distinguishing in an intellectual agency. All possible apriori diversity of quality, which may be made to appear in consciousness, and which is heterogeneous in itself, must be determined in an operation of Distinction. Sufficient attention has, therefore, already been given to the process for determining all possible diversity which is *heterogeneous.*

But in another point of consideration, the quality has a diversity in another manner. All the redness, or the coldness, or the grief, which is given as appearance from the same separate sensation, has in itself no contrariety but has similarity throughout. And yet there is diversity, for the redness of one place is diverse from the redness in another, and the coldness of one period is diverse from the coldness of another, and the grief rises or diminishes in diverse degrees; and thus in all, there is diversity which involves no contrariety of the reality itself, but which possesses similarity thoroughly. This diversity, then, may be termed the *homogeneous.* And as this has not at all, as yet, been considered, and as in the ordering of this diversity homogeneous in the appearance will be found all that belongs to the *form,* and in this also all that can come into an empirical intuition, and therefore all that may be embraced in the idea of the sense as in the empirical intuition, it becomes necessary clearly to apprehend this homogeneous diversity, and the whole process of its becoming an ordered *form* for the *matter* given in the sensation. The object in this section is, to determine this universal possible diversity of quality.

1. Of all possible quality which may be determined from an anticipation of content in the sensibility, a distinction must be made between it as a *reality*, and a void sensibilily which can give *no reality*. We may, therefore, take any reality as quality, and while homogeneous in itself, it may vary in amount indefinitely. The intellectual distinction from the non-real to the real has simply the limit, as zero, between them. On one side is the negative of all appearance and reality; on the other is a precisely discriminated appearance and reality; and this, it is manifest, may vary in amount from the least possible degree of that reality which can appear, up to the highest possible which can be given in an appearance. This difference of degree possible is a diversity in the anticipation, and includes all possible diversity of that reality; and as it is a diversity throughout in the same reality, it has similarity and not contrariety. It is thus a homogeneous diversity. And inasmuch as the amount is determined from the given sensation as degree of affection in the sensibility, it is a homogeneous diversity which should be characterized by a term expressive of its genesis. The amount of the pressure as heaviness, or of the color as brightness, is as the intensity of affection in the sensibility; the intensity of the sensation giving the amount in appearance, and thus hav-

ing a homogeneous diversity from the point of no sensation up to the given sensation. We may, then, as
characteristic of this homogeneous diversity, term it
a diversity as *Intensive*.

2. Though as reality, the quality may have a homogeneous diversity only as intensive, and thus
through all its amount, yet in another point of view a
homogeneous diversity is in another manner given.
The quality, as that of an external sense may occupy
more or less of space. The content given in sensation
thus considered stands in space as the homogeneous
through all the place it occupies, and it becomes thus
a diversity in the empirical intuition precisely as pure
space is a diversity in the primitive intuition. The
reality is homogeneous in the same place that the
pure space is homogeneous, and thus has a diversity of itself in every point of space in that place.
Quality, thus, may be homogeneously diverse in place ;
and as characteristic of this specific diversity, as it
fills more or less extended place, we will term it diversity as *Extensive*.

3. Quality may have diversity intensive and extensive, not only, but also in another manner there may
be homogeneity through a diversity. The reality as
appearance is given during the continuance of the sensation. So long as the content in the sensibility affects this sensibility in the same manner, the sensation is similar and homogeneous throughout, and thus
the homogeneous reality occupies the same succession

of instants in pure time for the empirical intuition, that the pure period does in the pure intuition. As the instants in the pure period are homogeneous and diverse, so the reality occupying this period is throughout homogeneous, and in each instant diverse. The reality is homogeneous in the same period that the pure time is homogeneous, and thus has a diversity of itself in every instant of the time it fills. Quality may thus be homogeneously diverse in time; and as descriptive of this manner of homogeneous diversity we may term it the *Protensive.*

Now an intellectual agency must *distinguish* the heterogeneous, and *conjoin* the homogeneous diversity. And this conjunction of the homogeneous will give *form* to that matter, which has been distinguished in the heterogeneous diversity.

SECTION IV.

THE CONSTRUCTION OF THE HOMOGENEOUS DIVERSITY OF ALL POSSIBLE QUALITY INTO FORM.

THERE are two main questions which may be asked concerning any anticipated content in sensation, and which must apriori be answered as conditional for all distinct and definite appearance in consciousness. The first is—*What* is the quality? The process for arriving at an answer to this, has already been indicated. It must be through the operation of *Dis-*

tinction. The intellect as discriminating agent must take up the sensation and determine it in its reality, particularity and peculiarity; and such agency places it in its own precise distinctness of quality immediately in the light of consciousness, and capacitates us to say directly *what* it is. Thus far it is properly observation, and this determining of quality in its *distinctness* is all that observation can accomplish. The sensation was not produced by the intellectual agency, but is an affection in the sensibility induced from the content in some way put within it; so that not the construction of the quality in its *existence* is given in consciousness, but only its distinction in its own precise reality in appearance. This precise distinctness as to what is the quality is all that an observation can propose to accomplish.

A second question is—*How much* is the quality? The process to the attainment of an answer here is by a different operation than that of distinction altogether. The quality is contemplated as having quantity, and the intellectual agency is to be employed in determining how much quantity. And now, in our first Division in this Chapter, we attained the apriori process for the production of all pure quantity through a conjunction in unity, the application of which to our distinct quality must be our only method for determining how much it is. All quantity has its quality, and all quality has a quantity. The only quality which any quantity may have is, that it is *extended;* and, as all

extension is determined only by a conjoining agency,
so both the quantity and its quality are given in the
same constructing operation. A conjoining act gives
both a quantity and also that the quantity has extension. There is, therefore, in the determination of
quantity no operation of distinction demanded, for its
precise quality is given in giving itself. There is
nothing to be discriminated in extension itself as a
quality, but only that it be determined whether the
extension be pure or empirical.

But not thus with the quality. The agency which
discriminates this and thus gives it precisely and distinctly in the consciousness, has not accomplished the
whole work demanded. The operation of distinction
has given quality only, and quality has quantity which
no distinguishing agency can determine. In addition
to the operation of distinction there must also be the
operation of conjunction. While, therefore, we could
finish our work in the construction of quantity by one
operation of conjunction, in relation to quality we must
apply both operations. To find the precise quality,
what it is, we must distinguish; and then, to find,
how much it is, we must conjoin. The distinguishing
process has been already given, we have here to apply
apriori the conjoining process. This will demand a
constructing process in a three-fold order of operation,
inasmuch as the homogeneous diversity to be constructed is three-fold. The question, How much is
the quality? may mean, How much as *Intensive*, as

Extensive, or as *Protensive?* i. e. how much in the sensation? how much in space? and how much in time? Only in the answers to these three inquiries, do we exhaust the quantity which is to be found in all quality. The operation in distinction we have said to be *Observation;* we shall now find the operation in conjunction to be *Attention.* Attention not only extends the intellect to the content in sensation, but includes the operation then performed in constructing it, and which puts the *form* of the content in clear consciousness. The applying of the intellect to the content in sensation may be an act of the will, or it may be spontaneous, as must have been the first agency in childhood and as often is in adult life. But the attending act (ad tendo) is the intellect *stretching* or *extending over,* and thus circumscribing or constructing the content in its complete form ; and this is none other than the operation of conjunction in unity.

In pure space and time the definite form as quantity is to be constructed by an intellectual agency in its spontaneity, moving over the diversity in its manifoldness and conjoining it in unity. The same work must also be effected for the content in sensation through its three-fold diversity as intensive, extensive, and protensive. The difference is only in this, that the pure diagrams in space and time must be constructed according to some scheme in the productive imagination ; but the empirical forms must be constructed according to the content as given in the sensation ; the work of construction is precisely the same in both—*the conjunction of the diversity in a unity, plurality, and totality*—and thereby giving completeness to the quantity of the quality already distinguished. The act of observation is thus to give *distinctness* to quality ; and the act of attention is to give *definiteness* to quantity : in observing, we distinguish it from all other quality ; in attending, we limit it in its own quantity : in the first, we get the *distinct matter* of the phenomenon ; in the last, we get the *definite form* of the phenomenon. We will now at once give the latter process in its three-fold application to the homogeneous diversity.

1. The diversity as *intensive*, is given wholly within the sensibility, and is the manifoldness of degree from no sensation upwards to the intensity of any given sensation. In order to attain the form of the quality, as to how much in amount ? this diversity in the sensation must be conjoined in unity into one total quantity. The intellect, as constructing agency, must commence from zero in the sensation, and conjoin the diverse degrees of intensity through all their multiplicity up to and terminating in the degree that limits the intensity of the given sensation, and such completed product is the quantity, or form in intensity, of that given quality. Such construction, as attending agency, brings the quantity of the intensity into immediate consciousness, and we perceive how much in amount the quality is.

Thus, I have the sensation of a *pressure*, and by observation I distinguish the sensation as *heaviness*. **By** attention I go over and conjoin the diversity from **no** heaviness up to the intensity of pressure as given **in** sensation, and I perceive there is *so much* weight.

So also, I have a sensation which in distinction **I** observe to be sound, and in further discrimination **I** observe that there is a great variety of sounds, **and** this is the utmost which any distinguishing **agency** can here accomplish. But I attend to these **various** sounds, and thus construct their quantity, and **I** at once perceive their various degrees of intensity, **and** can now discriminate, by other faculties which **need** not here be noticed, what is going on in these **sounds** and binding them in unison as a definite harmony in- to their tune.

So, with an anticipated content in the organ **of** vision inducing sensation, I discriminate and **observe** light; and at different times distinguish the peculiari- ties of sun-light from moonshine. Here is the **com-** pletion of what appears from observation. But I **at-** tend in a constructing agency and conjoin the **degrees** of intensity in the sun-light, and again in the **moon-** light, and I thus perceive *how much* light in both **se-** parately, and can now determine that it requires, **say** two thousand times the intensity of the moon-light **to** equal the intensity of the sun-light.

Thus of any inward sensation; I distinguish, **and** observe myself to be grieved; I construct the **degrees** of intensity in attention, and determine the amount of my grief.

Thus, in all diversity as intensive, the operation of distinction can give only the quality in its peculiarity; the operation of conjunction must be conditional for bringing the amount of the quality into consciousness. Except as this conjoining agency goes through the entire diversity of the sensation, it is impossible that the quantity of the quality should be perceived.

2. The diversity as *extensive* is the manifoldness of the points in the content of sensation, as occupying so much space. The precise quality having been discriminated, the question is, not how much as intensive, but how great as extensive? The matter having been determined in distinct observation, the form must be determined in definite attention. A conjoining agency must pass over these diverse points and bring them in unity in the same manner as before shown in pure space, with this difference only, that in pure space the constructing agency is guided in its work by some scheme in the imagination, but in the anticipated content it must be conditioned by the sensation. This construction completed, determines the form of the quality as figure in space.

Thus I anticipate a given sensation in a resistance to touch, which as precisely distinguished I term the quality of *solidity.* Without determining the form as intensity, i. e. how hard it is; I only seek the form as extension, how large it is. I must pass my organ of touch over the matter and bring it successively in the sensation, and the attending agency must construct the whole by joining the diverse points in unity and thereby give definite limits to this solidity ; and then affirm the quality to be of such a figure, and to fill so much of space. The matter has thus a definite form, as so great extension.

So again, with an anticipated content in the eye, as organ of the sensibility, which in distinguishing I term color; and in further observation I attain the varieties of the color, say now specifically green and white. I must now apply a constructing agency, and in attention I conjoin the greenness into figure, and determine the magnitude and outlines of a verdant courtyard ; and I conjoin also the whiteness, and determine the size and proportions of the dwelling-house, and its position relatively to the outlines of the yard in which it stands. I have thus brought the matter, as quality in sensation, into definite form.

Thus with all quality that can have extension. Distinction gives the quality, conjunction determines how great a space it occupies; nor can the form as extensive otherwise be determined. Without observation the consciousness would be "void," and without attention the matter in consciousness would be "without form." Sensation may be perfected, but it is utter chaos except as an intelligent spirit, in its distinguishing and conjoining agency, broods over it.

3. The diversity as *protensive* is in the manifold-

ness of the successive instants through which the appearance as quality is prolonged. Of any distinct quality, we may enquire, not merely, how much? as intensive; nor how great? as extensive; but also, how long? as protensive it endures. And for the determination of this, the same process of conjunction in an attending agency is necessary as in the construction of period in pure time, except that the conjoining agency is conditioned to the sensation in its beginning and termination, and not to any scheme of the imagination.

Thus an anticipated sensation in the ear, as organ of the sensibility, may be taken and distinguished as *sound*. I do not now enquire how loud, nor how distant it may be, but only how long does it continue? I attend to the passing affection of my inner state, and conjoin the instants from the beginning to the termination, or to any given instant in the prolongation of the sensation, and thus determine the period which the sound occupies; and thereby affirm that it has endured so long. And in the same way, for the form of all possible quality for duration in time; my attending agency must conjoin the diversity, and thereby construct the definite period.

And now, in these three diversities, as the manifoldness of degree, of extent, and of duration, all possible quantity which any quality may possess may be constructed, and thus all possible form be determined for all matter. Intensity in the sensibility, extension in space, and prolongation in time include all possible mensurations of quantity. If we would term motion and force to be qualities, their determination will be included in the above methods of conjoining in unity; for the motion must be measured as so much extension occupying so much time in passing, and the force as so much intensity of resistance or so much motion produced; all of which have their diversities as above, and may as above be all conjoined and made to appear in an attending agency. There can be no other possible quantities in any quality, and the form as giving definiteness to the matter cannot be determined in any other possible manner. We may thus give the apriori condition for constructing all possible quality into form, viz: that the intellect in attention must conjoin the diversity as conditioned by the sensation, —whether as intensive, extensive, or protensive—in unity, plurality, and totality. The concise form of expressing it is—*that the attention must produce the form in all possible quality.*

There are a few apriori cognitions involved in what has been here attained, which it may be of importance to notice in this place.

1. Inasmuch as all constructions of form must take place singly, and thus no two forms can be in process of construction together, it follows that an accurate and exact comparative mensuration of quantity cannot be effected in attention simply. In pure space I may construct two circles, and in sensation I may

have the matter for two rings which I construct into form, but I cannot exactly compare the two constructing operations together in either case, and say that the two circles or the two rings are of precisely the same quantity. In the above cases I may come near to exactness, though precisely how near I cannot determine, for I have no capability of constructing the diversity which their difference in quantity contains. In many other cases, the degrees of exactness may be necessarily much wider apart, especially when the contents must be given in different senses, or in the same organ at different times. Thus with the precise difference in the extension of a quantity as seen and as in the touch, or of the degrees of heat or of weight at two different experiences, their comparative quantity must be still less accurately given in attention simply. If I know that the circles, as above, have been constructed by the circumvolution of two lines of the same extent, the judgment at once decides that they must be equal ; but a difficulty would here again occur, how shall any attending agency simply be competent to determine the exact equality of the two lines ? But, now if I may bring the forms in both cases to one common standard, I may then determine their equality, or the difference between them exactly. Thus if I may apply the same material line as diameter to the two rings successively, or the same index to the two experiences of heat ; their comparison in this common application may determine their equality, or amount of inequality. We may thus apriori see the necessity for empirical standards of mensuration, and the principles on which we must move to attain them. Their exactness can be made an approximation to the perfection of an intuition, by so much as the mechanical execution and practical application of the common measure can be perfect. It is easy to see how the experiment, if not intuitively perfect, may yet be far more nearly exact than any construction in attention simply. Thus for the various degrees of intensity in different senses organically, we have photometers, thermometers, barometers, ballances, &c.; and for extension in space, rods or chains to determine length, with gallons, bushels and guaging rods to determine capacity; and for duration in time the various chronometers, as dials, hour-glasses, clocks, watches, &c. In no one of these diversities in quantity can any mensuration be absolute, but only as a reference comparative with some common standard.

2. It is apriori manifest that all quantity may be divisible beyond any possible experience, both in amount, extent, and duration. The intensity may be any amount of all possible degrees at any place and in any time. A given amount of light, or of heat, may thus be diminished in the same place to any assignable degree, and yet the space in extent be still a *plenum ;* nor can this be so far carried in any experiment, that it may not be conceived as yet possible to go further in the exhaustion, without at all inducing a

14

vacuum in any portion of the space. And as in amount, so also in extent; the diversity in the quality is as the diversity in space, and hence no given diminution may be, which is not also capable of a further diminution. And the same again in duration; the diversity in the duration of the quality is as the diversity in time, and hence no given contraction of a period can be, which may not also be still farther contracted. The process of divisibility, thus. in all quantity, is truly infinite. It cannot be carried out to a limit which has not yet a limit beyond.

3. While the heterogeneous diversity may come within the operation of distinction, it is only the homogeneous diversity that may come within the operation of conjunction. The heterogeneous in *kind* must be a content for the sensibility in different organs, and the constructing agency cannot thus conjoin the diverse kinds in unity. A sound and an odor cannot be conjoined in unity so as to give a total, nor either of these with a color. And the heterogeneous in *variety* must be at different times or in different places in the same organ, and therefore incompetent to be conjoined in unity. A distinct bitter and sweet taste, fragrant and fœtid odor, or a red and blue color, can not be conjoined in unity. The place or period which both occupy may be conjoined, or there may be a blending of the heterogeneous, as in the rainbow; and the whole, as undistinguished quality, constructed into form. So also, and for similar reasons apriori, the different

orders of homogeneous diversity cannot be constructed in unity. The degrees of intensity may not be conjoined in one form with the points in space, nor with the instants in time; though the same quality may separately admit of a conjunction, in all the orders of homogeneous diversity. A redness or a hardness may have degrees of intensity, figure in extension, and duration in time; but all these must be constructed in separate acts of attention.

SECTION V.

THE CONCLUSIVE DETERMINATION OF THE SENSE IN ITS SUBJECTIVE IDEA.

From an apriori position we have now passed in review the whole field of the sense in its ideal possibility. The operation of Conjunction for the construction of pure figure and period in space and time has been completely expounded, and all definite forms which may occupy space and time determined as possible. Other forms for phenomena, than such as may be constructed in space and time, cannot be; nor, can these be constructed otherwise than through the process of conjunction in unity, plurality and totality. By an apriori anticipation of content in general for the sensibility, the operation of Distinction, for the precise matter of any phenomenon which can be given through sensation, has also been fully exposed, and thereby

the possibility of all distinct qualities determined.
There cannot be other matter for phenomena than
that given in sensation, and this cannot otherwise be
discriminated than through the process of distinction
in reality, particularity, and peculiarity.   By attaining
all the apriori orders of a homogeneous diversity of
which quality is capable, as the intensive, the extensive, and the protensive, and the operation of conjunction in its applicability to them all, we have, moreover, determined the possibility of ordering sensation
in all the forms which the matter for phenomena may
assume.   Quality can have no forms but those of
quantity, and these can be only of amount, extent, and
duration; nor can these be otherwise constructed
than through the process of conjunction, as before determined in the pure intuition.

In these several apriori conclusions is involved the
complete idea of all perception of phenomena in its
possibility.   An empirical intuition is thus possible.
Phenomena may be given, as appearance distinct and
definite in consciousness, in this manner.   A Faculty
of Sense may so be, and perceive objects.   And if objects are given in space and time, as appearance in
consciousness, it must be through this same process
now apriori determined.   The comprehensive *formula*
for expressing the Sense in its complete subjective
Idea, may in conclusion stand thus—*Sensation must
be discriminated in observation, and thereby give distinct quality as the matter—and this distinct quality*

must be constructed in attention, and thereby give definite quantity as the form—of the phenomenon.

It is important to note, that as yet we have subjective idea only. There is a complete conception of the sense, and thus a true thought but still a void thought, and no knowledge of the faculty of sense as an actual existence. It is cognition to this degree, that such a faculty is determined apriori to be possible in conception—the thought is every way self-consistent and in unity—but as yet it is wholly the creature of the productive imagination. That there is any cause which may give actual being to such a faculty, our complete possession of the idea by no means enables us to affirm. This only is determined —the archetype after which the sense must be moulded, if any causation generate such an existing faculty of intelligence. In our subjective imagination, we make it to *seem* but we have not in our consciousness made it to *appear*.

It may, perhaps, conduce to give greater distinctness, though not more completeness, to this subjective idea of the sense, if we add here *some of the representations made of it by distinguished Philosophical Thinkers.* As the first and lowest form of intellectual action it is important that we apprehend it aright, and so be competent to make the sharp distinctions which separate it from higher faculties, as well as that we may attain an adequate comprehension of it in itself.

The very ingenious representation given by **Plato**, in the Republic, Book VII., commonly little understood or rather often misunderstood, is worthy of our first notice. In the latter part of Book VI. he has been speaking of *the Good*, which, as supreme and absolute, cannot be brought within any forms of representation. but can only be affirmed through analogies; and he represents that pure science has the same relation to it, that our knowledge of phenomena in sense has to pure science. The intelligible species has reference to the good, as the sensible species has to the intelligible; and his resemblance of both in their analogy, according to the Pythagorean mode, is by the division of a mathematical line. Let a line be divided unequally, and then divide again both these unequal parts in a ratio in each to the original division of the whole; and when these parts, in their proportional divisions, are set over one against the other, the larger in its proportional division may be taken to represent the intelligible, and the smaller in its proportional division the sensible species. The *first* has its own larger division, and this represents pure intellect or reason giving the axioms and apriori truths as the foundations of pure science; and it also has its smaller division, which represents the intelligible process, or *dianoetic* part, in a pure geometrical or mathematical demonstration. The *second* has also its larger division, and this represents the generalization which as universal rule is assumed from some broad induction of particular cases; and moreover this has its smaller division, which represents the sensible phenomena themselves as the facts in the induction. We have then the empirical facts given in sense, and which are the mere phenomenal shadows and images of the things themselves; and these bound up in an assumed general law, which can have verification no farther than the inductive experience reaches, and is thus as universal law resting upon hypothesis and faith only and not science; to be represented under the divisions of the *smaller* part of the original line: and then we have the successive steps of a mathematical demonstration, and which are pure intuition; and these, held in their axioms and necessary truths of the pure reason, giving rational science; to be represented under the divisions of the *larger* portion of the original line. And now, the inductive science of the former is analogous to the rational science of the latter, in this respect, that the inductive is the mere resemblance of the rational, as the rational is the archetypal emission, or educed paradigm, of the absolute and ineffable Good.

From this, in the beginning of Book VII. Plato proceeds to the representation which is of immediate interest in the present place. For the purpose of showing how far short of true science all attainments of sense must be, he gives his conception of what the sense is in the ingenious representation referred to. A subterraneous Dwelling is adduced, with an entrance expanding to the light and giving an opening to the entire cave. The persons within are chained by the neck so as to be unable to look except upon the wall of the cavern opposite to the opening. A bright light without, far above and behind them, illumines the opposite wall, and a road, over which perpetually passes men bearing statues and vessels and figures of all animated and material nature, lies along without the cave and between the bright light and the entrance. The shadows of all these passing figures projected upon the opposite wall are seen by the dwellers within, and any voices of the world without come to them only as echoes from the cavern wall, and seemingly as the voices of the moving shadows. To them, thus, nothing is true but shadows and echoes. These they regard intently, watching their appearance, and deducing the general laws of their successions and changes.

Should one suddenly be loosed and turned towards the light, he would be wholly confounded, and it would be long before he could comprehend the true position of things, know the realities, and bear the direct splendor of the sun-light in open vision. When this was thoroughly effected, and he should again talk with the chained inmates of the cave, his pure knowledge would be but transcendental ravings for them, inasmuch as to the prisoners of sense the eternal verities *above* sense are but simply as *nonsense*. How sincerely would he pity their conceited empiricism! How willingly would he forego all the encomiums, honors, and rewards which they were lavishing upon any who more acutely observed the passing shadows, discovered a new one, or best remembered how they were wont to succeed each other or appear together! This is an outline of the method in which Plato exhibits the manner of phenomenal appearance, and to which it might be added, that to each prisoner his own shadow is all that he can make of himself to be objective to his own vision. The qualities of things perpetually occupy the attention, and the sense is forced to absorb its entire functions in attaining the *appearances* of things, while an apriori philosophy alone can reach the living and eternally abiding *verities*.

A position for an *apriori* investigation of the sense would be given in this imagined cave of Plato, by supposing the man who had attained to the realities of things in the bright sun-light without, to come and sit down before the vacant back-wall of the cavern, and from the conditional principles of the transmitted light from without, determine how the shadows must there arrange themselves, in any anticipation of an inner content being given.

But a more complete illustration is given in some of the suggested analogies by Coleridge, in which, for the wall of the cave, we substitute a broad mirror. There will be the resemblance of whatever comes before the mirror, to the eye placed in a proper position; and so far as the mirror reveals the appearance, it can only be the resemblance of the thing and not the thing itself. The eye, thus, is to the mirror, as the intellect to the sensibility. The mirror has its own pure space, as primitive intuition; but that space is subjective to the mirror, and of no significancy to the thing itself which may give its resemblance within it. Some content must be given to the mirror, or no resemblance can appear; nor can this appearance be the thing itself, but only a phenomenal envisagement of it. The eye can by no means see itself, but only its resemblance. A faculty for perceiving the thing, and not merely its resemblance, would demand the capacity to receive and construct the content into form, other than within the illuminated space of the mirror; or, that the mirror should become transparent, and the thing apprehended directly through it.

As analogy for the *subjective* idea of the sense, the mirror only is conceived, and its content taken as anticipation in general; and then, from the conditioning principles of all reflection and representation of images, an apriori determination is made, of how the resemblances of things in a mirror is possible. This will give the complete thought of how any resemblance of things may be; but this can be only an imaginary *seeming* for the subject thinking, and not any *appearance* either for himself or others.

The method of Kant is to give the functions of the sense, not by any illustration, but in a direct statement of the process of perception. With his terminology fully understood, there is no farther difficulty in attaining his meaning than what is necessarily incidental to so abstruse a subject. With him, the sense is solely the faculty of envisagement, or of representing things themselves in their phenomenal appearances. The intellectual operations of discriminating and constructing, he refers to the work of the understanding; and thus excludes from the functions of the sense, that which gives distinctness and definiteness of figure to the phenomenon. The sense is the illuminated wall of the cave, or the reflecting surface of the mirror; but the chained prisoner, or the fixed eye before the mirror, is the conjoining agent, not as in the field of the sense but in the field of the understanding, and this operation of conjunction is not at all distinguished from an operation of connection, which we shall hereafter see is the alone proper work of the understanding.

With this functional instrumentality for envisaging, which the organism of sense supplies, the process of perception, as a work to be accomplished, then goes on in the understanding; and it is simply *his* method of describing the operation of conjunction, which we have already given after *our* manner of investigation. The conjunction of the content in sense gives to it unity; and that there may be this unity in the product, it is necessary that there be a higher unity in the understanding agency producing it. This unity in the product, he terms " Synthetic Unity," or, inasmuch as it is one member in his category of quantity,

sometimes he calls it the " Categorical Unity." The
higher unity in the understanding, inasmuch as it gives
the unity to all quality as product, is termed " Qualitative Unity." In this higher unity lies the capacity
to accompany all representations, so that each may, to
the mind, be *its* representation and thus all be in one
consciousness. This accompanying and uniting all
representations in one consciousness, and which yet
can not itself be represented in any appearance, he
calls technically the "*I think ;*" and there is thus the
same "I think" for every representation, and which
holds all in its own original unity. This he terms
"*the original unity of apperception.*" Except for this
original unity of apperception, every representation
would have its own separate "I think ;" and therefore,
as he says, "I should have as many colored different
a self as I have representations of which I am conscious." This bringing of all representations under
the one "I think," is the highest principle of all cognition, and the faculty in virtue of which we are competent to unite the diverse in one, and, therefore, as
in one consciousness, make each representation to be
an object as *my* object. "It is the highest point to
which we must attach all use of the understanding ;
in fact this is the understanding itself."

We will refer here but to one other explanation of
the function which brings phenomena into distinct
consciousness, and thus would render the perceptions
of the sense intelligible, and that is the method given
by Descartes.

His whole theory is contained in the germ which
has its concise expression in the noted formula " *Cogito, ergo sum.*" This has been interpreted in two
ways, having their meaning and use very distinct from
each other.   One makes it to be a *logical proof* of the
reality of my existence.   It is an ontological syllogism,
and concludes in the demonstration of real being.
Now in this method of interpretation, and which has
been the most commonly made, it has really no interest in, nor connection with, any inquiry after the
functions of the sense.   Its sole use is to prove the
real being of myself.   But it may be proper, here, to
say that in any such application, it can be nothing
other than an empty sophism.   It covers an absurdity,
and has thus no logical force except in its delusion.
If we postulate " *the thinking*," and would thence deduce the *I* as existing self, the conclusion is a non
sequitur ; inasmuch as the fact of a phenomenon of
thinking does not give the existence of the subject
which thinks.   And if we say " *I think*," meaning—
myself to exist thinking—the whole is a petitio prin-
cipii ; inasmuch as the existence of the *I* who thinks
is the very thing to be proved.

But another interpretation brings it directly within
our present use, as explanatory of the *process for attaining* to distinct consciousness.   The " Cogito," in
this meaning, simply involves the process by which I
come to know myself, or to awake in self-consciousness.   By the act of thinking I come into a state of

self-consciousness. I think—meaning thereby that I perform the intellectual operation of conjunction already apriori given, i. e., I attend—and thereby construct definite objects in consciousness; and such subjective operation, giving such objective phenomenon, determines a distinction of my object from myself as subject. By thinking, I find myself. Cogito, ergo sum, not as process of logical demonstration that I exist, but as practical process of coming into self-consciousness. A letter from Descartes himself to Gassendi would seem to fix this last meaning, as that which the author intended. " The very moment there are phenomena of any kind within our consciousness, that moment the mind becomes cognizant of its own existence; and that were there no consciousness, there would be no possible evidence of the existence of an intelligent principle. The scientific form of this truth was meant to be presented in the sentence, Cogito ergo sum."

Here, then, we conclude our first Chapter in the Sense, embracing the two divisions of the pure and the empirical Intuition. We have a completed Idea of how a faculty of sense for perceiving phenomena in consciousness may be. The whole is a *seeming* in the Imagination, and not an *appearing* in Consciousness; and is thus subjective only. Yet is the completed thought no fanciful and arbitrary combination of conceptions, but attained altogether through conditions necessary and universal. While we know that the product is ideal only, we know also that so the real is possible; and if at all actual, that so it must be.

It yet remains, to find this whole process of the sense as now determined in its subjective idea apriori, in actual being and operation. The facts must be gathered, in which we can ascertain a Law of perception as binding them up within itself, and expounding their being and combination. And when such law, as objective in the facts, is determined to be in full accordance and correlation with the subjective idea, we shall have answered the claims of a criterion of science, and may of right take possession of the whole field of the sense in the name of philosophy. This will now be the business in hand for our *Second Chapter* of the Sense.

CHAPTER II.

THE SENSE IN ITS OBJECTIVE LAW.

SECTION I.

TRANSCENDENTAL SCIENCE IS CONDITIONED UPON A LAW
IN THE FACTS CONFORMED TO AN APRIORI IDEA.

An arbitrary or a mere random construction in the
productive imagination of any complex conception,
would be but a chimera with no possible significancy.
But when constructed according to the conditions of
an apriori cognition, although still only a seeming in
the imagination, yet is it a seeming which has an intelligent systematic unity, and has significancy as a
self-consistent thought. Thus, any random aggregation of all the elementary conceptions conditional for
the complex conception of a steam-engine, would be
wholly without signification; yet when combined according to the conditions of an apriori cognition,
though still a seeming in the imagination only, they
will possess significancy. The whole is a unit, and
becomes a consistent *Idea* of a steam engine in virtue
of this apriori unity. But such consistent and signifi-

cant seeming is only mental, and a steam-engine merely as *void thought*. Such systematic construction of the mental steam-engine can by no means produce the real for our knowledge. The real can be found only in *facts*, (*res gestæ*.)

But mere facts as appearance, though real, will possess no significancy. All the materials for a real steam-engine in any manner of aggregation can give mere appearance, while yet there is no meaning in the appearance. It is the materialism only of the steam-engine as *void thought*. This material must be held in systematic unity as one whole by a law of combination, or the steam-engine is not known. And now, it is the competency to take this law of combination in the material, and cognize it as the correlative of the systematic unity in the void thought as ideal, which determines our knowledge of the steam-engine to be *science ;* i. e., knowledge intelligently expounded.

But again, science is of two kinds, differing not in the correlation of idea and law which all science must have, but differing in the manner by which the idea has been attained. If it is a mere arbitrary production, imagined in view of the facts as that which might perhaps explain the facts, then is it impossible that it should ever become a completed thought except as having completely in view all the facts that must be accounted for by it. The facts are a riddle; the solution begins by taking some that are obvious and inventing a law to expound them, and then as new facts are

15

taken up still ever modifying the law that it may embrace them, and so perfecting the law only as the successive facts are given; and even if persevered in until all facts should be given, the last modification of the law to embrace the last fact would be a mere *guess* that such was the real law of combination.   Thus with the attempt to explain the solar system by the stroke of a comet upon the sun, thereby knocking off melted masses of which the planets are composed; or the nebular theory, that matter was originally diffused through space, and has come together as it now is, through all its modes of organization, by some inherent law of progression.   Inasmuch as no such process can attain to either a completed idea, or a perfected law, and can therefore never give their correlation, it should never be termed *science*; but, when the most ingenious and plausible should be held as *opinion* only.

When, however, there is some hypothesis assumed, which it is expected will account for all the facts and bind them up in harmony, and is thus in itself a consistent and systematic thought; and this thought, as hypothesis, is carried out in the examination of facts and found to classify and arrange them in accordance with its own unity, and thus the hypothetical idea and the inductive law are found in correlation, this may properly be called one kind of *science*.   It is termed *Inductive* science, and is made universal by assuming that nature has universal laws, and deducing from the particulars in the induction, in which the law has been found in correlation with the idea, that their law is the veritable law of universal nature, and, therefore, that the hypothetical idea is also correlative with the universal law. All inductive science, thus, has its idea as a distinct and self-consistent thought; and, in the assumption of a universal law, makes an induction sufficiently broad to deduce the conclusion that it has found this universal law in the facts of the induction. The correlation of idea hypothecated and law deduced is thus perfect, and science is so far complete. But the occasion here for skepticism is two-fold; one, that the uniformity of nature is universal; and the other, that any empirical induction may find the universal law. The skepticism is wholly incorrigible while the first is only *assumed*, and the last is a deduction only from the partial. It is not a matter of probability, opinion, or faith, which we are here considering. The skeptic may admit probabilities to the highest requisition made upon him; but it is *science* for which we are now seeking, and of which only as being every way conclusive is it, that he affirms himself to doubt; and such doubt cannot be subverted in the one case by an assumption, nor in the other by a deduction from any induction which is partial.

But now if the idea may be so attained as not to be at all hypothetical, but necessary and universal in its own light, and therefore wholly an apriori cognition, it must give occasion for banishing all skepticism effectually from the whole region of facts embraced within the law of which it is the correlate. If the facts are, their law is not at all hypothetical; for we apriori know that it must be the correlate of our attained idea, and we only need the facts with their law simply to elevate the ideal into the real. It is not a deduction from any induction more or less extensive, but an apriori cognition that if something is it must have such a law; and then, finding that something is with such law, and that therefore the ideal is also a reality. If, in the process, it may also be apriori demonstrated that nature must have uniformity, then must all skepticism be doubly demolished. This last is, therefore, science of another *kind*, and of a higher description than Inductive science. As giving the idea in an apriori cognition, it is properly *Transcendental science*. The transcendental idea as conditional for the facts is not that which alone is found. This would be empty thought only, and the highest attainments of pure intellectual processes must end in a mere systematic seeming in the productive imagination alone. All striving after the real, either as a Soul, a universal Nature, or a Deity, in pure subjective rationalism solely, can possibly never advance the intellect beyond its own ideal productions, and must therefore be hopelessly ineffectual. But, it is much, if in this process we can attain the possible, inasmuch as here we have the idea to which all law in realities must stand in correlation; and we have thus only to find such reality in its Law, and at once we have an apriori demonstrated universal science. The idea, even in its complete systematic unity, is at most the knowledge of the possible, and can rise to science only through its correlation to an actual law; and on the other hand, the phenomenal, as appearance alone, is at most the knowledge of the material, and can rise to science only through an intellectual process which shall give to it form, and determine the form as idea and the form as actual law to be correlatives.

A fair illustration of much that is above said may be found in the history of Astronomy. Very early the heavenly bodies were grouped together in space within fancied outlines and arbitrary figures in the heavens. To these shapes in space and their included stars names were given, conformable to the things or animals which they were supposed to resemble; and these names, convenient for some purposes, have been perpetuated to the present day. This grouping of the heavenly bodies conformed to notions of astrology, or convenient as a nomenclature for fixing positions, can have no title to knowledge even, and much less to science. The figures at the most are only seeming, and cannot be made to appear. As early as the age of Pythagoras, and perhaps derived by him from Egypt, the sun was placed as the center of the starry system, and the planets supposed to have circular motion. Upon the hypothesis of Epicycles, Hipparchus and Ptolemy could arrange many of the heavenly bodies in such relations as to very well give a plot of the po-

sitions and movements of the planets according to the
real appearances. Much later, Copernicus from careful observation had fully settled the fact that the sun
was the center of the planetary motion, and that these
planets revolved quite regularly around it. A century
still later, Galilleo, in the prosecution of similar observations, attained other appearances and explained
more of the phenomena in the positions and motions
of the heavenly bodies; and Kepler, following out the
same work, found the orbits, of the planets to be
elipses, and by an almost incredible extent, minuteness, and accuracy of investigation in the study of phenomena, could make a diagram of the solar system as
lying in space, and moving in its orbits within itself,
very nearly perfect. This was as much as observation alone could accomplish, and gave completeness to
formal astronomy. Here was knowledge widely extended, and very accurate, but merely knowledge as
appearance. So the solar system was seen to be.
But no dynamical law, working in the system and
working out these results, was at all as yet apprehended. Neither the Idea nor the Law had been attained,
and hence no explanation of the phenomena could be
made, and therefore no proper science had yet been
reached.

The grand thought was first stricken out by the
genius of Newton, that perhaps all matter gravitates
towards all other matter, and following out the thought
in application, and attaining the ratios, direct as quan-

tity and inversely as the square of the distance, he
finds a complete solution of many difficult problems,
and from the extent of the induction assumes it to be
the universal law in the facts which must reconcile
all paradoxes, expound all anomalies, and combine in
systematic unity all the facts of past, and of all future
observers. This one thought, simple as truth, universal
as matter, convincing in its application as light, is assumed as correlative with a law running through the
material universe, and determining to every portion of
matter its position and relations. Henceforth there is
a *science* of astronomy which rests in its correlations
of idea and law universally and perpetually. Further
observation and calculation may work on under this
law through coming generations, but the whole pathway was determined in the thought, and the science
completed in the genius of Newton.

But genuine as is the science of astronomy, it is *Inductive* science only. It assumes a uniformity throughout nature, and from an induction, very broad though
yet partial, it deduces the universal law in its being
and its ratios, and, therefore, deep as it may fix the
conviction of probabilities, it is not competent that it
should silence the skeptic who doubts the every way
completeness of its demonstrations. But suppose the
practicability of attaining this idea in its whole systematic unity through an apriori cognition, and thus
in the idea itself seeing the conditions of the possibility
of a n ture of things, and that if a material universe

at all be, it must be under such a law in its ratios
and none other, and we should have a complete seeming universe in its ideal perfection, and needing nothing but the facts which should give an embodying of
a law that must every where be the correlate of the
apriori idea, and there would at once be a Transcendental science of nature from which all possible skepticism would be forever expelled.   Such an attainment
is by no means hopelessly impracticable, and when it
shall have been completely reached, the Law, assumed
by Newton as universal and which necessitates that
nature should be as she appears, will itself be seen to
stand in necessity, as conditional that a nature of
things determined in space and time may be possible.

And now, such an apriori idea for all possible functions of a Sense, which may give phenomena distinguished in quality and conjoined in quantity, has been
already attained.   In itself it is only an idea, and
therefore a mere seeming in the imagination through
all its systematic unity, and yet the labor in attaining
it is by no means thrown away.   It capacitates for
standing in a position relative to all facts which may
be given in an actual perception in the sense, as would
such an apriori idea of gravitation as above, capacitate
for standing in reference to all the facts of universal
nature.   It enables us to say what the law must be,
as conditional that the facts may be; and, therefore,
in finding that the facts which embody such a law as
correlate to this idea truly are, we are capacitated to

give an every way demonstrated exposition of our knowledge of these facts, and which is more than inductive, even an apriori demonstrated science. Without such an apriori investigation of the sense, it might certainly be very long ere we should come to an inductive science of perception. Phenomena in the functions of the sense might, indefinitely in the future as already in the past, be observed and classified under various fanciful or arbitrary forms of arrangement, without the seizing upon any systematic thought in its unity, which as complete idea should lead to the *in*forming law as its correlative, and thereby bring all the facts at once into an ordered science of this department of human knowledge.

How the knowledge of the Faculty of the Sense is without such apriori conditional idea, may be illustrated by many other departments in natural philosophy, where no correlative idea and law have yet been found. In such cases, not only are the single facts unclassified and without arrangement, but the facts as an aggregate have no definite circumscription, and it cannot be said that there is any precise field which ought exclusively to be given up to them; even as in the functions of the sense it is not known otherwise what facts altogether belong to it, nor whether there is any precise and definite region among mental functions that should be considered as solely the domain of the sense.

As sufficient for such illustration take the as yet altogether undetermined philosophy of Life. In anticipation that a science may yet come of it, it has been termed *Biology*, but it is a mere description of some of the phenomena, and not at all an attainment of the idea and law of life; a phenomenal biography, not at all a philosophical biology. A vital principle has been assumed, and many of the phenomena of its healthy and morbid action have been observed. The sympathies between different parts of the same living organization; the processes of assimilation and accretion, of exhaustion and purgation; the development of the whole and each distinct member of the organism from some inner force, according to some rudimental germ as given in the genus and species; the longer or shorter continuance in the vigor of maturity, and subsequent decline; the resistance to dissolution and corruption, and the recuperative energies supplied when any part of the organization has been injured; these and other phenomena have been collected, and some form has been given to them in different methods of classification; and some distinction has been apprehended between living forces and electric or magnetic influence, chemical agencies, and mechanical powers; but no law which may bind up within itself the vital phenomena through the vegetable and animal world, and make a distinct department, shutting out all that does not belong to it, and including all that has place within it, and arranging all in its conditional order and unity, has even been approximately attained. All these phenomena stand waiting for the wise man to come with his idea, which shall detect in its correlation the secret law that informs them, as nature waited long for its Newton; but that the Huttons or Keplers, as the necessary fore-runners of such a philosopher, have as yet fulfilled their mission may perhaps well be doubted. The science of life may perhaps find its birth amid the apriori study of distinguishable forces, rather than in any collection and arbitrary grouping of vital phenomena.

Even thus might all the phenomena in the faculty of the sense lie long waiting unsystematized and unexpounded; but by the attainment made in our previous investigation, we are now competent to say that thus they need not be left ungathered. The sense is completely attained as ideal, and from this we are prepared to collect the facts and find the law in which they are conditioned as real.

This is then our remaining task in this First Part of our work, *to find the Law in the facts of the sense as correlative with our apriori Idea.* The best and probably the most satisfactory method will be, to take our apriori idea, and for the present dismissing all regard to it as an apriori cognition, assume it only as hypothesis, and go out under its guidance to question the facts we may attain. This we will do in two ways, as giving a modified form to substantially the same method, and yet tending to augment the conviction of its conclusiveness. One, to assume the law as correlative of our idea, and with it go out and gather many facts which we may successively bind up in it, and which we may term *the Colligation of Facts*. The other, by taking apparently very distant and disconnected facts, and seeing how they leap unexpectedly within the law, and which we will term *the Consilience of Facts*. In the end we shall have full occasion to say, that our Idea of the possible is also the Law of the actual.

SECTION II.

THE COLLIGATION OF FACTS.

WHEN any self-consistent idea, at first hypothetically assumed, may be so applied to many different facts as to bring them all in unity within its circumscription, and bind them within itself that they may thereby belong to one organized system, each portion of which may be adequately expounded as determined in its place by this applied idea, we have then an instance of what is termed a Colligation of Facts. In such a result we no longer hold our applied idea to be hypothesis, but affirm that the facts themselves must possess within them a formative principle, which has controlled in their production and is the complete correlate to this idea which we have applied to them and that has collected and expounded them so completely; and that, therefore, there is within them an actual law, the exact counterpart of our applied idea.

We now proceed in this way with our apriori attained idea of the sense, to apply it to various facts in the process of perception as actually occurring in experience; and in proportion as we find it to hold these facts in colligation, and thus expound their peculiarities, shall we be competent to affirm that we have found the law which must inherently have regulated their formation, and which thus really exists as embodied within them. This law thus found, as the exact correlate of the idea, enables us completely to explain our knowledge of the appearances in the facts, and thus becomes properly a *science* of the facts.

We do not now insist upon the necessity and universality of the idea, as having been attained through an apriori process, but will use it for the present as mere hypothesis for interrogating experience, and ascertaining how completely it may collect the facts within itself. If it be found to possess the power of such colligation, it would, as mere hypothesis, be then verified and give to us a science as valid as any induction could afford; but we may then bring out its apriori characteristics of necessity and universality, and thereby give to the science a much higher foundation than in simple induction, viz: that of a transcendental demonstration.

The idea, therefore, which we now adopt as hypothesis is, that all the facts in the process of perception must stand within the law which demands the *intellectual operations of Distinction of quality and Con-*

junction of quantity; and consequently that where this law is complied with in its demands, there is clear perception. The process of application might be to take any facts in the perceiving of phenomena, promiscuously as they might come to hand, and dispose of them within the circumscription of our hypothesis as the facts themselves might permit; but the more philosophical and satisfactory course must be to order our induction of facts under separate heads, and see how completely the hypothesis binds up all the varieties of facts under the different captions. We shall make the induction sufficiently comprehensive to be a safe ground for deducing a real law and not a mere casual coincidence, but yet with no attempt to exhaust the facts; other minds may pursue the same process to an indefinite extent, as far as any facts which an experience in sense may furnish.

1. *Facts connected with obscure perception.*—A great variety of facts may be attained connected with some obscurity in the perceptions of the sense, and which lead to a popular way of accounting for the obscurity on a great variety of grounds, but when carefully examined they will all stand within the circumscription of our hypothesis, as the highest and most comprehensive reason which can be given, viz: that either the operation of Distinction in quality or that of Conjunction in quantity could not be accurately and completely effected. Sometimes it may be said that the sensibility of the organ is impaired; or, that the medium

through which the content is given, as the light, or
air, &c. is defective; or that the object is too minute,
too far in the distance, too much confused amid other
things, or glancing upon the sensibility too transient-
ly ; or, that the mind was too intently engrossed with
some other occupation ; but all these and other popular reasons for the obscurity will at last resolve themselves into this—the intellect did not exactly distinguish, or did not completely construct them.   It might
be easy to arrange our facts under the separate heads,
so that the obscurity from indistinctness and that
from indefiniteness might hold each their own facts,
but such subdivision is not necessary.   The example
will in each case give immediate opportunity for deciding to which, or whether perhaps to both, it belongs.

When the eye rests upon some landscape replete
with diffused and diversified lights and shades and
colors, we are conscious of a very inadequate perception of its different objects until the eye has roved
over the scene repeatedly and deliberately, and as this
process goes on the perception comes out with more
and more distinctness of the colors, and more and
more definiteness of the figures, there presented, and
the obscurity of the first look passes into clear perception.   So, still more, when we first enter the thronged
street of some strange city, from which new and un-
accustomed sensations are very confusedly given in
the thousand moving colors and forms of men and

animals and carriages, and the blended sound of feet
and wheels and jarring wares and percussion of tools
and human voices perhaps of different languages, is it
impracticable at once to perceive all, or perhaps even
any one appearance completely. Again, we cast our
eye upon the printed page of a book, and especially
the more to our purpose if the characters belong to an
unknown language, and with these multiplied and
blended sensations of lines and angles and curves and
points, the letters cannot at once stand forth as clear
perception in consciousness. Or, only once more as
an example, when the strains of distant music from
many voices and instruments strike upon the ear, and
the complicated and modified harmony is so obscure,
that we cannot catch the tune which combines all
these tones in unison, the whole is but a rhapsody of
diverse noises in which nothing distinct and nothing
defined is perceived. In all these, it is at once manifest that the operations of both distinction and conjunction are incomplete, and that the obscurity is removed in proportion as these operations are effected
by the intellectual agency, nor can any thing else secure a clear perception.

There may be noticed also such facts as the following. A blending of the quality so effectually that
though many peculiar varieties may be known to be
there, yet can no one be distinguished exactly not
even by deliberate trial of the intellectual agency.
We are conscious of the appearance of the peculiar

colors in the rainbow, yet can we neither discriminate nor construct them precisely, and hence they
must remain confused and obscure in our perception,
though it be easy to distinguish the whole bow from
the surrounding cloud and to conjoin it in a definite
figure. So we may take into our mouth food or drink
compounded of various ingredients, and while we may
be conscious of several peculiar tastes, yet may we
not by the greatest care distinctly separate them, nor
completely conjoin them so as to give the amount and
proportions of any.

And then, at other times, not from the confused
blending in the sensibility, but from the impracticality
of attaining a complete outline, we have obscurity of
perception. Thus the letters on a distant sign-board,
or on the stern of some departing ship, or the wheel-
house of a steam-boat passing at a distance, may be
wholly illegible though the colors as quality may be
very distinctly apprehended. An object, also at the
bottom of some clear lake or stream, when the surface
is gently ruffled by a breeze or the undulations of the
current, may be completely given in the sensation, and
the quality distinctly apprehended, and yet it may be
utterly impossible that the form should be definitely
perceived. So, again, when the content is given to
the eye through the medium of glass or chrystal,
which though transparent is so curdled and the substance interfused with waving lines, that the sensation is interrupted and distorted, the quality may be
16

very well discriminated and distinctly perceived, and yet no function of the sense may be able to give definite outline and figure to the object.

And certainly all these facts come within our applied idea. Precisely where we cannot discriminate, there we cannot have distinct quality; and where we cannot construct, there we cannot have definite quantity; and when either the matter or the form is imperfectly given, there is at once obscure perception, but which passes to a clear perception immediately upon the completion of the operations of Distinction and Conjunction. The law for the process of an actual perception is here abundantly realized. An exclusion made of the law from the process, and the negation of perception follows, and to just the amount of the exclusion; and the control of the law admitted, there is at once a distinct and defined perception of the object. The hypothesis as ideal, finds its counterpart here embodied as a reality.

We may much enlarge our induction, by taking such facts as are given when only a broken and incomplete content in sensation is effected. The portrait of some person may have a portion of the coloring or delineation of features faded or defaced by age or exposure, and the observer finds it wholly impracticable to perceive what peculiar face and expression of countenance the original picture represented. The intellect is incompetent to discriminate and construct from the sensation a complete image. But an old

friend and former companion of the person represented may stand before the portrait, and the few faint
lines and touches which remain are sufficient to
awaken long gone conceptions and to quicken familiar
recollections, and at once the features of his friend are
there, glowing vividly upon the canvass as the painter
originally gave them, and he dwells upon the picture
with deep and saddened interest. The well remembered countenance of the original avails to the re-con-
struction of the effaced lineaments of the painting, and
what to other eyes it were impossible to find he perceives distinct and well defined, because his own
agency has brought out anew the faded colors and
obscured lines of the picture, and in the restored portrait the likeness of his friend has found a perfect re-
surrection.

Again, some old manuscript, or an engraving on a
monument, or an ancient coin may be taken, some
portions of which may have become so obliterated as
to be utterly unintelligible to ordinary readers. The
sensation is too incomplete for the intellectual agency
to make out the construction, and if no help be otherwise afforded for restoring the defaced portion there
must unavoidably remain a perpetual hiatus in the
record. But if long habit in deciphering obscured in-
scriptions, or an acquaintance from other sources of
the facts designed to be here recorded, help the intellectual agency along the lost lines that it may fill up
the chasm through its faintest tracings, the whole is

to that mind again restored and he reads again aright the old record. To a practised antiquary, even the the slightest remnant of the old chisel marks on the monument, or the touches of the pen upon the parchment, are sufficient for filling up what must otherwise have been unavoidably wide gaps in the inscription. Champollion could read the much effaced Hieroglyphic upon a Theban tomb or column; and Belzoni, the faint traces on an Egyptian papyrus or mummy covering, when to an unpractised eye the whole was faded beyond recovery. The intellect, indeed, fills up a chasm which was merely a void in the sensation, and by re-constructing restores again the original, guided by the content which is given; and is an agency very similar to that, which from long study in comparative anatomy enabled Cuvier to restore a complete antediluvian animal, whose entire species has long since been extinct, from a solitary fossil bone as the only remnant of the skeleton.

Obscure perceptions, presenting what facts soever, will invariably be found to originate in an incompetency to distinguish quality when the obscurity relates to the matter, or an incapacity to conjoin the quantity when the obscurity relates to the form of the phenomenon. The intellectual agency cannot go out under the guidance of its conditional law, and therefore the product of a clear perception cannot be; but so soon as the distinguishing and conjoining agency may be carried into complete execution all obscu-

rity of perception is effectually avoided. Thus far in
our induction, our hypothesis collects all the facts and
binds them up in systematic order, and determines
for us that the law actually embodied in the facts of
perception is the exact correlative of the hypothetical idea which we have been applying to them.

But we may pursue our induction further, under
another division of facts connected with perception,
and examine,

2. *The relative capabilities of the different organs of
sense.*—Different organs of sense give their diverse
sensations as content for different kinds of quality,
and each in its own manner and degree capable of the
operations of distinction and conjunction to be applied to it. The eye receives its content for colors,
and the ear for sounds, &c., and these may be discriminated and constructed according as the peculiarity of the sensation in the organ may capacitate for
it. It is not designed under this division to notice the
intellectual agency in distinction so much as in conjunction, as our object must rather be here to attain
facts which reveal their law for form, rather than for
peculiarity of the matter. If, then, we find the facts
to be arranged under our hypothetical idea, so that
the capability of perceiving form or quantity through
the sensation in any particular organ, is precisely as
that organ is adapted for conforming its functions in
sensation to the demand of our hypothesis as conditional for an intellectual construction of the quantity

we shall in a deeply interesting manner enlarge our
induction of facts, whose actual law is the correlative
of our hypothetical idea. This will require that we
shall find the facts thus to be, that the organ which
from its functions gives the highest capabilities for the
passing of the intellectual agency in attention over the
content in sensation, and constructing it according to
the operation of conjunction, shall also be capable of
attaining to the clearest and most complete perception of the forms of its phenomena, whether of figure
in space, period in time, or amount of intensity in the
sensibility. For the purpose of thus questioning the
facts in experience on this topic, let it be recollected
that extension in space has three dimensions, length,
breadth, and thickness; that prolongation in time has
but one measure, as in the flowing along through a
series; and that intensity in amount has also but one
measure, as in the line of a continually augmenting
sum of degrees; and we shall be prepared to go out
and gather the facts which we may find under this
division.

We will first look at the relative capabilities of our
organs of sense for securing the perception of forms,
as extension in Space. The Eye, as the organ of vision,
is the most complicated, and as the result the most
completely adapted organization, for securing the construction and thereby the perception of extension in
the figures of phenomena. The intellect is best capacitated through its sensation to attain the most com-

plete perceptions of the shapes and relative positions
of objects in space. In order to use the facts which
should be gathered in this induction it is necessary
that we take a cursory glance at the material structure of the eye. A bare reference is sufficient for
those who have some understanding of its internal
structure and conformation, without any minute descriptions and explanations. The entire organ of the
eye, including its component elements of humors aque-
ous and vitreous, its lens, its pupil dilating and con-
tracting in proportion to the amount of light transmitted, its expanded nervous membrane as the retina,
with the large optic nerve passing out on the back
side thereof to the brain, its complicated apparatus of
muscles for moving the entire ball of the eye or fixing
it steady in one position, and its lid for lubrication,
cleansing and protection, is altogether most skillfully
adapted to the ends designed. The light is admitted
and the rays diffused over a most sensitive surface
within, and forming the images there as on a canvass
for the use of the intellectual agent. The sensation
is therefore conditioned by the rays of light, transmitted by reflection from the external object, which give
their content as the matter for the phenomena in perception.

In this arrangement of the organ, the whole content
conditions itself both in position and outline to the
place occupied upon the retina, and the sensation is
modified accordingly. The whole field of the sensa-

tion is spread out in order, and the constructing agency in attention may spontaneously move over the entire outlines given, and bring the forms of every part within the light of consciousness. The content is itself topical in the sensibility and the affection as sensation conforms to it, and this conditions the constructing agency accordingly, and thereby the phenomena are determined in their particular and relative forms of appearance. Moreover, there is this further important fact, that in one point of the retina there is a spot of higher sensibility than any other portion. A small point as a center has this acute sensibility and from which on all sides the sensibility diminishes. This has been called by physiologists *the sensible spot,*[*] and is of peculiar significance in our present induction. The muscles of the eye make it competent in its own motion to bring any portion at a time, and all portions successively, of the content upon this sensible spot for a more delicate and complete sensation. When the occasion requires that the intellectual agency should make a more nice construction, there will be spontaneously the muscular movement for bringing the more delicate outlines of the content upon this susceptible point in the retina, and revolving it there until the most minute forms have been accurately conjoined. It is this work which gives to the eye

* Phil. Trans. 1823. Motions of the Eye. Bell's Bridgwater Treatise. Also, Whewell's Phil. of Inductive Science, Vol. 1., p. 119.—Perception of Space.

that peculiar searching motion, readily observed in another, and consciously noted in our own experience when the mind would attain some perception very critically and exactly. When the attempt is made to give to any object a very close and thorough inspection, the person may be made quite conscious of an uneasy and disquieted feeling until his eye is fixed in the right position towards the object, and the attending agency can move the most accurately and completely over the content as this is made to revolve upon the sensible spot, and in this way bring the form into clearer and sharper outline in consciousness. All that the motion of the eye, and the turning of the head to favor it, may take within the sensibility of the organ itself, and which in succession may be the whole hemisphere, can in this manner be successively brought to revolve upon this sensitive portion of the retina for its more exact construction in a perception, and the completeness of the form will be proportioned to the exactness of such a construction. All these facts in the capacity of the eye as organ for perceiving figure come remarkably within the circumscription of our ideal hypothesis, and manifest that their actual law is in entire correlation with it.

But we may extend our induction to the facts given in the capabilities of the Touch for perceiving form in extension. The organization here is not so nice and complicated in its arrangements as in that of vision, but to the whole amount of its capacity for giving sensation which may be conjoined into form, the facts come completely within the same hypothesis, and evince for themselves the same actual law. The fingers—and by use other parts of the body may be made to subserve the same ends—are the organs of sensibility in which are given the sensations of touch. The ends of the fingers have their delicate nervous expansion and which also have their connection with the central sensorium in the brain by as complete a medium as the optic nerve, though a more extended communication than that. When these are brought in contact with any resisting object, a content is at once given in the sensation, and they become as the sensible spot in the eye, and condition the attending agency in the same manner. The content must be given to the organ through its contact with the outward resistance, and that the form as figure in space may be perceived, the fingers must pass over this resisting object as the content in the eye was made to revolve upon the sensible spot in the retina, and thereby the conjoining operation is effected and the form is completed in the attention. We do not here, however, find an expanded field of the sensibility for receiving topically the content for many phenomena at a time, as in vision. The broad landscape, the wide expanse of the distant heavens, with all their complicated outlines, are not within the capacity of this organ of sensibility. One by one, and within quite a limited range, must the objects gained by the touch be perceived, and thus in comparatively a narrow field alone is the operation of construction at any one time carried on.   But within these limits the perception of figure and position by the touch are very accurate.   When we have constructed the form through the sensation in the eye, almost instinctly do we reach forth the fingers to attain the content in a new sensation, and subject the same to a new construction.   Especially if the object be small, and near at hand, the intellect rejoices in the diversified manner of construction, and the confirmation of the perception by two operations.   The touch adds its own definiteness to the shape as it appeared in vision.   Though not over so broad a field, yet within its own scope, the sense of touch may give form in space as accurately as the sense of sight.   From the habitual exercise and cultivation of the sense of touch, the blind attain to a surprising accuracy of perception thereby.   They follow out raised letters with their fingers, and read with almost the facility that is given to others by the use of their eyes; and they have been able to trace the lines in sensation, such as those, say, in nicely joined cabinet work, where all perception of the eye completly failed.

We will extend the induction to the facts found in other organs of sense, and inasmuch as we shall find no capacity to perceive figure by them, so we shall find that they give no content in a manner that the intellect can conjoin its diversity, as *extensive*, in unity.

The operation of conjunction cannot be, and therefore shapes cannot by them be perceived.

The organs of Hearing are on opposite sides of the head, and thus quite favorable for giving the content in such a manner that it may be determined from what *direction* the sound has come. The ear which has received content in the greatest intensity will of course be an occasion for deciding that the sound has come from that side. The modifications in intensity through different experiences may afford the ground for some vague estimate of the *distance* from the center whence the undulations have proceeded. All such construction is necessarily comparative, and therefore quite imperfect, and yet complete precisely in proportion to the capacity of the organ to furnish the content in such a manner that it may be brought within an attending agency. But this vague estimate of direction and distance is all that can be secured of form in space by the organ of hearing. All conjoining into figure, and giving a determined shape and outline of object by the ear is impracticable. The sensation is not so spread out on any field, nor can the organ so go over it in contact, that the intellect may conjoin it into shape, and give form to the phenomenon. The organization may sometimes have its modifications in an elongation or expansion of the external portion of the ear, as in the horse or the hare, and very probably also a nicer construction and conformation of the inner ear may be given to some animals than to others. The intensity of sound may be thereby augmented, and direction and distance be more accurately apprehended. Such expansion of the outer ear and its easy movement in all directions subserves precisely the same end as the artificial ear-trumpet for the deaf, by which a greater volume of content is brought within the sensibility. But this avails nothing towards such a presentation of the content that an operation of conjunction may be effected, by which outlines may be constructed, and thereby figures in space perceived.

The organ of Smell is also in many of its facts very similar. The aroma may come into the sensibility in larger amount and thus with more intense sensation when the organ is in a given position, and thereby direction and distance may be vaguely estimated as the point from whence the effluvia have come. But nothing is here capacitated for giving the perception of shapes to odors. The organ may be more or less perfected in its conformation, and thereby a more intense sensation may be given, as in the dog or the vulture, and in this way distance and direction be more accurately apprehended, but no perfection of organization can in this way give the capacity of perceiving figure in space by the smell, inasmuch as there is no adaptation to the conditions demanded for the necessary intellectual construction.

The facts in the sense of Taste should also be put in the induction. From this organization there is not capacity for perceiving even position in space. The sensation is conditioned to the savory object coming in contact with the organ and being chemically dissolved upon it, and thus the sense of touch is to be wholly excluded. The quality discriminated may have form as amount, and as prolonged, but not extended. Not even position, and much less figure in space, can be perceived in any sapidity. There is nothing of the homogeneous diverse, as extensive, given in the content, and consequently nothing which may be conjoined into shape.

Thus, then with all our organs of sense ; the facts are held in colligation by our ideal hypothesis, and in all cases evince this actual law, that the capacity to perceive form as extension in space is found in the actual operation of conjunction, and where that cannot be effected, there it is impracticable that any figure should be perceived.

We will farther bring within our induction under this division, the facts connected with the capacity of the sense for perceiving phenomena in the forms of prolonged Time. The operation of conjunction is, in the protensive, in one measure only, and constructs period in the flowing series of successions. All sensation in any organ of sensibility is, as discriminated quality, a conscious affecting of my inner state, and thereby giving the homogeneous diversity as protensive in time. As the affection goes on in the continuance of the quality, or the perpetual alteration of qualities, the diverse instants admit of a conjoining operation which constructs them into definite periods, and the qualities are thus given as phenomena in their forms of time. One kind, or one variety of quality, is as much as another readily subjected to this operation of conjunction which constructs its form in time. No one organ has a different capacity in respect to forms in time from another.

Thus, take any color as quality in vision. Its topical arrangement on the retina, as the field of sensation, gives peculiar capacity for constructing its figure in space, especially in the capability for revolving the sensation in the whole field over the sensible spot, as before considered. But such facility for the operation of conjunction in extension avails nothing for conjunction in prolongation. The bare sensation in any organ may give diverse instants in the affecting of the inner state as completely as when the sensation is spread out topically upon an expanded field of the sensibility. I may thus as readily construct the period of a sound, an odor, or a taste, as a color or all the colors definitely arranged in a landscape. All sensation in any organ induces modified affections of the internal state, and thereby as inner sense come within time, and may thus fill the forms of time through a definite construction of them, and be perceived as phenomena having their exact periods; and no sensation, in this capacity for conjunction in the forms of time, has any advantage above another, nor in point of fact do we perceive the period of the quality in one organ, more readily nor more perfectly than in another.

We induce also the facts connected with the perception of Intensity in sensation. And here, again, manifestly the facts are that I can perceive degrees in the amount of the quality, as well when given in one organ of the sense as in another. The organ of vision or of touch has capacity for an intellectual constructing of figure in space, when all other organs are destitute of all that can capacitate for such an operation; but this does not give capacity for an intellectual construction of the degree in intensity, or amount, for the sensation in the eye or the touch any more readily or completely than for the sensation in the smell or the taste. I can as well perceive how much sweet or bitter there is in intensity, as I can how much redness, or hardness there is. And this fact manifestly comes within our hypothesis, inasmuch as all construction of intensity, or amount, must be of one measure in all quality, simply as a conjunction of degrees from void sensation up to the given intensity, and this as truly for quality in taste as for quality in vision. One organ has no prerogative over another, but each equally gives its content over to the attending agency, that the limits of its amount may be constructed for, and thus be brought within the light of consciousness.

Here, then, we have a very broad field of most interesting facts, all held in complete colligation by our ideal hypothesis. In all operations of conjunction the

form is given in perception precisely proportioned to the
capacity of the organ for giving the diverse sensation
to the intellect that it may be so conjoined in unity.
The organs of vision and touch give figure in space,
and they alone, inasmuch as no other organ gives the
diverse in extension as content in the sensation. But
all organs alike give phenomena in the forms of time
and amount, because they all alike have the diverse
instants of duration, and diverse degrees of intensity,
in their own sensation as content, and which, in each,
the intellect may alike construct within their respective limits. The ideal hypothesis and the actual law
in all these facts are manifestly correlatives. The
original conformation of our whole organization of the
sense must have had its regulation in such an idea as
its archetype. And in this we may see the beauty
and the truth of Plato's representations, so little understood, so often by an empirical perversion misunderstood and then derided as a visionary fancy, viz:
that the idea in the absolute reason—*the Divine Idea*
—has been breathed into shapeless matter, and thus
that which had otherwise been wholly amorphous,
and formless, has put on order and beauty; and this
idea, as if it were an infused soul, has given vitality
and unity. With all the wonderful elements in the
organs of the sense, how manifestly as inert and use-
less to all the ends of perception as the dust into which
they ultimately crumble, must they have been, had not
their Almighty Maker put this original idea into them,

17

as their upholding and *informing* law of combination
and functional operation.

There is still another division, including many interesting facts, which it is important should be brought
within the induction which we are now making and
which may be given as—

3dly. *Deceptive appearances.*—There are many facts
connected with deceptive appearances in the sense,
and delusive phenomena as perceived; which are held
in colligation by this same ideal hypothesis, and which
must therefore have their actual law as its correlative,
and which we will now proceed to bring within our
induction. In this division the facts are rather connected with the operation of conjoining into form, than
distinguishing in the matter, and yet so far as they
have any connection with the quality perceived, they
will confirm the conditions of the operation of distinction for all perception of distinct qualities. There is,
in these facts, an operation of conjunction effected, and
thus form appears ; but because the operation has been
other than the conditions of the matter demanded, the
form deceptively appears, and thus the perception is
partially or wholly an illusion. The facts are not of
obscure, but of false perceptions. A distorted medium, or a partial sensation, may condition the construction of the form that it shall be quite a false appearance. The ring of Saturn may appear as two handles
upon the opposite sides of the planet, from the conditions in which the content is given in the sensibility.

The agency in attention may thus be led astray by some imperfection in the condition of the sensation.

Thus, when in vision the content is received through a dense fog, or perhaps in the twilight, there may often be, not an indefinite appearance merely, but quite a deceptive and false perception. The content has not been spread upon the field of the sensibility with any sharpness of outline, and cannot, even when carefully revolved upon the sensible spot, give any exact conditions for the constructing agency, and the operation of conjunction is thus left very much to some scheme of the imagination. The habits, temperament, sympathies and emotions of the person may thus very much modify the shapes which the matter in sensation shall assume in their appearance, and may be of beautiful, or monstrous, or grotesque and ludicrous illusions. The old story of the gay young lady and the superstitious curate, viewing the moon in company through a telescope, is quite in point. " Those two shadows," says the lady, " which stand side by side together are surely two happy lovers in affectionate conversation." " Ah! I see," says the curate, " two lovers! not at all; they are the two steeples of a grand Cathedral." Personal experience and frequent observation may gather an indefinite number of effects of the same description, where the sensation has been constructed very deceptively through the influence of the imagination in its hopes or its fears.

So with the facts connected with tricks of legerdemain, or sleight-of-hand, which are often of so marvelous a description. The arrangement of surrounding objects, the lights and shades, manifestations and concealments, together with the attitudes and motions of the conjurer are so artfully contrived and skillfully managed that the attending agency of the spectator is induced to move in a certain designed direction, and thereby to construct the intended forms, and which thus appear in the consciousness as veritable phenomena. From the sensation as partially given, the productive imagination is induced to construct such forms as may seem to fill up the chasms in the content, and all this so readily and unsuspectingly that the completed product in appearance is taken to be entire reality, and the cunning delusion becomes the supposed perception of the most surprising occurrences, and the deceptive wonders are related abroad as the facts of eye-witnesses. When, through feints and artful management, the intellectual agency is induced to construct such products as the operator intended, while the actual content in the sense as given is not discriminated from that which is merely supposed, the delusion will be complete, and the credulity partake of the sincere conviction which belongs to a genuine perception. The distinguishing operation has been incomplete, and the constructing operation though complete yet deceptive, and thereby the most marvelous prodigies, ludicrous absurdities, and startling impossibilities except as miraculous, become the strange perceptions of our own eyes. The constructing agency of the spectator has been the real conjurer, but as that has been artfully deluded in its work, the deception which it has been induced to practice upon itself is wholly overlooked, and the cheat is not detected.

The vans of a wind-mill in motion, when the axle lies in such a direction to the eye that it is difficult to determine from the sensation merely which end of the shaft it is that is nearest to our position, may easily be made to turn in apparently opposite directions at pleasure. The vans may be arbitrarily constructed as now on this end of the shaft and again on the other end, and the vane is of course constructed as at the opposite end of the shaft to that on which the vans are fixed, and thus the shaft appears to lie now in one direction, and again in a reversed direction. In every such change of construction, the movement of the vans must accord, and consequently if the attending act give them now this and now that position, their motion must appear in opposite directions alternately. The apparent motion is wholly controlled by the arbitrary construction, and the facts are thus in colligation by our hypothesis.

So, again, with the waves running over the surface of the water according to the course of the wind, the constructing operation in attention passes along with them, and it is quite difficult to escape from the conviction that the whole mass of water must be flowing in that direction. The wind may be blowing strongly up the current of a broad river, and the undulations transmit their *forms* rapidly upward, while the *matter* is passing downward; the attention constructs these forms and gives them in appearance according to their succession, while the observation does not distinguish the matter which successively takes on these forms, but leaves it to appear as the same matter constantly accompanying the same form, and thereby the entire river is deceptively perceived to be flowing backwards in its channel.   But we look off upon some level meadow with its tall grass waving on the plain, or on the wide field of ripening grain—

> "That stoops its head when whirlwinds rave,
> And springs again in eddying wave,
> As each wild gust sweeps by;"

and the same form flows onward, and yet there our perception is not deluded.   We are forced to distinguish the matter as perpetually changing while the form moves along, from the present conviction that each oscillating top has its stalk permanently rooted in the earth, and this at once dissipates the illusion that both matter and form are moving on together. The observation in its discrimination gives the matter as merely swinging to and fro in its place, as the "eddying wave" careers over the landscape, while the attending operation follows the forms it constructs; and thus the forms flow, while the matter only swings back and forth in our apprehension.   The practised mariner, after long acquaintance with the mountain wave, dissipates all delusion in the same manner. He has learned to distinguish the matter as not the same in the same passing wave, and thus to his perception the waves may run in any direction, while he still apprehends the steadily setting course of the tides and currents.

Once more, only, under this division, we have the facts of deceptive appearances as they are given in cases of double-vision. The intellectual agency is here playing the same unnoticed delusion upon the appearance in consciousness as above. There is a content in both organs of vision, and from some derangement in the ordinary harmony of the sensations in both, the attending agency constructs each in its own definite form, and thus two objects like to each other appear in the consciousness. Ordinarily, the muscles of the eyes give to each such a direction that the content is topically in each after the same arrangement in reference to the sensible spot, and both the distinguishing and the conjoining agency operate according to an identity in the content of both the organs, and thus make but one phenomenon in consciousness; but when any derangement from concussion, a brain-fever, or other cause arises, or when the organs are imperfectly subjected to the muscular action, or the sensation distorted as in strabismus, or again when the object is placed between the eyes and too near to permit the axis of each to concentrate upon it, the sensation may be a condition for a double construction, and thus all the phenomena of double-vision occur. The single eye could not probably give the conditions for double-vision; at least in order that it might give such conditions, it would be necessary that its content so affect the sensibility as to induce a double attending operation.

A double perception is effected in the same way through other organs. The touch of different fingers of the same hand, or on the opposite hands may give a deranged sensation inducing a double operation, both of distinction and conjunction, and of course resulting in a double perception. One may be benumbed by cold, or a bruise, or there may be the crossing of two fingers with the object placed between them, and as the content in each may thus be separately constructed, two objects will seem to be perceived. Double sounds may be given from the different state of the two organs presenting their sensations so modified as to induce the separate construction of both; but inasmuch as the ear is without capacity for giving figure in space, the double operation could not give double object in shape. The doubling of the object as in reflection from a mirror in sight, or of an echo in sound, is not properly a double perception, inasmuch as the content given direct and that in reflection are really different, and their discrimination must be effected as in any difference of content. Where the organ is not double the perception is not two-fold, though in single organs the sensations may vary from the same occasions at different times, from some modifications in the state of the sensibility. Thus the same odors, or the same food, or wine, may differ widely in the perception in states of sickness from those of health.

Under all the foregoing divisions, we have now taken many facts, and many more might be readily brought within our induction, and it is here quite evident that they are all readily bound up in our ideal hypothesis with which we commenced, and are thus brought into complete colligation. All these facts have embodied within them one actual law of their being, and which law we now know to be in perfect correlation with our assumed hypothesis as idea; and thus far we have a science of these facts, because we can expound them in their own law of being and arrangement. And now, it would be safe, as an inductive science, to say here that our induction of facts has been sufficiently broad to warrant the deduction, that the law in these facts in the process of perception is the law for perception itself universally, and thus to conclude that all the facts which experience may give us in any perceptions will be found in colligation with those already attained. It is, however, competent to very much farther corroborate such a conclusion, by what we have termed *the Consilience of Facts*, and to which we will devote the next section, previously to any general deductions from the facts attained within the comprehension of our hypothetical idea.

SECTION III.

THE CONSILIENCE OF FACTS.

WHEN facts, which have apparently a very remote bearing from each other, and which at first seem widely disconnected, and would induce the expectation that if they are ever made explicable it must be from reasons and principles very diverse from each other, are yet found to leap together, as it were, in colligation with facts more manifestly allied, and which may have already been brought together in an induction, we have a case of what we here term the Consilience of Facts. The confidence in the general law thus deduced is augmented in proportion to the number of the facts and the distance whence they thus jump together within the same hypothesis.

An illustration of the force of such facts to corroborate the general law may be given in the example of the precession of the equinoxes as leaping within the law of universal gravitation. The longitude of the fixed stars, measured from the point where the sun's annual path cuts the equator, will from time to time change, if that point changes. Now the fact of such a change had been very early noticed by Hyparchus and observed by subsequent astronomers for near two thousand years. But for such a fact, no explanation was found. The phenomenon appeared, but stood quite anomolous among the other facts of astronomy. But when Newton had made the grand discovery of the law of gravitation, and had applied it to the explanation of many facts of planetary motion readily embraced within it, this remote and apparently wholly disconnected fact of the equinoctial precession was found very unexpectedly to leap within the same generalization with the apparently much nearer allied phenomena in the heavens. The equatorial diameter of the earth is greater than its polar diameter from the aggregation of matter accumulated about the equatorial region through its diurnal revolution, and of course the action of gravity which is as the quantity of matter must be thus modified. The disturbing force hereby induced is, when accurately calculated, precisely that which accounts for this change of point in the sun's annual path, and thereby solves the whole anomaly. The leaping of so remote and remarkable a fact within the same general law which had become readily applied to more obvious phenomena was an unanswerable confirmation of the general law, since no mere casual coincidences could have resulted in such extended systematic connection. It was a most beautiful manifestation of the comprehensiveness of the law and the harmony of its operation.

And, here, facts may be found which leap within our ideal hypothesis for perception, quite as remote from the others embraced as in the case of the precession of the equinoxes within the general law of gravitation, and though not as remarkable in themselves yet tending as effectually to corroborate the general law, within which they unexpectedly come in consilience. Some of these facts we now proceed to include in our induction.

The arts of drawing and painting have their facts which may readily be seen to come within this consilience of inductions. The two may be taken as one, in those respects in which both are designed to represent form as extension in space. The ideal creations in the mind of the artist, subjectively, are the product and proof of his genius; but when he would give to these ideals an objective representation, he is conditioned to just such a process of delineation and coloring as he would be in representing some original actually existing in nature. His idea, as a landscape, a face, or a group of objects material vegetable and animal, must be drawn and painted in the same method of operation as if he were actually taking some copy from nature. Separate from the creative invention of his genius, he is necessarily a copyist according to the conditions imposed by nature itself; and the completed product must be tested by its general conformity with these conditions of nature. If that which is put upon the canvas in its outline and coloring gives such an appearance as that ideal would if made to exist in nature, the operation is complete and the painter is perfect in his art. In the execution of this part of his work he must derive instruction from observation and practical experience.

Where the representation is to be made without the coloring in its lights and shades in painting, the result is effected simply by drawing lines in a skillful manner to give the figures and proportions of nature; and how exact the copy may thus be made, even in minute and very peculiar expressions, we need merely to glance at some finished production in sketching or line-engraving. How is this surprising resemblance effected? Certainly by copying nature in some way, and yet not at all in making the product itself like nature, but solely by inducing the spectator himself to construct such a product. In the picture there has been used nothing but certain lines with their curves and angles, while in nature, animate or inanimate, no lines are presented to the eye and only masses of color and combinations of light and shade. A definite portion of space is thus filled and, as content in the sensibility, is the condition for perceiving the object. Nature uses no pencil or engraver's tool to make outlines. She puts the mass of colors into space, and fills a definite portion, and leaves that portion surrounded on all sides by an outer space beyond it. When this is received as the content in sensation, the attending agency moves over it, and thereby conjoins it in the unity of figure which is perceived as definite object.

And now the same intellectual operation in the

spectator must be secured by the work of the limner. The attending process must be conditioned to the same track in the picture as in nature, and in this way the appearance is a representation of nature. But this is effected not as nature accomplishes it, by giving the whole mass of coloring terminating in exterior space on all sides, but simply by tracing that path in which the artist would have the spectator's attention move, by a simple line precisely where in nature the mass and the surrounding space meet together and limit each other. In this manner precisely the same constructing operation and thus precisely the same form is secured both in nature and art, and as the distinction of quality is not here regarded, the sameness in form gives the likeness in representation. Nature's law is followed, rather than that nature's object is copied. The intellect in attention is induced by art to move just where the content from nature would condition the movement. Hence the likeness often so very striking, from even a very few apt lines and nice touches. Here, certainly, are many interesting yet quite remote facts leaping directly within the induction which we had before bound in colligation by our ideal hypothesis.

And still farther, when the painter pursues his work and would imitate nature not merely in outline, but completely in the whole mass of color, and thereby secure the same sensation as nature's own objects would, the facts in this case have also a like remarkable consilience within the induction before attained.

The condition for constructing the figure of the object from nature is, that the masses of color shall fill their own places topically in the field of the sensibility. The limitations of the object in the surrounding space secure that the whole content in sensation shall observe this condition. But, as thus received, the outline is that of a plane superficies merely. Whether convex or concave, the outline is as of a plane surface only. Thus a sphere and a circle of equal diameters may either of them fill the same space; a column will have the same boundaries in space as a board of equal length and breadth; and each of these will also have the same outline as a concave body of equal longitudinal and lateral dimensions. Thus, also, of all angular forms; a square when turned obliquely fills in space the outlines of a parallelogram; a cube may have its visible sides in such a position as to fill, not equal squares, but oblong spaces; a circle may have the outline of an-elipse, by being turned obliquely in its plane, and when its plane is in the axis of vision it may even become a straight line in the appearance; and a cone fills the space of a triangle. The limits of all these in space are, respectively, like each other.

But in our experience a difference is perceived in all these forms. We distinguish quite readily plane from spherical bodies, squares from parallelograms, and cubes from solids of unequal sides. So, also, a small object near to the eye may fill the same place in the sensibility as a much larger and proportionally more distant body : and yet in our experience we shall readily distinguish the near and the smaller from the distant and the larger. The conditions for such an experience is what we need to find as explanatory of the results. The content in the sensibility must be so given that the peculiarity of forms and distance may be constructed. And when a careful examination is made of the facts, those conditions are readily found. When the outline, as given topically in the sensibility, is the same for different figures and distances, there are yet other conditions by which the right construction is induced. The sphere and the circle may occupy the same place topically on the retina, and be alike revolved nicely over the sensible spot, and if nothing but bare outline be constructed, no difference of figure could be perceived. But the sphere has, as a content in the sensibility, a diversity giving peculiar quality, as distinguishable from the content of the circle. The colors which give light and shade in the sphere are not in the circle. And thus is it with planes and convex or concave bodies, a board and a column, or a triangle and a cone, their content differs ; and as this is distinguished, the attending agency gives a differently constructed form, and thereby a perception of different figure. In painting, this difference of quality in light and shade needs only to be supplied on the canvas, and the attention gives the form as in the lights and shades of nature. With distances, again, there is not only the difference of light and shade, but also of sharpness and prominence of outline in the sensibility between the near and the more distant, which are to be *observed* in distinction; and as a still more remarkable condition, the capacity of getting the different optic angles for the near and the more remote object, by the position of the two organs in the different inclinations of their optic axes towards the object; or, when still more distant, the different inclinations when the head is in one place, and when moved to the right or left and the axes there directed to the object. Such optic angle as larger or smaller, gives the object as nearer or more remote, and this is to be *attended to* in the conjunction. By thus distinguishing the content in its lights and shades, its intensity and sharpness of outline in the sensation as different for different distances, and constructing the different optic angles, the less for the more distant and the larger for the nearer object, distance is conditioned in the perception as readily as figure from light and shade alone. The eye comes thus to perceive figures, magnitudes, and distances, with a most surprising exactness. The conditions for perceiving different shapes when the outlines are the same, and different sizes and distances when all are on one plane of the retina as given in the sensation, are thus made quite manifest. And that, through all

18

their complication and remoteness from the other facts in our induction, these do yet leap together within our hypothesis, gives great confirmation to the deduction of our universal law.

That the conditions for distance, magnitude, and figure, have as above been correctly given is also manifest from other facts, which also come leaping within the same induction. Thus for *distances* and *magnitudes* we have the following facts. When the eye receives its content in the sensibility through the medium of a spy-glass, the magnitude of the object is precisely in the ratio of the greater angle, which it is made to subtend through the more or less divergency given to the rays of light by the optic glass as a lens. The distance, also, is in the same ratio diminished. But if, now, we will invert the spy-glass and look at the same objects through the opposite end, the subtended angle is as much diminished as before it was enlarged, the objects are in the same ratio smaller, and also in the same ratio at a greater distance. It is not the intensity of the sensation or the sharpness of outline in the content, except as relatively in its own portions at the same time, for these may be exactly equal in the direct and the inverted spy-glass, but the constructing agency plots its distances and magnitudes from the angles which the objects subtend—the magnitudes directly, and the distances inversely.

Relatively to *figures*, we have the following facts.

When some medium for transmitting light gives the content in the sensibility a reversed location in the sensation, the outlines of the content become, of course, transposed to opposite sides throughout the whole field of the sensation. The reversed representation of the object must so appear. If, now, this object be a plane surface of homogeneous color throughout, the object as represented will appear as a plane, and though reversed as to its sides yet equable upon its surface. But if the object thus transmitted have characters, as letters or emblems, upon the surface, and these characters are in relief, standing out from the plane as in a coin or medal, the object will not only appear reversed, but all the outlines of its characters also reversed, and the lights and shades of the reversed characters transposed to opposite sides. This induces a construction in attention which directly reverses the characters in relief to engraved indentations beneath the surface, and they so appear in perception. And if we substitute the die by which the coin was struck, with its figures as depressions from the surface, the reversing of the outlines of the lights and shades gives the conditions for constructing convexities and not concavities, and thus the characters are perceived to be standing out in relief upon the surface. The whole perception of figure is as the attending agency is conditioned, and thus leaping in all its facts within the same colligation of our hypothesis.

And once more, only, when nature is exactly copied

in these particulars as above by the painter, the content given in sense conditions the sensation to be constructed as in nature, and thus the objects perceived in the painting appear as nature. We shall thus have this other remarkable consilience of all the facts of *perspective and dioramic painting* within our already very broad induction. The artist assumes a certain point, and arranges all his work in reference to it. The point in the painting is to be taken as the standpoint for perceiving the objects in nature, and the picture through all its several portions is made to stand at corresponding directions and angles from that point as in nature, and to receive such colors, and mo difications of light and shade, and clearness or indistinctness of outline, as shall condition the like construction from the content given to the sensibility by the picture as would be given by the original designed to be represented. The quality upon the canvas is thus made to appear standing out as in space with all the fullness and life of reality. The rules of perspective painting are thus taken from nature, not in her real forms as in statuary and carving, but only in her colors and angular proportions and bearings from the stand-point. The painter learns to separate nature as she is, from that which is given of her as content in sensation, and puts upon his canvas that precisely which is the counterpart to the sensation, and passes by all which the intellectual agency constructs in nature, leaving that operation to be effected in the same way as in nature from the conditions in the picture. In proportion to its perfection, the painting puts the same content in the sense as nature would, and the distinguishing and conjoining operations of the intellect give the same qualities and forms to the consciousness, and thus the picture becomes the resemblance of nature.

So, on the plane surface of his canvas the artist spreads out the conceptions of his genius before us. The sensibility receives the content, and we observe and attend. The quality is distinguished, and the forms are conjoined. The lights and shades through all the coloring, and the figures, magnitudes and disances over all the extension, are thus together constructed in consciousness, and give the perceptions in all their distinctness and definiteness, and, as a whole, the designed scene in all its completeness. Perhaps it is the interior of some magnificent temple; its massive architecture appears in all its grandeur, comprising long ranges of columns and broad and high arches, extended aisles, ascending stair-ways, and lofty galleries, with all their beautiful proportions. A throng of persons in all their variety of height and figure, of attitude and costume are seen to crowd its courts and porches, sit upon the benches, or walk over the tesselated pavements. With the single exception of motion the canvas gives all that nature does; or rather without exception, it gives all that nature does in one instant of the sensation, and the intellectual agency in its operation of distinction and conjunction puts within the light of consciousness the same appearance as would be conditioned by nature itself. The rules of perspective, and of dioramic representation in art, are simply a transcript of the conditions in sensation for open vision. All the facts jump together into the same conclusion of our general law for perception, and both the consilience and the colligation of facts alike find their systematic arrangement and adequate explanation in our assumed ideal hypothesis.

Perhaps it might now with safety be asserted, that no deduction of a general law from any induction of facts, could be more convincing, than that of the operation of distinction and conjunction for all perception. As an inductive science, we might here affirm that we have an idea correlative to an actual law in the perceptions of the sense.

But, our apriori investigation capacitates for a much higher ground of affirming this general law, than any induction of facts can reach, however multiplied they may be. At the most they are yet partial, and can give only probabilities, not realities, beyond the actual induction in the experience. In our apriori conclusions we demonstrated necessity and universality for our idea. We found that only in accordance with its conditions was any perception of phenomena possible. When we now find this apriori idea to have its correlative in an actual law in the facts, we are fully warranted in affirming for this actual law a universal extension to all the facts of perception, upon the high ground of an already demonstrated necessity and universality, and not merely as a deduction from a wide induction of particular facts. The apriori demonstration capacitates us to say, this actual law *is* so in the facts induced, not only; and *may be* deduced as general law from this induction, not alone; but much more than this, this actual law in the facts *must have been* as it is; and it must extend to all the facts which any experience shall give in the perception of phenomena *universally*. We have a transcendental demonstration of the *universality* of our law, as actually found in real colligation of facts.

Here, then, we complete our science of Rational Psychology in reference to the Faculty of the Sense. We have attained its *apriori Idea* both for the pure and the empirical intuition, and found it in this—that a content must be given in sensation, and that this must be Distinguished in its matter, and Conjoined in its form, as conditional for all possible phenomena in perception. This apriori idea has not only been attained as a *void thought*, but we have assumed it hypothetically, and questioned actual experience largely under its direction, and have gathered a wide induction of facts which are manifestly held in colligation by it, and from which it would be safe to make the deduction, that this law in the facts induced, as correlative with our ideal hypothesis in which the facts have been bound up, is a *general Law* for all the further facts of perception that any experience may give to us. The correlation of idea and general law gives us in this a valid *Inductive Science.* But, inasmuch as all skepticism cannot be thus excluded, because the deduction of the law is yet from a partial induction of facts, we have gone much farther than a mere deduction from the partial, and have given to this law actually attained, the apriori demonstration of necessity and universality, in which we have *Transcendental Science.* A valid *science* of perception in the sense is hereby attained, and we may from it not only perceive phenomena, but philosophically expound the process of perceiving. We not only may know as percipients of the phenomena know, but much more than this, we know how the perception *is and must be* effected. We know the appearance not only, but the *knowing* of that appearance. In this is science; and from its apriori demonstration is transcendental science; and thus a *rational,* and not merely an *empirical* or inductive Psychology.

Here our work as approriate to the first Part, would be terminated, inasmuch as the Psychology of the sense is here completed; but, as we have before indicated, the conclusions of Rational Psychology give the data for the demonstrations of Ontology; and as such a process of demonstration is of great importance, and leads to most interesting results in the determination of the *valid being* of the objects as known in that capacity which has been psychologically investigated, so we shall, in a separate form as an Appendix, give here an outline of the ontological demonstration for the *valid being of the objects*—the phenomena inner and outer—as perceived in the faculty of the sense.

APPENDIX TO THE SENSE.

AN ONTOLOGICAL DEMONSTRATION OF THE VALID BEING OF THE PHENOMENAL.

PERCEPTION we now know to be the taking of objects through the medium of sensation; and the process by which they are taken we know to be an intellectual operation, distinguishing the matter in its peculiar quality, and constructing its form in a definite measure as so much of space, so much of time, or so much in amount. This knowledge of what Perception is enables us to determine what objects Perception can attain, and thus to make an accurate circumscription of the whole field of knowledge which can come within the possession of the faculty of the sense.

All the *inner* exercises of the intellect, including also the emotions of the sentient and the actions of the voluntary capacities, as they directly affect the inner state and are thus a content in the inner sensibility, may be brought within the light of consciousness, and made to appear in their distinctness of peculiarity as to *what* they are, and their conjoined completeness as to *how much* they are. The conjunction of the inner exercises, inasmuch as they present no diversity as extensive, can give no figure in space, but only duration of period in time and degree of intensity in sensation. All the *outer* qualities, as affecting the organic sensibility, may also be made to appear in the light of consciousness, by the discriminating agency determining peculiarly *what* the quality is, and the constructing agency determining completely *how much* the quality is. In the outer sense, according to the capacity of function in the organ, is presented all the diversities as extensive, protensive, and intensive, and thus occasion for determining how much space and time and sensation the matter as quality fills. This is all that the faculty of the sense can accomplish in attaining objects, viz : distinguishing and conjoining into the forms of time and amount, the inner exercises ; and distinguishing, and conjoining into the forms of space, time and amount, the outer qualities ; and thereby giving to the consciousness distinct and definite inner and outer phenomena. Such constructed appearances in consciousness are all the objects which the functions of the intellect in the sense are competent to reach, and which must, therefore, consist of the phenomenal alone.

These phenomenal objects may be taken in our subjective conception, and constructions be made of them, by abstracting some part, or combining one with others, or comparing any two or more together, and thus a knowledge of their *relations* as matter in the sensibility and as form in space and time may be attained. This is the work only of the *re-productive imagination*, and is of the same kind as any distinguishing and conjoining operation in the sense, differing only in the conditions inducing it. The *productive imagination* distinguishes and conjoins in pure space and time, and its products are mathematical quantities, or pure diagrams. The *perceptive agency* is this same distinguishing and conjoining operation, but conditioned in the work by the content in sensation, and its products are the phenomena of our actual perceptions. The re-productive imagination takes the *conceptions* of any phenomena, thus re-producing them in the subjective thought, and then by the same distinguishing and conjoining operations, as above, reconstructing the whole through some process of abstraction, combination, or comparison, and the products are the relations thus brought into immediate consciousness as intuitively beheld; as, whole and part, single and compound, greater and less, &c. The whole work of the re-productive imagination is still within the field of the sense, and attains to a knowledge of different relationships in the conceptions of former phenomena. The productive imagination, so far as we may yet apprehend its operation as in the field of the sense only—inasmuch as we have not yet considered the understanding at all, within which we may still find the productive imagination in a modified form of operation hereafter—is especially called into exercise in the pure mathematics, as the constructor of all pure form; and the re-productive imagination, as yet apprehended only in the sense, is specially used in arranging, separating, or putting in new juxta-positions the phenomena of experience, as the re-con-structor of all new combinations and aggregates in the forms of space and time.

It is not important that we here have regard, for our present design, to any thing but the phenomena themselves as given in perception, since the sole end now in view is the demonstration of their valid being. These phenomena are inclusive of all the appearance given in consciousness, from the construction of the content in both the external and the internal sense—i. e. the affections of our inner state by our intellectual exercises, and of our organic sensibility by the con-tent from somewhere given within it.   These are thoughts, feelings, volitions, &c. as the phenomena of the internal sense; and colors, sounds, odors, &c. as the phenomena of the external sense.   The conditions of all perception carried out according to the neces-ary and universal law, which must be embodied in the actual process, gives such distinct and definite ap-pearances in the consciousness, and which we thus term phenomena, and of which as both inner and outer we now come to inquire—*Have they a valid being ?*

And here let it be understood that the validity of

being which is sought must not be taken as that which is independent of the subject perceiving the phenomena. The affection as sensation is in *my* sensibility, and the operation of distinction and conjunction is by *my* intellectual agency, and this gives phenomenon to *me*, not to another. *My* perception can give phenomenon only as appearance in *my* consciousness. The faculty of the sense is strictly confined, in all its perception, to the knowledge of phenomena solely in its own subject. What it knows, it knows only for itself, and is itself its own intelligent world, and cannot by any possibility commune with another faculty of sense in its subject. The redness, the coldness, the bitterness, &c. as perceived by me are my phenomena only, and from the functions of the sense I can never determine that the like, much less that the same qualities are perceived by another. We must have other functions than those of the sense, and other cognitions than those of phenomena or any possible abstractions combinations or comparisons of phenomena, in order to any participation in another's knowledge, or any communion in one common field of knowledge. The matter as distinguished in sensation, and the form as constructed from the sensation, and thus the distinct and definite appearnce as completed phenomenon in perception, all are in one object, and the knowledge is for one consciousness exclusively of all others in the same knowledge. We are not, therefore, to inquire for a valid being as objective to many, but.

for the valid being of the phenomenal as object only for that subject who constructs, and in whose consciousness it appears. In the sense, it were vain to attempt the demonstration of any valid being beyond this; and we must necessarily defer, till the consideration of the understanding, the demonstration of a valid being as common object of knowledge. Our data, from the attained law of perception, capacitate us to give a demonstration of the valid being of the phenomena in any subject perceiving them, and this is not merely all we *can*, but all we *need* here demonstrate.

With this full in mind, that the sense can only attain phenomena in their completeness as distinguished quality and conjoined quantity, and thus an appearance in consciousness of both matter and form; and this only for the percipient subject alone, in whose perception of phenomena none others can come in communion, but must each have their perceptions exclusively for themselves; we have the point to which an ontological demonstration must be conducted directly before us, viz: Is the phenomenon as appearance in my consciousness, a valid reality, or only a seeming to be? May I demonstrate that the matter and the form have each an actual, and not merely an imaginary being?

And here, inasmuch as this process of demonstration will be conclusive against the three forms of skepticism, as Materialism, Idealism, and universal Pyrrhonism, it may be advisable for a moment to recur to them respectively as delineated in the Introduction, that we may again have the grounds on which each of them rest clearly before us, and may thus see that while effectually demolished by this demonstration, yet could the data for such demonstration have been possibly no otherwise attained than through the foregoing apriori investigations of Rational Psychology.

Materialism doubts the real being of an inner agency, and resolves perception into the propagated actions of some outer object within the material organization of the sensibility: Idealism doubts the real being of any material content, and resolves all perception into the constructing intellectual agency: and universal Pyrrhonism founds upon the proved contradictions in our intellectual being, where consciousness and reason directly falsify each other, the utter incapability of all knowledge and the necessity of skepticism in every thing. Against none of these forms of skepticism can any appeal to experience in consciousness be availing, inasmuch as the skepticism is in each case based upon some assumption that calls in question the grounds of experience in consciousness itself. The science of perception, as the process for attaining to any experience in consciousness, must first be attained, and this whole process expounded in its necessary law, before we can attain a position for concluding against any form of skepticism that questions the very grounds of all knowledge in experience. For, suppose without such an apriori position, we only redargue his conclusions by pushing the skeptic out to the consequences. We force him to admit, as we certainly may, that his conscious experience of the fact of doubting is itself no more valid than the facts in experience which he assumes to doubt, and thereby oblige him to admit that he doubts the fact of his doubting, and is thus skeptical in relation to his own skepticism; but have we thus demonstrated to him that he actually has science? Have we not rather put him further back into the darkness of a deeper doubt, and made his skepticism the more incorrigible? He now admits that he doubts whether his own skepticism be a reality. Nothing can be known, not even the fact that he doubts every thing. But is this such a *reductio ad absurdum*, that it must legitimate the opposite conclusion? Can this demonstrate that he has knowledge? or, is it any direct subversion of the ground of his skepticism? Certainly such crowding him with his own principles is only to push him further back from all hope of ever coming to the light, or that to him any light can be.

Nor are we put in any more favorable position for reaching the skeptic, though gaining much in our own defence, when we plant ourselves upon an opposite assumption, that a clear experience in consciousness is valid for itself, and is never to be questioned, but is an ultimate fact that cannot be demonstrated only because, as ultimate, it does not need to be. We may put ourselves thus out of his reach, but his position is also beyond our assault. Our mere dogmatism cannot give us power to demolish his skepticism. All mere assumptions of the integrity of conscious experience must give a position, from which it were idle to attempt to demolish the counter-assumption, that reason contradicts this integrity.

But, the position which it is now competent for us to assume is neither surreptitiously nor dogmatically taken. It has been laid in an apriori demonstration and tested by the criterion of all true science. Perception in consciousness has been attained in its conditional idea, and verified in its actual law, and we thus know it as it *is*, and as it ever *must* be; and now from this higher position than any assumptions for or against its validity, we may wholly overlook the entire ground of all dogmatism and all skepticism relatively thereto, and, in demonstrating the valid being of the phenomena given in our conscious experience, may fairly extricate philosophy from all the skeptical conclusions of Materialism, Idealism, and Pyrrhonism. The demonstration must be restricted to the valid being of the phenomenal here, inasmuch as our psychological investigation has as yet embraced only the Sense, and which in its perceptions attains only the phenomenal; hereafter, as the result of our apriori investigation of the Understanding and the Reason, we shall be able to carry out our line of demonstration to the valid being of their objects, for which purpose we will add to each such Appendix. We shall find the

19

truth to be this, that Materialism and Idealism are simply defective, and erroneous only as they are partial. The Materialist supposes that he knows the material as the objective to have valid being, and he doubts only in relation to the valid being of the spiritual as the subjective; the Idealist, on the other hand, admits the inner and spiritual to be, but doubts the actual being of the material. Both are true so far as they go, and in what they affirm, but both are false in the points where they stop, and in that which they exclude. It is competent to demonstrate Idealism against Materialism, and thus prove a Dualism, viz: that both the subjective and the objective have a valid being. Both forms of skepticism are thus demolished, for that in which each has the truth is demonstratively confirmed, and that in which each is partial, and in which is the point of the skepticism, is corrected. Pyrrhonism, as expressive of universal skepticism, is wholly wrong, and founds upon a delusive appearance of contradiction between consciousness and reason, which delusion it is now competent fully to expose and thoroughly to dissipate, and thus make the false foundation for this highest form of skepticism utterly to fall away, and the superstructure so logically built upon it to sink beyond the possibility of a restoration. This may all be disclosed in the legitimate use of the data given in Rational Psychology, as the demonstration is progressively carried out to the valid being of the phenomenal. This we shall now proceed to accomplish.

1. *An outline of the demonstration of Idealism against Materialism.*— The celebrated scholastic dictum— *"nihil est intellectu, quod non prius fuit in sensu"*—is the starting point in the skepticism which doubts the knowledge of all being but the material. The materialist argues substantially thus—All knowledge must be through sensation. All sensation must be induced by something without the sensibility, which affects it by some method of impression upon it. And as this impression comes from the material, and is made upon a material organization, it is not competent that the sensation induced should be traced, by any process, beyond the organization affected. Perception must be completed within the sensibility as organic; and, therefore, as beginning with matter, and proceeding through matter, and completed in matter, it can be known as only material. Or, the process of argument may begin at the completed perception and follow back to its origin, thus—Inasmuch as that which is in the intellect has first been in the sense, and the sense can give only impressions from material objects; the object perceived may thus always be referred back to some representation of the material world in its impression upon the sensibility, and, therefore, if there be any perception which is not of the material world, it must be held as a delusion, and taken to be a mere chimera. Nothing can be known as reality,

save the outer objects by which the organic sensibility
has received its impressions.

Without attempting to directly traverse either mode
of argument, which certainly can be done with no advantage from any empirical data, we need merely to
take such data as have been attained in our apriori
psychological investigation, and we shall not find it
difficult to establish unanswerably the contrary conclusion, and demonstrate that we may know the inner
and the spiritual to have a valid being. We have attained space and time in the primitive intuition, as
wholly void of all content in sense and of all construction in unity by the intellect. We know their universal
necessity, as conditions that any possible phenomena
in the sense should be; inasmuch as without this
primitive intuition, there could be neither place nor
period for any phenomenon. Phenomena cannot be
without space and time, space and time may be without phenomena, and must be conditions for phenomena. The primitive intuition, while it may be wholly
void of all content as matter for phenomenon, can not
be void of the diversity in pure space and time.

Within this primitive intuition, as wholly void
space and time, we have also found that an agency
may enter and spontaneously construct definite forms
as pure figure and period, restricted only by the conditions which the very operation itself imposes, viz:
that it conjoins in unity a plurality into a total. This
whole work is within the immediate intuition; the

products are all within the light of consciousness; and
the relations and proportions of all such constructions
may be made intuitive demonstrations, over the whole
field of pure mathematics in geometry and arithmetic.
The internal state is here affected solely through an
inner agency, and yet is it really affected. The constructing, the intuitively beholding, and the mathe-
matically demonstrating, are as real phenomena in the
inner sense, as when the content in organic sensibility
is discriminated and constructed.   Although the forms
are wholly destitute of the material content in sensation, and are the results of the productive imagination,
solely; yet, while they are a mere seeming, the intellectual agency constructing them is not a mere seeming, but a veritable appearing in consciousness, and
valid through all the diversified operations as real phenomena.   Wholly irrespective of all outer impression,
the inner phenomena of the spiritual are given in their
own valid being.

It may be urged in objection here, that previous
impressions had been made from the outer material
world upon the organic sensibility, and that the whole
agency in perception was awakened in such impressions, and therefore that the material organism may
still be the sole origin of all the agency in the imaginary forms in pure space.   But in reply—that the intellectual agency is first awakened in sensation may
be admitted, yet if that agency may subsequently, in
any case, spontaneously go on in conscious operation,

without the concurrence of material impressions as its condition; and especially, if it may attain in its results, to products more complete and perfect than any material impressions can give; then is it manifestly an independent agency separate from all the organic conditions, and the inner phenomena are as real without as with the outward impressions. Were there nothing but material organizations acted on by outward material impulses, the process would be mechanical only; and when the impression from without was not, the organism must be quiescent. No material organism may acquire self-activity, from having been once put in operation by *ab extra* appliances. Beside, the product as pure form is perfect, quite beyond all impressions ever made upon the sensibility. What painter or statuary ever previously had impressed upon his organism, a form as perfect as his own ideal? or ever attained to it in his own labored production? No mechanical *copy* can rise higher than its original.

Here then are phenomena, independent of all organic impressions and material conditions. They are constructing exercises altogether peculiar; distinct from, and independent of, all material qualities. They are truly inner, mental, spiritual phenomena, as opposed to all such as are merely organic and material; and while their *pure products* only seem to be, yet do *they* truly appear in the consciousness, and are known in direct intuition. There are therefore some other

phenomena real, than such as are given in organic
sensation and are material; and in this Idealism is
fully proved against Materialism.

We have found, moreover, that it is practicable to
take the sensibility as wholly general and destitute of
all content, and by an apriori anticipation of content
determine what is necessary that any possible content
should be brought into distinct perception. It is competent for an inner agency in this manner to distinguish, as subjective operation, when no impression is
made upon any organic sensibility. When such a
prolepsis is made, and the operation of distinction is
effected through all the whole process of attaining the
result in a reality, particularity, and peculiarity, although the product is a void thought as pure conception merely, and has no other than a mere seeming to
be in the imagination, yet is not *the intellectual process
itself* a mere seeming, but an actual being. The whole
operation is in the light of consciousness, and as really
appears, and is therefore as valid phenomenon, as
when the same intellectual agency has done the same
work with a content really given in the sense. And
that this agency was first induced by some content in
the sensibility is not sufficient to secure that it should
at any time spontaneously be done, except as the intellectual agency is independent of the organic impression, inasmuch as mere material impulse cannot give
spontaneity to material organization, that it should
operate when the impulse has ceased and no new

material impression is given. The operation of distinction in such an apriori process is as truly a mental, spiritual phenomenon, as the operation of conjunction in pure space and time. The demonstration is thus again given, that the ideal in the productive imagination is the product of as real inner operation, and thus the offspring of what has been as truly valid phenomenon, as when the actual quality has itself been distinguished.

Again, we have a demonstration resting in the same conclusion, when we follow out the data given in the law embodied in the facts of perception. We have found that although material content be given in the sense, yet no phenomena can appear in consciousness except as both an operation of distinction and conjunction has been effected by the intellect. The impression upon the organic sensibility may be completed in the sensation, and yet in this alone it is impossible that perception should be effected. The content perfectly given in the sensation is wholly a chaos for the consciousness, except as elaborated intellectually into distinct quality and definite quantity. The content given in the vibration of the strings of a harpsichord are sounds perceived in the consciousness only as they are discriminated; and when thus discriminated they are still mere quality without measure, sound without form, except as they have been constructed in unity. Thus the sounds in a full choir, though distinguished accurately, are yet the matter only of which the tune is made, and that tune cannot be apprehended until first a conjunction of the matter into form has been effected. The observing and the attending agency is wholly of the inner intellectual being, quite separate from the organic impression. Sensation may be complete without any perception of the matter for a phenomenon, and the matter may be distinctly given in the consciousness and yet the form of the phenomenon not appear. The sensation is but the occasion for the spontaneous intellectual operation. With a material impression only, the organism of a living, is not more available to distinct and definite perception, than the organism of a dead body. The inner, intellectual, spiritual phenomenon is wholly distinct, even in an outer perception, from the material impression on the organ. No possible process of mechanical material agencies can constitute a phenomenon. The universal law of perception is a refutation of Materialism.

2. *An outline of the demonstration of Materialism against Idealism.*—Instead of the dictum "there is nothing in the intellect which has not first been in sensation," which the materialist uses ; the idealist, on the other hand, makes use of directly the opposite, "that all sensation is from the intellect." This latter dictum is viewed in two different aspects, and induces two different processes of reasoning, and thus gives to Idealism two modified forms.

One modification of Idealism is, that the intellectual

agency produces all that is phenomenal, and the entire
sense is but the product of the intellect alone. Beginning with thought, as it goes on spontaneously under
the control of its own inner law, it follows this up in an
analysis through its entire subjective process. The
merely spontaneous thinking holds the self absorbed
in the intellectual operation, and thus all self-consciousness is impossible. But, when any completed
perception, as product of the thinking, stands forth in
consciousness, it reveals itself as already a fixed and
finished product, and thereby conditions and limits the
spontaneity of thought and forbids that the process of
thinking should be any more in unconsciousness. The
product is distinguished from the process; the completed thought is separated from the thinking; the intellect comes to discriminate the conception from the
action; this at once puts the product as other than
and objective to the self, and thus in consciousness
there is a duality—a self, and a not-self; a subjective,
and an objective. This objective product, as other
than self, appearing in consciousness becomes at once
a phenomenal being in our apprehension, and is put
among the realities of an outer world. Thought, in
its spontaneous development, originates its own products which limit and condition its own spontaneity,
and which as thus made objective to itself become
the phenomena of an external world. The sense is
the intellect giving objectivity to its own creations.
All phenomenal existence is solely the product of an

intellectual agency, and can therefore possess no higher than ideal being. The only apriori existence is a LAW OF THOUGHT, and all perception is a consciousness of spontaneous activity, and a conditioning of this activity by its ideal creations. The material is solely the limiting of spontaneous thought by the ideal. The intellect creates its own material world by its necessity to objectify its own thoughts.

Another modified view of Idealism is, that as sensation is the only content from which the intellect can come to the knowledge of an outer world, the only thing possible to the intellect is, that it should know the sensations. But these sensations are nothing material, and can possibly be no other than mental affections. They are simply spiritual phenomena as they are only the mind's own feelings. Without at all explaining how the sensations come, it is enough to show that they are in the same mind which is conscious of them, and that this consciousness of sensations, of whatever kind or variety, cannot thereby be a consciousness of an external material world, nor give any data by which the valid being of such material world can be proved. The mind has its own sensations within it, and they are wholly of it, and these sensations are all it can know, and thus to it, all existence of an external, material world are simply the objectifying and materializing its own sensations. Perception of outer objects is a delusive and supposititious materialism for that which is solely a mental sensationalism.

We have the data from our apriori psychological demonstrations, for a refutation of all Idealism in both of these aspects and proving the valid being of objective phenomena, nor could such data have been supplied from any other source. We will now proceed to indicate the general outline of such Ontological Demonstration.

We have seen that it is competent for the intellect to construct all possible pure forms in the primitive intuition of space and time, and thus produce for itself all possible ideal figures and periods. When such ideal forms have been constructed, they stand out in the intuition as completed products of the intellect, and all of form that the intellectual agency may from itself produce is given in them. No possible intellectual agency, simply, can put any thing more into them as form, than to conjoin the diversity in unity, through a plurality, to a completed total. We may then take such completed pure product—say a circle in space— and most certainly it will stand out in the imagination as definite figure, and limit and condition all thinking relative to it, as much as any mere intellectual product can do. It were impossible to think it any other figure than a circle; in any other portion of space than that which the intellect has put it; or that any other constructions should be made that would not in some way be conditioned relatively to this. All that the intellect can do to it, to make it limit and condition its own further development, it has already done and has thus exhausted all its power to objectify this pure circle. And certainly, to a certain extent, it has been successful. It has given a product which stands out separate from the agency that produced it, and as other than itself is object to itself in its own intuition. But while as ideal form it is thus objective as far as the intellectual agency can make it, is there no difference in the consciousness between this ideal form, and the phenomenon of a material ring with its given content in sensation? Is the ideal here, in the same way a limiting of the spontaneous thought, and a conditioning of its development, and an objectifying of itself to its action, as is the real? Is there nothing in the material, as outer objective phenomenon, which is not also in the ideal? The intellect has given all it may to the pure form to make it objective, and yet, most manifestly, the phenomenal ring has something more in its objectiveness than the pure circle, and this something more must have been given to it from some other than a mere intellectual operation.

So, moreover, it has been seen that a content may be anticipated as a prolepsis in sensation, and thus an ideal quality may be attained by an intellectual operation of distinction alone. The anticipated content gives occasion for the simple operation of distinction, and the product is thus a distinct ideal quality, which may be also conjoined in form and thus become an ideal phenomenon in both distinct matter and definite form. I may thus by anticipation take a content which I distinguish as light, and may also so construct it in its form as to be an ideal of the moon in shape, and in this manner I may also construct its amount so as to have an ideal of the moon in brightness, and such operation of distinction and conjunction would give me the complete moon as the work of the imagination, and standing out from the intellectual operation as an ideal phenomenon. A Newton or a La Place might so construct the solar system in its ideal bright phenomena and pure forms, in all its beautiful relations and harmonious arrangements, and put the complete diagram in space and time as the reality stands ensphered in the heavens; and though the whole would be ideal only, and stand out in the conception as a mere void thought, yet would the intellectual construction have thus put within the ideal creation all that it was competent to itself to effect. Such an ideal system would limit and give conditions to spontaneous thinking, and be thus as truly and as completely objective as any purely intellectual creation could be made. But is there no difference in the objective being of a complete ideal solar system, and the reality as spread out by telescopic observation and scientific construction? To just this difference, surely, is the real beyond the reach of all attainment through an intellectual creation alone. The ideal is not, in any thing which may be completely constructed

in the productive imagination, the same nor the co-
equal, with that thing given in the reality of an actual
perception through sensation. In the ideal, however
complete in the construction, and vivid in the imagination, there is not what the real phenomena possesses. The first can only *seem* to be, the last actually
appears. The first is wholly void thought—an empty
conception—the last has a valid phenomenal content.
No possible action of the intellect can give an affection
in the sensibility, and induce the content of an actual
sensation.

And against the other view of Idealism, which
would make sensation itself wholly a mental phenomenon, and incompetent to sustain any conclusions from
it of any other valid being than that which is wholly
in the mind itself, we have the following data for a
sound demonstration. With a content in sensation,
we have seen in our apriori psychological examination, that an intellectual agency discriminates and
thereby attains the distinct quality ; and that this intellectual agency also conjoins in unity and thereby
attains the definite form of the quality, whether as in
space, time, or amount. But while it is not difficult
to determine this distinguishing and conjoining agency as wholly a subjective process, and the entire operation an inner phenomenon only, yet is there something antecedent to the operation which altogether
conditions it, and necessitates it to be as it is, and not
in some other manner. When we *anticipate the con-*

tent and make an ideal distinction, nothing conditions the kind or the variety of the quality we shall find, but it may be any possible quality as determined by any scheme in the imagination; and so also the construction of the ideal form is wholly unconditioned except by some scheme of the imagination, and may be any one of all possible forms in space, time, and amount. But *the content in sensation* excludes all direction from any scheme in the imagination, and necessitates that the operation be according to the conditions of the content. We cannot distinguish other than the given quality in its quantity, nor construct other than the given form. The ideal circle may be of any possible dimension and in any possible position in space, but the phenomenal ring can be constructed only where, and as large as, it is given in the sensibility; and the ideal moon may be of every size, position, or brightness, but the moon as real phenomenon is wholly conditioned to the matter and form determined by the content in the sensibility. This therefore becomes quite a peculiar objective and other than any possible ideal can be. It is an objective not at all as product of the Intellect, but as found by the Intellect. Antecedent to all construction by the Intellect there was already that in the sensation, which must determine all construction according to its own condition.

And now, these antecedent conditions in the content in sensation, which must determine the distinguishing and conjoining agency of the intellect, are no products of any intellectual agency in the same subject. The whole intellectual agency of the subject is exhausted in discriminating and constructing the content already given, and as given, and not at all in making or modifying the sensation. No intellectual act can give content to the void sensibility, nor modify the content as given. The sensibility is itself no agent, and possesses the capacity of a receptivity only, and not activity. It has its unity in the same ground or self as the intellect, but the intellect can only construct and apprehend what is already there, and can by no possibility put any thing there. When the intellect has done its whole work completely as productive imagination, and given any number or variety of complete ideal pure objects, it has not put any thing within the sensibility. The sensibility is wholly void and must forever remain so, if nothing but itself, or the intellectual agency, or indeed any thing which belongs in unity in the same subject, be depended upon to give it content. The content in sensation which possesses the conditions that must determine the construction, and thus also the perception, is therefore, wholly other than any thing subjective; it is the gift utterly of some *ab extra* agency, and therefore properly objective. The only point in which the subjective and the objective meet is in the affection in the sensibility. The content is from some where *ab extra* given to the sensibility, and induces its affection in the

20

sensibility as causality for it, wholly irrespective of all subjective agency. The sensibility is in the same subjective self as the intellectual agency and the conciousness, and has its distinguishable force as sentient superinduced upon the common vital force of the whole subjective being; and thus when the causality of the objective content meets it, its own distinguishable force as sentient capacitates it to be affected thereby, and when this effect as sensation is produced, and just as it is produced, the intellect as in the unity of the same subject with it may then distinguish and construct it into clear and definite phenomenon. The occuring of the sensation is wholly from the without, the constructing of the sensation is wholly from the within; but the subjective agency in constructing is wholly conditioned by the objective content which affects the sensibility. This peculiarity in the content in sensation it is, that gives to the phenomenon an objectiveness which no ideal may possibly attain, and which wholly forbids that it should be perceived as an inner and subjective phenomenon, or the product of any inner intellectual agency. The inner intellectual agency, in distinguishing and conjoining, only finds it as it already is.

Sensation, therefore, though an affection *in* the sensibility which is in unity with the intellect in the same self, is not *from* any thing in unity in the self, but wholly from some other and outer source, and is so far from being wholly mental, that it is given to the mind, and determines every mental and subjective agency by its own conditions. There is not only something other than a pure ideal creation in the mind, but something other than an inner mental affection, viz. a causality *ab extra* for that affection, and an objective determiner, in the conditions given, what the subjective agency may construct and perceive from it. And though we do not at all attempt here to determine whence the content in sensation comes, nor what at all is its causality, inasmuch as whatever is given in the phenomenal, in the clear light of consciousness, must be from the sensational content itself and not at all revealing that causality; yet do we abundantly demonstrate an objectiveness, which cannot admit that it should be known as only and wholly mental. And this is both all that is possible, from the data given in the Rational Psychology of perception, and all that is needed for meeting the skepticism which in any form of Idealism may attack the reality of the phenomenal as given in the sense. The determination of the *causality* for sensation must await a further psychological investigation in the domain of the understanding, whence we may gain data for this further ontological demonstration; but sufficient for the sense, and all skepticism relatively to it, is the demonstration that the phenomenon perceived, while distinguished and conjoined in the subjective, has its matter as content from without, and determines by its own conditions *what* quality, *where*, *when*, and *how much*, shall be perceived, and is thus truly an objective to the perceiving subject. Something other than subjective idealism, something more than mental sensationalism, is conclusively demonstrated. The phenomenon perceived has its valid being, and actually appears, and thus has its reality independently of all ideal creation and subjective mental production.

The sense, it is thus clear, may reach no further in its knowledge than to that which is put within its own field, and this field must ever be circumscribed within the self-consciousness. I may perceive my subjective acts as inner phenomena, and know their valid reality. I may have an intuition of my ideal creations, and know them to be empty thought, and only a seem-to be. I may perceive the phenomena conditioned in sensation, and know them as objective reality, which verily appear and not merely seem. But this can extend no further than within the sphere of myself. The color, the touch, the taste, the sound, the smell, and all the varieties in their distinct peculiarities and measures which I perceive, are phenomena to me only. They come within *my* sensibility, they are distinguished and conjoined by *my* intellect, and they appear in *my* consciousness; they are thus valid phenomena for *me*, and are truly objective in *my* experience, but my knowledge can possibly be no standard for any other than myself. Whether my perception of the warmth, or the weight, or the bitterness, &c. be as that of any other self, no possible function of the sense can determine. This would demand that I should have an organ for perceiving another's perceptions. I can know only my own phenomena, both inner and outer, but these I may know as valid and real for myself; and may make those of any oné time, a standard for a comparative determination of the matter or form of similar kinds or varieties perceived at other times. But all determination of a common objectiveness, and the attainment of an outer world which shall be the same in the experience of all, must from the conditions of the faculty by which it may be known, be deferred until the psychology of the understanding has been completed. We here demonstrate the phenomena of the sense to be both of the inner and the external sense; that there is both the spiritual and the material, the subjective and the objective; and we thus fully establish what is true, and demolish what is partial, in both Materialism and Idealism.

3. *An outline of the demonstration against Universal Pyrrhonism.*—This skepticism deduces its conclusions from the alledged contradiction of the consciousness by the reason. The undoubted universal conviction of consciousness is that we perceive external objects immediately, and not some image or ideal representation of them. Reason, on the other hand directly falsifies such convictions, and demonstrates that often at least the real outer object cannot be in the sensibility, and that when it does come in contact, it cannot be the object but only the sensation which may

be directly perceived. In all cases, not the object, but some intermediate representative thereof must be that which is actually perceived, and at best we must know the outer objects by this intermediate representative.

Here, then, two. original and independent sources of knowledge terminate in direct and unavoidable contradiction. Clear consciousness may not be questioned, nor its convictions resisted. A clear deduction of reason may not be gainsayed, but its demonstration must compel assent. One may not be permitted to correct the other, for they are both original and independent; nor can one expound the other, for there can be no exposition authoritative of one over the other. When one source of knowledge comes in different ways to opposite convictions, an exposition may be made by an independent examination of the media of knowledge. When I perceive the same phenomenon through different colored glasses, or as passing from a rarer to a denser medium, such explanation is practicable beween the two perceptions, but here the contradiction is affirmed to lie between clear consciousness and legitimate reasoning; and all that can be said is that they subvert each the other, and all ground of confidence in our whole intelligent being falls hopelessly away forever.

But, now in our apriori psychological examination of perception, we have attained the complete Idea of the whole process, and we have also found the actual Law of perception in the facts, and here we have found exact harmony and not contradiction. The

Idea in the reason, and the Law in the facts as given in consciousness, are in the accordance of perfect correlates; there must then be some false element somewhere in this alledged conclusion of inevitable contradictions. We may also affirm further, that the data are given by which we may detect the fallacy on which rests this whole superstructure of absolute doubt, and show just how and where the fallacy is made an occasion for surreptitiously bringing in so fatal a skepticism. This we will now proceed to accomplish.

The data attained in Rational Psychology may be used as follows: The content which is given in sensation becomes an occasion for a spontaneous intellectual operation of Distinction, and thereby the quality is brought into distinct consciousness and is perceived as the matter of the phenomenon. The constructing intellectual agency gives to it definite form in the consciousness, and thereby the perception is perfected and the phenomenon complete. The content as sensation, while it occasions the intellectual agency in discriminating and constructing, determines it also according to its own conditions, and is thus *objective* in its reality, as opposed to the intellectual agency which is *subjective* in its reality. All this is brought within the immediate consciousness, and is thus a direct and immediate perception. So far, our psychological conclusions confirm the *first* fact assumed by the skeptic as his preparation of the ground for his deduction of universal Pyrrhonism; viz. that the universal conviction of consciousness is that we perceive the object immediately.

But the fact further is, that this distinct and definite quality is all that the sense can reach, and all that consciousness can testify to as immediate in its own light. That causality, whatever it may be, that gave this content to the sensibility and thus in its affection induced sensation, is not itself given in the sensation, nor can it be known as immediately in the consciousness. It is not at all perceived, but must be attained, if known at all, through some other faculty than that of the sense. The qualities of the rose—color, fragrance, smoothness, weight, taste, &c. as given in any and all organs of sense—are immediately perceived; but what perception ever attained the rose itself, as other than its qualities? The rose, as causality for affecting the sensibility through the content given, is not an object for the consciousness at all, and is not, therefore, in the testimony of any consciousness immediately perceived. Reason only affirms that this causality, which is back of its perceived qualities, is not perceived; and certainly no consciousnsss contradicts this. Consciousness confirms this, so far as it may, by its negation of all testimony about it. It denies that any thing back of the qualities ever becomes an object to it. And the same might also be shown of the inner phenomena. The acts, as affecting the internal state in any mental exercise, come in to immediate perception, as they come immediately within

the light of consciousness; but whose consciousness
ever testified that his own mind, as causality for these
acts, had ever been immediately perceived? Consciousness affirms one thing, an immediate perception
of qualities ; and reason does not at all contradict this,
but affirms and apriori demonstrates it. Reason also
affirms one thing that, whatever it may be which is
under or back of the qualities, and is causality for
their coming within the sensibility that they may thus
be brought by the intellectual agency into the light of
consciousness, yet this causality as thing in itself cannot
be immediately perceived; and consciousness does
by no means affirm in contradiction, but as far it may,
sustains reason by a negation of all testimony about
it. The whole basis of the skepticism, so broad and
startling in its consequences, is thus found to be the
old sophism, *figuræ dictionis*, so often deluding us by
its fallacies, and which is at once demolished, when
our analysis enables us to see the false play upon the
phraseology. The *object for the sense* in its perception
is phenomenon as quality solely ; the *object for the reason* is the thing itself as causality for its qualities :
and certainly consciousness may very well testify for
its immediate perception of the former, and reason
very well deny an immediate perception of the latter,
without any contradiction between them. We are
thus able to utterly overthrow universal skepticism,
by being made competent, through the conclusions of

Rational Psychology, to expose the sophism on which it had been built.

The outlines of an Ontological Demonstration are thus clearly though rapidly traced, and their conclusive result against all forms of skepticism relatively to a knowledge in perception is made manifest. That the valid being of phenomena in perception is attained we here render indisputable against all the possible forms of doubting. We take in, at one view, the process against all doubting, and the demonstration is sound and unanswerable.

Materialism is partly true, and false only as it is partial. To this extent its dictum is safe, viz: in reference to all quality. A void sensibility must leave the consciousness utterly destitute of all quality. Whatever the intellect may construct in its agency, it can possibly give no quality to be perceived, but as a content has first been given in sensation; and thus, "whatever," as quality, " is in the intellect, has first been in the sensation." There is, in all such perception of phenomena, a valid, real, material content. But its partiality and exclusiveness is its false side, and on this rests its skepticism. It excludes all reality from that which has not been in sensation. Nothing in the intellect has valid being which has not been taken through an affection of the sensibility, and as this is wholly material, all that the intellect may attain, and man may know, must be the material alone. This excludes the whole phenomena in the inner operations of the intellect itself, and admits of no inner exercise that there can be knowledge, any further than it may be traced to a sensation induced by some material content. That the action in distinguishing and conjoining the content in sensation is as real as that content itself, the materialist does not admit, simply because his analysis has not enabled him to detect any difference between such an intellectual operation, and the natural effect of an impression from without mechanically upon the organization. It was the perception of this exclusiveness that induced Leibnitz to qualify the fundamental dictum on which materialism rested, by adding to it—"*praeter ipsum intellectum,*" and thus affirm that nothing is in the intellect which has not first been in the sense, *beside the intellect itself.* But even with this exception of "the intellect itself" from the necessity of having been in the sensation in order that it might be known, we shall still make the dictum more partial than the truth, unless indeed "the intellect itself" be made to mean all things that the intellect may any way attain. For, if we by any means may come to know space, time, causality for sensation, &c., we shall know not only what has not been in sensation, but what also is not "intellect itself." That the material phenomenon is known in sensation, and in sensation only, is true; but that this is all that may be intellectually cognized is not true, as our Rational Psychology has fully shown.

Again, Idealism is true in part, and because it is

partial and denying knowledge beyond what is attained in the subjective intellect, it is erroneous. It affirms what Materialism denies, and denies what Materialism affirms. Both are good in their affirmations, both are false in their negations. Beginning in subjective thought, and only developing thought in a logical process, the ideal is all that may be attained, and the subjective process is all that may be known as having reality. Even sensation is only the conditioning of the subjective, by making its own creations objective to itself; or, in the Berkeleian form, all sensation is itself purely mental. This is affirmed, only from the want of such an apriori cognition of sensation as may make it competent to show, that no possible intellectual subjective agency can induce sensation, nor give to any ideal creations the characteristics of real objective phenomena. That the inner development of thought is real, and that sensation is an affection of the sensibility as mental, both are valid; but that all valid being is thus subjective, and that the content in sensation is not wholly *ab extra*, is erroneous.

Universal Pyrrhonism is true in affirming that in perception we are conscious of an immediate knowledge of the object, and also true that reason demonstrates that we cannot immediately know the object; but the object in the first case is quality as phenomenal, and the object in the last place is the thing itself as causality for the phenomenal; and the falsehood is in the sophism of concluding as if both were the same. The contradiction alledged between two original faculties of knowledge is thus shown to be wholly a fallacy, and the validity of knowledge both in perception and reasoning is left wholly unimpeached.

We have thus a valid being of the inner spiritual phenomena against Materialism; and a valid being of the external material phenomena against Idealism; and a complete subversion of that Universal Skepticism which denied that we might know either of them.

We may also very well show how impossible it must be to attain to any such demonstration, or effect any such overthrow of all skepticism relative to our knowledge in perception, by taking the position of Reid. This is available only as a defense, not at all as a point of aggression against any skepticism; and it defends itself only in the dogmatism of an assumption. The argument from common sense was simply the conviction of consciousness which Hume alleged was contradicted by reason. While Reid affirmed that common sense was wiser and safer than all the conclusions of reason, Hume could still allege his proofs that reason flatly contradicted common sense notwithstanding. Hume could not thus be cured of his universal skepticism, nor so far as his philosophy could avail could Reid prevent himself from being dragged down into the same abyss, and only saved himself by prudently holding on to consciousness or common sense, and let philosophical reasoning go where it would.   And the same also is true in relation to the other forms of skepticism; it is not possible from mere counter-assumptions to do any thing effectual to extirpate them.   " In 1812 Sir James McIntosh remarked to Dr. Brown, that Reid and Hume differed more in words than opinion."   Dr. Brown replied—" Yes, Reid bawls out—' we MUST believe an outer world;' and then whispers, ' but we can give no reason for our belief.' "   " Hume cries aloud—' We can give NO REASON for such a notion;' and then whispers, ' I own we can not get rid of it.' "—*Progress of Ethical Philosophy, p.* 239.

That our knowledge begins in perception, and that our perceptions give valid realities as phenomena, may be thus demonstrated; but that any thing other than the phenomenal, and that within the sphere of our own self, can be real in our knowledge, the sense can furnish no data for proving.   How purely spiritual beings, without the organs of a sensibility, may know, we cannot from any facts in perception determine.   Such could not have the facts in consciousness of heat and cold, weight and weariness, sweetness and bitterness, fragrant and fœtid odors; and must know them as we experience them, without their own experience of them; as Omniscience may know what physical pain or remorse of conscience are to us, with no such phenomena in his own consciousness.

This phenomenal world of inner exercises and outer qualities, though single, isolated, and fleeting in all its objects, and wholly in a perpetual flow, is yet a world of reality, and not mere dreams nor ideal semblances. The actual content in sensation distinguishes all phenomena in perception from spectral illusions, mental hallucinations, or credulous clairvoyance. It is knowledge valuable for its own sake, and worth more for the use hereafter to be made of it. Its full explanation is science begun, a first and necessary step towards science completed. Other, and higher objects remain to be attained, but the higher are beyond attainment except as we avail ourselves of these here given. In this philosophy of the Sense, the door opens to more spacious and more splendid apartments, but we may by no means enter except through this forecourt of the Temple of Science.

PART II.

THE UNDERSTANDING.

I.

THE NECESSITY FOR A HIGHER INTELLECTUAL AGENCY
THAN ANY IN THE SENSE.

PERCEPTION in the sense gives to us phenomena in
real appearance, and not as mere fantastic illusion.
But such phenomena are in the sense necessarily fleeting, isolated, and standing wholly in one self. The
discriminating agency distinguishes only the content
given in the sensibility, and which is a perpetual coming and departing; the constructing agency conjoins
this distinct content as quality separately, and thus
in one form of its quality only as definite object at
once; and all this only for the self, in whose consciousness this distinguishing and conjoining operation
is carried on. Each phenomenon must thus occupy
its own space, and its own time, in the self-consciousness; its appearance disjoined from all other phenomena, its place from all other places, and its period
from all other periods, and the self-consciousness in

which the appearance, place and period are, disjoined from every other self. From the very functions of the sense in their law of operation, it must be wholly impracticable that it should give any thing other than definite phenomena, definite places, and definite periods, as single parts of nature space and time, and can possibly know nothing of any connection of these parts, as the components of one whole. All parts are to the sense definite totals, and the conception of a universe of nature, and a oneness of all space and of all time, is from any agency in the sense wholly impracticable. One phenomenon is gone when another has come, and its place and period came and went with it, and the conjunctions in the departed have no connection to the conjunctions in the becoming; and thus, neither phenomena, places, nor periods take hold of each other in their arising and departing in the consciousness, nor connect themselves into one nature, one space, or one time.

As in the perceiving self there can be no such whole of all phenomena, of all space, and of all time, much more must it be impracticable for the sense to give to different perceiving selves a participation in the same one whole of nature, of space, and of time; inasmuch as neither self can have a whole of nature space and time not only, but neither self can at all participate in any other's definite phenomena places and periods. In the sense, each one perceives for himself, and his phenomenon, figure in space, and period in time, are

21

each his own only, and in which none other may participate.   How come we then by such conceptions as one whole of all nature of which all definite phenomena are its parts, one whole of all space of which all definite places are but its parts, and one whole of all time of which all definite periods are but its parts? Certainly by no functions of the sense.   The operation of conjunction defines its object only so far as the conjunction in unity is carried, and then comes an hiatus, separating the next conjunction in unity from it, whether of appearance place or time.   If I construct a circle in the pure intuition, I know it as distinct from a triangle, as occupying a space, and as continuing a period; but when that constructed circle has departed from the pure intuition, and I now construct a triangle in pure intuition, while I know the triangle as distinct from a circle and as having place and period, yet do I not know this triangle and that circle as having any connection with each other in themselves, their place, or their period.   The circle, in its conception place and period, has altogether departed; the triangle, in its conception, place and period, has come in; and a chasm, which no construction by a conjunction in unity can bridge over, separates them; and my intuition cannot determine that the conceived circle and triangle, and their places and periods, have each with each any connection.   The being of the circle is gone, the place it occupied is gone, and the period it filled is gone; and that the conceived triangle now come, and its place, and its period, have any connection in a whole of all conceived being and of all space and of all time, with the conceived circle in its departed being and place and period, the intuition can have no possible functions for determining. And so, precisely, with the relation of a departed and a becoming phenomenon. The redness and and its place and its period have all departed, and a whiteness in its place and period is now in its becoming; but for the sense there is a chasm of nihility between the two, and an impossibility of saying that the redness and the whiteness are connected in one whole of nature, their places in one whole of all space, and their periods in one whole of all time. To the sense, every definite construction of phenomenon in place and period, stands only in its own isolation. It can construct definite phenomena in their distinct quality, in different figures and periods definitely; but it can only construct, and from one construction to another it can give no connection. Its definite phenomena, it cannot connect into one universe of nature; its definite places, into one whole of space; nor its definite periods, into one whole of time. Each intellect in self-consciousness must construct its own phenomena, and these will be perpetually departing and utterly disjoined from the becoming; and thus to no self-consciousness can there be in the sense any connection into one whole of nature space and time, nor can one self-consciousness in its constructions commune with any other self in its constructions. Were there no higher functions than the sense, phenomena in their places and periods would be a mere rhapsody of becoming and departing constructions, and in such a hap-hazard dance of appearances, that all conception of a connected whole of nature, of space, and of time, would be an impossibility. If we may know other than isolated phenomena in their separate places and periods, a higher faculty than that of conjunction in sense is necessary.

II.

THE EXPOSITION OF THIS HIGHER AGENCY AS UNDERSTANDING.

THE intellectual agency gives two different kinds of relations in the consciousness. One kind is that which has already been considered in the sense as the operation of conjunction. The diverse elements are taken in their manifoldness and conjoined in unity, so that they stand together within limits and become a total, and the bond which holds them in unity is both different from and external to the elements themselves. The elements are brought into juxta-position, and make a whole as an aggregate simply, and thus the relation is one of *collocation* only. When I construct a triangle in pure intuition, I merely conjoin the diversity within external limits, and the area of the triangle becomes a whole, simply in virtue of this external defining of the diverse points contained within the

limits. So also in the construction of any phenomenon in its form, the same relationship of collocation
only is effected. The content in the sensibility, as
color in vision, is conjoined in attention and thereby
defined in its figure, and thus becomes a definite whole
as colored surface placed within outer limits. Of this
kind are all the relations of the sense, pure or empirical, inasmuch as the operation of conjunction can effect no other relationships, and this is the only operation in the sense which may give any relations. These
may be termed *Mathematical relations.*

Another kind of relationship is that where the elements are held together by an inherent bond and all
coalesce in one whole, and which is thus not a mere
aggregation but a relationship of *coalition.* All the
parts are reciprocally inter-dependent, and together
constitute an organic total. Thus with the whole
plant or animal, the elements are not merely together
in a mass, but there is an inner bond in which they
all grow together. The union is not local or periodical, but dynamical; and as distinguished from the
former, we may term this kind *Philosophical relations.*

And precisely in this difference of the kind of relationship is the necessity of our present investigation.
Mathematical relationships can be given in the constructions of the sense, and the operation of conjunction can give only such relations. The construction
being effected, the relation of all its parts becomes an
immediate intuition; and the specific relation, as a

new conception, is seen in the construction; and thus the synthetic judgment is manifestly valid. If I construct a circle in pure intuition, the relation of its radii is immediately seen in the construction itself, and the new conception of equality thus attained is legitimately added in a synthetic judgment; and so with all possible mathematical relations, whether pure or empirical. The process is synthetical, viz: the adding of some new conception in a judgment through all the process; but this new conception is always attained, *in an immediate intuition in the construction itself*. An exact definition gives occasion for an affirmation of the exact relationship, and the same for a phenomenon in its empirical form as in a pure form in the primitive intuition. The judgment, though synthetical, is also *intuitive*.

But this cannot so be effected in philosophical relations. The new conception is not one that admits of becoming at all an immediate intuition. There can be no construction effected in which it may be seen. I may construct the form of two colors in space, and in the construction see all the relations in space of the two phenomena, and thus affirm that one is square and the other is circular, one is without or within, above or below, larger or smaller, &c., and in time earlier or later, of longer or shorter continuance, &c. than the other. But I cannot so construct any two phenomena, as to see in the construction that they both inhere in one ground, or that both originate in one source. The new conception is of an inner bond which will not allow of any construction, and cannot thus become intuition. That in which the phenomena coalesce, and by virtue of which they are held in one whole, is altogether supersensual, inasmuch as it is wholly beyond the conditions of any conjunction in unity. That the redness and the smoothness are in one place and period, may be affirmed from the sight and the touch, and a construction may be made to represent them externally, by a painting; but that they inhere in one ground as their subject, which we call a rose, we cannot make to be immediate intuition, because no construction can possibly give this supersensuous ground or common subject, to be immediately seen. That the phenomenon of heat, and that of evaporation, have a relation in their periods, and what that relation is, may be affirmed from a construction in the sense intuitively; but that they are connected as source and consequence, by an inner bond of causality, cannot be an intuition of the sense, inasmuch as no construction can possibly give this to be immediately seen. Philosophical relations are altogether of this supersensuous kind, and their inner bond, through which all coalesces in the unity of a whole, is beyond the practicability of any construction. The forms of space and time can have nothing in which it may be represented.

The philosophical relation always involves a new conception, which can not be attained by any analy-

sis of the phenomena that are held in relationship by
it, and thus the judgment is always synthetic. That
the two phenomena are affirmed to be thus related is
by reason only of this inner supersensual bond, and
the adding of this in the judgment is an extension of
the cognition, and as it is thus no product of an analysis, and as before seen is no possible intuition in any
construction, it must somehow be attained in its own
peculiar manner, and demand that for it a peculiar
function should be supplied, other than any thing which
the faculty of the sense can give. As conjunction only
puts together in collocation, while this gives internally
a coalition ; the first a collection, this a connection ;
I shall so distinguish it as the *operation of* CONNECTION.
And as the intellect *conjoins* in the sense, so its *connecting agency* belongs to the faculty of the understanding. This faculty of the Understanding, as that which
gives the relations of phenomena in their inherent
grounds and sources, and thus from being conjoined
into isolated qualities they become known as connected into existing things, it is now our business fully
to investigate. By this distinction of operation, as
connecting and not *constructing* agent, we have wholly
separated it from the faculty of the sense already examined, and in this isolation of being, the claim is, that
we attain an apriori cognition of how it is possible
that such an operation of connection may be effected,
and thus how an understanding must be regulated in
its functions if it is to have any synthetic judgments

of philosophical relations, and this will give the understanding in its *Idea*. It will then be necessary in another Chapter, to attain in the facts a *Law* in actual operation, the precise correlative to this apriori idea, in which we shall have a valid science of the Understanding, as before of the Sense. We may then use these conclusions for an Ontological Demonstration of the valid being of the objects given in the understanding.

CHAPTER I.

THE UNDERSTANDING IN ITS SUBJEC-
TIVE IDEA.

SECTION I.

THE UNDERSTANDING NECESSARILY DISCURSIVE.

Conjunction gives definite form in space and time, and thus all conception of its products is of that which is brought directly under an intuition either pure or enpirical. But such products can have no other relationship to each other in our knowledge, than that which belongs to the forms of space and time. They may be *conjoined* in space or time, but cannot thus be known as *connected* in their own internal being. A dynamical connection cannot be constructed, and cannot therefore, be accurately defined; it can admit only of a description which shall suggest, not of a definition which shall make to appear. The bond which constitutes the relation is thought as inherent in the conception related, and thus while the related conceptions are constructed, the bond as their inherent connective is not and cannot be constructed, but is a new conception of a very peculiar kind. Thus two billiard balls may be constructed in space, and the meeting of the one in motion with the other at rest and the consequent displacement of the latter may be constructed in time, and the point in space and in time of their actual contact may be given in an intuition by the construction ; but all this will not in the least serve to give the conception of the dynamical bond, which we may in this case call *impulse*, that inherently connects the impinging of the first and the displacement of the last together. This conception of impulse, here, is not only new numerically, but quite new generically ; the conception of the balls, and their contact, and their antecedent and consequent motion, all admitting of a construction and thus of an accurate definition in the immediate intuition, but the conception of impulse not at all admitting of such construction, definition, and direct intuition. It can only be *thought*, not *perceived*.

Precisely thus, with all connection as *ground;* it can no more be constructed, than can the connection of impulse above given as *source* of the displacement of the second ball. The form of the whiteness and that of the hardness of the ivory ball may be constructed in the vision and the touch, and both may be referred to the same place and the same period intuitively, and thus a definite conception of their relationship in space and time may be attained, but this will not at all serve to give the common ground in which both the whiteness and the hardness inhere, and which gives to them the relations of qualities in one thing. This last is a conception as connection, and not at all as conjunction; it is only thought, it cannot be perceived. It belongs wholly to the understanding in its work of connection, and cannot be attained by the sense in its work of conjunction.

And, now, to distinguish this conception of the bond as product of the operation of connection from the product in the operation of conjunction, we must appropriate an exclusive term. The whiteness and hardness, the motion, contact and displacement of the billiard balls we call *phenomena*, because they are made to immediately appear in a definite construction. They may differ as *quality* connected in their ground, and as *event* connected in their source; but all are alike phenomena, inasmuch as each is made to appear, and all are given in the sense. The antithetic term to phenomenon, from the same Greek language, would be *noumenon*; but as this has been much less familiarly incorporated into the English language we shall, at the expense of derivation from another tongue, take an equivalent term for this antithesis from the Latin *notio*, and call this new conception, which the understanding in its work of connection can alone supply, *Notion*. This is to have its exclusive application to this specific conception—the bond of relationship as product of connection; and never to be applied to any product of conjunction. Thus we shall not say a no-

tion of hardness, whiteness, motion, contact, displacement, &c., all of which come under the term phenomenon; but we shall say a notion of the ground, source,
&c., for the connection of phenomena. Phenomena
will be conjoined by phenomena, but can be connected
only by the notion. The phenomenon is wholly in
the sense, the notion is wholly in the understanding.

The notion, as supplied by the understanding, is
put under the phenomena as substratum in which
they inhere, or as source on which they depend; and,
as it is a peculiar operation of the Intellect which supplies this notion, and makes it to *stand under* the phenomena as their connection, so this function of the intellect, as faculty for connection, is appropriately
termed *the understanding.* The same intellect *conjoins* the diversity—and this is the faculty of the sense
—which *connects* the phenomena—and this is the faculty of the understanding.

This connecting of phenomena in their grounds and
sources by the understanding is the act of *thinking*,
and the product should be termed a *philosophical judgment*, distinguishing it from the process of conjoining in
unity, which is the act of *attending*, and the product of
which, as intuitively affirmed, is a *mathematical judgment.* Both are synthetic, inasmuch as both attain a
new conception in which the relationship is given;
but in one case, as the mathematical, the new conception is attained by an immediate intuition in a construction; and in the other, the philosophical, the new

conception cannot be constructed and thus cannot be intuition, but is wholly supplied as thought or notion from the understanding. This connecting of phenomena in their notion is *pure thinking*, when the phenomena are not given in the sense, but are merely the conceptions of phenomena by a prolepsis or anticipation purely mental. The whole work is thus entirely intellectual. The anticipated content is constructed in the sense when there is no actual sensation, and is thus a conceived phenomenon only; and the notion, as connective, is wholly supplied by the understanding as pure conception also; and thus the whole process, though combining both intellectual conjunction and intellectual connection, is wholly a mental conception and therefore pure thinking. *Empirical thinking* is, when real phenomena are thought as connected in their grounds or sources. This last is properly *experience*—the connecting of our perceived phenomena in their notions, as their ground or source of being. When phenomena are thought as connected in their ground, the product is called *a thing;* when as connected in their source, the product is an *event*; and when both thing and event are conceived simply as originated being, they are *facts—(res gestæ.)*

This connecting of things and events may go on indefinitely, and when it is pure thinking, the whole product is *a train of thought*; when empirical thinking, it is *an order of experience.* This thinking in judgments in the understanding, it is manifest can never be made intuitive. The phenomenal conceptions may be constructed in their conjunctions of space and time, and their relationship of conjunction intuitively apprehended; but the notional conception cannot be constructed, nor intuitively seen in any construction, and thus the relationship of connection cannot be intuitively apprehended. We can never so construct the whiteness and the hardness of the billiard ball as intuitively to see the ground in which they are connected, nor so construct the impinging and the displacing as intuitively to see the source in one out of which the other springs. Our construction of the whiteness and hardness may give the *roundness* in space, and we may thus call it a *ball;* but this is still only quality and not ground. The qualities of whiteness and hardness and roundness are all thought as in one and the same ground, which we call *ivory*; but this ground, called ivory, is wholly supplied as a notion, and not at all as an intuition. So also, our construction of the impinging and the displacing may give *succession* in time, and we may thus call one antecedent and the other consequent, and the whole in combination *sequence;* but this also is still event, not source. The events of impinging, and displacing, and their sequence, are all thought as in one point of connection which is a source that we here call *impulse;* but this source, called impulse, is wholly supplied by the understanding as a notion, and not by the sense as an intuition. So must it ever be in all thinking in

the understanding that the connective in the judgment
can never be supplied by a construction, and can thus
never be made an intuition.   The difference between
the mathematical judgment that a straight line is the
shortest that may be drawn between two points, and
the philosophical judgment that the whiteness and
hardness are qualities of the ivory, or that the displacement of the second ball by the first was from impulse, is at once palpable.   In the first, as mathematical judgment, we construct the conceptions and we
intuitively see in our construction the new conception
of relationship, which we name *the shortest;* but in
the other, we can possibly make no construction that
shall give intuitively the new conception of relationship, which we name *the ivory* as ground or the *impulse* as source; and from which connectives only can
we form our philosophical judgment.

In the philosophical judgment, we are obliged to
receive the notion, as connective, from the understanding; and then, the relationship is always apprehended only by a *discursus* through that notion; and thus
the judgment is necessarily *discursive,* not intuitive.
We go from the whiteness to the hardness, in our connecting of these as qualities in a thing, through the
notion of ivory as common substratum; and we go
from the impinging to the displacing, in our connecting
of these as events, through the notion of impulse as
source in the antecedent for the origination of the consequent.   The judgment can only be formed from the

process of connection; and the connection can only be made in the notion; and the notion is supplied by no possible intuition. We can thus connect, i. e. think in the understanding, in no other possible manner than discursively. The understanding is faculty only for connecting, not for constructing; for thinking, not for attending; for discursively concluding, not for intuitively beholding. It attains philosophical judgments, not mathematical axioms. Its judgments are truly apriori, inasmuch as they are conditional for all experience. That I have the sensation of warmth may be given in the sense, and when, and how much; but all this will be isolated sensation and not connected experience, except as I can connect that sensation with other sensations in their common grounds and sources, and say the sun or the fire warms me. But in order to such judgment in experience that the sun warms me, I must apriori assume the notions of both ground and source, and, discursively, through these conclude upon the judgment in experience. The experience does not and cannot give the notion, the notion is conditional for the connected experience.

That the notional is conditional for all experience, as a connection of the phenomena into things, should be fully apprehended, and may be very conclusively determined. Thus, I may have the definite and distinct qualities of a hardness, a coldness, a brittleness, a transparency, &c. as real phenomena in perception, but they are all, necessarily, separate from each other

22

as given in perception, and no conjunction can go any further than to give to each its complete form as phenomenon, and let them stand singly and separately in the consciousness. But when the understanding has supplied its notion of a ground common to them all, the thinking may then connect them all in it by a discursus from one to another through it, and give to this notion as connective ground a name as thing, and of which the phenomena will all be held in a judgment as common properties or qualities, and I may then say, *the Ice* is hard, is cold, &c. My perception in the sense has given the phenomena only; my thinking in the understanding has given me all the separate phenomena to be connected in one thing; but such a judgment that the one thing—Ice—contained in itself all these phenomena as its qualities, and which is essential to a proper experience of such qualities, could not be attained except I had first assumed this notion of a common ground, through which to make my discursus in thinking the phenomena respectively to inhere in it. So, in the same manner I may perceive the phenomena of a liquidness, limpidness, fluidity, &c., and by a supplied notional as ground I may connect them as the properties of one thing and call it *water ;* and then again, I may perceive the phenomena of volatility, expansibility, elasticity, &c., and connect them in a common ground in the understanding and call it *vapor ;* and as the result, I shall have the three things with their respective qualities, as ice, water, and vapor. Neither of these things could have been given in an experience, but only the distinct phenomena in perception, except as the understanding had supplied their notional connectives, and thought them in a judgment discursively thereby.

But, still further, with these three things distinct in a judgment of experience, I may proceed in the understanding and supply a higher notional connective as common source for them all, and think these three things to have successively come out of one and the same material substance, which has now been ice, and now water, and now vapor, and thus on through all possible changes. But it is manifest that no such connection in this comprehensive judgment of an experience could have been effected except as first this higher notional, as common source, had been supplied in the understanding. And thus ever, in all our judgments of experience, whether more or less comprehensive, the experience does not give the connection, but the connection produces the judgment of experience, and this rests wholly upon a supplied notional in the understanding. No possible thinking in discursive judgments can be effected, and thus no experience can be, except through the use of a notion supplied in the understanding. The judgment cannot be *in* the sense, for the sense cannot supply the notional, nor make the discursive connection through it; but the judgment is *according to* the sense, for it must be the connection of only such phenomena as are given in the sense. We may thus say of the understanding, that it is a higher faculty than the sense, but though transcending the sense, it yet is a faculty judging according to the sense. It connects only what is first given in the sense.

SECTION II.

SPACE AND TIME THE NECESSARY MEDIA FOR DETERMINING CONNECTION THROUGH A DISCURSUS.

THINKING is the intellectual operation of connecting the conceptions supplied in the sense through the conceptions supplied in the understanding. The sense-conceptions are of the phenomenal, the understanding-conceptions are of the notional. The intellectual process is ever from one sense-conception to another by a discursus through an understanding-conception, and the judgment resulting is wholly synthetical—adding the necessary connection of the phenomenal in the notional—and thereby giving universality to the ultimate judgment, as, that all phenomena must stand in some ground, or must originate in some source. And the great question is—how verify this synthesis? How show that the addition of the notional as necessary and universal connective in such judgments is valid? All experience and all inductive science rest alike upon such synthetic judgments, and the former is wholly an illusion, and the latter a mere straining of speculations through a fictitious notional which can leave in the sieve only an empty ideal, except as this whole process of thinking in judgments may receive an apriori determination.

If we attempt to explain such necessary connection, as did Hume, through the frequency of observation in experience, and thus that habit only induces the conviction of necessary connection, we leave the judgment to rest upon mere credulity; and all experience and all philosophical science stand upon no firmer basis than " a belief" engendered in " custom." If we say with Brown, that there are only the phenomena in a certain " invariable order of sequences," and that all conviction of necessary connection is from the constitution of the human mind alone, which is so made that by a ceaseless and infallible prophecy it simply foretells the coming of the consequent in the appearance of the antecedent, we leave again all validity to experience and inductive science wholly amid the mysteries of this constitutional and instinctive prophesying. To take, with Reid, this necessary connection as the mere dictum of common sense, and make this an ultimate fact in which all experience and all philosophy must begin and back of which no investigation can reach, is to admit at once that experience and philosophy have only an assumed original, and that neither can possibly return back and examine the source in which it originates, nor expel the bane of skepticism from either the fountain or its streams.

When we have demonstrated the reality of the phenomena by our foregoing apriori process, still all the above methods of accounting for the conviction of the necessary connection of the phenomena leaves the whole as a mere matter of credulity or assumption, and no thinking can terminate in a judgment that shall have any higher validity than mere opinion. The roundness, whiteness, hardness, &c. are veritable phenomena; but that they are all connected by an inherence in one notion as their ground, and which we call "ivory," and are thus qualities in one thing, we may believe or hold as opinion but can never determine. The motion of one ball, and its contact with another, and the retardation in the first and displacement of the last ball are real phenomena; but that the retardation and displacement are connected in one source with the motion and the contact which precede them, and which as connective notion we call "impulse," and thus that they are events held together by one agency, we may believe or opine, but we can never know. And all philosophy founded upon any induction of such facts, however broadly and carefully made, must also alike rest only upon mere opinion. We are in this position utterly precluded from all power of reply to that skeptic who shall affirm that he has examined all these sources of a necessary connection, and has satisfied himself that their whole induced conviction is a mere mist and fog-bank deceptively rising over a stagnant understanding, and which is utterly dissipated into thin air whenever the sunlight strikes upon it from above, or the ebb and flow of active thought agitates it from beneath. But, surely, the interest in the human mind for science, and the intellectual yearning for established truth will never permit an aquiescence in such desponding conclusions, until skepticism has itself become a demonstration; and the only truth found to be this, that man can verify no truth; and that the only foundation for science is at last seen to be self-contradiction and absurdity.

The success in our apriori investigation of the sense, and our complete exposition of the operation of conjunction, should encourage to the same effort and anticipated result in the field of the understanding and the apriori explication of the operation of connection, and under the influence of so well grounded a hope the attempt to realise it should not be easily abandoned. We are not to take the understanding-conception upon trust, nor merely because we need it as our connective conditional for all possible thinking, and which can give for philosophy no other basis than an unverified empiricism; nor are we to assume it merely as the condition and law of our subjective thinking, and thereby attain those splendid ideal systems of nature, the soul, and God, which have so highly distinguished the great masters of modern German Metaphysics; but which, denying any thing as legitimately in the possession of philosophy beyond the subjective process itself, have only issued and for the future ever must only issue in the emptiness of an entirely misnamed Rationalism, and which at last is nothing else than the absurdity of a transcendental **Panthe-ism.** Subjective thinking and an objective experience differ not in this, that the sense-conceptions are not connected through the understanding-conceptions, for this is conditional for any connecting in discursive judgments whatever; but they differ in this, that in subjective thinking the intellectual operation of connection creates its own judgments within the self, and only for the self who thinks them, while in objective experience the whole process and its result in a judgment is conditioned by somewhat already existing other than the self, and the determination of this other existence in the judgment makes it to be objective to the self, and competent in the same way to be object to any other self possible. One gives wholly an ideal, the other an actual thing in the judgment. And, here, the task which we are to accomplish lies directly before us, viz. that we attain the operation of connection itself in its apriori elements so completely, that we may determine how, and how only, an objective experience is possible. In this will be attained the entire functions of an understanding in its possibility, and will thus be the understanding in its Idea after which we are seeking.

Sufficient has already been said to show that no determination of connection can be reached through an intuitive process. The judgment is inclusive of somewhat not admitting of construction, and thus not possible to be brought under an immediate beholding.

Conjunction is restricted to the field of the sense, and can by no means project itself within the field of the understanding, and thus it is utterly impracticable that an intuitive passage should ever be opened between them. Connection is wholly another work than conjunction, and intuitive affirmations wholly other cognitions than discursive judgments. No exposition nor use of the former can be of any significancy in determining the latter. The sense cannot think nor give any exposition of the process of thinking. Conjunction which is for the sense, simply brings into *colloca-tion;* connection, which is for thought in the understanding, requires an inner *coalition.* One is function for cognizing juxta-position, the other for cognizing an inherent concretion.

Since, therefore, all attempt of an apriori exposition by an intuitive process is wholly excluded, the alternative must be to take some media, if such may be found, by which it may discursively be determined how such objective connection may be, or which is the same thing, how an objective experience is possible. Such media must be common to both our subjective constructions of phenomena in the sense and our objective connection of them in an experience, or they can afford no occasion for a discursus from one to the other and consequently no determination of any connection having been effected between them. They must, moreover, be apriori conditional for both subjective construction and objective connection in an experience, inasmuch as our determination of such connection in experience is to be wholly apriori, and thus necessarily conditional for all objective connection. Only in such manner can any connection in an objective experience be possible. And now, such media may be found in Space and Time. We have already seen that all definite phenomena must have their definite place and their definite period, and thus that all construction of phenomena must be in a space and a time; all subjective constructions thus must have a space and a time. On the other hand, all objective things and events, as connection of phenomena in an experience, must be in space and time; and thus all objective connection of phenomena must have a space and a time. Space and time are thus common to both a construction of phenomena in the sense, and a connection of phenomena into things and events as experience in the understanding. Space and time are also apriori, that is, they are necessary and universal conditions for both construction of phenomena and connection of things, and may thus be used in an apriori investigation. And now, the design is to show, in the use of space and time, how it may be determined that constructed phenomena may be connected into things and events in an order of objective experience, and how only this may be done, and which will be the Understanding in its Idea.

SECTION III.

SPACE AND TIME EXCLUDE ALL DETERMINATION OF AN
EXPERIENCE EXCEPT IN THE CONNECTIONS OF
A NOTIONAL IN THE UNDERSTANDING.

THE conception of Experience is that of perceived
phenomena determined in their places in space and in
their periods in time.   Except as phenomena are given
there can be no experience, inasmuch as there is nothing which appears in the consciousness; and except as
the phenomena are determined in their places and periods there is nothing connected, but a mere rhapsody
of coming and departing appearances is given with no
possible significancy.   And now, that it may be found
how such an experience determined in space and
time may be, we say, that only three suppositions are
possible in which we may have the conception of phenomena in space and time, and only in one of these
suppositions, to the exclusion of both the others, can
we possibly determine the connections of these phenomena in their own places in space and their own
periods in time.

1. *There may be the conception that the phenomena
only are given, and that the space and time are constructed from them.*—A content given in sensibility
and conjoined into definite figure and period, will be

cognized as occupying a space and a time; this content may pass from the sensibility and other content may be given, which in its turn shall be conjoined into definite figure and period, and thus known as occupying a space and a time; and thus onwards indefinitely. So long as the construction which terminates the one conjoins itself with the construction that begins the other, the place and the period of the one may be determined relatively to the place and period of the other. If, when I have constructed the perception of a rod a yard in length, and thus know definitely the place it occupies; and then, as that content departs from the sense, I go on to construct the perception of a chain five yards in length, and thereby know definitely its place; and then perhaps continue the construction of a rope ten yards in length, and know its definite place; I may very well determine that the rod the chain and the rope occupy so much space, and what the place of each is in this whole space in relation to the others. So also in reference to time. If, when I constructed the rod, my conjoining movement occupied one moment; and the chain five moments; and the rope ten moments; I can very well determine the time of the whole, and the relative periods of each in the whole time. And so for any constructions contiguous in space and consecutive in time. But I do not thus at all determine what is their place and period in a whole of all space and time as given in an objective experience. My subjective construction has so far determined relative place and period, but what their relation to a whole of space and time I have not and cannot so determine. They are continuous, but in what direction relatively to all space, and in what succession relatively to all time, I can thus know nothing. If my constructing agency had terminated with the rod, and then a chasm had intervened with nothing in the sense to construct, and consequently nothing in the consciousness, when I awoke in the self-conscious act of constructing the chain and effected it definitely in its own place and period, yet could I not then determine its direction and distance in the one whole of space from the place of the rod, nor in one whole of time from the period of the rod ; and so with all other constructions in sense. When the constructing agency ceases, then conscious extension and duration ceases ; and the places and periods can be determined only relatively to the uninterrupted constructions. All is isolated in its own definite place and period, and can never determine its relationship to a whole of space and of time.

This is so in reference to the self whose agency conjoins in space and time. There is a contiguity of places in space, and a continuity of periods in time, as the uninterrupted coming and departing of phenomena are definitely constructed ; but these are determined in place and period only relatively to such as are comprehended in the uninterrupted constructions, and this only in reference subjectively to the self who

constructs them. So *his* phenomena have been ; **and**
and as he has constructed them, so *his* spaces and
times have been ; but what phenomena, and what
spaces and times have been for other constructing
selves, we may not by any possible means determine.
His phenomena in their places and periods have been
for him and theirs have been phenomena place and period for them, nor can either say any thing what relatively one may be to the others.   Thus, from mere perception can the phenomena be determined in space and
time only relatively as comprehended in a continuous
construction ; and this, even, for no other self than
subjectively for the constructing agent. *Materialism*
must thus proceed, but must thus also fail to determine an experience in space and time.

2. *There may be the supposition that space and time, as*
thought in a whole of all space and of all time, may de-
termine the connection of phenomena in an experience.
—It may be seen that by beginning with the perception, as in the former case, it is wholly impracticable
that any whole of all space and of all time should be
cognized.   For every new construction there is a new
space and time which is cut off and isolated from all
other spaces and times, and no conjoining can bring all
places into one space, nor all periods into one time ; and
thus it must be forever impossible that coming and departing phenomena in perception should ever be determined in their places and periods in one whole of
space and one whole of time.   It may then be sough

to attain first a whole of all space and of all time, and determine the places and periods of all phenomena in them by space and time themselves, as each a whole. It is necessary, therefore, to examine this process which *Idealism* would take to determine an experience in space and time.

It is not difficult to think space and time in their totality, and to expound the process of the understanding in so doing. This we will first attend to and then show its utter incompetency for determining an experience in space and time. The conception of Space as a total of all spaces is attained as follows: by a process of pure thought in the understanding, not at all by a conjunction of places as in juxta-position in the sense. A notional connective is assumed as everywhere pervading all places, and in this thought of an all-pervading connective, all possible places are brought into a coalition and made to belong to one concrete immensity of all space. Not a conjoining act, which takes spaces as in the diverse and constructs them into a total space; but an all-pervading connective is thought as already in space, holding it in one universal immensity as first in conception, in order that any place may be taken as within space. There can, thus, be no chasm as a void of space around any definite place, as must ever be with all constructions in the sense; but this all-pervading connective of spaces is a universal plenum to space, and therefore all places are held by it as in the one whole of space, and readily

determinable in direction and distance each from any
other in the one whole.   There can be no separation
of spaces, inasmuch as the all-pervading connective
ever holds space in one whole, and while divisions
may appear *in* space, separations cannot be made *of*
space.   The understanding-conception of space is
not thus an aggregate of spaces in juxta-position, but
one concrete whole in its all-pervading connective,
inseparable and immovable both as a whole or in any
interchange of its parts.   Such notional connective
into one immensity of all space gives to its conception
in the understanding but one possible mode, viz : that
of *absolute permanence.*   Every place in space has its
own permanent position, in reference to the one immensity of space and to all other places.

The understanding-conception of Time, also, as a
total of all periods is attained in pure thought thus.
A notional connective as ever-abiding is assumed to
hold through all periods, and thereby making all possible periods adhere together in the one eternity of duration.   This, again, is no construction of a whole time
out of diverse times conjoined in unity by bringing
them in collocation, as in the sense ; but the perduring
connective of all periods already first holds all times
in one Time, in order that any period may afterwards
be taken as in the one whole of all time.   There
can, thus, be no chasms in time as if there were intervals in which is no time, thereby isolating definite
periods in their own times, as in the sense ; but this

all-abiding connective makes one eternity of time, and all possible periods to be in it, and each inseparable from it, and determinable in succession relatively to any other period. Time, thus, cannot be sun lered, but only things in time can be sundered in their different periods. Time in the understanding is not the conception of single, separate, and fleeting periods; but an ever-abiding, all-embracing duration.

The conception of time as one whole, is not like space restricted to *one mode* as permanence, but has *three modes*, which, as given in pure thought, it is here important should be clearly apprehended. When we take the conception of time in its ever-abiding connective, holding all periods within itself as the same perduring whole of all time; we have one mode of time which may be distinguished as the *perpetuity* of time. When, again, we have the conception of this all-abiding connective holding all possible periods within itself as a series, such that no one can be reached except in the coming and departing of all periods which precede it; we have another mode of time which may be distinguished as the *succession* of time. And, lastly, when we have the combined conceptions of the perpetuity and succession of time, such that in the perpetual, no period of the successive can be coetaneous with any other period, but that each stands for itself only in the same point of all time, and can thus only be in the same time with itself and not in the time of any other period; we have a third mode of

23

time which we may designate the *simultaneousness* of time.   These three, the perpetual successive and simultaneous, are all the possible modes of time, and are quite distinct each from each.   The perpetuity of time, is the mode of perduring in all periods; the succession of time, is the mode of a progressus through all periods; and the simultaneousness of time, is the mode of a standing in its own position for every period.   While in a sense-conception we should say, as *fleeting* as time, in the understanding-conception of the first mode we say as *lasting* as time; while, again, in the sense, we have the *alteration* of time, in the understanding as second mode we have the *continuance* of time; and finally, while in the sense we have the *indeterminateness* of time, in the understanding as the third mode we have the *exactness* of time.

And now, with this attainment in the understanding of space and time in their universality, so that all places may be thought as in one time, and thus all places be determinable in distance and direction each from each in the one space, and all periods determinable in their successions relatively to each other in the one time, it may be supposed that thus the phenomena given in sense can be determined to their places in space and their periods in time.   And so they might be if they were but *ideal conceptions* as in our thought of the modes of space and time.   When I conceived of a rod, a chain, a rope, &c. as before; I should put these conceived phenomena in some place of my understanding-conception of all space as a whole, and thus in thought their direction and distance could be readily determined in the whole of all space. And so also in time, I should put the conception of their appearing in some period of my understanding-conception of all time as a whole, and thus their ideal period could be readily determinable from all other periods in my thought of a whole of all time, as whether before or after, and how much in each case. But, this would leave the whole to be subjective merely. It is *my* thought of space and of time as a whole, and *my* conception of the phenomena to be put in space and time and their places and periods to be determined; and their determination is only ideal and subjective, for myself and with no possible significancy for any other self. In this way no objective experience can possibly be given, determined in space and time.

And further, should it be assumed that each self has, as understanding-conception the same space and time each as a whole; and that it is a law of thought that an understanding working any where should attain to just such modes of space and time;—which must be mere assumption that every man's space and time is precisely as every other man's space and time —yet could not the real phenomena, which each man should perceive, be determined to their places and periods in an objective experience. The same space and time would be for each man, but his perceptions of phenomena would differ, and appear in different places and different periods, and each would have his own world for himself, with no community of common phenomena in the same place and in the same period as others. The appearing of the phenomena would determine all the connections in space and time, and this would differ as the perceptions came and went with every individual. The permanent mode of the one space, for all, could not determine the connections of the phenomena appearing in it, for all; inasmuch as while the phenomena were perceived, the space could not be perceived, but could only be thought. And so with the three modes of time, which it is now conceded all might have alike, they could not determine the connections of the phenomena appearing in time to be perduring, successive or contemporaneous; for while the phenomena were perceived, the modes of time could only be thought, and cannot be made to have phenomenal appearance. I can determine the place of one phenomenon arising in a lake and then sinking, compared with another phenomenon afterwards arising and sinking, and can tell their bearing and distance; but this is because the lake is itself perceived, and connects and determines the places of the appearance; but such is not space and time as a whole; they are thought, not perceived.

While, then, it may be admitted that the understanding in pure thought might attain to the modes of space and time as each a whole, yet could not this possibly avail to connect the phenomena appearing in space and time and determine their places and periods in an objective experience. If all might have, from some inner law of thought, the same modes of space and time, this could not give to them a common experience in perception; for their ideal subjective space and time, though admitted to be the same in all, yet can be perceived by none, and only thought, and cannot thus be any media for connecting and determining in their places and periods, the phenomena which may be perceived by each. It is not necessary that we expose the assumption of a universal law of thought, that would give to every understanding the same space and time from each one's own pure thinking, which resolves all into an arbitrary constitution of an understanding, and knows no reason for such a law rather than any other, and which involves the teacher of the doctrine in dogmatism and his disciples in credulity; but we may pass it all by, since when admitted, it is yet utterly in vain for all objective experience.

3. There remains only this other supposition possible, *that perhaps a notional connective for the phenomena may determine these phenomena in their places and periods in the whole of all space and of all time, and so may give both the phenomena and their space and time in an objective experience.*—By using the conception of space and time as the media for ascertaining how an experience in space and time may be possible, we have now already excluded the two methods of *Sen-*

sualism and *Idealism*, and found that neither the perception of phenomena, nor the thought of a whole of space and of time, can by any possibility give an experience determined in its connections in space and time. We are thus shut up to the one remaining process of conceiving a notional connective for the phenomena, which shall condition them in their appearance and thereby in their places and periods, and thus determine their connections in space and time objectively. It is much to have now found the only possible medium of connection between the sense and the understanding, and that if the passage be at all made it must be at this point and through this medium. And that it may here be effected is quite probable from the advantage over the other suppositions, that in this we may use both the sense and the understanding, and combine perception and thought in one process; the impossibility of which, in the former cases, having been found as the source of their helplessness. So far as appearance in perception is concerned, we may conjoin the diversities as space and time, and the conjunction is the sum or aggregate of the diverse brought into unity. The two conceptions of quantity intuitively give the third as the total in combination. But we do not inquire, in determining an experience in space and time, *how much* space or time is occupied? but *where*, in a whole of all space and of time, the phenomenon is? We have here three terms demanding for their combination the interposition of a fourth, and that fourth cannot be attained by intuition, but must be sought as a medium through which, by a discursus, the three may find their connection. We have the three conceptions given in the different phenomena, and the conception of their place or their period; and we need to find that which shall determine their connection in all. The phenomenal and the place or the period cannot determine the *connection* of each other, but can merely stand in *conjunction*. If now we may assume a notional as connective for the phenomenal, and determining also the connection of the place or period in a whole of space and of time, so that the notional as existing thing determines both the connection of the phenomena and the place or period at the same time, we shall have in this notional the fourth conception which the exigency of our problem demands. We will in the next section, give the method of demonstrating apriori such a possible connection, and thus a possible experience determined in space and time; and in this will be exposed all the *apriori* Elements which enter into the operation of connection, and which give the functions of an understanding in its idea.

SECTION IV.

THE APRIORI ELEMENTS OF THE OPERATION OF CONNECTION, GIVING A POSSIBLE EXPERIENCE DETERMINED IN SPACE AND TIME.

EXPERIENCE is the connection of the phenomenal as determined in space and time. The perception of the phenomenal cannot give such determination, inasmuch as the one whole of all space and of all time cannot so be attained. In perception we can only conjoin the diverse in unity, but we cannot connect all such constructions as in one concrete whole. Nor by mere thinking of the places and periods as in one whole of space and of time can we connect the phenomenal in an objective experience, since the phenomenal is a real appearance which will not conform to our assumed modes of space and time and give uniformity of experience to all, and also because that our whole of space and of time is but ideal and the product of pure thought, and cannot thus be perceived so that the ideal of space might connect the phenomena in their places or the ideal time in their periods. And as the whole of space and of time can be no media in perception for connecting phenomena, so it may, moreover, be added, that in the thought space and time can be no dynamical connectives for any phenomena. We can neither see the connections of the phenomena in their places and periods in space and time, nor can we think the phenomena to be connected in their places and periods by space and time.

But one possible method now lies open. The phenomena must themselves be so connected in their grounds and sources of being, that every perception of them shall be conditioned by this notional ground to its place in space for each, and by this notional source to its period in time for each. It is now the design to show how, in this way, an experience determined in its connections in space and time is possible; and in the process we shall attain the complete operation of Connection in all its apriori Elements.

First we will attain to a possible determination of experience in *Space*.

Let there be the conception of a *force* in a place, which maintains its equilibrium about a central point and completely fills a definite space, and which forbids all intrusion within its place except in its own expulsion from it, and we will here call that conception of force *the space-filling force*. Its equilibrium every way upon its own center secures that it must remain steadfast in its own place, unless disturbed by some interfering force *ab extra*, and thus constancy and impenetrability are the necessary apriori modes of its being. This space-filling force is altogether a notion, and impossible that it should be other than an understanding-conception, and yet it is manifest that it may be an occasion for phenomena as appearing in consciousness. To the sensibility in an organ of touch it opposes a resistence to muscular pressure, and may thus furnish the content in sensation for comparative hardness or softness, smoothness or roughness, and for figure and motion as yielding to pressure. It may also give content to the sensibility in any other possible organization when the requisite conditions are supplied; as through the light, colors; and through the air, sounds; and through an effluvia of its own, smells; and through a dissolving sapidity, tastes. It cannot itself become appearance but thought only, and yet it may manifest itself through a sensibility in all possible quality, and while its mode of being in the understanding is that of a force constant and impenetrable, its mode of being in the sense is that of its perceived quality in the manifold phenomena it occasions. The occasion for its own manifested mode of being in the sense is determined in its mode as given in the understanding, and this, when the conditions are supplied, to any sensibility that may bring its content within any self-consciousness. It thus determines its own content in all sensibility as conditioning the constructing agency, and secures its phenomena to be objective in each, and itself as ground the same object to all. The place in which the conjoining agency must construct the figure of its phenomena in the vision or the touch, is the same in the same self-consciousness at every repetition of the construction, inasmuch as the space-filling force is constant in its place and constant as occasion for phenomenal content in the sensibility ; and for the same reasons, the place must be the same to all possible self-consciousnesses within which the figure of the phenomena shall be constructed. Whether, then, the content be constantly in the sensibility or not—i. e. whether the eye be constantly in the direction of the object or not, or whether the touch be constantly upon it or not—the constant space-filling force in the understanding determines the constructed phenomena to be in the same place at every appearance, and for every percipient.

Not, then, as in the sense only, in which every phenomenon must come and depart in its own appearance and disappearance and its own definite figure in place come and depart with it, and thus the places be as isolate as the phenomena with no possibility of determining them in one whole of all space ; but, with the coming and departing phenomena in the sense, we have here the space-filling force which occasions them conceived to be constant in the same place, and thereby determining their appearance to be in the same place, and this same place fixed in its one position in the one immensity of universal space. And now, it matters not how many such space-filling forces be conceived as each in its own place, and giving occasion each to its own phenomenal quality in the sense ; since all will be in a determinate relationship each to each in direction and distance in the one space which contains them all, and this also for all who shall perceive their phenomena. This determination of the relative bearing and distance of different objects in space from each other still, however, is conditioned on the same conception of the space-filling force in the understanding. If there be concieved any place in which there is no space-filling force, then in that place there is nothing which may occasion phenomenal content, and as nothing can there be perceived, so it is manifest that nothing of place can be determined. Such a chasm of all space-filling being would necessitate an utter void of all experience, and it could never be determined how broad such chasm·is; in what direction from each other the phenomena on each side of it were; nor where in the one universal space, such chasm as a void of all being was situated. A chasm of all being in void space of a cubic yard would as effectually cut off all experience on one side from all determinate relationship to any experience that might be on the other side, as would a void which might receive a thousand suns and their several rolling systems. Whether there may be such voids of all being in space or not, or whether all of being may be circumsphered by such a void space, is not at all affirmed or denied here, but only this, that a determined experience in spaee can be possible so far forth only as a space is occupied by a space-filling force, giving occasion in its own constancy of being for constant phenomena to appear in the consciousness. The conception of a removal into a void space beyond all occasions for perceiving a phenomenal universe, would preclude all possibility for determining the place in the immensity of space which that universe occupies. Only as space is filled with that which, as understanding-conception, is competent to furnish constant occasion for that which, as sense-conception, may constantly appear, is it possible that any determination of space should be given in experience? Communication from one phenomenon to another, and thus from one determined place to another, can only be thought as possible where a plenum of being in space gives occasion for a continuous appearance from place to place.

In this manner, and in this only, is it possible that experience should be determined in space. A ground must be given in the space-filling notional for the construction of the continued phenomenal, and the space-filling ground will determine all its phenomena constructed in their definite places to be in the same place; and this, occasioning continued appearance, will determine its place in one universal space.

But, it is now manifest that this space-filling force is the constant subsistence in which the phenomenal qualities inhere. The connection is that of *subsistence and inherence.* But this subsisting notional, which in the understanding is constant, is the same conception as that of *Substance;* and the inhering phenomenal, which, though having occasion for a continual appearing, may yet come and go in the sense and may therefore be quality as accidentally inhering, is the conception of *Accidence;* and thus we have the apriori condition, that the determination of an experience in space rests upon the connection of subsistence and inherence, and which necessitates the being of Substance and Accidence. The first apriori Element in an operation of Connection is, therefore, that of *Substance and Accidence.*

We will next examine how an experience determined in *Time* is possible.

All consciousness of time depends upon the modifications of the internal state. Except as changes occur in the inner sense, it must be impossible to apprehend that a time is passing. This capability of the inner sense to be modified lies already as primitive Intuition in the self, and the capacity of the intellectual agency to move over the inner sense and thus modify the internal state, makes it possible that a subjective time should be brought within consciousness and constructed into definite periods. Thus, I may conjoin the primitive diversity in space in unity and thereby construct a definite figure in space, as a mathematical line. The movement of my intellectual agency in such construction would change the inner state, in the passing of the intellectual agency through the diverse points in the primitive intuition of space, and thereby give in the consciousness the apprehension that a time was passing. This, it is mani-

fest, must be wholly subjective, and the consciousness
for myself only that a time was passing, inasmuch as
it would be only *my* affection of inner state and by
my intellectual action.   Both the definite time as figure in space, and the definite period in time in which
the constructing agency was passing, would be of no
significancy except in *my* self-consciousness.   Every
point in the diversity of space through which the conjoining agency passed may be conceived as that which
the moving agency successively occupied, and as thus
standing in it, each point may be called an *instant* of
time; and each interval from point to point may be
conceived as that through which the intellectual
agency in the construction of the line moved, and
which may thus be called a *moment* of time; the diversity in the primitive intuition of time may thus be
considered as instants or moments, according to a
conception of the points in the inner state to be affected or a conception of the moving agency from one
point to another.   As the agency stands in the point
it is an instant, as it moves from the point it is a
moment; and as each moment is a new modification
of the internal state, there is a succession of affections
going on in the inner sense, and thus the consciousness of a passing time.   So long as my intellectual
agency is thus passing from moment to moment a
time is passing in my consciousness which I may construct into a definite period; but when my intellectual agency ceases, all apprehension of passing mo-

ments must cease, and I can be no longer conscious that a time is passing. If again my intellectual agency pass from moment to moment, and I construct again a definite period, this last can have no determinate relation to the former, for a chasm of all consciousness of a passing time separates them, and it were impossible that I should bring them into any conjunction in self-consciousness. Every period, as subjective time, is thus separate from all other periods, and all determination of any period in relation to one whole of time is impossible. The pure sense can only give its pure periods as separate, and thus the conception of time in it cannot be of the one time but the manifold times.

And so also with respect to phenomena in their periods. When any content in the sense is constructed in a definite figure in space, the intellectual agency gives the instants as it stands in the diverse points and the moments as it passes from point to point, as it does in a pure construction, and thus there is the consciousness that a time is passing; and when this is constructed in a definite period, it is known as the time in which the phenomenon appears in consciousness. But this phenomenon thus constructed is *objective* in this, that the content in the sensibility has not been produced by the intellectual agency, and has only been constructed in its figure in space and its period in time by it. The quality, as real appearance, has from somewhere beside the agency of the self been given to it, and the agency of the self has constructed its form in space and time. Yet, while as real appearance the quality is objective, yet is the space and time in which it appears *subjective* only. It has been constructed in its definite period by *my* agency only and as it has affected my inner sense, and thus its period has no significancy except in *my* self-consciousness. When, therefore, I have constructed one phenomenon in its period, and that phenomenon has passed, the constructing agency ceases and thus the internal state ceases to have any successive modifications, and thereby all consciousness that a time is passing becomes impossible. Where some new content in the sensibility is again constructed in its definite period, that phenomenon in its period is wholly separate from the former phenomenon in its period, and the chasm of all possible conjunction of time between them prevents all possibility of determining their relationship in one time. Phenomena in the sense cannot be conceived as in one time, but their times are manifold. How, then, may phenomena, in their definite separate periods, be conceived as possible to be determined in their relationship in the universal objective time? And here we answer, as before in reference to determination in Space, that it is possible only as the phenomena are themselves necessarily connected in their relations. How this may be in reference to the three modes of Time, the perpetual successive and simultaneous, must now be explained; and such explanation com-

24

pleted will give to us the apriori Elements of the operation of connection, and thus complete the Idea of an Understanding. Each mode of time must be taken up separately, inasmuch as the manner of connection between the phenomenal and the notional must in each be different.

1. The apriori determination of an experience in *perpetual Time.*—The conception of a space-filling force giving occasion for continual phenomena, and which is substance with the phenomenal qualities inhering, is sufficient for determining a possible experience in space ; but though a necessary preliminary, this is not sufficient for determining a possible experience in time. The substance being constant in place, and giving occasion for continual phenomena in that place, is a sufficient condition for determining the bearing and distance in space of any other phenomenon, which may appear as inhering in its substance in its place, and which can be perceived in communion with the former phenomena. Such phenomena will be determined as in the same one objective space, and in their relative positions in that one space. A constant substance, as of a star in the heavens, giving occasion for a continual phenomenal brightness in that constant place, is sufficient for determining that any other brightness in its place which may appear in communion with it, is in the same universal space, and the bearings and distance which it has with the first may also be readily determined. But, if that

substance, constant in its place and occasion for continual phenomenal brightness, never give occasion for any alteration in its phenomenal brightness, all the change that would be possible to be effected by it in the inner state would be the modification of appearance and disappearance, i. e. of perceiving and of not perceiving the brightness. When the organ was so directed as to receive the content and construct the phenomenon in space, a time would be apprehended as passing in self-consciousness, but when the content had gone from the sense and no constructing agency was modifying the internal state, all apprehension of a passing time would be impossible. The modification of inner state would be only that of consciousness of a time and that of no consciousness of a time, and this simply as the modifications occurred in the inner state of the subject-self perceiving and not perceiving. That any such modification of internal state was occasioned by the substance and its phenomenal brightness could never be determined for any other self-conscious subject, but only for the perceiving and non-perceiving subject-self, and hence the passing of any time in the self-consciousness must be *subjective* only. That there was any one universal objective time, which must be the same in all subjects of self-consciousness, could not be thus determined.

But, now, we will conceive that this space-filling force, constant in the same place, becomes somehow so modified inherently as to be occasion of continual phenomenon but yet phenomenon in alteration. The same substance gives occasion now for perceiving one quality as phenomenon inhering in it, and again for perceiving another quality, and thus varying the mode in which the substance manifests itself in the sense. The substance itself thus conditions its phenomena, and the conditioned variations of phenomena condition a modification of internal state, and thus of a passing time in the self-conscious percipient; and this not merely from the arbitrary attention given by the perceiving self, but must be the same in all perceiving subjects of a self-consciousness. The substance itself conditions the variations in the phenomena perceived, and thus of the alterations of the inner sense and thereby of the apprehension of a passing time, and this for all possible percipients of the varied phenomena; and, therefore, for all possible subjects of self-conscious apprehension of this passing time, it must be the same time and objective to them all. Moreover, this same substance perdures through all modifications, and thus through all variations of its phenomena, and thereby determines them all as they arise and depart still to inhere in the same substance; and they, therefore, are all in continuous connection in their perpetual variations. The period of each varied phenomenon is connected in the one time through which the one substance perdures, and thus all the periods of continuous varied phenomena are in the one perpetual time through which the substance perdures, and this for all possible percipients of these varied phenomena in their varying periods. One perpetual time embraces all the periods which can come up in any experience of these varying phenomena, and thus this substance constant in place is not only space-filling, but perduring through all periods is also a time-filling substance. The determination of any phenomenon in this continuous variation, to its relative period with the periods of all other phenomena in the one perpetual time, is in this manner manifestly possible. Let all phenomena, as they come and depart in continuous alteration, be thought as the varied appearances of the same one perduring substance, and it is possible to determine their whole experience to its proper periods in the one perpetual time, and only in their connection of phenomena can an experience be so determined.

And now, the connection here is manifestly still that of subsistence and inherence, inasmuch as it is substance and accidence still, but this connection is given in a modified manner, not as constant substance and accidence, but as perduring substance and varying accidence. The qualities inhering in the same substance alter, and thus the substance becomes in the thought *perpetual source* rather than *constant ground* of the phenomena; and the phenomena coming and departing are, in the thought, *depending events* rather than *inhering qualities*. The substance becomes the notion of source, and the accidence becomes the phenomenon of event, and the connection is that of *origin and dependence*, rather than as before of subsistence and inherence. We shall thus have the apriori element of connection in time to be a modification of the element found in connection in space, and which, though still substance and accidence, we may distinguish in its modified conception as Source and Event. The *first* apriori Element of connection is, in Space, Substance and Accidence; and this as still the same though modified in the conception is, in perpetual Time, *Source and Event*.

2. The apriori determination of an experience in *successive Time.*—The perdurance of the time-filling force, as source for all the varying phenomena which as event depend upon it, would be sufficient for determining all their events in their several periods as occurring in the same perpetual time. The period of one could not be when the period of another was, but the events must come up singly into the experience, and thus be alternate in every self-consciousness. But with no other conception than that of source and event as element of connection, it would be impossible to determine any fixed order of succession in the one time for all percipients of the events, or precisely where in one progressus of all time the period of any event in our experience was. That the phenomena of fluidity, of congelation, and of vapor may all be the altered events from one source which I call water, is sufficient to determine that when one is the other can-

not be, and thus that all must somehow belong to one perpetual time, but if I have nothing further than the conception of the connection of origin and dependance, I cannot determine these alternations of events to any fixed order of succession in their period. That the phenomena alternate with each other at hap-hazard must leave the alternations of their periods in an equally indeterminate rhapsody of a coming and departing time, and when all phenomena are thus conceived as simply alternating each with each in their perpetual sources, it were impossible to determine that any experience was proceeding either backward or forward in time, or whether it were not a perpetual oscillation to and fro in time. There is no fixed point in the thought, and thus no determining of period as before and after in a whole of time. All experience, as it originates in one perduring source must be in one perpetual time, but as nothing determines the flow of period in time and only the alternation of periods, it were impossible to determine any order of succession to our experience in time.

But, if we will now conceive that a modification of the source gives the condition for the alteration of the event, and that this modification has a fixed order of progressus, such fixed order of modification in the thought will necessitate the order in the varied phenomena, and give the capability of determining the flow of experience in time, and the relative position of any period in time in which the experience occurs

Thus a substance, as water, may be an abiding source for the alternating phenomena of congelation, fluidity, steam, &c., but if we have the conception of source and event only, and thus the connection of origin and dependence alone, we can never determine from the mere alternations of events any order of progress, inasmuch as these alternations may be desultory, and go from fluidity to vapor or from fluidity to congelation with no necessary connection in the order of the series, though always originating in the same perpetual source. Such alternations of phenomena would condition corresponding variations in the internal state of the percipient subject, and the period of each might be definitely constructed and apprehended as in the same perpetual time from the connection of all in the same perduring source of being; yet these periods could not be determined in one progressive flow, but must conform to the alternating phenomena. There is nothing in the inner sense to determine the order of succession, except as some fixed thought be given as notional connection in the understanding. Let, therefore, the substance, water, be so modified as space-filling by combination with another distinguishable force, as caloric, that the congelation cannot appear except under such a given modification of the substance; and thus also with the phenomena of fluidity, and of steam; and at once a fixed order of succession in the phenomena is determinable, and thus also a fixed order in their periods in the inner sense, and the series must proceed in accordance with the progressus of the modifying force, caloric. The perception of the phenomena must be conditioned by the inherent modifications of their source. The determination of a fixed order of modifications in the thought will determine a fixed order of connection in the phenomena, and thus a fixed order in their periods and thereby a progressive flowing on in time. Some standard, as a perpetual on-going of modification of substance in the thought and of corresponding phenomena in the perception, must be taken, and it will render determinable in time the period of all possible varying phenomena that may be held in communion with it. If the series can only be a progressus and never a regressus; as for example, in the modifications of the expressed juice of the grape, through the sacharine vinous and acetous fermentations; or the order of the seasons; then an order of successive time may be determined, and all possible periods in which the phenomena may appear may be determined in their relative positions in this successive time, but impossible in any other connection.

This connection is that of *efficiency and adherence*, inasmuch as the modification of the source makes the variation of the phenomenon, and this as event is not mere sequence but necessary result as dynamical adherent. The substance thus is not mere source for an event, but an efficiency is thought to be in it which necessitates the kind of event, and thus the source becomes the exact conception of a Cause and the necessitated event is the precise conception of an Effect; and we have thus, as condition for determining phenomena in successive time, a *second* apriori Element of connection as *Cause and Effect*.

3. The apriori determination of an experience in *simultaneous Time*.—The connection of origin and dependence in the notion of source and phenomenon of event is sufficient for determining phenomena in perpetual time, and the connection of efficiency and adherence in the notion of cause and phenomenon of effect is sufficient for determining phenomena in a successive time; but quite another element of connection must now be attained for determining phenomena in simultaneous time. The modified source as cause makes the event to be what it is as an effect, and as the modifications in the source proceed, such also is the necessitated succession of effects; and as these phenomenal effects must modify the inner sense in the perception of them, so the periods of their appearing may be constructed and must be thought as in a fixed order of succession in time. But any number of such series of cause and effect may be conceived as passing on each in its own fixed order of progressus, and when the perception of these phenomenal effects is promiscuous from one series to another, it will be impossible from the connections which only run up and down the separate series to think any connection in communion each with each, and thereby to deter-

mine that any of the phenomena in each are contemporaneous, or, as the same thing, are in simultaneous time. Each can be determined to its position in its period according to the connections in its own series, for the thought has fixed the order of the progressus in that direction up and down the succession, but no one series has fixed any order of progressus in another series, and it cannot thus be said whether one event in one is before or after any event in another series. The thought has no fixed connections athwart the series, and it is therefore impossible to determine the period of one in its time as having any relation in time with the period in another. Thus, I may have the different modifications of the substance, water, giving the varied phenomena as successive events of congelation fluidity and steam, and when I think them as connection of cause and effect in a necessary order, I may determine the periods of each effect in their appearance in successive time. And, again, when I have the varied modifications of the substance, caloric, in the successive temperatures of cold, agreeable warmth, and hot, and think them in connection as cause and effect in a necessary order, I may determine the periods of such effects in my experience in successive time. But if, now, I can think no connection between the ice and the cold, the fluid and the agreeable warmth, the steam and the heat, I can never determine the contemporaneousness of either, because I can only determine the periods in each in their own successive time, but not at all determine the periods in each to be simultaneous.

Let, however, the conception of reciprocal modification be here entertained, so that the substance, water, modified by the caloric successively as causes for the effects of ice liquidity and steam, also modifies reciprocally the substance, caloric, as successively causes for the effects of cold agreeable warmth and heat; and thus, that while water as modified by caloric is the source of congelation, caloric so modified by water is the source of cold, and thus on reciprocally through all successive effects in each: we shall thus, from this reciprocity of modification, determine a necessary connection of effects in each, and that the period of the one must synchronize with the period of the other, and that the phenomena of the ice and the cold, the fluid and the warm, the steam and the hot, must be together simultaneously each with each. The series of effects and thus their periods in time are connected as concurrent and concomitant, and the determination of coetaneous in time is as readily made as before of perpetual or successive in time. If every event in its series is not thus connected by a reciprocal efficiency with every other concurrent event in its series, it were wholly impossible to determine them to be contemporaneous. All effects must be held in communion by a reciprocal efficiency, as necessarily as in succession by a direct efficiency.

And now, this last species of connection is that of

reciprocity and coherence, inasmuch as the efficiency each way makes a mutual variation of the phenomena, and these as effects are not merely adherents as successive but coherents as in communion. The conception, therefore, of such reciprocal causation is precisely that of *Action and Re-action.* This is the *third* apriori Element of connection.

Through the media of Space and Time we have thus attained all the apriori elements of connection, and which must be that of substance and accidence having the connection of subsistence and inherence for determining an experience in Space ; and which, for determining an experience in Time, becomes modified into source and event, having the connection of origin and dependence for perpetual time ; into cause and effect, having the connection of efficiency and adherence for successive time ; and into action and re-action, having the connection of reciprocity and coherence for simultaneous time. No conception of an experience determined in space and time can be, except as the phenomenal in the sense is thought to be connected according to these apriori elements as the notional in the understanding. The operation of connection must, therefore, be universally conditioned upon the notions in an understanding of Substance as ground in space, and of Substance as source in time ; which last, as modified for succession, becomes Cause ; and again modified for concomitance, becomes Reciprocal Causation.

SECTION V.

SOME OF THE APRIORI PRINCIPLES IN A NATURE OF THINGS.

As apriori conditional for all determination of objects in Space and Time, the phenomena must inhere in their permanent substance, depend upon their perpetual source, adhere to their successive causes, and cohere by their reciprocal influences. It is not possible that the phenomena of the sense can be determined in space and time except as they are thus connected among themselves, and thus condition the order of their experience in the understanding; and wherever there is such a determined order of experience, there must be real phenomena standing in their valid substances causes and counter-influences, and constituting through such connections a systematic and organized whole of things which we properly term, as distinct from all ideal connections in our subjective thinking, an objective world. Separate and fleeting appearances are connected in their sources as events, and in their reciprocities as concomitant occurrences, and this every-way connection in our experience gives a *nature of things*, and considered as a whole of all such connected things we term it *Universal Nature*.

This is the province of the Understanding, to take the perceptions of the sense and determine their connection in a judgment of a nature of things; and except in such field of operation it is impossible that an understanding should effect any judgments. If there may be existence which is not subjected to the space and time-determinations, and not bound in the connections of substances causes and reciprocal influences, it must be held as utterly without signification for an understanding which can operate only in the connections of the phenomenal through the notional. The supernatural is as nothing for an understanding judging according to the sense. It would be as preposterous to put the understanding to the work of determining the supernatural, as to put the sense to determining substances and causes which are wholly supersensible. If we have no faculty which may transcend the cognitions given in an understanding then, truly, must we be ever shut up within nature, and that any existence may lie beyond nature must be wholly inconceivable.

But this whole field of nature, as of the conception of phenomena connected into a universal whole of all possible experience in space and time, is the legitimate province of the understanding, and all that is possible to be known of it must be contained in such discursive judgments. Having now attained the process for all such judgments through all the different methods of connection which are apriori possible in an experience determined in space and time, and thereby explained how it is possible to verify the synthetical judgment in its addition of a new conception in the notion which the understanding supplies, not intuitively but discursively; we may further take the conception of such verified judgments, and by an *analysis* of their conditions we may find many predicates for an analytical judgment, which will give to us so many necessary and universal principles as conditions in a nature of things. This we will now proceed to accomplish through each of the connective notions made use of in their methods of discursive connection, viz: the *Substance*, both as ground and source; the *Cause*, as conditioning changes; and the *Reciprocal Agency*, as conditioning concomitances.

1. *Substance*—This, we have found, is a notion wholly supplied by the understanding; impossible to be reached by the sense; standing under all phenomena as their ground or source; and yet which may be verified, as objective being and not mere subjective notion, from the determination in space and time which it gives to experience. As primitive conception in the understanding it is ground for all quality and source for all event; and as verified in a determined experience, objectively, it is a space-filling force in its ground for all perceived quality, and a time-filling force in its source for all changing events. As no construction can place it in the light of consciousness, so no immediate intuition can take cognizance of

it; but through the media of space and of time, it has been apriori found to be a necessary condition for all determination of an experience in the relations of space and the relations of perpetual time; and, therefore, wherever an experience determines itself in its relations in a whole of space, there must be a space-filling substance as permanent ground for the phenomena which appear unchanged in the same place; and wherever an experience determines itself in its relation to one perpetual time, there must be a time-filling substance as perduring source for the changing phenomena there occurring.

And here, if we will take the conception of this verified objective space-filling and time-enduring substance, and analyze it as connective notion for qualities in one space and events in one time, and thus standing as the substantial essence and thing in itself of material nature, and of which all perceived phenomena of quality and event are but the modes of its manifestation through the different organs of the sense, we shall in such analysis be able to find many apriori principles of nature, as the analytical elements and conditions without which a nature of things as given to an experience determined in space and time cannot be.

Let us then take the conception in the *first* place, of substance as *space-filling*, and find the analytical content which must apriori belong to it. Our analysis must be of that which is wholly supersensual, and

25

not at all phenomenal but notional as the transcendental ground and condition for all phenomena; and
thus, an indispensable pre-requisite to such analysis is
a distinct conception of this understanding notion of a
space-filling force. All conception of force involves
action, but a mere pure act does not give the conception of force. Action in one direction, meeting no
other action, could have nothing answering to the conception of force. Except as action meets action and
thereby counteraction takes place, no generation of
force is conceivable, and hence all conception of force
is truly that of a product from an antagonism. It is
not original pure act, but the resultant of pure counteraction. At the point of counter-agency, as pure notion in the understanding, shall we first attain the
conception of force as pure understanding-conception.
Such a point becomes an occupied position in space
and resisting all displacement, and to the extent to
which the diverse points in a space are contiguously
thus occupied by pure forces is there a filling of space,
and a resistance to all foreign intrusion within such
space. And here, with this conception of pure force
as occupying a space, we have all that is now necessary to be considered as sufficient for the pure understanding-conception of a space-filling substance. This
pure space-filling force, as thing in itself, cannot appear in the sense, but may very well be occasion that
there should be phenomena in the sense. It may readily give content in the sensibility, and thus occasion

different affections which may be both distinguished and conjoined, and thus become distinct and definite phenomena. To the sensibility of the touch and muscular effort, it may give content for the phenomena of resistance, figure, superficial smoothness or roughness, hardness or softness, and weight or pressure, &c. And so, also, through the intervention of other media it may give content to vision; to hearing, smelling or tasting; and this in all possible ways of such organs of sensibility becoming affected, according to the modifications internally of the space-filling force. The phenomena are thus the modes in which the one space-filling force manifests itself through the perceptions of the sense. This permanently fills its space, and stands in its position, and is constant occasion for the like content in all organs of all sensibilities. It thus must determine its own place, and its relation to all other space-filling substances in their places, and become objective experience as the same thing in its place for all occasions when its phenomena are perceived, and for all subjects of the self-conscious perceptions.

And now, with this pure understanding-conception of the space-filling substance, it is quite manifest from a mere analysis thereof, that a permanent *impenetrability* must belong to it in the space which it occupies, and that this will be a valid index in the sense, that a space-filling substance occupies the place into which the phenomena of another substance cannot be introduced without a displacement of the phenomena al-

ready there appearing. The principle of impenetrability must thus belong to a nature of things, and the
conception of such impenetrability must be essential
to the conviction that any phenomenon has substantial
objective reality. The determination of substance to
its place may be thereby effected when an impenetrability is determined in that place, and the sameness of
a substance may be determined for the sense when
the same phenomena are occasioned from the same
impenetrability.

And again, that *infinite divisibility* is an apriori predicate of all material substance is clear in an analytical judgment. The space-filling force is a point in
the antagonism of a pure counteraction, and has thus
as the mathematical point it occupies, position only
and not magnitude. And the entire space filled by
the substance is so filled only, as every point in the
space is position for the point of an antagonism engendering force, and thus the substance is as divisible as
the space which it fills. It is also manifest that the
intensity of the counteraction is the measure of the
force engendered in every point of the space filled, and
therefore that the same space may yet be filled, while
the quantity of the substance filling may differ in an
infinite degree. Every point in the space may have
its occupying force, and the intensity of the force may
be from the point $=0$, onwards to an infinite amount.
The intensity of force concentrated in one point may
give sufficient substantiality for filling infinite space.

Substance is thus divisible without limit in two ways; in the extent of space filled, and in the intensity with which the same space is filled. The atom of matter is thus no possible phenomenon in the sense-conception, but a notion in the understanding-conception. It is the force engendered in one point of pure counteraction, and while it may not occupy space except as simple position without extension, it yet may be of an infinite diversity in its intensity, and thus some one atom might have an intensity which should equal the aggregate atoms of a world. Not only infinite divisibility as diminution of space filled, but also infinite divisibility as diminution of intensity in the same place, may be apriori predicated of all material being; inasmuch as an evanishing in the same place may as truly pass through infinite degrees, as a dividing of the place may pass through infinite limits. In this respect, space and substance differ in the thought: space is divisible only as extent; substance is divisible both as extensive and as intensive.

We may also, in the *second* place, analyze the conception of substance as *time-filling*, and determine some of its apriori principles in this direction. This same space-filling force indicating itself in its constant impenetrability, may be conceived as giving its content to the sensibility and in this manner its phenomena to the perception, and these as changing in their definite places, or as themselves changing in the same place; and in either case a filling of time will be determined. The moving of the phenomena from place to place in the perception must affect the inner state, and thus induce the consciousness that a time is passing; and this may be conjoined into its definite periods, while the constancy of an impenetrability in the changing places of the phenomena will give a perduring substance through all these changes, and thus determine these definite periods to be in one perpetual time. Or, the changing of the phenomena in the same place must also affect the inner state by the perception, and thereby induce the consciousness that a time is passing; and this may be conjoined in definite periods, and the constancy of the impenetrability will give the same substance as permanent source for the changed phenomena, and thus determine the definite periods to stand in the one perpetual time. In either case, therefore, the permanent substance perdures through a time, and is thus time-filling.

And now, inasmuch as the perpetuity of the one time is determined only by the perdurance of the one substance as source through all its changes, and that as the one time endures so the one source of all changes of phenomena must endure; it follows, that the understanding can admit of nothing which is new to come into its conception. That which arises and departs is the phenomenal, and is new only as a sense-conception; but it has come up from some perduring source, and when it has departed there has not been a void left in the understanding, for the substance still

is, as the constant source for new phenomena; and
thus, for the understanding neither a coming nor departing can be, but a perpetuity of things endures.
Origin from nothing, and extinction in nothing, are
both inconceivable. It would be a void of all being before and after the phenomenon; or, a chasm of vacuity
between phenomena; which would cut off all possible
connection in the determinations of the understanding,
and in the admission of which the understanding
would annihilate its own functions. Neither nature
nor time could be thought in their unity, nor that nature had any determinate position in time. This is,
therefore, an apriori principle of nature—that no change
of phenomena can arise from non-being, and vanish
again into non-being, but must ever originate in some
permanent source, and depart with that source still
perduring. The old dictum of the ancient philosophers is peremptory, viz :—

> " E nilo, posse nil gigni;
> In nilum, nil posse reverti."

Whether substance itself may begin, and thus the
creation of a thing in itself be effected by that which
is free personality and not a thing, is a question for
quite another faculty than the understanding. So far
as an action of the understanding can reach, it must
be by discursive connections through the medium of
the notional, and it were as absurd to attempt thinking phenomena into a nature of things without a permanent substance, as to attempt perceiving the shapes

of phenomena without place. The conception of the substance as notion in the understanding is conditional for all function of an understanding; and of course the inquiry, whence is the permanent substance? must transcend all action of the understanding as the faculty judging according to sense. The substance, as space-filling force, verified in the determination of an experience to the space-relations, and the substance also as time-filling force, verified in the determination of an experience to the time-relation of perpetuity, being given; the understanding may use it for connecting a universe of nature in the immensity of one space and the eternity of one time : but, when it would transcend connections through this substance, and inquire for an origin of the substance itself, it is abolishing the very notion which determines the immensity and the eternity in their oneness, and obliging itself to think another substance in another immensity and eternity, of which this system of nature in its space and time is but a modification. It is an understanding attempting to overleap itself by issuing its agency outward into some higher understanding, and could even thus only employ itself in an endless leaping from sphere to sphere, without the possibility of resting in a final landing-place.

The perduring source of these changing phenomena is conceived to be before the first phenomenon, and to continue still in the departure of the last, and thus to hold all the phenomena within one perpetuated du-

ration, and neither beginning nor ending nor as at all
exhausting itself in any of these perpetuated successions. The substance persists through all modes of
its manifestation without beginning or end, augmenta-
tion or diminution. The force in one point may be
modified by any combination of forces in other points,
but the space-filling force once given, its modifications
in any part can only occasion new phenomena in the
sense, not any creations of new nor annihilations of
old substances. It is thus an apriori principle of Nature, that within itself *nothing is created nor annihilated;* but itself remains the same whole through all
its transformations. If any thing may be added to it,
or taken from it, it must be by some *ab extra* interference; and is, of course, the introduction of some supernatural agency which can have no conceivable
significancy in any Judgment of the Understanding.

And this conception of the permanency of the substance of nature, and the coming and departing of the
phenomena of nature, discriminates between some
other conceptions which are often confounded. The
conception of *change* is that of any modification in
the permanent substance; the conception of *alteration*
is that of the departing of one phenomenon and the
arising of another; and the conception of *variation*
is that in which one phenomenon is made distinct
from another. Thus the permanent substance
changes and thereby *alters* its phenomena, and these
phenomena *vary* one from the other. There can

be no change but in a permanent which neither alters nor varies. We may change the mode of the same thing, alter one thing for another, and vary different things among themselves.

We have also in this the conception of *chance*. It is the origination of phenomena from no permanent source. It is no positive judgment, but a negation of the connective conditional for all judgments, and assumes an origination from a void of all being. It is the absurdity of thinking through the sense; of discarding the notion and thus vacating the understanding, and yet attempting to account for the connections of phenomena. It is a negation of the law of thought itself, and thus such an experience of nature is an absurd and impossible conception. A Nature of things cannot admit of Chance.

2. *Cause.*—This we have already found to be an apriori Element of connection and thus a primitive understanding-conception, wholly supersensible, and yet possible to be verified as objective being in the determination of an experience to successive time. We shall find a clear conception of cause to admit of an apriori analysis, which will give the predicates of a nature of things in an analytical judgment in several important particulars; and which, as involved in the apriori connections of nature itself, must be the necessary and universal principles and conditions of a nature of things. The first requisite is, the attaining of a clear and complete conception of Cause. No

construction is possible that it may be given in a definite intuition, but its conception must be wholly within the thought of the understanding.

When we recur to our conception of substance, we have a force in every point of space which the substance occupies, and is thus space-filling; and a perduring through every instant of time that, as source for coming and departing phenomena, the substance continues, and is thus time-filling. This substance, as time-filling, is the conception of a modification of the internal space-filling force so that as thus modified it becomes occasion for an altered content in the sensibility, and consequently of an altered phenomenon in perception; and we say that the same thing has become changed. But, manifestly, this space-filling force as substance will hold itself at rest in each point of its antagonism from the constancy of the counteraction, and thus nature will hold itself in utter inertion throughout, if the force in one portion of space does not intrude upon the places occupied by other forces; or, which is the same thing, if one substance does not become combined with, or make an impulsion upon another substance. In all such cases, the combination of forces must work an inner modification of the antagonism in each point of counteraction, and thus necessitate altered contents for the sensibility and consequently altered phenomena in the perception, and we shall have *chemical* changes; and the impulsion of the forces must modify the intensities of the points of counteraction, and we shall have *mechanical* changes. In all such modifications of forces as space-filling, while the perduring impenetrability will indicate the substance which is the permanent *source* of these altered phenomena, yet will that substance which obtrudes its modifications upon this permanent source be a distinct conception; and it is this obtruding of one space-filling force upon another in its modifications which, precisely, is the conception of *cause*. Thus the permanent substance which we conceive to have been constant in all the alternations of congelation, fluidity, vapor, &c., we conceive as the *source* of these alternating phenomena; but the substance which has obtruded itself in its modifying force, and thus produced the changes in the permanent source, we conceive as the *cause* of these alternating phenomena. The substance, caloric, is combined with the substance, water, and thus as one space-filling force so modifying the other space-filling force, that in its various modifications the caloric is cause and the water is source now for congelation, again for fluidity, and again for vapor, &c., as chemical changes; and the ivory of the billiard-ball at rest as space-filling substance has been so modified in its intensities of counter-agency at each point in the space it filled, by the obtrusion of the ivory of the moving ball upon its place, that the first has become source of continual displacement in the resulting movement, and the last has been the cause of such movement, as mechanical change. Thus in all cases of causation, the conception of a cause is that of a space-filling force as one substance obtruding itself upon the place of another space-filling force as substance, and by the modifications induced securing chemical, mechanical or other changes in the latter, which manifest themselves to the sense in the altered phenomena.

It is, therefore, clearly involved in the very conception of a cause, that as the changes induced in the permanent source by the modifications of the cause, pass along according to the conditions of the combination of the substance-cause with the substance-source, so the altered phenomena springing from these changes in their substance-source must pass on in the same conditioned succession. The modification of the source by the cause is the condition for the altered phenomena, and this alteration of phenomena must correspond to the changes in the source. The perception can, therefore, be but in one order, and this conditioning of an ordered series of perceptions is an index of an ordering series of causation. When the phenomena in their successions in the sense can be perceived in one order only, and not the reverse, then it is that an ordered series of changes is going on in the substance-source as conditioned by the combination with it of the substance-cause; and in this may we determine an objective succession as distinct from mere successive appearance in the subject perceiving. There is in this an alteration of phenomena, and not a mere succession of perceiving acts.

Thus, when in a hemisphere of the heavens, I perceive one star in succession after another, and as one passes from my sight another comes into vision, the perceiving agency is as truly successive and may be constructed into its definite periods as completely as if one star had been the condition of my seeing the next, and thus on through the whole series. Merely such a succession in perceiving will determine nothing in relation to an objective succession in the phenomena themselves, but if I find I may reverse my order of perception, and see the same stars successively in a retracing of my series of perceptions; I then know that not the stars themselves are successive, but only my perception of them. But if I follow my perception of the tides as ebbing and flowing, and thus at any one point as rising and falling successively, and I cannot perceive in an inverse order that the water is either rising or falling at pleasure; I then determine that it is not a mere successive perceiving, but an objective succession in the phenomena themselves. And in this objective succession of phenomena, I shall have an index of a conditioning series of causes. And here, that I may determine the cause and the source of these successive phenomena, I must be able to determine the objective reality of their substances, and in these, which is the cause and which is the source. I may very readily determine a perpetual

impenetrability in the rising and falling water, and
know that to be permanent source for the flow and ebb
of the tide which appears; but it may be much more
difficult to determine that the force of the revolving
moon modifies in combination with it the space-filling
force of the substance water, and thus makes the latter to be source for the ebbing and flowing tide; and
yet except as I have so determined, though I may
have determined that there is causation, yet have I
not found what is the cause. I may very readily determine that the phenomena of sacharine vinous and
acetous fermentation are objective alterations and not
merely successive perceptions, for I cannot vary the
order of the perceptions; and I may also determine
the source of these altered phenomena of the sugar,
the wine and the vinegar, by determining a permanent impenetrability constant in one substance through
them all; and though I have thus clearly determined
that this substance-source must stand in combination
with some substance-cause and be modified thereby,
yet it may be impossible for me to determine what that
permanent space-filling force in its perpetual impenetrability is, which is the substance-cause for these
changes; but until such is found, though some cause
must be, yet what the cause is has not yet been determined.

That a cause is, has a safe index in this—an ordered
succession of phenomena perceived in a determined series; *what* a cause is, must be determined in this—a per-

petual impenetrability that marks the substance, which
by combining with the substance-source of the phenomena modifies its changes, and thus conditions its successions of phenomena. One space-filling force cannot im-
pinge upon or combine with another without so modifying it as to induce some changes in it, which must manifest themselves in the sense by some alteration of the
phenomena, and this competency to so induce changes
is the essential of causality, and which we term the
power, or the *efficiency* of the cause, and which is the
causal nexus, as notion in the understanding, for connecting the successions in the phenomena. If, then,
we sometimes find the phenomena in the substance-
cause and those of the substance-source to be together; we shall still determine that to be cause in which
the efficiency is, and cognize it as necessarily first in
the understanding-conception, though both may appear together in the sense. Thus I may first perceive
a vapor, and then perceive a heat as phenomenon of
the notional caloric which causes the vapor; and
though I may perceive that the heat and the vapor
are together in the sense, yet inasmuch as I determine
the efficiency to be in the caloric of which the sensation of heat is phenomenon, I judge the heat to be
truly first in order and the vapor to succeed it. And
so, moreover, when I simply perceive varying phenomena in some source, but cannot perceive any phenomena of the substance-cause, the determination that
there is an efficiency inducing these changes in the

source is quite sufficient that I should judge some substance-cause to be present, although it does not manifest itself by any of its own phenomena in the sense, but only to the understanding through the changes which it is effecting in the source of these coming and departing phenomena. Thus, I may perceive the altered phenomena which magnetism is effecting in some substance-source, as the movement and disposition of the steel-filings after an ordered arrangement; and though no phenomena mark the presence of the magnetic substance in the place where the steel-filings have been arranging themselves, yet my understanding at once concludes that some permanent space-filling force is present, and that the sharpening and perfecting of some organic sensibility might be sufficient to receive its content as a sensation, and capacitate the intellect to discriminate and construct it into a complete phenomenon. In my understanding, I therefore conclude magnetism, and so also electricity, galvanism, and even gravitation, to be space-filling forces, although they manifest themselves to the sense in no other way, than by the altered phenomena which they produce in other substances.

The efficiency in any substance-cause may be conceived to lie in the substance as an inherent property, even when it is not in combination with any other space-filling force as actually inducing changes therein, and it is such conception that we mark by the term *latent power*, implying that it would induce

26

changes were the occasion given for its combination with some other substance. We thus conceive the steel and flint as possessing the latent power to produce the spark, though no occasion of collision has occurred; yet ought we not to hold such notion of latent power to be that of cause, but only that on occasion of their combination in collision, there would be cause, viz: a modification of the space-filling force. The steel and flint are no more cause for the spark than a chip and leather, except as brought in combination ; for without this the phenomenon of the spark can no more appear in the sense from one than from the other.

An analysis of this conception of Cause will also expose some important distinctions in reference to occurring events which are often very confusedly apprehended. Thus, when I conceive of a series of causes and effects passing on in their order, and some phenomenon extraneous to this series and not at all accounted for in it comes suddenly in, and interrupts the process of thinking in its connections as going on in the experience, I term this intruding phenomenon a *casual* event, and perhaps, as if surprised by it, I say, it somehow so *happened;* or, that it was an *accident.* The meaning is, not that any such occurrence has come without both its source and its cause as space-filling substance, but that its connection is quite in another series of cause and effect from that which we were then determining in an experience, and in proportion to the suddenness, supposed disconnection, and difficult explanation of the intruding phenomenon is our surprise, and the mystery in which we leave the casual occurrence.

When we follow the conception of connected phenomena in one *source* through their successions, as of the juice of the grape through its successive stages of fermentation, we have the judgment of *a change in things*. When we follow the conception through the successions of a series of *causes*, we have the judgment of *a train of events*. Thus, in the return of the sun from the winter solstice, and the dissolving of the snow and ice, and the overflow of the streams, and the deposition of organic remains upon the fields, and the augmented business, wealth, population, &c. we have a successive *coming out* from different sources of new phenomena which we term *events;* and these are all conditioned in their order of occurrence by their series of causes, and we therefore say, that they occur in a *train*. These successions have no connection in one source, but the phenomena vary the substance in which they originate with every step, and their connection is only through a varied combination of substances, of which one becomes an occasion for the next, and thus onward through all the efficiency of the changes by their causes. And again, when we conceive the antecedent not as the efficient, but only as a preparative occasional for an efficient, we may deem both the occasional and the efficient to be causes, but their distinction in the conception must be noted by some qualifying phraseology. Thus in the overflow of the streams as following the dissolving of the snow, the dissolving is only a preparative, occasional for and not an efficient for the overflowing. The disengaging of the fluid by the dissolution of the congelation prepares the way for the efficiency of gravitation to come in combination and produce the overflowing; and then this overflowing is again a preparative occasional for the deposit of its sediment, inasmuch as the quiet state of the waters which ensues permits again gravitation as an efficient, to bring the suspended particles to the bottom. We may mark this distinction by calling the one *an occasional cause*, and the other an *efficient cause;* and in many cases such distinction leads to very important philosophical consequences. The old scholastic distinctions are not unworthy of careful preservation; as *causa causans, causa cuusata, causa efficiens, causa sine qua non, &c.*

This clear conception of Cause gives opportunity for a further analysis, by which still more important apriori principles in a nature of things are determined. The conception of *fate* is that of a cause in utter blindness; competent to originate effects, and yet utterly without determination of what the effect must be. It is a blind giant in its power, irresistible and inexorable, under which, the doctrines of the Stoic become the highest wisdom, viz: that there is nothing to pray for and nothing to pray to; nothing to be feared

or hoped; and the part of virtue is to receive all things
in perfect equanimity, inasmuch as while something
must come, there can be no possible fore-seeing by
any what is to come. The cause is positive, but all
conditioning of the effect in the cause is negative.
The understanding has simply the connective of efficiency, and therefore it may determine that one thing
shall make changes in other things, and successions
of phenomena shall flow on; but it has no connectives
for judging what changes shall be induced, and thus
no determination of what phenomena must appear.
But if we will here analyze our conception of cause,
we shall find a nature of things no more admitting of
Fate than, as above seen, of Chance. The space-filling force as substance in a nature of things already is,
and the conception of cause is the efficiency of one
substance in combination with others to induce changes
therein, and thus condition the phenomena which
must appear in the sense. But the given combination,
from the inherent forces of the space-filling substances
as cause and source, can produce only a given modification and thus a given change and thus also a given
phenomenon; and every change must also be conditional for its next combination of substances, and thus
onward in endless development, but with the inherent
principle in every succession as an intestine law of
what every subsequent succession must be. In nature there can no more be a blind fatality of result,
than there can be a resting of causation. Both the

cause must go out into effect, and must go out in such
effect, and the whole is given in the germ as truly as
any part in the past development.   Causation has its
connections in intelligible inherent law, and knows
nothing of a blind Fate, which would annihilate all
function of an Understanding in Experience.

Again, the conception of *liberty* is that which may
propose to itself as cause an alternative of ends,
and go out in its agency for the one in the possession
of an efficiency for its alternative.   It is positive of
agency and positive of conditions, but as having an
alternative of conditions it is negative of a necessitated
order of effect.   But in the causation of nature an alternative of conditions is an impossibility.   No combination of space-filling forces can induce but one modification in any point of efficiency, and the cause
must as necessarily go out into its own conditioned
effect, as it must go out in effect at all.   In Nature
there can be no Liberty.

And, lastly, the conception of *a leap* in nature would
be that of passing from effect to effect without an intermediate efficiency, and thus in one stage of development reaching an advanced position without passing
through the intermediate changes.   Such a conception would break up all intelligible connection in nature, inasmuch as any cause which was efficient for
other than its own effect must leave all intermediate
effects unconnected by any cause.   Nature would
have some changes which were not connected in any

development of nature. A nature of things can never admit of progress *per saltum.*

3. *Action and Re-action.*—This is another pure understanding-conception, and may be verified in an objective reality by the determination of an experience as contemporaneous, or as occurrence of events simultaneously. A clear conception of this manner of connection will also give occasion for a further analysis by means of which some other apriori principles of a nature of things may be obtained.

The conception is that of two substances in combination or collision, which cannot occur but it must modify the space-filling force through every point of the space filled. But while such modification must be made in one substance from the combination, the combination must as surely modify the other substance, and thus the change must be reciprocal. And this is not merely in single instances of combination, but inasmuch as all of a nature of things may be determined in the relations of one space and of one time in experience, it follows that all things as co-existing in space and time must stand in this reciprocal intercourse and communion each with each. Were some one substance isolated from all reciprocity with all other substances, it could not be determined as in the same universal space and time with other things, and thus could not stand connected in the same experience.

This mutual commerce between all portions of the co-existing universe gives the occasion for perceiving

the phenomena of different substances in one order
and then in a reverse order of perception. If, when
the perception of one phenomenon had passed, the
phenomenon could not again be repeated in the sense,
it would indicate that the modification in the substance which occasioned it had also passed, and a
change had been induced which must now give occasion for the perception of some other phenomenon,
and such succession would indicate that the connections were those of cause and effect, and could not
admit of reversed perceptions, inasmuch as all occasion for the preceding perception had wholly passed
away. But when the apprehension of one phenomenon has passed and another has been apprehended,
and then the apprehension of the first may be again
repeated at pleasure, it manifests that the occasion
for such phenomenon remains, and the order of apprehension each way is the index that the connection is
that of reciprocal influence, not of cause and effect.
When, therefore, all co-existing things reciprocally influence each other, such influence gives occasion for
the same phenomena in each, so long as the modifications of any one does not make its changes in all.
Thus, when the presence of the sun acts and re-acts
in the modifications of its light upon all, my perception in the organ of vision may be from one co-existing
substance to another in the phenomena thus occasioned, and in a reversed order of apprehension arbitrarily, and I determine them as contemporaneous;

but when the sun is withdrawn and such action and re-action ceases, and such modifications have passed away, and I can no longer pass in my apprehension from one thing to another, I can no longer determine their contemporaneousness, but only the successions that have passed since they all disappeared.

With this conception of the reciprocity of influence throughout nature, and that no one thing can be changed in its inner modifications but it has been acted upon by all, and that thus one portion of nature acts through every other portion while every other portion is also acting through it, we have the analytical judgment apriori, and thus a primitive principle of nature, that it can be no *concervum* of particular things which are merely in apposition in space; nor yet a mere *concatenation* of various series of things, in independent lines of cause and effect; but that while all have a perpetual source, and a conditioned order of succession, this warp of all lines of causation is also woven across with the connecting woof of reciprocal influences, and thus that nature has its complete *contexture* which may be held as one web of a determined experience, and which no more adheres continuously than it also coheres transversely.

And lastly, the conception of a *vacuum*, is of a space destitute of any force as substantial source, cause, or reciprocal influence. It is the negation of all being, and the affirmation of an utter vacuity in the midst of nature. And now such a void may be conceived, just

as ideal space may be conceived, but not at all con-
sistently with a determined experience in space and
time.   If there is somewhere a rent in nature, which
causation does not pass through, or action and reaction
pass across; then cannot that chasm of vacuity be at
all determined as any place in the one objective space,
nor any period in the one objective time; nor can the
threads that run out in it, and come up from it, be possibly determined as in the same one whole of space
and time with each other.   The understanding has no
connective notion by which to carry its thought across
it, and once to sink into it would be to lose all possibility of coming out of it.   The functions of an understanding would be lost in it.   Nature not merely ab-
hors but utterly forbids, within itself, a vacuum.

   With the phenomenal as sense-conception already
given, we may now completely apprehend the Understanding in the entire province through which all its
possible functions may operate, and in this we have
attained the perfect Idea.   Phenomena are given in
their definite but also isolate singularity, and no possible function of the sense can connect them in an experience as belonging to a universal nature.   This
must be a work exclusively for an understanding,
which, by an operation of connection discursively
through the notional, holds all nature to be one concrete of universal being.   The possibility of determining the phenomenal in all the space and time-relations affords an apriori distinction between all sub-

ective idealism and objective being; for, except as phenomena stand connected in their constant substance there can be no determination of them in the one immensity of space, and except as they stand also connected in their perpetual source, their successive cause, and their reciprocal influence, there can be no determination of them in the one eternity of time. A determined experience in space and time is utterly impossible except through such connections. The media of space and of time give the occasion for a complete demonstration of the necessity of the notional as connective for the phenomenal, in order to any possible experience determined in space and time.

From this apriori demonstration of the connection of all possible experience determined in space and time through a notional as the being of things in themselves, we have the valid synthetical judgments in their universality and necessity of comprehension—that qualities must inhere in their substances—events must depend on their sources—effects must adhere through their causes—and all concomitant phenomena must cohere in their reciprocal influences—and thus all of Nature be possible to become an experience determined in space and time. A perpetual impenetrability will indicate the being of Substance, in its position in space and duration in time; a continual and irreversible order of apprehension will indicate the being of Cause; and an order of apprehension reversible at pleasure will indicate the being of Reciprocal Influence. An Understanding thus, is a faculty for connecting phenomena in a determined experience in space and time, through the notions of substance, cause, and reciprocal influence. The complete Idea concisely expressed is—*The Faculty for a universally determined Experience in the connection of the phenomenal through the notional.*

SECTION VI.

FALSE SYSTEMS OF A UNIVERSAL NATURE EXPOSED IN THEIR DELUSIVE APRIORI CONDITIONS.

A COMPLETE apriori idea of an understanding induces at once a conception of the true Intellectual System of the Universe. Its application to all false systems will enable us to detect their fallacies at the very point of their departure from the apriori conditions of the understanding itself, and thereby to trace their self-contradictions and absurdities to the source in which they become unintelligible. It will be the conclusion of this first Chapter of the understanding when, in this section, we have applied our idea of an understanding to several erroneous conceptions of a Universal System of Nature, and thereby exposed their fallacies in their apriori sources.

From the earliest history of philosophy, we find the traces of a very earnest conflict perpetually occurring between some who have restricted nature wholly within the phenomenal, and others who have affirmed a notional as altogether beyond the region of the phenomenal, and wholly supersensible. The authority of Plato settles the great antiquity and the ardor of this contest. In the Sophista he affirms that the doubts in which essence, or being in itself, is involved has induced a gigantic battle. On one side, "catching hold of rocks and oaks with their hands they degrade all things from heaven and the region of the invisible, and because they may touch such things they contend that only to exist which may be handled, and thus that tangible body and true being are the same; and if any one affirm that there is being beside body, they rail and will hear no more." But, on the other side, "discreetly and piously contending from the region of the invisible, they maintain that the notional and incorporeal alone is the true being, and logically break up the body which the first call true being into atoms, and show this to be perpetual flux and not essence. Here a fierce war has always raged." Aristotle, though philosophizing more concerning the phenomenal than the notional, yet no less explicitly than Plato, teaches an essence supersensible; separable from all phenomena; a substance indissoluble and indestructible. And certainly, this everlasting battle between the sensualists and super-sensualists can never be composed to peace except by an apriori science. The impossibility of an experience determined in space and time, except as the phenomena stand connected in their grounds

and sources of being as substance cause and reciprocal agency, must be demonstrated, or we can never
fully settle the controversy, and show that the phenomenal is the mode in the sense of that which, as
thing itself, is the notional in the understanding.

But this idea of an understanding determining experience in space and time, is much further available for
the exposing of many fallacies and philosophical delusions which have very much multiplied themselves
about this operation of connecting the phenomenal in
universal judgments by the interposition of a notion in
the understanding. The great difficulty, as before noticed, lies in the verification of a synthetical judgment.
This is readily effected in all cases where, by a construction of the conception, we can bring all its relations within an intuition. But when we are to judge
of *existence* and not of *appearance;* of things and not of
qualities; of inherent connections and not of external
appositions; all construction in an intuition is out of
the question. Our philosophical principle cannot be
made a mathematical axiom. The judgment is synthetical but necessarily discursive, and the only possible method for verifying its validity is by subjecting it
to the demonstration, that the connectives of the notional are a necessary condition for determining all experience in one whole of space and of time. In this
we have the true and complete idea of an understanding. But these fallacies and delusions have originated
from a method of philosophizing, that completely ex-

cluded all consideration of these necessary conditions. The nature of a discursive synthetical judgment was wholly overlooked, and thus, instead of applying all the force of an apriori intellectual investigation to the point of verifying the validity of the notional and the conclusions in the judgments thus connected, there has arisen the various attempts to attain to a Universal System of Nature, sometimes by an analytical process; sometimes by an arbitrary generalization; sometimes by mere assumption on the ground of common sense; and sometimes by the arbitrary omnipotence of divine interpositions.

The delusions we would here seek to dispel may be found in the ambiguity, on one side, of using the phenomenal as if it were a valid notional; or, on the other side, explaning the notional in its use by only the characteristics of the phenomenal. One intellectualizes the phenomenon, and then philosophizes as if this were a true notion in the understanding; the other sensualizes the notion, and then proceeds as if no substratum in an understanding were at all necessary. The understanding is made *to conjoin*, or the sense *to connect;* and from these opposite fallacies, philosophy has been involved in the grossest absurdities. Either Atheism or Pantheism must be the conclusion of all such processes of thinking in judgments, and it may be one as readily as the other. If the philosophy elevate the phenomenal to a notional, it may keep out of sight that any supernatural connective is wanted; or, in the manifest emptiness of all thinking without a verified notional, it may arbitrarily introduce the supernatural simply because it is wanted; yet when so introduced as the connective in nature, it is impossible that its divinity should be any thing other than nature.

It is not a little amusing to watch the delusions induced by this ambiguous use of the phenomenal and the notional, from the position we have now attained, and see how the philosophy is forced to balance itself by an amphiboly, in which the ball is made to play from hand to hand according to the delusion which it is obliged to practise upon itself. We will pass the varieties of these two ambiguous uses of the sense and the understanding before us, sufficiently extended to detect their ever recurring fallacies; and this not so much for our amusement as to expose the ambiguity and dispel the delusion it has occasioned. The first sublimates the phenomenal to a notional in the understanding, and the last degrades the notional to a phenomenal in the sense. By keeping this examination ever within the light of our apriori Idea for all possible thinking in judgments, the detection of the deceptive ambiguity will be readily effected.

1. *The general process of physical philosophy where the phenomenal is elevated into a notional for the understanding.*

The common conception of material being, as the starting-point for philosophy in building up a System of the Universe under this general process, may be thus described. The material world as given in vision or by the touch is an extension in space, and by resistance to muscular pressure is apprehended as impenetrable body. This extended impenetrable body is capable of successive divisibility up to the primitive particles of which the mass has been compounded, and such particles in their ultimate analysis are deemed to be the primitive elements of material nature. As thus uncompounded, primitive and distinct they are known as *atoms*. The phenomenal has in these atoms disappeared, inasmuch as the analysis has gone too high to give a content in the sense, and that, which from its sublimation has passed out of the reach of the sensibility, is now taken to be valid thing in the thought. And here the first fallacy, the πρῶτον ψευδος, is found. This sublimated phenomenal, as having passed from the sensibility, is no longer considered to be phenomenal, but is intellectualized into the essential being of matter as thing in itself.

And now, with all matter given in its atomic elements, the labor of philosophically accounting for its combinations and systematic connections commences. How are these atoms combined in a body? How are bodies brought into system? How are systems held together as one universe? Here is the salient point for many diversified modifications of this general process of philosophizing. A few of the more prominent will cursorily be noticed.

(1.) There is an Atheistic scheme, according to which

27

an attempt has been made to build up a system of Nature, that dates far back among the earliest annals of Grecian philosophizing, assigned to such names as Leucippus, Democritus, and Protagoras, but which can hardly claim to possess more than a semblance of systematic philosophy. The atoms were assumed to have not only position and hardness, but weight; and thus a fall of all atoms in the void space gave to matter an original motion in space. With these primordial atoms in motion, it was deemed a necessary consesequence that resistances, percussions, collisions and attritions should ensue; and thus aggregations of atoms would be induced, which would be bodies of diverse magnitudes, shapes, and movements in space. And inasmuch as such aggregations must take to themselves some position, and stand to each other in some relationship of figure, motion, density, &c.; and as the present actual composition of nature is one among the indefinite number of possible arrangements; it is only required that we admit the component atoms to have come together as they have, and this fortuitous concurrence has made nature what it is. There needed only primitive atoms enough, and their own weight put them in motion, and the present system of the universe has come into its own arrangement, and quite as readily this as any other among all possible combinations.

But aside from all questions of the origination of the atoms, and of their diffusion through the void, and of the assumption of weight as an inherent property of the atoms producing motion; the impossibility of all collection in any aggregates is manifest from this, that the atoms in their fall must move in right lines, and each moving by itself, there must still be preserved the same diffusion and separation notwithstanding their assumed motion.

(2.) Epicurus, standing in the midst of the increased light which had been diffused by the Socratic philosophy and especially the physical investigations of Aristotle, was obliged to modify somewhat the atomic theory of Democritus, which he seems to have adopted from considerations springing out of his ethical system, to which the atomic philosophy could be made more readily to harmonize.   He saw that the atoms must in themselves be invariable, or their weight and motion and other sensible qualities could have no permanency; and that they must be infinite, or in the infinite void a finite number would be scattered and dissapated in a disorderly movement.   The void offers no resistance, and thus all atoms must be precipitated with equal velocities, and could therefore no more be brought into juxta-position than if each were falling in its own separate tube.   Hence, Epicurus gave to the atoms an arbitrary inner energy, by which slight deviations from a perpendicular descent could be effected.   In this assumption he attained two benefits for his own interest, the introduction into the system of another agency than that of mere necessitated action (which his ethical system demanded) and the supplying of a physical want by a conception which might bring the atoms in collocation. All combinations of the falling atoms depend upon the deflections which this inner arbitrary energy in each may occasion; and, as this is wholly unconditioned, an infinity of worlds similar and dissimilar to our own may eternally be combining and dissolving. The formation and dissolution of worlds is with no order, and dependent upon no law. Both in physics and in ethics purely arbitrary consequences may occur from these arbitrary deflections. With this assumed slight convergency of direction, the atoms are perpetually colliding, repelling, and rebounding; and Nature happens now to have the combinations of figure, place and motion which belong to it.

And here, again, independently of all inquiry into the origin and weight of the atoms, and also wholly aside from this inner arbitrary deflection in the descent from a perpendicular; the emptiness of the whole as a philosophy of nature is manifest, in that no nature of things as universal system can be so attained. The atoms fall together and become a mere coacervus of separate particles. Each atom is as truly disconnected and independent as if separated in the void from all others. They merely come in external contact and have solely conjunction in space, but there are no inherent dynamical relations in virtue of which all phenomena coalesce into a universal nature of things. A phenomenal has been sublimated into a spurious notional; and such atoms can only touch each other, not at all infuse any connective agency through each other. They are really no more a notional in the understanding than the unanalyzed phenomenon itself. Accordingly, so soon as we attempt their use as a notional, and as if we had entered the region of the understanding are about to think the atoms into a nature of things in a discursive judgment, we are at once admonished of the emptiness of our notional as a connective, inasmuch as we cannot make the phenomenal stand in it nor come out from it; and immediately an amphibolous play is necessary to steady ourselves, and we throw the ball at once into the other hand as the notion of *weight* which is now to give motion to the atoms. We are then, ready to try the process of thinking in a discursive judgment once more; but alas! the same empty notional and the same delusive amphiboly recur. The weight is itself phenomenal, and it is impossible to make the motion of the atoms to be originally conditioned by it; and the attempt is made to steady the reeling thought, by throwing the ball again back into the empty hand as some inner deflective agency which may turn the falling atoms in convergency and bring them in contact. Here Epicurus stopped short; but another attempt at a discursive judgment must have repeated the same delusive fallacy by striving to ballance the factitious understanding with another assumed notional. If this inner arbitrary energy be other than a phenomenal quality, it is gratuitously assumed merely because it is wanted, and may prove to be the very energy of an interfering Deity which Epicurus would so much dread; but if it is only a property of the atom as Epicurus conceived, like some deflection in an ascending flame or a zigzag movement in the lightning, then are we still as far as before from any thing to stand under our thinking, and of course as far as ever from all entrance into the region of the understanding. The play of a false notional may everlastingly thus delude us, and we should still abide only in the phenomena of the sense, while we deemed ourselves in the process of thinking discursively, and just about to conclude in a valid philosophical judgment.

(3.) A modification of the same delusion is found in the physical system of the Stoics. Zeno, Cleanthes and Chrysippus are the most noted among the founders of the philosophy of the Porch. The principles of Heraclitus, who flourished before the Socratic Era, were in many particulars adopted and embraced in their application by the Stoics.

The incorporeal essence of Plato and Aristotle, as supersensible being, was rejected by the Stoics, and all true being was held by them to be in the corporeal. The corporeal was, however, made to include a broader signification than the atomic bodies of Democritus and Epicurus; inasmuch as both a passive and an active being was ascribed to it. The weight which induced the fall of the atoms and the inner

agency by which the slight deflection in their course
was effected, in the Epicurean philosophy, they ascribed to body itself in its active capacity.   A vacuum,
place, time, and merely logical relations, when taken
as abstract generalizations, were the incorporeal ; but
in their definite particularity, they were considered to
be body.   A definite cubic foot in vacuo, or in pure
space, inasmuch as it excluded all other extension
and rested permanently in itself, had both an active
and a passive and was thus truly body, as much as
when possessing sensible content.   The phenomenal
content in sense was analyzed, not merely by dividing
it into atoms, but by separating its distinct quality
and its definite quantity, and in this was attained a
complex of action and passion and not merely the
atoms as separate from each other and inseparable in
themselves.   The properties of bodies were thus made
themselves to be body, and thus more than one body
might occupy the same place at the same time ; they
interpenetrated each other.   The *hardness* of a cubic
inch of gold and the *yellowness* of it had each quality
and quantity, content and form, action and passion,
and were thus each alike body, and interpenetrated
each other in the same place.   The analysis was only
of the phenomenal, but this as content and form ; the
content was the passive side and was matter, the
form was the active side and was spirit ; but that
matter should be body it must include spirit, and that
spirit should take form it must reside in matter.   The

Soul and God are spiritual, and by these man and the universe have their development into bodily form; while the material, as the passive in which the active spirit resides, is that which is being developed; and thus the content and form, the passive and active, matter and spirit, are ever in unity and together constitute the only true being and which is ever corporeal being. Thus, the seed cannot be developed without its active spirit, the active spirit cannot effect the development except it reside in a material germ. God is the seed-relation (ςπερματικος λογος) of the universe, and must reside in it that its development may be effected. The spirit and the matter are a perpetual unity, and the development is perpetual flow and change. The active, however, works in a non-resisting passive, and is therefore wholly unconditioned and no reciprocity can be admitted. The movement is not, thus, connected cause and effect in which the substance-cause and the substance-source mutually modify each other; nor is it the chance without cause of the Epicurean; but a Stoical Fate, as causality with no conditioning from the substance on which it works.

The light of the true idea of all connection in an understanding will readily expose the deceitful ambiguity of this attempted philosophizing. It is merely an analytical process, and can give no valid synthesis. The notional is wholly an analytical element of what is corporeal in the sense. The phenomenal body has matter as quality, and form as quantity; the first as passive in the sensibility, the last as actively constructed by the intellect, and the unity of these is the essence of the universe. This, therefore, as a sublimation of the phenomenal, becomes an assumed notional in the understanding, and consequently a false notional; and that it may have a dynamical connection, an analysis is made which attains the form as of the active, and the matter as of the passive. The false notional in this way becomes again the phenomenal, and the form is not the active itself but a product of an active farther back, and the matter is not passivity itself but a phenomenal quality of something farther back which is the passive; and now this second amphiboly of phenomenal and notional is made to furnish the occasion for the connectives of a discursive judgment. The active is put as notional for the cause and the passive as notional for the source of all change and development of the universe, and the whole is thus thought to be brought into a philosophical system. The working of one in the other is the development of nature.

But when we come to rest the understanding upon this spurious notional, its insufficiency is at once betrayed. Properties have been made things; and now, when we would think the active cause as about to develop the passive matter; behold! this cause is but a mere phenomenal activity having no source on which it may depend for the efficiency of its causality, and we are forced, in order to balance ourselves and

save the understanding from sinking into the emptiness of mere chance, to put the analyzed active again
in composition with the passive, and let that stand as
the substance-source in which the causality resides.
Our cause is thus taken as efficiency residing in a
passive substance, and we would now think it to be
the central force for the development of nature. But
again, when we come to rest the thought upon nature
as being thus developed; behold! once more we are
sinking into emptiness, for our substance in which the
causality exists, and on which it is to work, and out
of which as source is to come all the development of a
nature of things, is but mere passivity—a negation of
all possible conditioning of causality—and we have
escaped from Chance only to rest upon Fate as a blind,
unconditioned, undirected efficiency. And then, inasmuch as such a conception is a negative of all intelligence and an annihilation of the understanding itself,
since it can only be causality without any counter-
agency, the delusion is still kept up by throwing the
ball once more back and making this efficiency to be
itself caused, which is the same as making fate to be
fated. In this as the ultimate analysis the old Stoical
philosophy rested; reposing all things upon a blind
power which controlled gods and men and things.
There was a force controlling the highest force, and
a physical power put behind Jove himself. And yet
the last was wholly analytical, and no more a valid

connective for synthetical judgments than the first. It was but the vain attempt to make the sense think.

(4.) Pythagoras lived more than an hundred years before Socrates, and his name is connected with the earliest systems of philosophy extant. It is quite evident that he had a very full acquaintance with the ancient Egyptian philosophy and sciences, and may perhaps in many things be taken as a representative of the Egyptian method of thinking. It is only from the writers of the Pythagorean school who lived immediately precedent to the time of Socrates, that we attain a knowledge of the Pythagorean doctrine; as it is evidently from these that Plato and Aristotle drew their descriptions of this philosophy. These were mainly Philolaus, Eurytus, and Archytas, the first of which, more especially, gave shape to the Pythagorean system.

Their whole system is clothed in a mathematical garb, and their conceptions of things are expressed in the formula of numbers. Their first principle is " that number is the essence of all things;" and as all numbers have their combinations, and their relations in such constructions in a general harmony, so a principle nearly equivalent to the above was, " that all things exist through harmony." But the real meaning clothed in this mathematical dress is all we now need, in its most summary form, for the purpose of detecting another phase of that delusive amphiboly before noticed between the phenomenal and the notional.

The process of this philosophy was wholly analytical, but in a different direction from the Atomists or the Stoics in the passive and active of bodies. The phenomenal alone was used in discursive thinking, and which must have induced for synthetical judgments some double use of the phenomenal as a spurious notional; and this it is our design here to expose. The analysis proceeded in this direction : taking the phenomenal body as having length breadth and thickness in space, we have as a first analytical result, surfaces ; and when we further analyze surfaces, we have lines ; and when we analyze lines, we have ultimately points. Points, as the ultimate analysis, are atoms. But these atoms or points are only limits, and not limited. In order that there should be a finite or limited body, there must be the point with an interval terminated by another point. All bodies are thus originally points and intervals, or atoms separated by a vacuum. The one point in vacuo is an atom ; two points, with their intervening vacuum, is a line ; three points and their interval, when not continuous, is a surface ; and four points, when any one is out of the plane of the other, is a solid. Here is the explanation in what way " the essence of things is number." The unit is an atom ; the dual, a line ; the triplicate, a surface ; and the quadruple, a solid. Definite numbers are also given for cubes, pentagons, hexagons, &c.

The system of nature is constituted of these elements of atoms and intervals ; i. e. of points and voids.

These are the ultimate results of an analysis of all phenomena, and all being is thus taken as compounded of
atoms and the voids interposed. With these, the philosophy commences to connect its system of universal
nature. A generalization of all atomic being as including all existence is termed, the One; and a generalization of the voids includes all the intervals inter-
jacent to the atoms, and which is known as the Inexistent. The first One, standing in the infinite void, is
known as the Odd; and assumed as spontaneously
tending to a self-limitation by an inhaling of the cir-
cumjacent void within itself, which is called the inspiration of the Infinite; and this bringing of the infinite void into the One makes it to be compounded,
extended, self-conscious, and all-comprising; and is in
this the supreme force and essence of the universe
now called the—odd-even—inasmuch as the limiting
atom and the separating interval are now in unity
within itself. Here now, as a triad, is in this odd-
even the capacity for the beginning, the middle and the
end; and as thus including the entire elements of being it becomes THE ALL. The All is now competent
to divide and separate itself indefinitely by inhaling
the void between the atoms, and thus extending and
limiting itself and thereby distinguishing in self-consciousness; and this limiting itself in its distinct and
definite portions secures that it becomes Uranus, or
the world. The different elements of nature—as fire,
air, earth, water,—are the products of different com-

pounds of atoms and intervals, and which have their expression in numbers; and the arrangement of all was with a cube or a pyramid of fire, as the altar of the universe and the watch-tower of Jupiter, at the center; and from which goes constantly out the flame which pervades and encloses the worlds, and constitutes the grand vortices in which all the discriminated compounds of atoms and voids are kept perpetually moving about in their orbits. This movement was after the law of harmony, and supposed to be attended by sounds too sublime for mortal ears to hear, but which to the gods were the perpetually ravishing music of the spheres.

Now, without enquiring into the genesis of the primary atoms, and which by inhaling the void and thereby being rendered capable of self-conscious limitations become monads; and not at all seeking the validity of the generalization, which can give only an *ideal* unity to the atoms as the Supreme One, and an *ideal* combination of the one existent and the infinite inexistent as the odd-even or the ALL; we only need to trace, in the light of the true idea of an understanding, the ambiguity here involved, and all the delusion is at once exposed in its primary sources. The atom, even as generalized to the universal One, is but the phenomenal carried beyond all perception and made a pure intuition; and this, taken from the field of the sense, is assumed to have entered the field of the understanding and thereby a mere intuition is delusively used as a notion. But when the thinking discursively commences, the false notional has no subsistency, and hence to save the fall, the ball must be thrown into the empty hand as a higher assumed notional, which is a force seeking after a self-conscious limitation. The atom has thus an inner causation which moves it, and in this way has become again phenomenon, and the inhaling or self-limiting energy has been put as the connecting notional. But this again, though assumed as the supreme governing force of the universe, inasmuch as it may act only upon the passive void which it inhales into itself has no force nor reaction, and thus can give no connection to the atoms. So soon therefore as the mundane force is to be used for connecting the combined atoms into a universe, to save the fall again the ball must be thrown forward as a newly assumed notional in the vortices of the central fire which is made to pervade the spheres, and to float them about in its gyrations.

Here the Pythagorean system stops short, but it is quite as little self-balanced as before it commenced its delusive philosophizing; for the next step upon the vortices must at once make them to be as truly phenomenal as the spheres which they carry about, and we must still seek another balance-weight in some new notional which shall condition the gyrations of the flaming vortices. The philosophy cannot be completed, because an analysis of phenomena can never supply an understanding-conception, as true notional connective.

(5.) Another modification of the atomic theory, to provide for this defect in the impossibility of an ultimate analysis, is effected by Descartes; and would fill up the void in the notional by at once interposing the supernatural. The outline of the Cartesian physical philosophy is as follows. Material being has its essence in *extension*. All external phenomena are in some way qualities of extension, and thus only different modes of extended being, while the simple extension itself is the sole essence. This indefinite extension, as the original essence of the material universe, is separable and moveable and therefore capable of a division into definite parts. The first modification of material essence was the breaking up of this indefinite extension into angular portions, and which in the movement of their breaking up pressed against and were made to grind upon each other, and this attrition rounded the fractured parts into small spherical atoms. Interposed between these small spherical atoms, was every where the still finer dust which worked off in the grinding. This finer dust is the *first* component element of nature, and the spherical atoms are the *second* element.

The original disruption of the mass and the consequent concussions occasioned whirls and eddies in which the finer dust of the first element was carried about in different vortices; and this prepares the way for the philosophical connection of the elements into a system, and which is thus effected. The fine dust of the first element, in its exceeding minuteness, thus whirling about, naturally tends in its motion towards the foci of the vortex in which it is carried around, and is thus subtracted from the matter of the second element, leaving the spherical atoms diffused through the heavens, and which, as thus cleansed from all the floating dust, become the medium of light. The first element, so far as carried into the foci of the vortices, becomes there condensed and steadfast in position except as turning about its own center, and thus constitutes the different suns of the different vortical systems. And yet very much of this fine matter of the first element tended to cohere ere it reached the centers of the vortices, and such incipient coherences become a *third* element, more dense than the spherical atoms of light as the second element, and according to its different densities came together in masses at different points in the vortices from the suns at the center, and formed the planets and comets as they are carried about in their respective systems. In process of time the larger vortices absorbed the smaller and controlled them in its own, and the sattelites while carried about their primaries were all carried about in the great solar vortex ; and thus our solar system, and in like manner all other systems of the universe, became completely established in their bodies and their revolutions.

And now, all this, as in the Pythagorean system, is wholly phenomenal, so far as the being, figure, arrangement and revolution of the material world is considered. Extension is solely a sense-conception, and thus the very being of matter is given only in the sense, and the understanding supplies no notional at all as a connective. The Cartesian philosophy can know nothing of substance and cause as space-filling force existing in nature, and even the negative of substance as a vacuum is an impossible conception. Descartes thus reasons against the possibility of a vacuum —that if there were any such thing it might be measured, and all measure implies extension, and all extension is essential matter, and thus no vacuum can be. And in this, precisely, is its peculiarity. Altogether unlike the Pythagorean philosophy, when it has analyzed the phenomenal and found its highest analytical predicate in the conception of extension, and denied that any extension can be a void but must be material essence, and thus wholly phenomenal; it does not, like that, attempt to sublimate the phenomenal into a notional. Descartes had already provided for such want, in beforehand preparing for himself a connective wholly supernatural, and which allowed that he should utterly dispense with all function of an understanding, and connect directly by the reason. The phenomenal is held together not through substance and cause, but immediately by the Deity. Indeed, that the phenomenal can at all be known to be, depends upon having first demonstrated the spiritual to be; and all physical science originates in the previous science of

Theology. This, so peculiar a method of building up a nature of things by making its whole connective supernatural—and yet in such a way, as we shall see, that an amphiboly introduces its delusive play in another form though as really as in any of the preceding which has been noticed—demands that we carefully examine it, and be able to make a fair exposition of its fallacies.

Cartesianism, then, begins in universal doubt, and seeks for a first verified truth. In this very casting about for what may dispel all doubt, there is an action which may be called thought; and in this very thinking, there is an awaking in self-consciousness. Thus, in the thought itself, the mind becomes cognizant of its own being. Here then, is the first truth for all possible science—I think, and in thinking I cognize my own existence. "Cogito ergo sum." Having thus the existence of mind, and having found that this mind has many thoughts, which are named all as alike ideas, it makes *clearness* and *distinctness* the criterion of the truth of our ideas; and then finds this one grand idea as more obtrusive, absorbing, and unavoidable in the clearness of its presence than all others, viz: an all-perfect Infinite Being. Such an idea, so controlling and necessary, could not be in the mind from the mind itself nor from any other source, except as it originates in the actual existence of this all-perfect Being himself. The prominence, clearness, and necessity of the idea of a God is proof apriori of the actual existence of a God.   Thus the thinking soul is, and God is.

And now the sense gives us an outer world; but the sense can verify nothing, and only make phenomena to appear.   But we have already cognized an all-perfect Being, and his veracity must be manifested in his works.   The outer world, therefore, exists, or God has falsified his own veracity in making man the subject of perpetual and helpless deception.   The truth that the outer world is, rests upon the truth that God is, and that his works do not deceive.   In this way we come to the demonstration of an outer world as phenomenal reality.   This outer world is then, in the last analysis, found to be extension; and this, as the essence of all matter, is brought into its present arrangement as system of the universe, according to the foregoing process of the atoms in the vortices.

Thought is the Cartesian essence of mind, and extension that of matter, and in these is included all possible being.   They are utterly unlike, and can have no reciprocal communion with each other.   No-connection is to be thought between them, as if one could act upon or be affected by the other.   The essence of matter is wholly inert; thought only is active.   And in this is the provision made for all the dynamical connections in nature.   The breaking up of the inert essence of matter, the attrition into the first and second elements, the vortical revolutions and the connections of finite mind with matter, are all resolved into the immediate interposition of the Deity. The doctrine of " Divine Assistance" is made to account for all the movement and changes of nature.

And here, so far as the physical connection of the phenomenal universe is regarded, this philosophy has the merit of a logical consistency. It does not as in the preceding, attempt by an analysis of material phenomena to attain a notional in the understanding, by which to connect into a judgment a nature of things. The connective is supplied in another manner, and the supernatural is immediately introduced as the constituting force on which a system of nature depends. But, though not in the same direction as in the former theories, yet still from another quarter a similar ambiguity is introduced, and a delusion is effected which is to be dispelled by applying the true idea of an understanding. The false notional is not at all attempted from the material, but is derived from the spiritual phenomenon. The whole Cartesian philosophy founds upon Thought, as its first given fact. The phenomenon of thinking induces consciousness, and this is made evidential of a self, or an Ego, which thinks. That I have self-consciousness in thinking is taken as valid that I have in this, myself, as notional subject of thinking. Self-consciousness is sublimated into an understanding-conception of a permanent substance, as the causal source of thought. Here then, is the first deceptive ambiguity. The thinking in consciousness is wholly phenomenal; and an analysis of the exercise in the thinking and of the thought as product, and one put as the subjective and the other as the objective, deludes into the conviction that the supersensual subject Ego is truly attained. And then the speculation is still further advanced, that inasmuch as the analysis of the subjective can be carried no higher, therefore the Ego, as soul, is simple, indivisible and immortal.

But, inasmuch as the soul, which is thus surreptitiously assumed as an understanding-conception and permanent notional source for all thinking, can be source only for the thinking as inner phenomenon, and not at all source for the phenomena of an outer world, and therefore no knowledge of a nature of things can be attained through such connections; the philosophy returns to the phenomenal thought, and demonstrates the being and connections of an outward nature of things by another and entirely independent process. One thought as product is separated in an analysis from the thinking as intellectual activity, and because it is more prominent, absorbing, and necessary than all others, is taken to be more distinct and clear than any, and on this account the most true and valid of any, viz: that of an All-Perfect Being; and in this assumed validity of existence from the necessity of the idea, the being and perfections of God are considered as apriori demonstrated. The phenomenal in the inner sense is made available here, not merely for a notional source of thinking as self or soul, but taking the though as product, is made available for attaining immediately the supernatural as substantial ground for the thought; and the phenomenal is at once elevated to the divine. The sense is made to perform the functions of the reason.

But inasmuch, again, as the philpsophy needs only a physical substratum and connection, so this Deity, assumed *to be* from the clearness of the thought of the All-perfect, is used only as philosophical source for constituting a universal system of nature, and degraded to a mere physical force, as cause in an understanding-conception, for breaking up the original essence somehow unaccountably generated, and grinding it into its atomic elements, and whirling the subtle vortices which are to shape all things in their individual forms and systematic revolutions. While avoiding the absurdities of attaining its false notional connectives from a sublimation of the *outer* phenomena, it runs into even more gross fallacies and violent subreptions, in attempting delusively to attain its notional connectives wholly through a sublimation of the *inner* phenomena. The ambiguity of the phenomenal for the notional is the same as in the former theories examined, and the fallacy heightened in absurdity by elevating the phenomenal immediately to the supernatural, and then degrading the divinity of the supernatural to the bond-age and perpetual servitude of the natural. The Deity is needed only for holding nature to its place.

Malebranche simply carried forward Cartesianism to its ultimate results, without the addition of any important new principle; and the necessity for supernatural interpositions in nature became with him a completed doctrine of "Occasional causes," and the vision of all things in the Deity, and a resting of all evidence of the reality of an outer world upon divine Revelation.

(6.) Spinoza so far modified this philosophy in its foundation-principles as to make indeed a new system of the physical universe. The two essences of thought and extension which had been conceived as so heterogeneous that they could not come into communion, and hence demanded supernatural interpositions, were by Spinoza generalized and identified in a higher essence, which was assumed as ultimate, indivisible, and eternally immutable, and thus the Absolute Substance. God is not a personality, acting according to the imperatives of reason in view of final ends; but a simple essence, in the absoluteness of its own being developing a nature of things in the perpetual unfolding of itself. Extension and thought are merely analytical conceptions of this infinite substance in which they are identical. The absolute essence is both infinite thought and infinite extension, and thus all mind and all matter are but the modified development and modes of existence of the All-Perfect Being. A supernatural interposition is not needed to constitute and hold together a nature of things; the supernatural is developed into nature itself. An unfolding Deity is the universe.

And here, Spinozism is unquestionably more philosophically consistent than Cartesianism. It does not attempt to explain nature by getting a supernatural apriori to it, and then absorbing all of nature in this supernatural; but entirely reversing the process, it goes through nature up to the absolute substance, and then accounts for nature by evolving it from the absolute. Both may be termed Pantheistic; but Descartes' God is diffused as causality through nature, and Spinoza's God is the substance which in its own development becomes nature. But, in this last, there is the same ambiguous use of the phenomenal for the notional—a delusive substitution of the faculty of the sense for the faculty of the understanding—and thus attempting to think in discursive synthetical judgments with no valid medium through which to make the discursus, and therefore no valid connection in which to legitimate the conclusion in a judgment.

The thought and extension are simply the sublimations of the phenomenal, and not at all a valid notional supplied in the understanding; and instead of vainly attempting to think them into a nature of things by the interposition of whirling vortices, which again are but interpositions of supernatural agency, the attempt, equally as vain, is made to think them into connection by a higher sublimation of the phenomenal, and assuming it to be a valid substance as notion in the understanding, and then arbitrarily educing a nature of things from it, merely by a development of it. Let it be demanded to think in a judgment a connected order for this development, and all the philosophy of Spinoza is wholly impotent. It will then require a further sublimation of this assumed notional as absolute substance, and which is no more space-filling force, as substance cause and reciprocal influence, than the phenomenal thought and extension themselves. It stops with this assumed substance, but it is a mere delusive stopping-place; for philosophy as much demands an intelligent development of nature in a conditioning source, as a resting of nature upon an ultimate substance. Only a true idea of an understanding verifying its notional in a determined experience in the space and time-relations can do this.

(7.) The genius of Leibnitz, penetrating powerful and comprehensive beyond that of most philosophers, apprehended clearly the difficulties in the Cartesian system, and that they were still left unresolved in all the modifications of Spinozism; and in a manner evincive of the superiority of his intellect, he set himself to work a reformation in the very first principles of this philosophizing. But, manifestly, from the want of a true idea of an understanding in its operation of discursive connection, he only modified the system, but did not at all change the order of the thinking. It is still an attempt to sublimate the phenomenal to a notional, and to think a universal connection in a nature of things by only notionalizing the phenomenal. The acuteness and fertility of his mind is astonishing, but in the absence of the true light, it only changed the point of the delusive ambiguity, and still retained all the false play of the deceptive amphiboly before noticed.

The grand difficulty in the Cartesian system was the inertness of all physical essence. Causation could nowhere be used as a connective in nature itself, but must every where be superinduced upon nature, and thus perpetually demanding the supernatural. Nor did Spinoza's generalization of all thought and extension into the different modes of one assumed absolute substance help this difficulty. It gave a specious unity to nature, but provided for no intelligible exposition of the successive on-going in the changes of nature. A substantial ground was assumed, but because it was only a sublimation of the phenomenal, it could give no understanding-conception of force as a cause for change in a space-filling substance, and which might thereby condition an alteration of the phenomena in the sense. This deficiency was to be supplied, and somehow the notion of causality introduced into nature. This is the leading interest in the Leibnitzian physics, and the stand-point from whence to take an examination of this philosophy; and yet we shall find this causality to be merely an intellectualizing of the sense, though with much ingenuity, and giving much plausability to the fallacy.

The analysis of matter which Leibnitz assumed to be always given to us compounded, was the first step, and from this the atomic theory was necessarily adopted. The last analysis attained to an indivisible, indissoluble portion; and this atom, as thus wholly unextended and impossible to come under any outward determination, can only be distinguishable from other atoms in virtue of something within itself. Hence the principle of "the indistinguishable" in matter by any thing external. But changes are perpetually occurring in the atoms, and some "sufficient cause" is to be found for them; and as this cannot be from any outer conditioning but must be determined from the inner, and the inner can have nothing of extension or composition, so nothing is left but that it must be distinguishable in virtue of its inherent energy. A sort of representation-force, analogous to that which is an inherent property of mind, must be possessed by all atoms, and in the modifications of this only can one atom be determined as distinguishable from all others. Thus, the atoms are not inert and passive, as with Democritus and Descartes, but possess an inherent energy as power of inward representation, and in virtue of this inner causality they are not dead atoms, but monads. Each had its own particular representation-force, and in this is its principle of identity; and as each also is competent from this inner energy to represent all others within itself, every monad is competent to become a little world in itself and is "a microcosm." Some monads have their inner representation-force in utter unconsciousness, and are the elements of material nature; others are partially awakened into consciousness, and have indistinct representations, and are the elements of animal spirits; and others again have this inner energy developed into full and distinct consciousness, and are the elements of the rational human soul. God is the ABSOLUTE MONAD; and his existence, we are forced from the apriori laws and conditions of all thought to admit, and he stands as "sufficient reason" for the existence of all others. Thus, the elements for an intellectual system of the universe, all stand ready for a philosophical putting of a nature of things together.

In this particular possession of inner representation-energy, the whole must give all possible phases of being, and in such universality of representation there must be "perfection." Inasmuch as essential monadic being can have no determined external relationship, but only inner representation, so space can be no apriori condition of nature, but wholly consequential upon its being and representation. The representation-force is first, and space is produced in the representation—as if to the mirror there was no outer, then the mirror must first be, and the represented space consequently produced within it. In such production of space there is, of course, occasion given for the position, figure, and relative bearings of all that the monad shall envisage; and this in the case of all monads; and thus all things appear in space. But how is it that the relations correspond in time? The energizing causality is wholly inward, and not that one monad can act outwardly upon another; how then shall their separate and individual representations conform each to each? This demanded, not "the occasional causes" of Cartesianism which would require a perpetual interposition for each case, but an original arrangement which should harmonize all in their representations forever. And here is introduced the doctrine of "a pre-established harmony," in which all monadic representation-forces, as so many mirrors each representing the state of all the others, are made to tally precisely each with each. The entire universe of conscious and unconscious monads thus go on in their inner causal representations, not from any community of influences reciprocally among themselves, but orderly and successively in their periods from the wise arrangement of all in an original predetermination.

With all our interest in such surprising creations of genius, still how amusing to watch the double-play perpetually going on between the sense and the understanding! The sense gives to us every thing compounded and thus confused; and the mere analysis of this, according to this method of philosophizing, takes it out of the sense, and gives to us the things themselves in their essential being in the understanding. Thus the atoms become things as understanding-conceptions; and yet when we would think them in discursive connections, we are forced further onward for our real notion of things, and must endow them with an inherent causal-energy. Then, inasmuch as it must be an analysis from sense, and we have analyzed the atom beyond all outer relation, we take the causal-energy from an analogy of what may be attained in an analysis of our inner phenomena, and make it to be a representation-force. And when we would use this as the medium for a discursive connection, it is wholly impotent and we are again forced forward for our notional to an independent and unexplained pre-determination, which is the original connective for this harmony. The notional is ever thrown forward, and when we essay to step upon it, it straightway fails altogether as a support for the thinking, and the judgment is ever thrust forward into the void hopeless of all support. It thus, also, makes every principle it uses delusive. The principle of "the indistinguishable" is found in the use which the understanding makes of this false notional throughout. The phenomenal is analyzed beyond all outer determinations, and as if now it were the substantial thing in itself, its distinction from all others is to be found in the inner only. Difference of identity cannot be determined by place, for space itself is the product of a representation. The principle of " sufficient cause" is, for the same reason delusive, and no no true notion of force can be conceived but only harmonious representations. The representations cannot counteract; their opposition would be simply irregularity in time, as if the clock should not strike just when the hand points the hour. And finally, the principle of "pre-established harmony" leads to the same delusion, on the same account of a use of the false notional; for this harmony is simply conformity of representations, not an agreement of interacting dynamical forces. The system is, after all, simply the regulation for representing appearances, not the control and arrangement of acting and resisting substances. It is no more a nature of things than the accordant reflections of two mirrors face to face.

We will now give attention to the other method of philosophizing, viz:

2. *That which degrades the notional to a vague phenomenal, or entirely dispenses with it.*

In this order of building up a physical system, nothing is permitted to enter as conception of valid being which has not been attained through the sense. A supposed supersensual is to be held as delusory, and though accompanied by irresistible conviction can be determined as resting upon no valid basis.

The philosophy of Locke in accounting for the origination of all our knowledge, is the source of all this order of philosophizing in physics. The elements of all knowledge and the essence of all being are given to us according to Locke, through two sources only, viz: Sensation, giving to us that which is material element, and Reflection, giving to us that which is mental element. All our simple elementary knowledge is thus provided for. The simple elements, passively received, may be in various ways modified through the activity of the mind itself, and thus known in various determined relations. The mind is competent, having attained the simple elements, to combine, compare, and abstract; and through such mental operations we may know the elements as united, contrasted, and isolated. Hence our conceptions of double and single, even and odd, greater and less, higher and lower, general and particular, &c. All conceptions, not themselves elementary as given in the sense, are to be thus attained by a mental operation upon what is given in the sense; and all such operation is confined within these three functions, combination, comparison and abstraction.

From what we have already gained in our former investigation, it is manifest that all those immediate intuitions which are given in the definite constructions of the phenomena of sense, may in this way be accounted for; but the system of Locke greatly errs in its partiality and incompleteness, in supposing that any conceptions, conditional for discursive synthetical judgments, can be thus attained. Conjunction may thus be effected, but not connection. Relationship in space, time, and amount, may thus be determined; but not the inner dynamical relationships of being itself. The notions of substance, cause, and reciprocal influence, are no combinations, comparisons, nor abstractions of any simple elements attained in sense. Here is the grand defect of the sensualism of Locke. It would get along with only the functions of the

29

sense. Sensation gives all phenomena; reflection gives all the intuitive relations of phenomena; and no distinction is recognized between conjoining and connecting—mathematical and dynamical relations—intuitive and discursive judgments. Hence it would obtain the conceptions of cause and substance as it would those of likeness and difference. The philosophy begins in the sense, as all knowledge must; but it also ends in the sense, as no true philosophy can be permitted to do. Instead of any intelligible dynamic connections, we have really only juxta-positions and sequences. All understanding-conceptions are forced to be, in some way, the determinations of sense.

From this philosophy diverse theories have arisen in reference to various topics of speculative interest, such as are designed to explain the manner of perception; the foundation of moral obligation and responsibility; and the capability of attaining the data for a natural theology; but we have occasion now to consider such only as relate to a universal nature of things. A few of the more prominent cases will be sufficient to expose the illusion which comes in on this side, and show the deceptive ambiguity in the point of degrading the notional to a mere phenomenal, as connective for a universal physical system.

(1.) The first to be here noticed is the theory of David Hume. Whether the philosophy of Locke induced the skepticism of Hume, or whether the skepticism was itself congenial and the philosophy adopted as the means of justifying it, is not incumbent upon us here to decide. This much is clear, that he most acutely detected the skeptical tendencies of this philosophy, and as legitimately as intrepidly pushed the issue to the entire subversion of all philosophy in physics and of all science in theology. Nature and Religion have no other foundations than such as must be laid in faith, and which in each case may easily be convicted of credulity; and therefore to the consistent philosopher there is nothing so natural, so logically consequential, and thus nothing so noble, as to avow his doubts of them both.

The process in Hume's philosophizing is very plain and direct from the premises given. Knowledge, as given direct through the perceptions of sense, is experience; and all such sensible objects are termed "Impressions." The recalling of such impressions by the memory, or the anticipation of them in the imagination, he terms "Ideas." The ideas are the copies of the impressions, but as secondary they must be more faint and indistinct than the primary perceptions. We can have "impressions" of only that which is given in experience; and no "ideas" in the memory or the imagination which must not also be the copies of experience. These "impressions" and "ideas" are the mind's entire stock of original elements for all knowledge; and by the functions of combination, comparison, and abstraction, these elements may be brought into various propositions and judgments; and such modifications of them must constitute the sum total of all that man can know.

And now, " the relations of ideas," as given in the comparisons and combinations of the mind, are demonstratively certain; inasmuch as they are intuitive, or immediately beheld; and in this field lie all the conclusions of mathematics. Here is exact science. But "matters of fact" cannot be made to stand together in any such relations, and cannot therefore be brought within the demonstrations of science. How clearly in all this, did Hume see that no intuitive process could legitimate a discursive judgment! That any present fact in our experience should be connected with another fact which is to follow it, cannot be made intuition; and yet, by calling the last an effect of the first as its cause, we assume that there is a necessary connection, and then carry our convictions quite out of experience, and assume to determine how other facts and events must be, which have not at all been matters of experience, and perhaps are not yet at all in being. By what legitimate principles are such connections in judgments effected? All apriori demonstration, that such a connection must be in order that experience should be determined in the space and time-relations, was unknown to Hume, and utterly impossible to be effected by any philosophy based upon experience; and thus his skepticism in physical science stood impregnable. The effect cannot be immediately seen in the cause; no possible construction can give an intuition from one to the other; and thus there cannot be any predetermination of what the consequent shall be from any thing given in the antecedent. All reasoning from effect to cause or from cause to effect is thus wholly an assumption. All that can be said for it, and the clearest explanation of any conviction attained through it, is simply resolved into the result which a repetition of experience induces in the mind.

The *philosophical explanation* of the process is this; a first experience of such connection was like all other experience, an "impression" as a primary fact of sequence without any conception of necesity in the order of connection. Frequent repetition of the same sequence as "impression," induces its copy as "idea" in the memory, and this also is put as copy in the anticipations of the imagination; and this copy as idea, faint at first, ultimately becomes strong and confident "belief" that such connections are necessary. The conception of cause is an "idea," as it is a copy of an "impression," and is thus a mere offspring of experience as truly as any other copy in the memory or the imagination. The experience has given the idea of cause; cause has not determined the order of experience; and hence all reasoning from causes, as any apriori conditioning of nature, must be mere sophistry. Both Natural Philosophy, and Natural Theology are at once convicted of building a structure without a basis.

And, here we may detect the fallacy of the philosophy in its very source, and dispel the delusion which
has given so much speciousness to this skepticism, by
applying our apriori idea of an understanding as faculty for connecting phenomena in a system of universal nature. And this fallacy will at once, in this light,
be seen to lie in the ambiguity of using the same conception as both in the sense and in the understanding.
Here the understanding-conception is sensualized into
the phenomenal, whereas in the former order of philosophizing, the sense-conception was intellectualized into
the notional. The "impression" is wholly of the sense,
and is thus phenomenon only. The sequences of events
are phenomenal sequences altogether, and they account
for our *convictions* of necessary connection simply
through their repetition in experience. But no account is attempted for any necessary order in the
events of nature itself. The connectives for phenomena into a conception of a universal nature of things
are themselves mere copies of the phenomenal. Cause
and effect in their own necessary connections do not
condition our experience, but the repetitions of our
experience condition all our "ideas" of causation.
The same also must have been true of the connectives
of substance, and of reciprocal influence, as of cause;
only that the skepticism did not philosophize broad
enough to encounter the necessity for their explanation.
The notion in the understanding is degraded to a mere
copy of the phenomenal in the sense, and gives to

philosophy a nature of things which only seem to be connected in universal order and system, because the phenomena as original "impressions" have in the sense had their juxta-positions and sequences. Nature is merely a mass of appearances, and not a connection of existences; a continuance of "impressions," and not a series of things. And without a true notional in the understanding, as apriori demonstrated from the conditions of determining an experience in the space and time-relations, this is all to which philosophy could attain. Science could not go beyond sense. Mathematics only could be exact; philosophy and theology must be opinion and faith. All judgments of a nature of things must rest upon mere phantasms as the copies of those "impressions" which we deem them to connect; and all the conclusions of natural philosophy and theology rest solely upon the credulity which our habitual experience has induced. The supercilious sneer of the skeptic springs spontaneously from his clear perception that both philosophy and religion have no foundation.

(2.) Another example of this delusive method of discursive thinking is given in the philosophy of Brown. The understanding-conception is degraded to a mere illusion of the sense, and then rejected as an empty figment. The order of nature in the connected series of cause and effect is reduced to a mere fact of invariable sequence which the human mind is so made as unavoidably to anticipate.

This entire theory of causation is expressed in the following statement. According to Brown, simple invariable succession is the entire conception of cause and effect. The conception of *power*, as some bond which connects the antecedent and the consequent, is affirmed by him to be an illusive phantom of the imagination ; and though common to all former philosophers with the vulgar, is yet a mere chimera. That an illusion of some third thing, called power, stands between the two sequences and connects them, he explains as having become a general admission from various sources. The structure of language; a false identity between a thing with and without a particular predicate, as if the sun shining and the sun, or the man thinking and the man, were respectively the same; and the imperfection of the sense which is perpetually finding higher antecedents ; all these are made to explain the fact that the delusive conception of power has become so common. But when the mind is disabused of this delusion, then the whole process of cause and effect ceases to be so mysterious and inexplicable. There is no such mysterious something ever present in all sequences and never appearing, which has been called power, for connecting them together.

Such an illusion of an intervening connective does not help to explain our conception of cause and effect, but in truth gives another antecedent altogether more inexplicable than the phenomenon itself. Expel such a delusion, and then there remains simple invariable

sequence. The whole real meaning of power is, therefore, this invariableness of succession. To say that a
certain degree of heat applied to a metal will have its
invariable consequent of liquefaction; or, to say that
a certain volition is invariably followed by muscular
motion; or, that the divine fiat, "Let there be light,"
is inevitably followed by the coming of light; is in
each case the same as to say that the first has power
to produce the last, and which again is the same as to
say the first is the cause of the last. Invariableness of
sequence is the whole conception of power and of
causation. Having thus taken away all intrinsic dynamical connection, the natural inquiry for the origin
of this universal conviction of invariable succession is
met by cutting, without any attempt at untying the
knot, and resolving the whole into an arbitrary constitution of the human mind. We are so made as necessarily to imbibe such a conviction. It is an instinct implanted in human nature, operating as an "internal revelation," and is "a voice of ceaseless and
unerring prophecy."

Locke had attempted to account for the genesis of
such a conception as power, and thus for causation,
from sensible experience. But Brown, more clearly
than Locke, saw the impossibility of attaining any
proper conception of power as phenomenon in sense.
Obedient to the philosophy, therefore, since the
conception of power cannot come from it, it is taken
as wholly a delusion and its reality discarded alto-

gether. If it were at all possible to be used, he knows of no other method than by interposing it as another phenomenal antecedent to the effect, and thus merely perplexing the matter without at all explaining it. It is made the mere shadow which coming events cast before them, and the mind from its conformation anticipates the consequent as wholly an unexplained prediction. The notional, as understanding-conception, is wholly abolished in the mere sense-conception of an invariable sequence, and the conviction of such invariable order is an instinctive prophesying.

But, how impossible thus to attain to an intellectual system of universal nature! The separate phenomena are as really independent of all inter-agency as the particles of dust floating in the sun light, and simply *have* such an invariable order but nothing which efficiently *produces* it. Nature is a mere congeries of phenomena, and as destitute of all connection and reciprocal communion as the letters of the alphabet.

(3.) There are two other modifications of this method of philosophizing, having an immediate reference to *mental* phenomena, and out of which have originated two theories for giving to the mind systematic unity; and which are of the more interest for American Psychologists, since their respective authors were Divines of great distinction and high reputation in the religious community of New-England while they lived, and their influence upon all metaphysical speculation will not cease with the generation that now succeeds them.

We need have no reference to any theological doctrines to which these theories may have been applied, either for explanation, defence or refutation; nor to any other religious or philosophical tenets of their authors, but solely to the methods in which mental phenomena are sought to be connected into a system in the Understanding.

The *first* to which we will here attend, though later in age, is the theory of the late Dr. Emmons, so venerable while living, and so much revered since his death. This theory has been familiarly called " the exercise scheme ;" and when referred to the true idea of an understanding as above attained, will be found to follow that order of philosophizing which we are now considering—making the phenomenal to be the essential being, and wholly dispensing with the notional or introducing an arbitrary and illusory figment

The outline of this theory is as follows. The specific acts of thinking, feeling, loving, willing, &c., come within consciousness, and each one for the period of its duration is the soul in its essential being. There is no true substance, which as constant substratum or perpetual source permanently exists, and that changes in its mode of being so as to occasion the altered events; but when the thinking is, that is the soul; and when that departs and a feeling or a willing is, the exercise is all there is of the being and the soul exists as one and simple in every act. The voluntary exercises make the moral man, and all such acts in dis-

tinction from intellectual acts are known as the heart.
" The heart consists in voluntary exercises, and voluntary exercises are moral agency." "There is no mor-
ally corrupt nature distinct from free voluntary sinful
exercises." The phenomenal is the sole being of mind,
and nothing is but that which is the exercise itself.

And here, with all existence wholly in the exercise
and utterly exclusive of any substance which may be
thought as perpetual source for the exercises, the inquiry must arise—whence are these exercises? Is
there a void of all being between them, and thus does
each as essential existence come up from a vacuity of
all existence? This would seem to be the necessary
conclusion, since no substantial being is, which may
perdure through all the exercises. To escape from
such a chasm of all being and an origination of the
phenomenal being of the exercise utterly from a void,
as must follow when the notional is discarded and an
understanding is vacated, the supernatural is immediately interposed, and the exercise comes up as a direct production of the Deity. " Since all men are dependent agents, all their motions, exercises or actions
must originate from a divine efficiency. We can no
more act than we can exist, without the constant aid
and influence of the Deity." The supernatural is thus
made to take the place of the notional, and all the phenomena immediately originate in God, and are connected in unity by the direct efficiency of God. The
human agency is the exercise itself, and the Divine

agency is the efficient producer of it; and thus it is affirmed that "human agency is always inseparably connected with Divine agency." "He not only prepared persons to act, but made them act." "There is no possible way in which he could dispose them to act right or wrong but only by producing right or wrong volitions in their hearts. And if he produced their bad as well as good volitions, then his agency was concerned in precisely the same manner in their wrong as in their right actions." "His agency in making them act necessarily connects his agency and theirs together." The Divine efficiency is thus made to subserve all the purposes of the notional in an understanding, and the phenomenal exercises come up from it, and adhere together in a series by it.

But the delusiveness of such a false connection in the understanding is at once exposed, when we step forward upon it and trust our philosophy to it. For all that we possibly know is the phenomenal only, and all our conceptions must conform to the phenomenal, and although we have used the efficiency of the Deity as the origin and connective of all human exercises, yet must we now degrade this supernatural, used as a notional, at once to the phenomenal only. How may we conceive of the Divine agency in any other manner than as phenomenal exercise? Divine efficiency in producing our exercises is but an exercise, single and simple in being as our own. This, in other connections of the theory, is fully admitted and even directly argued, though when fully apprehended in its bearings upon the philosophy it shows its whole basis to be a mere delusion. The Divine efficiency is wholly ambiguous; it has been used as a notional, but when we come to rest upon it, the fact that after all it is only the phenomenal betrays itself. God exists just as we exist, in exercises only. "There is no more difficulty in forming clear and just conceptions of God's power, wisdom, goodness and agency, than in forming clear and just conceptions of human power, wisdom, goodness and agency. Power in God is of the same nature as power in man. Wisdom in God is of the same nature as wisdom in man. Goodness in God is of the same nature as goodness in man. And free voluntary moral agency in God is of the same nature as free voluntary moral agency in man. To say that God's agency is different in nature from our own is as absurd as to say that his knowledge, his power, or his moral rectitude is different from our own. And to say this is to say that we have not and cannot have any true knowledge of God." God's agency is as our own agency, with his whole existence in the single exercise for the period of its duration; phenomenal and fleeting from exercise to exercise; so that we are just as far from all originating source and connecting efficiency of the exercises as before. We have deluded ourselves by the use of a divine efficiency, as if it were a legitimate notion as source and connecting cause for our human exercises; but when we now come to rest upon it, we find it to be mere appearance and not be-ing; a sense-conception of the phenomenal and not at all an understanding-conception of the notional ; and the reeling philosophy must at once fall, or betake itself to some other and farther advanced delusion of using the sense for the understanding.   Such a philosophy can-not possibly attain to a conception of the efficiency it so much uses.   It calls it Divine efficiency ; Deity ; but it is used only as an originating source and con-necting cause for human phenomenal acts.   If it were validly attained it would be mere physical connective for the exercises ; but as ultimately apprehended, it means only a higher exercise single and isolated, and equally as devoid of all possible conception of efficien-cy as the human exercise.   There is no connective for mental action, either as human or Divine ; and the very notion of efficiency, to say nothing of a free per-sonality and independent Deity, is a surreptitious ta-king of a passing phenomenon in its place.   Such ex-ercises could no more be determined as an experience in time, than the exercises of our dreams can be con-nected in the unity of existence with our waking hours.

The *other* theory belonging to the same process in philosophizing, and the last which we shall here feel disposed to notice particularly, is that which is ad-vanced by Pres. Edwards, in answer to an objection against the doctrine of Original Sin.   His acceptation of the doctrine of original sin, in systematic theology, is that of an imputation of Adam's first transgression

to all his posterity in this sense, that in all there is a
" liableness or exposedness, in the divine judgment,
to partake of the punishment of that sin." The objection which he conceives as being brought against
such a doctrine is, " that such imputation is unjust
and unreasonable, inasmuch as Adam and his posterity are not one and the same." The objection is removed by affirming just the opposite, viz : that Adam
and his posterity are one and the same; and then
comes in the philosophical theory to which we here
have reference, to show the identity of the race with
the progenitor in the first transgression. With such
identity understood, the punishment is apprehended
as both just and reasonable, inasmuch as their action
is involved as truly as his act. But without any concern here with the theological doctrine, we look only
at the philosophical theory to account for the personal
identity of all with Adam.

There is first a somewhat extensive reference to
different analogies in the perpetuation of identity in
other cases; as of a tree an hundred years old, and
that tree as it first sprang from the ground ; the adult
body of forty years, with the body in its infancy; the
identity in one person of the body and the soul ; and
perpetuated consciousness as throughout the same
consciousness; after which comes a more explicit an-
nouncement of the theory. It is made to have a general application to the phenomena of both the material
and the mental world. These phenomena are ever

separate and fleeting, and the difficulty is, as thus isolate, to account for their identity in any one thing.
Thus we have the brightness of the moon shining in
the clear evening sky, and that shining appears constant and in perpetual being. But when this is intellectually considered, it is manifest that nothing here
is permanent; but that all is only a repetition of coming and departing appearance. The rays in one instant of the shining are not those of the next instant.
A new effect comes into being with each successive
moment of the shining, and this coming and departing
of one new effect after another is the same in all its
qualities; in the gravity of the moon as in that of its
shining; and this also in the case of all the phenomena
of an outer world. All nature is but a continual repetition of new creations. Nothing is for a moment the
same, but its perpetuation is a continual repetition of
new products. That there is any perpetuity to any
thing depends wholly upon perpetual creations, and
identity of object in any thing is an arbitrary establishment of the Deity. A divine constitution is given
to nature in these incessant and orderly new creations.
The sameness or identity of any thing, from time to
time, consists solely in the keeping of an onward flow
of these new products. Nothing is the same in nature
from one period to another, but just as the flowing
river is the same ; a continual coming and departing
of the new elements of which the thing is constituted.

By the like arbitrary establishment of the Deity
30

through a perpetual divine efficiency, the personal identity of every human being is constituted. One mental phenomenon departs and another comes, just as the efficiency of God keeps on the perpetual series; and inasmuch as this is the sole ground of all personal identity, nothing hinders that this perpetuated divine constitution should run on from one person to another and up through all persons to their first parent. No man would be the same from hour to hour, and on from year to year, except for this divine constitution; and this may just as well give identity from age to age as from year to year, and to all individuals of the race as to all the phenomena in each individual. This is what gives to the human race its unity, and humanity is thus constituted one identity through all ages. The first transgression is therefore an act belonging to all, and as sinful, throws its guilt and liability to punishment upon all; inasmuch as in this divine constitution an identity is perpetuated, making all to be truly one.

How clearly is all this method of philosophizing based upon the principle, of bringing in the conception of a supernatural to perform the part of a notional in the connections of the understanding. Phenomena are taken as the true being, and a divine efficiency connects them; and this not only in nature but in personality; and not only in one person but identifying all persons. How shall such an efficiency be attained except as a mere assumption? How shall its own connections in any identity be determined? How shall phenomena be determined in the experience as in one space and in one time, without shutting up this connecting divine efficiency also within the determinations of space and time ? The Deity must in this way be degraded to the phenomenal. And in the same manner may we detect the fallacies of all philosophizing, where the phenomenal is forced into the place of the only true being, and the notional is discarded ; or the supernatural is made to take its place, only in the very next step to be forced in subjection to the constructions of the sense. The phenomenal can never be connected into a system of nature and determined in an experience in space and time, by any false playing off of the conjunctions of the sense for the connections of the understanding ; nor by surreptitiously introducing a divine efficiency, which can itself have no other predicates than the apriori elements of quantity.

We may, then, affirm the partiality, incompleteness, and thus the error of all philosophy which deludes itself by an ambiguity, on either side, of elevating the sense into the region of the understanding or of degrading the understanding to the functions of the sense. An amphiboly necessarily follows, and the ball is tossed from one hand into the other, as every changing step destroys the balance thus vainly sought to be preserved. Certainly, with very few exceptions, philosophy from its earliest history has kept itself one-sided on one or the other of these extremes ; and to help itself out of its difficulties, either nature has been made God or God has been made nature. The English mind has best maintained its balance, since the great lights of Grecian philosophy in Plato and Aristotle have been obscured or perverted, and this not so much from the clear and intelligent apprehension of the manner of doing it, as by an almost instinctive mother-wit or good judgment, sometimes called common-sense, which forbad the putting of all things upon either foot at once; and feeling the awkwardness of all such attempts it has striven, at least, to make its philosophy stand on both feet. Cudworth has introduced his conception of "*a plastic power*" into nature; and this, though neither a space-filling substance nor a time-filling source; neither successive cause nor simultaneous reciprocity; yet, as a connective notional in an understanding, merely general and which might be made to accomplish what any occasion for its use should require, has preserved his intellectual system of the universe from falling into the gulf on either side, through an annihilation of the sense, or an emptiness of the understanding. It gave a real dynamical connection to the phenomenal universe, though with no possible determinate order apriori; and his whole atomic contrivance is just so much surplusage, inasmuch as all notional connective is supplied in the "*plastic power*," and the atoms become the mere "chips in the porridge," the philosophy being wholly made up without them.

So also, Newton's good judgment, cleaving to facts
rather than speculation, and taking these in their intellectual laws rather than merely observed appearances, kept both the constructions of the sense and the
connections of the understanding in their proper
spheres, and performing their proper services in the
conception of universal nature; but without any apprehension of an apriori psychology, which gave to
each their necessary and universal conditions. The
notions of substance, cause, and reciprocal influence,
were understood to be the laws in nature, while the
diagrams in pure space and time gave the intuitive
forms for all phenomena; and thus was a nature of
things truly constituted, with no ambiguity of either
the functions of the sense or those of the understanding. And so more emphatically with the philosophical genius of Lord Bacon; accurately distinguishing
the laws and forms in nature, from all qualities and
events in appearance; and thus perfectly separating
the work of the sense, from all operations of the understanding; analyzing nature intellectually and not
chemically; it has established forever the highway o
all inductive science, though all unconscious of an apriori road which, in its misapprehension, it affected to
despise as emptiness and absurdity. The idealism it
condemns is that which its own good judgment taugh t
itself to shun—a mere arbitrary hypothesis, not tha t
which has its ideals in the conditional laws of all
thought, and which must necessarily be in nature, if

nature herself may be subjected to a determined experience.

We here complete the Frst Chapter of the Understanding, having attained it completely in its Idea and also seen how in the light of this idea, we may detect the errors of false and defective processes of philosophizing, in those very points where the fallacies originate; because they are seen to depart from the apriori elements of all possible connection, and to violate the conditional principles of all thinking in discursive judgments, and thereby render themselves helpless in all determination of an experience in space and time. But, as yet our attainment is only an Idea. It is the demonstrating how an understanding, that may determine its experience in the connections of space and time, is possible to be; and in order to science, it is now necessary that we find such an understanding in actual operation, and so connecting in judgments its whole phenomenal experience. This will be effected in the Second Chapter.

CHAPTER II.

THE UNDERSTANDING IN ITS OBJECTIVE LAW.

SECTION I.

SPACE AND TIME, EACH AS A WHOLE.

THE Faculty of an Understanding is to so give connection to the phenomena gained in the sense, that they may become an order of experience determined to their places in space and to their periods in time. Our apriori idea of such a faculty, that may operate such a result, has been found to include the notion of constant substance as ground for connection in space; perduring substance as source for connection in perpetual time, consecutive cause as efficiency for connecting in successive time, and reciprocal influence as condition for connecting in simultaneous time. This is subjective Idea, or possible understanding only; for demonstrative science it is still incumbent that we attain a Law in actual facts, the correlative of this idea, and in such determine the real operation of such a faculty.

In effecting this, we shall take our attained apriori idea for the present as hypothesis only, and will apply it to actual facts in a sufficiently broad induction to induce full conviction, that our necessary and universal idea has its counterpart in a veritable law of intelligent action. We shall need to gather facts in respect both to the determination of an experience in *one whole* of space and of time; and the determination of it to *particular places and periods* in this one whole of space and of time. It will be requisite to appropriate a Section to each.

That we in fact do determine experience in both ways is manifest from our forms of expression and the universal adaptations of language. We speak of a universal Space as inclusive of all spaces, and in which all experience is in the same one space. So, also, we speak of a universal Time inclusive of all times, comprising *eternitas a parte ante* and *eternitas a parte post*, and in which all experience of ourselves or others is embraced. We speak of space as one void expanse, which in its immensity gives place for all phenomena; and of time as one open duration, in which is period for all events. We talk of the unfolding and unrolling of time; that which has been as already spread out, that which now is as just opening, and that which is to come as yet shut up: and so also of the stream of time, all the parts of which pass any one point successively; and of the ocean of time, which as one all-embracing flood bears all events along together. Space is thus a whole enclosing all spaces, and not an ever-growing conjunction of parts; and time is one whole embracing all periods, and not an endless adjunct of portions of time. We speak, moreover, of experience determined in its particular places, as of the map of human experience in which all phenomena have their place; and also determined in its particular periods, as of the chronicle of human experience in which all events have their own order of occurrence.

With the fact manifest in all forms of communication that we determine experience both in a whole of space and of time, and each fact of experience to a particular place and period in this whole of space and of time; we have this as the end of our present investigation, to answer the inquiry—How is this effected? Do the facts in the case show that such determination is made under a Law, which completely corresponds with our apriori Idea? This we must make to be apparent, both as determination in *one whole* of space and of time; and as *particular* in place and period.

SECTION II.

THE DETERMINATION OF EXPERIENCE IN ONE WHOLE
OF SPACE AND OF TIME.

WE will here make an induction of facts, which will be seen to come under the conditions of our hypothetical idea, viz : that we determine an experience to be in one universal space and time, *through the connections of the phenomenal in a notional.* We will take an experience in space and an experience in time separately, inasmuch as the facts in each case must be of a different class and indicating a peculiar notional connective for each; that of experience in universal space, conditioned upon the connection of space-filling substance, and that of experience in universal time, conditioned upon the connection of time-enduring source. The substance is known as space-filling, by the apprehending of a constant impenetrability in the same place; and as time-enduring, from the perduring of this impenetrability through its different places or its altered phenomena in the same place.

1. *Experience in universal space.*—Let us *first* take the facts given us in our *pure intuitive reasoning.* It would be the same in numbers as in the pure diagrams of points in space; but the illustration will not be so perspicuous from the use of numbers, as from that of definite pure figures in space. When I construct any

diagram by my sole intellectual agency in self-consciousness, I have in the apprehension of the pure diagram necessarily the apprehension of a space also. Every repetition of the constructing of similar pure diagrams is necessarily connected with the apprehension of a space for each completed construction. Our facts, therefore, may here be multiplied to the extent that we can have different constructions of pure diagrams, all giving an apprehension of a space in the fact of their own pure apprehension.

But none of these pure spaces are determined as in one universal space. One construction is produced and dismissed after another and at different periods intervening, and as the pure diagram departs from the self-consciousness, the space apprehended also departs with it; inasmuch as neither the diagram nor the space had any significancy except in my subjective consciousness. We can by no means determine that these spaces are in one universal space, and only determine from the primitive unity of our self-consciousness, that they have been constructed and apprehended by one self. There is no constant substance, as space-filling, whereby to determine constant sameness of place, and we do not, therefore, determine different constructed pure diagrams in their places to be in one and the same universal space.

Much less is it practicable, to determine the pure diagrams constructed in different self-conscious subjects and their apprehended spaces to be in one universal space. The constructing agency is conditioned only by the scheme in the productive imagination in each subject; and we do not determine one man's pure diagrams in space, to be in the same universal space with the places of another man's diagrams. We cannot say that the triangles, circles, &c. of one, are the same as those of another; nor that they are together in the same one whole of all space; inasmuch as there is no one space-filling substance, which occasions the constructions in all persons to be of one thing, and in one and the same place, and this in the one universal space. The law for *construction* is here found, but the law for *connection* is utterly wanting; and hence, while we have the intuition we can have no judgment in the understanding, and while we have a subjective experience, as seeming phenomena, we can have no connection of these seeming phenomena into an experience determined in one universal space.

We will *next* take facts in mere *organic affections.* —The organ of vision is the most appropriate, though sometimes facts of the same class may be found in the organ of touch, or that of sound. It is practicable, by a pressure on the eye-ball, to attain changeable floating colors in our self-consciousness; and which keep up their appearance for a longer or shorter period. We may construct them into figures more or less definite, and though often unlike any shapes of reality, they yet have their places and relationships each to each. Some permanent organic defect or in-

jury may make such affections permanent, as in cases
of clouded spots and rings in the sight, and moving
appearances as if of some discoloration in the humor of
the lens, known as *volitantes muscipuli;* or perhaps,
for a few moments after having turned the eye aside
from an intense light; or the dreadful phantoms of
some brain affections, as in *delirium tremens.* In all
such phantasies, we have as truly the apprehension
of a space, as we have of the shades or colors which
come and go as organic illusions; but inasmuch as
the affection is simply organic, and having no significancy except for the self-conscious subject whose organ it is, such illusions and their spaces are as wholly
subjective as the pure diagrams of mathematics.
They are not conditioned in their construction by any
scheme in the productive imagination, but altogether
from the affection in the internal state of the organ ; and
as these change or are permanent from the state of the
organ, and not from any occasion in a constant space-
filling substance, so we never determine such spaces
to be in one universal space, nor that the places at
different periods of the appearance are the same places.
And much less do we determine the spaces, in all the
different self-conscious subjects of such affections, to
be in the same universal space. The occasion for a
construction in figure is given, because the conditional
law of all conjunction in unity is here; but the conditions for a connection in the judgment of an understanding are not here given, and we can bring no such

experience within the determination of a universal space. All such facts are fully explicable from our hypothetical idea, and prove it to be the law for the determination of experience in one space.

We will *again* take facts occurring in *reflected vision*. The same illustrations might be found in reflected hearing, as an echo in the sense; but inasmuch as hearing has the conditions for only a very imperfect construction of space, it cannot be made so convenient for our design. We have appearances in vision from any medium that may subserve the purposes of a mirror—the calm surface of a lake; the prepared plate of glass with its quicksilver coating on the backside; or some metal with its highly polished surface. In any such arrangement, the occasion is given for a content in the sense, and the construction into definite figure is complete, and readily effected. In all such constructions, a space is apprehended as necessarily as the figure constructed in the consciousness. But this space is signficant only as relative to the particular mirror. The mirror is conditional for it; it is produced in it, and destroyed in its destruction. There are as many different spaces as mirrors, and it is impracticable that there should be one universal space embracing all mirrored spaces. Such appearance is objective, inasmuch as the mirror is no part of the subject-self but occasions the same appearance for all subjects of self-conciousness in the same circumstances; and thus the space is objective and independent of the peculiarity of the subject apprehending it, and is the same space for all self-concious subjects of it. But though objective and the same space to all that may apprehend it, yet is it space in that mirror only and not the same space with that in any other mirror; since the removal or destruction of the mirror, abolishes its space, without any interference with other mirrored spaces. We may thus very well speak of the definite figures in the same mirror as all appearing within the same space, for there is the constant substance of the mirror through which to connect at each different period of observation and for every different observer. But another mirror has its own space, for each period of observation and for every observer; and it would demand an including mirror of all mirrors, to bring the spaces of all mirrors into one universal mirrored space. And precisely because there is no such all embracing substance, which, as universal mirror, might hold all mirrored spaces in itself, there can be no determined universal whole for the spaces in all mirrors. It is thus impossible to determine the experience in reflective vision in one universal space; and this precisely in conformity with our hypothesis; for, so far as constant substance may be thought in the mirror, there is one whole of space, but because constant substance for all mirrors cannot be thought, therefore the spaces in all mirrors cannot be connected in one universal space.

And still further, the mirrored space may be con-

sidered in reference to the space in which the mirror
itself is. Each mirror is itself in a space and has its
own space in itself, and the space within the mirror
cannot be the same space with that in which is the
mirror itself; for the removal or destruction of the
mirror is an abolishing of the space within it, but no
interference with that space in which was the mirror
itself. To make the mirrored spaces one universal
space would demand a universal substance as constant mirror, which might contain all others ; but such
universal mirror would still demand its own place in
which it might be, and could never identify the place
in which it was, with the universal mirrored space
that was in it. Were it true, therefore, that an experience of reflective vision should be determined in
a universal whole of all mirrored spaces, by the occasion of an including substance as mirror for all mirrors, it would still be impracticable to determine such
experience in one universal space; for the spaces in
which the universal mirror must be, could not be
thought connected in one space with that universal
mirrored space which was in the mirror itself.

And still further, the space in which the mirrored
appearance is, may be considered in reference to the
space in which the phenomenon is, of which the mirrored appearance is the reflection. The reflected appearance is not the same as the phenomenon reflected,
for the removal of the mirror abolishes the first but
has no interference with the last; and in the same

way and for the same reason, the space in which is
the reflected appearance is not the same space as that
in which is the phenomenon reflected. Should some
universal mirror, therefore, give all reflected appearance to be an experience in one universal mirrored
space, we should not thus connect this experience in
the same space with an experience of the phenomena
reflected. The one, though universal of its kind,
would still leave the other altogether unincluded.
The substance which filled the space and occasioned
the phenomenon reflected would be no substance in
the mirrored space of the reflected appearance, and
on this account the two spaces cannot be connected
in a judgment of the understanding, into the same
space. Thus, in all the many and very diversified
facts of reflected vision, we find them all held in colligation by our hypothetical idea, as their actual law.

We will, in the *last* place, take the facts which occur in *open vision*. The illustration will be the same
in any organism, that may give occasion for definite
construction in space; but as the organ of vision gives
such occasion the most perfectly, the facts connected
with vision become the most appropriate for our purpose. Mere appearance in consciousness necessitates
the apprehending of a space; but mere appearance
does not give an occasion for determining all as in one
space. When I simply perceive the stars in their appearances, I see them to be in a space; and I may
make constructions, that shall give me their bearing

31

and distance from each other in that space; but something more than appearance must be given, as occasion for connecting them in thought in the one universal space.   I cannot perceive in the sense, but only
judge in the understanding that all appearance is in
the one space. If I sail on a smooth lake in a clear
night, I may perhaps be wholly unable to perceive
the surface of the water, so perfectly does it reflect all
that is above it.   In such a case I shall perceive the
appearance of the stars above and beneath, and so far
as perception is concerned I am ensphered in a heaven
of stars, and the mere appearance cannot determine
for me which hemisphere is direct and which reflected appearance.   It is only where in the understanding
I fix the constant space-filling substance, that I come
to determine this one to be the existing heaven and
the other its perfectly mirrored reflection.   And my determination of appearances in this one space is only
as I think it to be filled with constant substance.
The space-filling substance of the stars has been constant through the day, though the more intense sun-
light has wholly absorbed their phenomenal being;
and when they appear again on the succeeding evening, because their appearance is occasioned by the
same constant substance, I judge them to be the
same stars, and in the same space.   So, also, when
the voyager has sailed to the opposite side of the globe
and on the opposite side of the equator, he perceives
a heaven in which the stars have wholly another ap-

pearance; but he judges them all to be in the same one space, not because he so perceives them, but because he conceives a filling of space by some existing substance from the place of the stars in one hemisphere to the place of the different stars in the other. A chasm of all substantial being as notional space-filling force would cut off all communication from one phenomenal world to the other, and we should be unable to determine them in the same one space, but only as each in its own space.

All the facts, both as negative of a connection in a notional and as positive for such connection, come together in our hypothesis—that we never determine experience in one universal space except in the thought of a connective notional, and always when we have such connection. No fact can be found in any experience determined in one whole of space, that may exclude itself from the colligation of this universal Law.

2. *Experience in Universal Time.*—I can have no apprehension of the passing of a time except through some modification of my internal state. When that varied modification is going on, a time is apprehended as going on in my consciousness; as that is quickened or retarded in its flow, the apprehension of an elapsing time is faster or slower; and as all such modification of inner state ceases in consciousness, all apprehension of a time ceases in consciousness likewise. It is, thus, ever the fact that some modifying process is going on

in the internal state, and this apprehended in the light
of consciousness, or we do not consciously apprehend
that a time is passing; and, that we do apprehend
the elapsing of a time, in conformity with the flow of
such varied modifications of inner sense. This fact
full in our apprehension will facilitate the acquisition,
and ready application, of many other facts to our present purpose.

We will *first* gather some facts in purely *subjective
experience*. There are many instances of an experience going on wholly within our own minds, and in
which we are ourselves our own world. The inner
sense alone is active in perceiving and constructing a
train of passing events as they take place wholly
within our own subjective being. This may be a passing of one emotion after another, or one thought after
another, or perhaps a varied flow of thoughts emotions
and purposes which stand only in our consciousness
and pass only in our inner sense, while all attention
to any thing external is withdrawn. In such a case
there is the consciousness of an elapsing time, but as
it has been apprehended only in relation to the coming and departing of the inner events, its correspondence with the time which has been going on in the
flow of passing events external to us has not been at
all regarded; and as we have had no apprehension of
the external events and the time of their flow, it is
impossible that we should put one within the other
and determine them to the same one universal time.

We are obliged, when we are roused from our subjective thinking to recur to some standard which indicates how the flow of passing outward events has progressed, and thus determine the period of our musing by putting it within a definite period of an objective flowing of events; and we are sometimes greatly surprised at the ascertained disparity between them.

We may suppose some pure geometrician as Euclid or Archimides, or some Newton or LaPlace constructing his pure diagrams of the heavenly movements, and so wholly intent on the intuitive processes which are going on in his own pure creations, that the phenomenal events of an outer world are utterly lost to the consciousness. To such a mind, absorbed in its own action, there will be a progressive modification of the internal state as the process of pure construction and intuition goes onward, and thus consciously a time is passing; but the only time apprehended is that in which this inner agency may be brought, by constructing into definite periods the instants in which it has stood or the moments through which it has passed. Were there no other conception of the modification of an inner sense but such as was subjectively experienced in its own constructing agency, we should have a time but it would be our own subjective time only; nor should we be able to say that it could be at all within any universal time of an objective duration. When the philosopher awoke from his profound study and went out from

the consciousness of an inner sense to the consciousness
of an outer movement, he would be wholly unable to
identify the subjective succession with an objective duration, except as he could fix on some constant substantial being as a source of successive changes in the
alterations of its phenomena, and from that determine
how an objective time had passed since his subjective
time had been going on, and thus putting the period
of the latter within the definite period of the former.

While it thus is manifest that time subjectively can
have no identification in an objective time; except
through the determination of the one within the other
by the connections of phenomenal events in a perduring substantial source, so it is the more manifest
that the mere passing of a time in subjective consciousness can never be determined in any universal
time. My inner agency in its modifications of my
internal state is subject to perpetual interruptions.
When it is in process, then a time is passing; when
it is interrupted, then is the flow of time in my subjective consciousness broken up; and it is not possible that I should conjoin the periods as in one time
across these breaches. Within my subjective experience there has been only separate periods as I have
been conscious of the varied internal modifications of
state, and those separated by intervals when no subjective time was passing; and surely, without some
perduring source marking its changes in perpetually
altered phenomena, and which I can never find in

my subjective being, I can never connect these separate periods across their fathomless voids of all time,
and determine them to belong to one universal whole
of all time. To my subjective experience they are
so many separate times. And I have nothing in me,
as the subject of their self-conscious apprehension, by
which I can connect them all in one universal time.

Other subjects of self-consciousness may by their
own inner agency be modifying their own internal
states. And coming to the consciousness that a time
is thus passing on in their inner sense; but there is
nothing to connect the periods in their interruptions
into one time in each self-conscious subject, much
less any thing to connect all their periods into one
universal time for them all. There must be a perduring source, whose changes shall be marked in continually coming and departing phenomena which arise
as events from it, and thus give a continually flowing
time objectively as common standard for all their subjective times; and only thus may all be determined
in the same universal time. No one subject can connect his own periods across their frequent interruptions by any permanent standard in his own subjective being. And neither one nor all can bring the periods of their separate selves into one time, from any
common standard found in their subjective being; nor
is this in fact ever done but by referring them all to
some permanent objective source of changes. There
would be as many times as there are subjects of self-

consciousness, did we not determine our own and each others times by some permanent objective notional, which as substantial source connects the changes in their periods and gives one time for us all.

We may *next* take facts in our *subjective organism.* If we confine the modification of our internal state to the coming and departing appearances or the motions in some delusive organic affections, we shall attain a large class of facts for our purpose. The deceptive phantoms before mentioned in some diseased or deranged organ—as the colors from the pressed eye-ball, or a ringing sound in the ear, or a pain in the nerves— would give occasion for a constructing agency and thus for a modification of internal state, and thereby secure the consciousness of a passing time. But inasmuch as this sensation originates in the organism, and gives occasion for the self-conscious possessor of the organ only to be thus internally affected, the passing of the time can be of no significancy beyond his subjective being, and as exclusively his own time as above in the purely mental movements. So far, therefore as there are such periods in organic experience, they may furnish their facts for our purpose.

Perhaps the facts of dreaming may here give the best illustration. A dream may be taken as a sensation in our subjective organism generally, inducing such intellectual constructions as the state of the organism occasions; and such, though only of the re-productive imagination, do yet induce a modification of the internal state, and thus the conscious passing of a time. But none of us can bring the times of our dreams into one connected whole of a dreaming time for ourselves subjectively, much less put all the times of all dreaming in all persons into any one time, or identify the times passing in our dreams with our objective universal time, only as we have some substantial source for phenomenal successions, and subject the times of our dreams to this one common standard which marks the progress of one universal time for all.

We may *lastly* take the facts of any *real phenomenal experience*. My perceptions of phenomena through any organism are, so far as they are appearance in my consciousness, subjective only. The color, the sound, the touch, the taste, and the smell, are all in me subjectively; and the modification which their distinction and construction in consciousness occasions in my internal state gives the consciousness of a passing time, but, this phenomenal passing in its periods is in my subjective consciousness only. I am not conscious that such modifications and such periods are passing in others. This would demand that the others consciousness should become phenomenal in my consciousness. I have my own phenomenal coming and departing in consciousness, and another subject may have his; but no consciousness of either can put the interrupted periods of one subject into one time, much less the periods of the two subjects of self-consciousness into one common time. Every subject judges that what has occasioned his perception of the phenomena is the same permanent substance occasioning the like perceptions for all; that the changing events originate in a source which is a common occasion for perceiving the same series of events by all; and that the occasions for modifications of internal state are given alike to all; and thereby the periods are the same to all, and are connected in the same one time for all. The substantial time-keeper gives the phenomena of moving hands over the dial-plate, and the tick of the seconds, and the periods of them in their series, as a standard for common experience; and although the perceptions are only subjective and separate in the sense, yet the permanent sameness of substantial source in the thought connects them all in one nature, and in one time. Thus, in all the above facts is the colligation of our hypothesis verified as universal Law.

SECTION III.

THE DETERMINATION OF AN EXPERIENCE IN ITS PARTICULAR PLACES AND PERIODS.

ALL experience is but a medley of appearing and disappearing phenomena, except the phenomena are determined in their particular places and periods. And that we do judge phenomena to be each in its own place and period in universal space and time, and determine their relative bearings and distances from each other, needs no illustration; since our experience has no connection in itself as a whole any further than such determination of particular phenomena in space and time is effected. The point for investigation is, to find the Law in the facts for such particular determination. Will our hypothetical idea bind up within itself all the facts of a determination of particular phenomena to their places in space and their periods in time? If so, the induction will manifest it to be their law; and thus that the understanding does determine the particulars of an experience in place and period, in accordance with our apriori idea of an understanding already attained. We shall, as before, take the particular determinations in space and in time separately.

1. *Particular determination of places in space.*— All the phenomena of experience, we judge to be in one universal space; and the law for this as already found in the facts is, the connection of these phenomena in a constant space-filling substance. We shall now show, that the law for all *particular determination in space* is the fixing of the phenomena in their relative spaces, by their inherence in the constant space-filling substance.

In all determination of particular phenomena in space there must be some movement. The place occupied must be determined in bearing and distance from other places, and we never take such bearings and distances without an intellectual moving agency which in its progress constructs the places and the lines between them. But no movement can be apprehended, except in reference to somewhat that is permanent. I only determine that I move, by a reference of myself to something which does not move. It thus becomes the condition in all determination in place, that we have some permanent stand-point.

But I find no permanent stand-point in my subjective being. When I am conscious of an inward constructing agency producing pure figures in space, the *movement* is apprehended only in the passing of the agency throughout the diverse points in the primitive intuition. Subjectively, my pure diagrams have a relative bearing and distance from each other, but no determined relation to the places of any phenomena in universal space. Nor, from my subjective sensations any more than from my subjective pure intuitions, do I attain to any permanent stand-point. If I press my eye-ball and fill the organ in consciousness with the floating fantastic colors, they may have bearings and directions from each other, but they give no permanent point for determining themselves in universal space. And this would be precisely the same with our real sensations, were only the subjective sensations regarded. That I had a real sensation in touch, and this continued so that in my consciousness I attained the construction of some definite figure and thus a place in space; yet, if the sensation were all that was given, I should not be able at all to determine where in the universal space that place was, nor what direction and distance from the place of any other construction by the touch. The result would be the same in the construction, whether the organ of touch moved over the resistance or the resistance moved over the organ, and the mere sensation would give no permanent stand-point from whence to take any bearings and distances. Sensation can give only the subjective; and the subjective can never attain to any permanency from whence to determine particular places in space. All the facts of our merely subjective experience are bound in this law, that we can determine them only in a subjective space, for that only has permanency in reference to our subjective self; but what relation this bears to any places in universal space we cannot determine, precisely because we can attain no permanent objective.

But, if now I take my own body, and think all the phenomena which it occasions in the sense to inhere in it as a constant space-filling substance, and thus that this body permanently occupies a place; I can in this determine the bearing and distances of all these phenomena inhering in the permanent substance of my own body, and say what are their relations in their places to each other. The direction and distance of the appearing head from the appearing foot through any sense of vision or of touch may readily be determined; because there has been given the permanent space-filling substance in the understanding, which as fixed position in objective space occasions its own phenomena to appear in their own relative places, as inhering in it each in its own place. Just so far as you fill a space with the permanent substance, you determine the relative places of its phenomena; for so far, and only so far, you have the hypothetical law for it.

But such determination, of the relative places of the different phenomena of my own body, can determine nothing of the relations to any places in universal space beyond it. I cannot determine my relative position in the room I occupy, by any permanent filling of a space in the substance of my own body alone. That will only avail to determine the relative places of the phenomena in my own body, and not the places of any phenomena beyond the space so occupied. I must first judge such phenomena to be the inhering qualities of a space filling substance beyond and enclosing my body; and I may then very well determine the relative places of the phenomena in my own body with those in the substance of the wall of the room in their particular places. All the hypothetical conditions are so far given, and so far a determined experience in particular places is effected. But still, all determination of place is confined to the space of the room, and we cannot yet say where in space the room itself is. I look from the window of my room, and various phenomena appear to be moving past the space of the room which the window occupies; but I cannot determine whether the space of my room and myself in it are moving past the outer phenomena, or whether the phenomena are moving past the window of my room. My room may be the cabin of a steamboat, and I readily determine the relative positions of all the places in the room ; but I cannot yet say where in universal space the phenomena beyond are, in reference to the place of my room. I may find them to be the phenomena of another steamboat, but I cannot yet say whether they are permanent and we are moving, or the contrary ; or whether both are not moving in opposite directions ; or, perhaps both in the same direction, though one be more rapid than the other and thus the more rapid passing by the other. Until I can attain some permanent space-filling substance in the judgment of the understanding—as a tree, a house, a hill upon the shore—which I at once recognize as occupying permanent place still beyond, I cannot determine the relative bearings of any phenomena external to my own room. The permanent substance on shore gives occasion for determining the direction and bearing of all the phenomena intervening.

But facts in the same direction will still further confirm our hypothesis to be the universal law ; for this permanent substance on shore may be still transcended. We cannot tell where in space the phenomena on the shore are, except as we have extended our thought to the earth itself, as permanent space-filling substance, and determined its phenomena to be connected in it as permanent ground for their appearance, and thus as fixed at determinate bearings and distances from each other in their particular places. And then, if we would know the place in space of the earth itself, we have the higher stand-point to attain in the permanent space-filling substance of the sun, which determines all the phenomena of its planets and their sattelites in their relative positions. And then, yet again, this planetary system can be determined in its place in space only by a higher permanent substance in the fixed stars, which considered as occupying each the same place in space beyond the region of our planetary system, may give the same law for the understanding to determine the place of the system as, in the first illustration given, the place of any part of my own body. And then, whether all the fixed stars are indeed fixed in the same invariable place in universal space, or are not perhaps themselves planets carrying each their unseen systems around some higher center, can only be determined by attaining such phenomena as evince their inherence in such higher space-filling substance. Our hypothetical principle is thus a universal law. The notion of a permanent space-filling substance, connecting all the phenomena in their relative places through their inherence in this substance, must be given, or no determination of experience in particular places in space is ever effected; and at once, and always, where such connective is given, the determining judgment in the understanding is readily and confidently made.

The point for an absolute determination of all places in universal space would be some fixed substantial center, which never changes its place by a revolution around some higher center; from which all centrifugal force goes out, and to which all gravitating force tends; and thus making the universe of nature to be one sphere of substantial being with its inhering phenomena ever occupying as a whole the same place in universal space, and only turning itself on its own center in its own place. Shall we ever determine such fixed center, which unmoved itself yet ever moves all else about itself? Surely not from experience. No experience can possibly rise to the absolute in anything; therefore can never attain to an absolute determination of space. It can only determine the relative places within the space which is occupied by a permanent substance, and in which the inhering phenomena are fixed in their connection to their respective places. If we were placed upon the supposed absolute center about which all revolved while itself was steadfast, it would be impossible for us to determine in experience our steadfast position. The understanding may *think* such a permanent stand-point; but place the sense there and it could not *see* if it stood, or whether it moved about some higher unseen center.

32

2. *Particular determinations of periods in Time.*—
Time has three modes of relation to phenomena, and
we need to gather the facts in each, and see if they
all come within the circumscription of our hypothesis
for determining particular periods in time.

(1.) Facts in the determination of particular periods in *the perpetuity of time.*—This general fact is every where apparent, that there is not a perpetual apprehending of a time in any self-consciousness. When
there is a progressive modification of internal state,
we may be conscious that a time is passing; but
when there is any interruption of the conjoining agency, there is an interruption in our conscious apprehending of a time. Such interruptions are frequently
occurring in every experience. The intellectual agency is often so completely absorbed in other constructions, that we take no note of time. There are also
reveries and musing meditations, paroxysms of delirium and fainting fits and the stupor of disease, and
more especially the occurrence of sleep from the necessities of our animal constitution; in all of which,
the consciousness of an elapsing time is interrupted.
To our subjective being these intervals in our consciousness have no significancy, and are a void of time
as truly as a void of all inner affection. Such chasms
in any elapsing time effectually break up in our consciousness the perpetuity of time. It is nevertheless
a fact that we somehow determine time to be perpetual, and to have been continually passing during these

interruptions in our consciousness of all time, so that
we as truly determine a period to our unconsciousness as to our conscious exercises. This can be no
intuition of the sense, but must somehow be a discursive judgment formed in the understanding. If I am
sailing with the current of a stream in my conscious
apprehension, and am then wholly unconscious of
any such movement through sleep or otherwise,
and again awake in consciousness of the similar fact
that I am sailing with the current of a river, certainly
my interrupted apprehensions cannot be so brought
together, or the chasm of consciousness so bridged
across, that I can *perceive* that I have been perpetually sailing with the current, nor that the currents in
the two periods of apprehension are the same perpetual stream. If I determine such facts at all, it
must be through some discursive judgment in the understanding. I must *think* the connections of these
experiences through some media, which as data lie
beyond the subjective experience itself. And here all
the facts, in our determination of the interrupted periods of our experience to be in perpetual time, will
be brought into complete colligation by our hypothetical condition of a perduring source, as the time-filling substance to which the phenomena in their different periods all adhere.

Thus, after a period of activity in consciousness, I
fall asleep in my study-chair. After this interruption
of consciousness, I again awake and would fain deter-

mine the continuity of time in this interval when time had no significancy to me. Certainly I do not attempt to make my intellectual agency pass through this chasm, and thereby construct the periods in consciousness that I may *perceive* a time has been perpetually passing. I have no diversity of instants in that interval of unconsciousness which I may conjoin in unity and by this bring in conjunction the periods before and after, and thus make the time perpetual. I take a very different course; laying aside all function of intuition, I seek to connect the periods only by a discursive operation of the understanding. I find some permanent source of varying phenomena which has existed through the interval, and whose coming and departing events have had their periods in this interval, and which have thus connected the periods through this subjective void of all time; and I at once conclude that time has been perpetual. Any such perduring source for coming and departing events will give a datum for such a discursive judgment, and all the facts of a determination of the perpetuity of time through such a chasm will invariably rest upon it.

Thus, I may take my watch, which has been a perduring source of varying events in the movements of the different hands over the dial-plate, or the undulations of air from the stroke at each swing of the balance-wheel. Those events as phenomena have not appeared in my experience, yet has the occasion for such phenomena perpetually existed, and I must thus think them connected in their continual periods varying as the changes in the source went on; and in the judgment of the understanding, I at once determine that a time has been perpetually passing, though in my subjective consciousness it had no significancy. I conclude thus, only in a discursive process that has gone from period to period through the notion of a perduring source in the undertsanding. As another fact, I may look at the falling sands through the permanent waist of the hour-glass; and though I have been all unconscious of the varying phenomena, yet is this perduring source of such successive appearances for any perceiving sense that might have been present in consciousness, a sufficient datum for the understanding to determine that the occasions have had their periods, and that the time has been perpetually passing. The shadow of the gnoman on the sun-dial may give another fact within the same conditions. The perduring source as notional in the understanding has been in existence through the interval of my unconsciousness, and given occasion for a continual perception of the moving shadow to any sense which might have received the content and have had its perpetuated time through all the moments; and the void of time in consciousness is thus a perpetuation of time in the understanding. Only by such connection of adhering occasions in a perduring source, do we determine any particular period to be in a perpetual time.

And when no artificial chronometers are at hand, the same conditions are given in a thousand ways, each of which would be a new fact coming under the same hypothesis. Thus, I awake, and find the sunshine from my window has changed its position; or, perhaps the twilight of evening has succeeded to the clear daylight when my sleep commenced; or, the diminished warmth of my room from the neglected and expiring fire in the stove; or, the diminished light and exhausted oil in my lamp; any one of these or numberless other such occasions give the datum in a permanent source of continual variations for the determination in the understanding, that a time has been perpetually passing through all intervals of our unconsciousness. So in that void of all time to us which precedes our existence as self-conscious beings, or, that which is yet to come beyond the present instant in consciousness; we readily determine a perpetuity to time and embrace all the experience of humanity in one perpetuity of duration. The permanent substances which give their phenomenal brightness in the heavens are lasting sources of adhering events for a continual experience, and thus become data for the determination of a perpetual time, which flows on in uninterrupted periods, independent of all consciousness of it. They are thus, what their Maker in the beginning designed they should be, "lights in the firmament of heaven to divide the day from the night, and that they may be for signs and for seasons, and for days and years." As far as we may think the perduring source to exist with its adhering occasions for coming and departing phenomena, so far we can carry out our determinations of particular periods in a perpetuity of time, and give the chronology of nature; but when that notion as necessary condition of all connection in time drops from the understanding, the vacant thought has nothing for its support, and all determination of perpetuity to time is wholly impracticable.

We thus affirm, that all the facts in an actual determination of particular periods to perpetual time, come completely within, and are wholly concluded by our hypothesis—that the connections of adhering events in one perduring source is the necessary condition for all such determination of an experience in perpetual time. We have in this no longer a mere hypothesis, but an actual universal Law.

(2.) Facts in the determination of particular periods in *the uniform succession of time.*—We judge time to be in uniformly progressive flow; that its stream does not turn back upon itself, nor wheel itself about in one perpetual cycle; and that it is not by desultory leaps, nor paroxysms of quickened and retarded movement. But when only the subjective apprehension of a time is given, we determine nothing in reference to the *ordered progress* of its movement. Our dreams may give an apprehension of successive periods in any direction; and our memories may follow back the tide of events, or begin at any past point and follow down again the old stream of our experience. Were there nothing but our subjective constructions of periods, our apprehension of time must be backward or forward according to the contingent modifications of our internal state by the constructing movement. There is nothing in the subjective consciousness, which may serve as a permanent from which to determine the absolute direction or the rapidity of the current of time. How then do we determine the particular periods in time to be in an ordered and uniform succession? The facts will all be bound up in our hypothetical condition—that an ordered series of causation alone gives the datum for the determination of particular periods as uniformly progressive.

Thus, as before, when I awake from my sleep, and would fain know how much of time has passed, I need to determine, not only as before that there has been a perpetual passing of time and which is effected by any perduring source of adhering events, but, moreover, now I need to determine that this perpetual passing of a time has been in an ordered and uniform succession. A perpetual movement from period to period might be as the pendulum to and fro; or, as the wheel on its axis revolving without progress; or, as the waves on the surface of the lake varied indefinitely; and there would be the notion of one perpetu-

al source in which adhering events in their periods
were continually recurring, and we might determine
that all the periods belonged to a perpetual time ; but
we must have some other data for determining that
all the periods are in one uniform progress, as an
ordered and even succession of time. When I look
at my watch to determine *how much* time has passed,
the datum which I get for my judgment is not merely
that the substance is source for perpetual coming and
departing events, but, moreover, is cause that the
events can be only in one order and in uniform rapidity of succession. It is the abiding source and its
events which suffices for perpetuity of time, but it is
the series of cause and effect which can alone suffice
for the determination of an ordered succession of time.
If the watch might go either backwards or forwards,
or in a progressus of irregular rates of movement,
there would be no datum for determining the onward
flow of time, and none for determining uniformity of
process by it. Thus with the hour-glass, the sun-dial,
or any other artificial chronometer ; we take the notion
not only of a perduring source, but also of an ordering
cause, necessitating the source to give its altered
events in uniform succession. So far as we attain
such a datum, we possess a chronometer ; and so far
as there is any deficiency in these conditions, the capability of an accurate determination of successive
time is defective. I may know that my stove has
been gradually diminishing in warmth while I was

sleeping, and thus the cause of the gradual settling of the mercury in my thermometer; and in this case I could determine the movement of the mercury and its periods to be in one direction, and so far it would be chronometer for the progress of time. But, I must also have the datum of uniformity of causation, before I can make it chronometer for the rapidity of time. Any notion of causation is sufficient in its varying events to determine a progressus of time, but only uniformity in the variations can make it practicable for us to determine the uniform successions of periods in time.

Thus, although we readily determine that time is a progressus and never a regressus, we attain to only a comparative and not an absolute determination of the even flow of time. We find it necessary to bring every chronometer to some comparative standard of an ordered series of causation. The great standard is the revolution of the earth on its axis. Taking the earth as perduring source of the varied phenomena, and the cause of its revolutions as ordering the same in progressive and equable successions, we have the great chronometer by which all artificial time-keepers are to be regulated. As this revolution of the earth divides itself into the two portions of light and darkness, so it has been found convenient to give to the ordinary chronometers two revolutions to one revolution of the earth, thereby separately measuring the day and the night. An hour-glass may take any

equable division of this as a twelfth, and be truly an
hour-glass; or a twenty-fourth, and be a half-hour
glass. But in all the datum is the same—a causation
ordering successive phenomena in accordance progressively and equably with the revolutions of the
earth. And now, that this is perpetually progressive
is readily manifest. The causation is ever onward
and not backward. One point of the earth's surface
comes under the meridian after another, and these
points cannot alternate in the periods of their coming
to the meridian, each with each. We thus determine
the periods to be progressive and never regressive.
But inasmuch as the movement is a revolution, and
each day repeats its causal variations in the same order; how do we determine that time has any other
progress than a repetition of cycles? The facts bring
us again within the circumscription of the same hypothesis. Had we no causation but that which orders our diurnal revolution, we should not be competent to determine our regular progressus in time and
each day would be to us the old day over again; as
with only a whirling balloon in the open air of heaven,
each turn would to the æronaut be in the same space.
But as a sight of the objects on the earth would give
the data for determining that his revolutions varied
from place to place, so do the thousand onward moving events give the data for determining that the diurnal revolutions of the earth vary in their periods,
and are each a time further on in the opening of eter-

nity than the last. The on-going of the objective
events in nature are right onward from day to day,
and not wheeled into cycles as the earth rolls on her
axis, and thus each day though a periodic revolution
has a different period from its predecessor. Were all
the causes in nature only repeating a certain circuit,
and coming about again as in a vortex only to go over
again the same effects in the same order, their experience could only induce the repetition of the same circuit of inner modifications, and time could be determined only as a perpetual revolution in the same cycle. So also, should nature at any monent cease the
onward development of cause and effect and turn directly back upon her order of connections, making
every where what had been the consequent to an antecedent to become the antecedent to the same,
the determination of time could only be that of a
regressus, and yesterday would return again to our
experience, and life roll itself backward through
the consciousness in an exactly reversed order of periods as of phenomena. But, while the earth repeats
her revolutions, the causes in nature do not turn from
a direct on-going in their developed effects, and we in
these attain our data for determining that every recurring day is a new day further on in the period of time,
and not the same day repeated, nor a return again to
the old day which had passed. The successive progress of time is thus readily determined from the successive on-going of events.

But an absolute equality in the onward progress of time is not thus determined, nor indeed can in any way be determined from any possible experience. Here are facts so much aside from the class before given, and which would so little have been expected to come within the same connection, and yet which do surprisingly evince themselves to stand bound in the same hypothesis, that they may be well considered as an example of a consilience of facts leaping within our hypothetical condition from a distance—and thus add the stronger confirmation that our hypothesis is the universal law for all determination of successive time in an understanding. Thus, I may very well determine that the pulsations at my wrist go on in an ordered succession, for I have a perpetual cause in the the palpitating heart for successive pulsations in their progressive periods. But I cannot say that the pulsations and their periods are equable in their successions, precisely because I cannot determine that the development of the causation into effect is equable. The phenomena as effects come into experience, but the notional cause can never come into experience. I may trace the phenomenal pulsations up to the alternate action of the heart in systole and diastole, and determine that this contraction and dilation is in successive progression, for I think the same cause for this as phenomenal effect that I do for the pulsations ; but yet it is only the phenomenal that has come within consciousness, while the causal efficiency is necessarily notional in the understanding and can never be made appearance in the sense. I have no means, therefore, of determining the absolute equality of the succession in the cause, and can only attempt such determination of equable succession in the effects. I compare the phenomenal effects with those in another series of cause and effect. I find, on comparison with the on-going phenomena of my watch, that the pulsations for one minute are, say seventy-five; and, in some minute of another hour, I find them to be less or more, say seventy for the less and eighty for the more numerous. How shall I determine which successive periods are the true successions in time? Only by taking the causation in the one case or the other to be an assumed equable efficiency, and thus judging the phenomenal effect of that to be equable in its periods, and then determining the phenomenal effects in their successive periods in the other compared with that as a standard. If my watch is taken as having kept on its equable efficiency in developing its successive effects, I shall determine that the pulsations have been faster or slower in the different periods, from some inequality of causation in the heart.

But, how determine that the causal efficiency of the watch has been equable? I may compare it with the falling sands of an hour-glass, or the oscillations of a pendulum regulating the descent of the same weight, and may assume that the efficiency of gravitation is an equable cause in the same place on the earth, and thus, if the watch agrees thereto, that its efficiency has been uniform. But, if now I should compare that watch, thus tested, with a sun-dial through the year, I should find perpetual inequalities of movement faster and slower than the dial, varying in extremes of fifteen minutes, and making the difference between mean-time and apparent-time on any given day in the year. How shall I determine where is the equable efficiency now? The watch has been tested by the constant efficiency of gravitation in nature, and yet it disagrees with the revolutions of the earth in their periods which are the phenomenal effects of the same causal efficiency. Is the same cause in nature contradictory in its own effects? But all these conflicting phenomena leap together within the same conditions, when we know that the earth is running its eliptical course about the sun; and that in proportion as in aphelion or perihelion its revolutions on its axis will be retarded or accelerated by the equable efficiency of gravitation, to just the degree and on the very days of the year indicated by the facts of disagreement between the clock and the sundial; and that, therefore, those different days in the year are just so much longer or shorter in their periods in absolute time. We determine the equable succession of time on the hypothesis only that the higher causation of gravity, in its force from the sun, is equable in its production of effects in succession.

It might here be said, that for all which has yet been determined of the equable succession of time, there may notwithstanding be as wide variations between a correct chronometer and some years, as between this chronometer and some days in the year. And so it may be. And if this were so found as a fact from any comparison of widely different years with the same accurate time-keeper of centuries, it would only the more confirm our hypothesis; for we could only determine the equalization of the discordant times, by taking the higher stand-point of causation, and thinking our sun, with its whole attendant system of worlds, to be wheeling on in its grand elipse around this causal efficiency in one of the foci of its orbit, and conditioning the same disparity of years in this great cycle, as before of days in the annual circuit of the earth in its orbit. Nor should we then be any nearer the attainment of an absolute measure of time. The only position for such determination would be the absolute center of all gravitation, fixed in its one position in the immensity of space, and ensphering and revolving all phenomenal being about itself. And if we stood at just such central point with an eye to perceive the rolling universe about us, how should we see that our own position did not move in absolute space? How see that the revolutions were not unequal in absolute time? Causation may be producing the faint pulsations of an artery or wheeling the universe on its center; but in all cases it is the connected series which determines the periods to be an ordered progress in time, and the even working of the efficiency which determines the equable progress in the successive periods. We have, therefore, a sufficiently broad induction of facts to determine that our hypothetical condition is a universal Law, and needs to be held as hypothesis no longer.

(3.) Facts in the determination of particular periods in *simultaneous time.*—We have varied phenomena each in their own periods, and which are alternately appearing and disappearing in the sense, so that when one appears the other has disappeared, and when the last appears again, the first has also again disappeared; and, though they are never given in consciousness together, we yet determine them to be together in the same time. This cannot be from thinking them to be the adhering events of the same source: for that can only determine them in the judgment as perpetual in the same one whole of universal time, not that they are together in the same one period of universal time. Nor can it be from thinking them to be the dependent effects of the same cause; for that can determine them only as successive in the universal time, and thus that they cannot be simultaneous. Since, then, the perception never brings them into the conscious experience simultaneously, and no datum yet considered gives them in the judgment of the understanding as simultaneous, the inquiry yet to be made is—under what law do these facts of a determination to particular periods as simultaneous events arrange themselves? Our hypothetical condition is—that they

33

must be connected in *the communion of a reciprocal influence.* This last induction of facts will exhaust all our hypotheses for determining particular periods in time: and if the hypothetical condition be found to be the actual Law, our task will be completed.

Thus, when I have the phenomena of continuous motion over the graduated points on the dial-plates of two clocks, in such a position that when I perceive one the phenomenon of motion over the other is not perceived, and thus, alternately; I may say of each when thought to be events from a perduring source, that their periods must belong to one perpetual time; and also, when thought to be effects from an ordering series of causation, that the periods in each must be in progressing succession; but, as I cannot see the phenomena of motion in both together, I cannot perceive the moments of motion in both to be simultaneous; nor, can the notions of perduring source and perpetual cause enable me at all to determine, that the motions in both pass any given points in both at the same moment. But if now these phenomena of motions over the graduated points of the two dial-plates are apprehended as on opposite sides of a tower, and that they are the two faces of the same chapel-clock, and have each a communion reciprocally so that one cannot be modified in its motion but the same modification must be communicated also to the other; I have then a datum in the understanding by which I may well, discursively through this datum, determine that their moments are simultaneous. With such a reciprocity of influence I can, and without such I cannot, and in point of fact it is only by such that I do, determine any phenomena of alternately perceived movements to be simultaneous.

Again, I may have the phenomenal brightness of two stars in opposite points in the heavens, so that when one appears the other shall have disappeared from the consciousness; but since I cannot perceive that the shining of one is together in the same instant with the shining of the other, how then do I determine that they are shining contemporaneously? Not that there is a perduring source for continual shining in each, which can determine only perpetual time; and not that there is perpetual cause for modifying my organ of vision alternately, which can determine only successive time; but, some other notion must enable me to determine that any instants in their shining are simultaneous. If, however, I apprehend the shining of these two stars as reciprocally in communion with an influence from the sun or other fountain of light, so that whatever should modify the shining of the one in my vision must also modify the other in the same communication of influence; I shall in this find a medium for the discursive judgment, that both have their periods of shining in the same time. The perception may alternate in either direction at pleasure, inasmuch as the influence which gives condition for the shining in both is simultaneous in each. Should any thing break up this reciprocal communion, and cut off the light so that my perception could not thus alternate at pleasure, the notion of reciprocity would be lost and I could no longer determine their shining to be contemporaneous. This reciprocity in the communications of influence, by which all phenomena of colors in vision are so modified that we may alter the order of our apprehension of them at pleasure, is the condition for our determination of the objects of vision on earth or in the heavens to be contemporaneous. That we may apprehend them alternately is not seeing them together simultaneously; but it is the index of a reciprocity in communion and not an efficiency in succession, and thus the condition for the understanding to determine in a discursive judgment, that the phenomena exist contemporaneously and not as antecedent and consequent; nor can simultaneous period in vision be otherwise determined. So I may touch the opposite scales of a balance, or the counter-weights suspended on each side of a pulley alternately—and the same will also apply to alternate vision, or perception through any organ of sense—and my apprehension may be, that when one scale or one weight has been raised the other has been found lower down, or the reverse; and if I had nothing more than the alternate perceptions in the positions of the phenomena, I could not determine whether these alterations of place were successive or simultaneous. The interval in perception will admit, that the displacement should be in either a successive or a simultaneous time.

If I should somehow get the notion of two alternate causes each producing its own effect, one lifting and the other depressing the weights; this notion of alternate cause in the understanding would necessitate the judgment, that the displacement was also alternate and thus successive; but, when the notion of the communion of reciprocal influence is assumed in the understanding so that the action and re-action must synchronize, the judgment must conclude in the simultaneous displacement of the weights. And precisely the same hypothesis applies where no phenomenal connection, like the scale-beam or the pulley-rope, brings the communion within the intuitions of any organism of sense.

Two voyagers, at opposite sides of the earth, find each a high tide in the ocean, but surely no human perception can settle the determination that they are contemporaneous. An accurate chronometer, when the two men should subsequently meet and compare their experience, might be the medium for determining that the tides were simultaneous; but the accuracy of the chronometer must ultimately be tested by its comparison with the action and re-action of gravitating bodies in the diurnal revolution of the earth. And such notion of the reciprocal influence of gravitating forces, acting and re-acting upon the ocean according to the positions of the sun and moon, exclusive of the chronometer, would be sufficient for determining the simultaneousness of the tides by each man at once and in his own place. This wholly imperceptible force of gravity is, as notion in the understanding alone, an efficient connective of the phenomena ; and as valid a condition for the judgment of contemporary being in the tides, as if it could be made phenomenal like the scale-beam. The reciprocity of influence must produce the tides coetaneously. Aᴜᴅ precisely this medium of communion in the reciprocal action of gravitation pervades the universe. It is the grand and only law, as notion in the understanding, by which we can determine the times of any phenomena of revolutions, and transits, and eclipses, and occultations, and full and change, through all the heavenly bodies. What is now going on in regions of space unseen, coetaneously with the phenomena which now appear ; and what events in all past history were contemporaneous in occurrence with some remarkable phenomenon in the heavens—as an eclipse, or the full moon—and thus often the settlement of long lines of events in disputed chronology ; and what phenomenal occurrences in the revolutions of the earth, the tides of the ocean, the appearances in the heavens, and even the coming and departing of comets, simultaneously with each other ; all are determined on the hypothesis alone, of the fixed connections through all the phenomena of nature of a universal and everlasting communion in the reciprocities of causation, which modifies all from each and each from all simultaneously. Cut off in thought the departing comet from this reciprocal communion, and you have cut it off from all connection in the understanding ; and you can no more determine its sameness of time with the phenomena of nature, than you can its directions and distances in space from the places occupied in nature. Its law of all connection is gone, and it is no longer a part of our system nor is it any more even a determinate part of the universe. It is somewhere its own universe, in its own space and its own time ; but it is not ensphered and turning in unity with universal nature in its space and its time.

It is, then, sufficiently shown in the facts, that the hypothesis of a communion in the notion of a reciprocal influence, for the determination of phenomena as simultaneous in their periods in time, is no longer hypothesis but a veritable Law in the facts. And inasmuch as we have now found the law in the facts comprehensively for all determination of phenomena in place and in period, and can now see that the law in the facts is precisely the correlative of our apriori idea of an understanding ; we may unhesitatingly affirm, that here is a true and valid psychological science. We know the Understanding completely, both in its transcendental Idea and in its empirical Law.

APPENDIX TO THE UNDERSTANDING.

AN ONTOLOGICAL DEMONSTRATION OF THE VALID BEING OF THE NOTIONAL.

PSYCHOLOGY is the only basis for Ontology. Psychological science is completed in any department, when we have attained the intellectual operation in its apriori Idea, and then in its actual Law, and determined their correlation. On such completed science may be rested a demonstrated doctrine of valid being; and as we have now advanced our psychological science beyond the department of sense, so our ontological demonstration may be proportionally extended.

In the sense, our psychological science gave us the idea and the law for all possible construction of forms and all possible distinction of qualities, and on this as a basis we rested the doctrine of the valid being of both inner and outer phenomena, by giving the outlines of an ontological demonstration. But we could not make such phenomena take an ordered systematic existence. The inner phenomena could not be brought into one system of thought as understanding, nor the outer phenomena into one system of things as nature. There was not, therefore, the foundation laid for an ontological demonstration of nature's laws in the universe of thought and the universe of things.

But in the province of the understanding we have now attained the complete psychological science of all possible connection in thoughts and things, and thus the entire process for effecting all possible discursive judgments, both in the apriori idea and the actual law; and on this as a sound foundation we are now prepared to advance the ontological demonstration for the valid being of an inner energy with its inherent laws of development in thoughts and judgments, which is the permanently existing Understanding; and also for the valid being of an outer force with its inherent laws of development in things and events, which is the permanent existing material Universe. It should be here noticed, that no attempt can yet be made towards an ontological doctrine of the Soul and of God. This would now be as preposterous, as to have made the attempt to rest the doctrine of an understanding and of nature upon the mere constructions of the phenomenal in sense. From the science of Conjunction, we attained the ontological demonstration of inner and outer real phenomena; from the science of Connection, we now shall give an outline of the ontological demonstration for essential mind and matter; but we must first attain the science of Comprehension, before we can give an ontological demonstration of a free Soul and an Absolute God.

It will be necessary only that we indicate in a mere outline the process of this Ontological Demonstration, in reference both to the valid being of an in-

ner Law of thought as Understanding, and an outer
Law of things as Nature.

1. *Valid being of an inner Law of thought as an
Understanding.*—We have already found that the intellect is competent to make itself the subject of its
own speculation, and while it cannot bring its own
essential being into the light of consciousness and
make itself appear to itself, and can only make its exercises and products to be perceived as phenomena,
yet it may attain completely its own laws of operation
in all its separate functions, and thereby wholly comprehend itself from what it finds within itself, and
the data for effectually demonstrating its own valid
existence as distinct being from its objects of knowledge.   This demonstration has already been indicated, in its general outline, for the reality of the inner
phenomena of sense against the partial conclusions of
Materialism, and thus that there is as truly an inner
sense with its real phenomena as an outer sense with
its phenomenal outer world.   Our comprehension of
the intellectual operation of Connection in its apriori
law gives equally the capability to demonstrate the
valid being of an Understanding with its inherent law
for all thinking in judgments.

It is competent for us to think in pure judgments
arbitrarily, in many respects.   We may connect
thoughts in pure judgments *when* we please, and we
may vary the order of connection *as* we please.   Thus,
nothing hinders at any time, in the subjective intel-

lectual energy, the agency from going forth in the connection of conceived phenomena in things and events,
and therein possessing an ideal world at pleasure.
And we may also vary the order of these conceptions
in their connections at pleasure, and now put them
in one place in space and again in another place and
in different positions and distances from each, and so
also at different periods of time as a whole or in the
order of their occurrence among themselves, as we
will. The work of ideal connection in things and
events is no more conditioned by any objective experience, than the operation of ideal conjunction in the
primitive intuition. We may construct mathematical
diagrams where and when we will, and equally at
pleasure may we construct conceptions of phenomena,
whether as qualities in things or events in their series. But, while thus unconditioned both in respect to
period of operation and order of arrangement, yet is
there an invariable condition in the method of operation. It is not possible at any time nor in any order
of connection that we should conceive the phenomena
as quality to be determined to their places in space,
except through one *modus operandi*, viz: the connection of subsistence and inherence. If the conceived
qualities are not connected in a conceived permanent
space-filling ground, and thus fixed in their places as
the accidents of a common abiding substance, it is not
possible that we should conceive that any determined
judgment of their places in space can be effected.

And so also, if we conceive of phenomena as occurring
events to be determined to their periods in time, we
are shut up to one conditioned method of operation,
and this invariable through the three modes of time.
Unless we conceive the occurring events as connected
in a perduring substance, it is not possible that we
should conclude in any judgment which determines
their periods in perpetual time; and unless we conceive
the events as the progressive effects of continual causes,
we cannot attain a judgment determining them in successive time; and unless we conceive the events as
connected in the concurrent reciprocities of action and
re-action, we cannot conclude in any judgment which
determines them to be coetaneous in time.   Here is a
permanent conditioning of all thinking in judgments.
The intellectual energy which may at any *time* operate in connection, and which may connect in any *order* in space and in time, yet cannot connect in any
other *manner* for the determining of place in space and
of period in time than by the apriori elements of all
connection.   This permanent conditioning of all thinking in judgments and thus an inherent law of all
thought, which does not come and go as the phenomenal thoughts arise and depart, is the understanding
itself as perpetual source of all discursive judgments.
The same intellectual existence in its perpetual law of
conjunction is the sense, which under its inherent law
for connection is the understanding.   The permanency
of this law of development in thinking in judgments

demonstrates more than a reality of phenomenal appearance in the consciousness. The thoughts come and depart as inner phenomena; the abiding law as function for all thinking in judgment neither comes nor goes, but perpetually is; herein is the existing Understanding for all discursive judgments.

And that this permanent understanding exists independently of all objective phenomena, and thus wholly irrespective of all sensible experience, has its complete demonstration in this; that we may at pleasure build up ideal worlds of things and events, which are not only no copies of anything which nature has given us in experience, but which are altogether the perfect archetypes for determining the imperfections of experience from nature. The ideal of a machine, as a steam-engine, can never find its perfect pattern when embodied in the rough vestment and clumsy workmanship of a material mechanism. The human features may be given in higher perfection and beauty in painting and statuary, than actual experience ever found; but the paintings of Zeuxis never glowed on the canvas, and the statues of Phidias never swelled in the marble, to the completeness of the ideals which the artists' own genius had created. The point or line or ring in matter is never the perfect mathematical intuition; the combination of qualities or connection of events in experience, never equal the pure philosophical conception. We always make the pure judgments of the understanding our criterion for testing such as we find in experience. Our ideals are the pure products of the intellect according to its own perfect inherent law of operation; our experiences are the conclusions conditioned by the rude material in which nature must work out her developments. The inner law of thought is utterly independent of the outer development of nature; it is not conditioned to nature; it is more perfect than nature.

But a still higher demonstration of the valid being of the understanding, as independent of all experience from nature, is found in the fact that its judgments as connections in pure thinking are wholly apriori. They have the characteristic of necessity and universality. By experience we can conclude in judgments as to what *is*, but experience can never judge beyond that which *is*; the pure understanding in its own subjective law alone concludes in judgments as to what *must be*, and this *universally*. It gives the conditions of all possible experience in space and time, and determines the connections it must have in order to judge of places and periods in time. Its pure judgments are no derivatives from experience, but the apriori conclusions after which all experience may be expounded. That the Understanding in an inherent Law of all thinking in judgments has its own permanent and valid existence, is thus from the attainment in Rational Psychology a complete and irrefragible demonstration.

2. *Valid being of an outer Law of things as Universal Nature.*—Let it be admitted that an intellectual force truly exists with an inherent law of operation as function of an understanding; such understanding in actual being can by no means produce phenomena connected in their notional law as determined in space and time, and thus give an experience of universal nature.

If such understanding may think space to be one whole of space, and all places in it determinable in direction and distance each from any other; and may also think time to be one whole of all time, and all periods in it determinable as in perpetual, successive and simultaneous time; yet cannot such understanding make its thinking of space to become actually space-filling substance and connect qualities in their places; nor its thinking of time to become time-abiding substance, as perduring source successive cause and simultaneous action and re-action, and connect events in their periods.   No thinking of constructed places in space and periods in time into a connected whole of space and of time, can at all avail to put a universe of material nature into this immensity of space and eternity of time.

Or, if such an understanding may have a conception of the varied phenomena of sense, and may think them in connection according to its conditional law for all discursive judgment; yet this could be only subjective and a mere semblance of a nature of things.

The *manner* of thinking would be conditioned by the inherent law of the understanding, but such ideal world of nature might have any *place*, and occupy any *period*, and its phenomena might be of any *variety*, according to any arbitrary scheme of the re-productive imagination. A real objective nature of things con-ditions the thinking not merely in the manner of con-nection, but in its place and period, and its particularity of phenomena and occurrence of events. No possible ideal system of nature can attain for itself those uni-versally conditioned connections which belong to a veritable universe, and which fix it in its own space and time, and all its single facts in their own places and periods.

Or, again, were real phenomena given in the sense, such an understanding in its own action could not con-nect them in their places in the one space and their periods in the one time, if they were not already con-nected in their own grounds and sources of being. The one space and the one time which such an under-standing might think subjectively, could not determine the real phenomena objectively to their particular pla-ces and periods in this one subjective whole of space and of time. No possible operation of an understanding can make real phenomena to be connected as inherent adherent and coherent, if they are not already so con-nected in their own substances causes and counter-influences.

Or, lastly, suppose appearances to be given with

some order of connection wholly preternatural, such as a credulous or superstitious fancy has in all ages been prone to figure to itself. Let there be appearance in space with no substantial filling of space, as in all the marvelous stories of ghosts and spiritual apparitions; or, events appear as coming and departing with no perduring source out of which they arise, as is the illusion induced by the legerdemain of jugglers and the magic of conjurers; or, an intellectual apprehending of future events without their causal connections, as in the pretensions of fortune-tellers; or, finally, let there be communion with no reciprocal media, as of mind with matter in the assumptions of clairvoyance and of mind with mind in the mesmeric sleep. In all these delusive connections, which together exhaust all possible forms of "lying wonders" inasmuch as they apply themselves to all possible functions of false judgments, we have the attempt to find and enter a world which is neither nature nor the supernatural. The notional connectives of the natural are discarded, the miraculous interventions of the supernatural are not claimed, and all the mystery lies in somewhat aside from nature as the preternatural. If a veritable nature of things already determined in space and time does not exist, such appearances if presented must be phantoms in a maze and belong to a world impossible to be any way intelligible. There must first be an objective space-filling substance determining place, or we could not say *where*

34

the ghost was; and also an objective time-abiding substance . determining period, or we could not say *when* the ghost appeared.

The conclusion of all this is unavoidable, that no subjective action of a veritable understanding can possibly give the conditions for determining a nature of things objectively to its places in space and its periods in time. Even if an understanding could create its own world of phenomenal qualities and events, it could not determine their places and periods in one immensity of space and eternity of time, if it did not also make them to inhere in their substances, depend upon their sources, adhere through their causes, and cohere by their reciprocities. A nature of things in determined space and time must have its inherent laws of connection, and such laws can no more relax the constancy and stringency of their control, than space may break up its own immensity or time may sunder its own perpetuity. The nature of things as they exist is thus demonstrably an intelligible Universal System. Not an accumulation of atoms but a connection of things; not a sequence of appearances but a conditioned series of events; not a coincidence of facts but a universal communion of interacting forces. Nor is such a conclusion merely assumed; nor the credulity induced by habitual experience; nor the revelation of an instinctive prophecy; but a demonstration from an apriori Idea and an actual Law which logically and legitimately excludes all skepticism.

PART III.

THE REASON.

I.

THE PROVINCE OF THE REASON.

THE Sense and the Understanding have both been circumscribed within the limits of their respective provinces, and thus subjected to an apriori investigation. It was necessary that each should be apprehended in its own identity, in order that each in its individual capacity might be brought within a demonstrated science. For the same end, it is now necessary that the specific province of the Reason be accurately ascertained, and this last and highest faculty which we are to consider be apprehended in its own separate being and operation. This may not be so readily effected in the case of the reason as in that of the former faculties, inasmuch as it has been in the use of the reason that we have been enabled to make out an apriori investigation of the sense and the understanding. If we were not endowed with the higher faculty of reason, though we might perceive in the sense and judge in the understanding according to sense, yet could we not subject the functions of either the sense or the understanding to an apriori examination and secure for them a demonstrated science.

The sense as faculty may in the exercise of its own functions distinguish the content given in the sensibility and thereby attain distinct quality, and may conjoin this into complete form and thus attain definite quantity, and this may appear in the light of consciousness and thus there be a complete conception as phenomenon in space and time. But this is all spontaneous operation, with no interest or capacity in the sense that it should overlook its own action and expound the conditions of its own working. These conditions of all perception of phenomena lie back of the phenomenon perceived, and cannot themselves become appearance. The sensibility ; the light of consciousness ; the self, as common ground for the higher unity in self-consciousness; these cannot be perceived by sense, and it is only in a higher light than that of consciousness in the sense, that they can be known as conditional for all functions of sense. A higher light than consciousness gives space and time as *primitive intuition ;* and from this apriori position as condition for all sense, it is competent to oversee the whole province of the sense and determine all the conditions which make perception in sense possible. It is thus that we know there must be sensibility in order to perception, though sensibility cannot be perceived ; and that consciousness is necessary to all phenomenal appearance, though consciousness cannot itself appear. In this higher light of the reason we have examined all the conditions of the sense, and determined how a sense is possible to be, by an organ altogether higher than any which sense can use.

So, also, the faculty of the understanding connects phenomena in things; and thinks in conclusive judgments; and thereby attains to a knowledge of nature as a connected whole. But the understanding spontaneously operates in this work of concluding in judgments, and has neither interest nor capability to overlook and expound its own processes of thinking. Substance, cause, and reciprocal influence are conditions for all connecting in judgments discursively; and these cannot therefore be given in a judgment of the understanding. This would be the absurdity of making substance itself the accidence of a higher substance, and causality itself the phenomenal product of another cause, and thus in a perpetual series of finding a first in a second, and dooming the understanding itself to rest only in a higher understanding. But, in a higher light than any judgment of the understanding, the *pure notions* of substance, cause, and reciprocal influence for determining phenomena in space and time have been attained, and thus all the province of the understanding has been readily overseen, and all the conditions which make an understanding possible determined. The understanding could not bring within its judgments the conditions of its own judging, but the whole has been brought within the demonstrated comprehension of a higher faculty.

In the use of reason we have thus come to a science of both the sense and the understanding. In the sense we *perceive ;* in the understanding we *judge ;* but in the reason we have *overseen* both the process of perceiving and the process of judging. The same intellect in the capacity of the sense *envisages,* in the capacity of the understanding *substantiates,* and in the capacity of the reason *supervises.* The sense *distinguishes* quality and *conjoins* quantity; the understanding *connects* phenomena ; the reason *comprehends* the whole operation of both.

And now, since neither the sense nor the understanding have any interest in their own comprehension and no capacity for effecting this, but the whole work has been in the interest and the light of the reason, much more is it manifest that only in the interest of the reason can there be any promptings to the work of investigating the reason itself, and expounding this operation of *comprehending.* It is wholly because man is rational and not altogether mere animal that he has any interest in philosophy, and having carried out this interest through all the phenomena of the sense and all the notional connectives of the understanding, it becomes a want of science in its highest and truly most important region, that this faculty of the reason be itself fully examined, and its whole process of intelligent action subjected to a rigid apriori demonstration. It is now quite plain how the sense and the understanding may be comprehended, but there remains yet the more difficult task to be accomplished in expounding the process by which the reason may come to know and comprehend itself. In this is the grand γνωθι σεαυτον of the ancient philosophers, the most difficult yet the most important of all sciences, and comprehending within itself all philosophy.

The point of difficulty is exposed in this, that inasmuch as it is the comprehension of that by which both the operations of the sense and of the understanding have been comprehended, its whole field must therefore lie wholly without the province of either. It is not possible that its objects of knowledge may be constructed within the forms of space and time, and be made to appear within the light of consciousness; but they must be wholly *supersensible* : nor, is it possible that they should be connected within the conclusions of any judgment of the understanding, and be determined in place and period within a whole of all space and of all time, and thus be given as bound up in nature; but must be wholly *supernatural*. No intuition in space and time can help us, for what we seek cannot be constructed; and quite as little can any connections of discursive thought help us, for what we seek cannot be connected in the conditions of substances and causes. The overseer of nature must not be shut up within nature. We are to comprehend nature and this is not to be effected by any connecting of things in nature.

It deserves very particular notice, how impossible must ever be the attempt to reach this region and know any thing of the province of an all-comprehending reason, by an understanding in any of its processes of discursive thinking; but which has hitherto been the course usually pursued. It lies wholly out of nature, how then shall any processes of the understanding which may only follow the connections in nature issue out and enter this region of the supernatural! We may as well make the sense to think and judge, as the understanding to oversee and comprehend; as well make mathematics dynamical and invade the region of natural philosophy, as to make natural philosophy transcend nature and enter and explore the world of the supernatural. The intuitions of sense have their own field and their own science; the discursions of the understanding have their field and their philosophy; and the reason must have its field and its peculiarity of science above them all. And yet so constant, and determined, and apparently incorrigible is the attempt to reach the province of the reason in some way through the processes of thought or reflection in the understanding, that it becomes quite an interest on behalf of the reason very thoroughly to expose its absurdity, and thus the hopelessness and helplessness of all possible efforts in this direction. The prison of nature is the destined dwell-

ing of the understanding, and if there are no higher
processes of operation competent to intelligence than
the connections in discursive judgments, then verily
will those prison doors never be opened. All that
nature needs, or rather all that an understanding
wants in thinking a nature of things in connected and
concluded judgments, is just to be allowed to push
out her pathway and carry her line of connections
from condition to conditioned interminably. She may
run along down this process, and think nature in constant and indefinite development; or, in reflection,
may make her regressus up the chain from conditioned to antecedent condition, in a constant and indefinite retracing of what has been already unfolded in
the connections of nature. But how thus make the
leap, from the perpetual births and deaths in mortal
nature, to a region of immortality? How thus escape
the fixed necessities and linked connections in the iron
chain, and emerge into a region of free originations,
and find the Being who acts in his own liberty?
How rise from nature as universally connected, to nature's independent Author and Governor?

Such an attempt may begin in *subjective thought*,
and postulate a law of thought; or an antithesis of
being and non-being; or an identification of subjective and objective; but in all cases the thinking must
go on in its interminable series of fixed conditions,
and the present thought can only be as condition for
the next, with no interest in nor aim towards any end

as ultimate consummation. An assumed generalization of all thinking is here the only possible method
of attempting to reach the supernatural. But how
shall any arbitrary generalization comprehend a perpetual and interminable process? How, if it could,
shall a generalization of endless conditioning become
an unconditioned? How such an unconditioned be a
free personality? How the interminable process of
thought in humanity become Deity? Or, should this
subjective thinking attempt to turn back upon itself,
and beginning with the thought that now is, take its
regressus to that which conditioned it, and thus step
by step retrace its upward way to find some unconditioned landing-stair, then an arbitrary assumption at
some step must be made, that *this* is the supernatural;
and, as the discursive understanding can possibly find
nothing in this thought which may relieve its search
for a higher condition, so it can only stand on this assumed highest stepping-point, staring anxiously into
the void with one foot thrust forward in vacuity. Or,
should this subjective thinking find itself conditioned
by some thought as product of itself, and thus the
process, limited in its own product, take this to be
something other than itself and thereby objective to
itself, and in this deem that it has found an outer
world which now stands forth distinct in consciousness; then this is to be made the starting-point for attaining the supernatural. But such ideal objective
can truly be followed up to no other source than the

thinking in which it originated, and from thence the only processes have already been given, viz: an assumed generalization of all progressive thought, and an arbitrary positing of a conditioned for an unconditioned; one of which must be taken, and neither of which can reach to a comprehending Author of all. No possible discursive thinking subjectively can attain to a Deity.

The attempt may be made by beginning in *objective nature* as real existence. But thus the understanding can go from phenomenon to phenomenon only through their substances and causes. The speculation either backwards or forwards runs an endless race, for if it stop at all it must bring its first phenomenon from, or lose its last in, an utter void. Should it attempt to run all back to an original absolute substance, out of which all phenomena as nature have been evolved; this would still find only nature in its germ, and all the rudiments already conditioned in the order of their necessary development. Should it trace all back to a first cause; it could find nothing else in this cause but a conditioned efficiency which must pass out into effects and in just such an ordered series, and thus merely the inner power which works out a universe. If it assume this cause as so making a universe, that the universe does not as much condition it as it does the universe; then is there a chasm made between the First Cause and Nature which nothing in an understanding can possibly bridge over, and the only altar it can set up must be "to the Unknown God." If it does let its conditions down into nature, and which may be followed up from nature and then go back within the causation itself, still we have found no supernatural Divinity, but nature still runs up her linked regressus in the bosom of the Deity.

In subjective thought, we may thus run the race of speculative Idealism; or in objective being, trace the entire process of philosophical Materialism; but the fixed connections of discursive judgments forever exclude the understanding from the promised land. The region of the supernatural cannot be so entered. It is a false generalization or an empty abstraction, on the one side; and a development of the Deity into nature or a crowding back of nature into Deity, on the other side. Reason still presses all her interest for some deliverance, while no tortured speculation of an understanding can bring any relief. The region of the supernatural lies still in darkness; the spirit-land is all unknown. The interest of reason alone urges to the discovery, and we may at the outset conclude that only reason can be the discoverer.

II.

THE REASON AS ORGAN FOR ATTAINING TO THE SUPERNATURAL.

THE common consciousness is the light in which all our constructions of both pure and empirical intuitions appear. This can avail in perception for nothing except what the intellect has conjoined within it. There must, therefore, be a higher light in which is given to our knowledge that which will not admit of being constructed. Whatever is neither a pure nor an empirical object, neither mathematical figure nor phenomenon of either external or internal sense, cannot be object in common consciousness, but must be revealed if known at all in the light of a higher organ than any thing in the sense. This is the Reason ; and concerning its cognitions we sometimes say, to express our conviction of their difference from any perceptions of sense, that we have them in our " minds eye." The apriori conditions of perception must be so given, since as necessary *to* perception they cannot be given *in* perception. So, also, the notional connectives of substance, cause and reciprocal influence, must be given to us by the reason as an organ apprehending in a higher light than ordinary consciousness. The functions of sense, and of an understanding judging according to sense, the animal as well as the man may possess and exercise ; but no animal can take these operations and separate the apriori conditions from the products, and distinguish space and time from the objects which appear in them, and substance and cause from the qualities and events which they connect, and thus overlook in a higher light the whole process of perceiving and of judging and expound the whole as demonstrated science. A higher organ is given to man and hence man can philosophize, and

subject his very functions of knowing to science. He
may systematize not merely what he attains in perception and thought, but the necessary and universal
conditions for all perceiving and thinking. Without
this higher organ though he should perceive and
judge, yet could he not give the apriori processes of
operation.

And here is the place which gives the first opportunity for explaining the meaning, specifically, of the
term *Idea*, which has kept company with us from the
beginning of our work, and as correlative with law
in the facts, has been made the criterion of all science.
The explanation of this will also go directly to show
the reason to be the organ for attaining to the supernatural. In the use of reason we attained space and
time in the primitive intuition as the necessary and
universal conditions for all perception, and with these
apriori conditions we determined the process for the
intellectual agency to construct all possible quantity
within them; and also in the use of reason, we attained the apriori elements of all connection in discursive judgments, and with these, we determined
how it was possible to connect all phenomena in universal nature. To these *systematic apriori processes*
we gave the name Idea, and called the first the sense
in its idea, and the last the understanding in its idea.
An Idea is, thus, a systematic process in pure thought
by which it is possible to secure a specific result.
When that process appears objectively in actual facts,

we term it Law. And when the Idea and Law accord, we have Science.

But as yet, this conception of a systematic process of knowing has been attained only in the possibility for a sense and an understanding. Reason as organ has availed to overlook and give the complete idea of the operation of *conjunction*, and also of the operation of *connection;* but we have yet remaining the operation of *comprehension,* for which we have not the conception of a systematic process, and of which on that account we have not yet attained the Idea. From all analogy with the former processes, it may be assumed that the reason as organ is first to attain that which is apriori conditional for all comprehending of judgments, and in this higher light oversee the whole process, and attain it in its pure systematic conception, and which will thus be the complete idea of the operation of comprehension, or which is the same thing, the Reason in Idea. In the sense we attained the process for constructing phenomena; in the understanding we likewise attained the process for connecting phenomena in nature; we must now seek the process for comprehending universal nature. This demands that we get for nature an origin and an end, and thus some existence above nature, and reaching beyond nature. The reason as organ, must therefore, give to us something other than space and time in *the primitive intuition,* by which we attained a comprehension of the conjoining of phenomena; and

something other also, than substance and cause in
the pure notion, by which we attained a comprehension of the connecting of things in nature; even that
by which we may attain a comprehension of nature
itself. This apriori condition for all comprehension
we will here term, in distinction from primitive Intuition and also from pure Notion, *the pure Ideal* What
this apriori condition is which, when attained, we shall
term the pure Ideal, we now defer to a more favorable point for consideration and need only say here that
it must be *the supernatural*, It is essential that we
transcend space and time, as also substance and cause,
and find a position not merely apriori to phenomena
and apriori to the connection of phenomena in things,
but also apriori to substance in its causality through
which nature is connected. We must be able to stand
intelligently and firmly on the *super*natural, and which
will be a pure Ideal. How this may minister to the
interest of Reason in comprehending nature may be
partially illustrated by the use which the painter or
the sculptor makes of the ideal which his genius creates for itself, and after which archetype he must as
an artist direct the whole process of his work. He
makes it comprehensive of all that his pencil or chisel
is to embody. It is only in " the mind's eye," but in
its light he may arrange the whole systematic conception of color or outline, and determine the possibility
of the product in idea.

The necessity for such an apriori process is seen in

the very proposition to be expounded. That nature must have an author and a governor is wholly a synthetical proposition. No analysis can get from nature this, that it must have an author. That nature must have substance cause and reciprocity of influence is analytical, and each of these may be taken from the very conception of nature and added as distinct predicate in an analytical judgment; and such would be the only author and governor which an understanding could find for nature. When put to the task of attaining a Deity, the understanding must from the very law of its functions give to us some compound of physical substance and cause; and hard and long has thus been the labor to get the conception of a Divinity from an analysis of nature, but in every result it has been as it ever must be, nature still. It is a synthesis and not an analysis that is demanded. A God of nature must be found above and independent of nature, and be wholly a new conception to be added to the conception of nature, in the proposition that He is nature's author. The apriori process is for the same reason necessary here, as in the idea of the sense or of the understanding. That sensation must be constructed into phenomena; and, that the phenomenal must be connected in a notional—i. e. every quality must inhere in a substance—every event must a have cause, &c. —these are synthetical propositions, and we have been obliged to find an apriori position for the sake of attaining the new conception which could be no product

35

of an analysis. We found the *first*, in the primitive
intuition of space and time, and from that position we
could *directly behold* that a conjunction of the sensation in consciousness was possible, and was necessary
in order to any product in perception. We found the
second, in the conception of one whole of space and of
time, as *media for demonstrating* that the notions of
substance cause and reciprocal influence were necessary to the determination of phenomena in their places
and periods in the one space and the one time; and
thus that the connection of the phenomenal in the notional was possible in the conclusions of a discursive
judgment: and we must now find the *third*, in a conception of one whole of space and of time to be transcended and comprehended in a pure ideal, which as
wholly unconditioned to the forms of space and of time,
may circumscribe nature in its own space and time,
and as the maker of nature may be the *compass for
comprehending* how both nature and nature's space
and time may begin together and end together. Such
a process of comprehending nature will be a complete
attainment of the Reason in its Idea. We must then
find facts in colligation by a Law which is the correlative of this idea, and we shall thus possess a Science
of the Reason. An Ontological Demonstration of the
real being of the Soul and God may then follow.

CHAPTER I.

THE REASON IN ITS SUBJECTIVE IDEA.

SECTION I.

THE ATTAINMENT OF THE ABSOLUTE AS AN APRIORI POSITION FOR THE REASON.

When we trace backward the work of the understanding in connecting phenomena into a system of universal nature, we find every event to be conditioned to an antecedent, and inasmuch as the series in nature could be given in a discursive judgment only through the connections of the understanding, so in our regressus we can only retrace the very pathway of antecedents and consequents which the operation of the understanding has previously cast up in its connecting agency. It were in vain, therefore, to attempt any regressus in the pathway of nature's development except as we must step from the conditioned up to the condition perpetually. The function of the understanding is wholly employed in the work of concluding in discursive judgments, and in reference to phenomena it can do nothing but connect them into a nature of things through their appropriate notions, and, thus, were there no other and higher functions in exercise, we should never find any higher want than that there should be given an unhindered development to nature in the connection of cause and event, and an unobstructed passage to the march of thought down the series in an indefinite progressus or a reflex returning up the series in an unbroken regressus. The understanding finds no disquiet from its confinement within the conditions of nature, for its endowment of function capacitates it for moving only within the fixed series of nature and it can possess no interest beyond it. Our intuitions would as soon seek to overleap and circumscribe space and time, as would our discursions to go beyond and comprehend nature.

But that there are the functions of a higher faculty in action is quite manifest from the earnest inquiry spontaneously and perpetually coming up— *Whence is nature? and whither does it tend?* There are the strugglings of a faculty within whose interest it is to overleap nature, and which may never be made contented by running up and down the linked series in the conditions of nature. Discursive thinking up to the highest generalization and down to the lowest analysis cannot satisfy. No possible conclusion in a discursive judgment, whether in the abstract or the concrete, can fill this craving capacity. There is demanded for it a position out of and above the flowing stream of con-

ditioned changes, whence may be seen the unconditioned source in which they have all originated, and
the strong and steady hand that holds all suspended
from itself and gives to them their direction towards
some ultimate consummation. But this interest of the
higher faculty always exceeds the capabilities of the
lower to satisfy. The sense, in its pure operations,
can only construct for itself a pathway by conjoining
the diversity in space and time, and can, therefore,
never issue out beyond the line which she carries onwards herself and which is limited in her own movement. The pure understanding can have foothold only
as it may step from the conception of some phenomenon as event to an antecedent phenomenon in connection by its cause; and it may, therefore, never put
down the foot beyond the conception of that which is
an attained condition for its present standing, and
which could be no safe stepping-stone were it not itself
conceived to be linked to a still higher condition. The
aspirings of this higher faculty and the efforts of the
inferior to reach and satisfy it, throw the human mind
upon a tread-mill which forces it to a perpetual but
vain toil, compelling to a continual stepping while
each stair must ever slide away beneath and disap-
point the hope of any permanent landing-place. We
can, in this way, find no link in the series which will
permit that it should be taken in the judgment as the
origin of all others, and itself unoriginated from a high-

er; and if we assume that there must be such somewhere at the head of the series, this is merely because
the higher faculty demands some ultimate point upon
which all are dependent, but which is only assumed
to be and never reached because the lower faculty can
never attain unto it.

This endless search is also just as empty labor in
the conditioned series of *design* as in that of *causation*.
Design indicates a designer; but when we seize upon
this conceived designer as condition for the produced
design, we find it adapted to the making of just such
products, and this adaptation at once becomes a conditioned, demanding for itself a higher designer of which
it must be a product.   Whence is the independent unconditioned spring of all design?   This is the question
which the interest of the higher faculty asks, and is ever
seeking that it should be answered, but which all the
tasking of the functions of the lower faculty can never
accomplish.   We may assume there is such underived
designer, because the interest of the reason as faculty
cannot else be quieted; but we are forced to stop and
rest in a mere assumption, making our very want the
only evidence of the real existence, while it is impossible to bring it within the conclusion of any discursive judgment.   If on the one hand reason objects the
absurdity of an endless series, so on the other hand the
understanding objects the impossibility of taking any
position from which it must not still ask, what next?
Whence is this? and what is above it?

An interminable dialectic is thus opened from the
very faculties of the human mind, and all attempt to
stop the demand in the interest of the reason, that we
should somehow issue out of nature and find its author and governor, is in vain; and all effort in any
possible use of the functions of an understanding to
meet this demand is equally in vain. The reason is
too enterprizing, to submit to any circumscription
within nature; the understanding is too limited in its
capacity, to be able that it should ever unbar the
gate and point the way to the supernatural. The
discursive faculty must ever keep within the conditions of the space and time-determinations, and must,
therefore, ever pass through the connective notions of
substance cause and reciprocal influence in concluding
in judgments; and that which may not be brought
within the conditions of such connectives must forever, to it, be not merely the unattainable but the utterly unintelligible. We are thus forced to dispense
in this part of our work with all use of the understanding, and can see that if the supernatural may in
any manner be attained, it must be in the use of the
reason only. The faculty in whose interest the want
originates, must rely upon its own resources alone to
attain to that which may satisfy it. It is its own
operation for *comprehending* universal nature that we
wish to attain in a complete and systematic process,
and thus possess the entire faculty of the reason in
its idea. In this we shall find how it is possible that

a nature of things may be comprehended; and according to which, if in fact this ever is done, nature necessarily must be comprehended. The finding of such a *fact* must belong to the second Chapter of the Reason, while here we are intent only on attaining *the systematic process* as idea. As preliminary to all progress in this work, it is first of all necessary that we attain our apriori position for overlooking this whole province, and in the light of which our whole investigation must be conducted.

We make abstraction, then, utterly of all that is phenomenal, and therefore dispense with the use of all the functions of the sense both in the sensibility and in the constructing agency. By thus making abstraction of all that is phenomenal we dispense also with all the operation of the understanding, which must go from phenomenon to phenomenon through the connecting notion. The phenomenal is gone and there is nothing to connect, and the notional as connective only remains, and the functions of the understanding have not the necessary conditions for their operation. They can connect in judgments only according to the sense, as that may give its phenomena; but here nothing of the sense remains. We have then the notional only, as the reason had supplied it for the use of the understanding in the connecting of the phenomena in the sense. We thus have nature in its substances, causes, and reciprocal influences, as things in themselves, and as they must be determined to exist

by any intelligences who should know things directly
in their essence, without any organs of sensibility to
give to them a mode of appearance as phenomena.
Having thus wholly done away with the phenomenal
and the coming and departing of appearances ever
varying, and retaining only the notional which is permanent, we do away with all significancy and use of
the separate places in space and the separate periods
in time which the definite phenomena severally occupied.   Substance in its causality is, but no inhering,
adhering or cohering qualities are.   The true ground
and essential being of nature is conceived, but not the
mode of its appearance as phenomenal world in the
sense.

We have already made ourselves somewhat conversant with this pure understanding-conception of
space-filling and time-enduring substance, which the
reason supplies for the understanding in order that it
may determine phenomena in the one space and one
time.   We would now take it more immediately within the mind's eye, and endeavor to attain a clear reason-conception of what it must be.   We have simply
considered it as *force*, which in its very conception
involves an antagonism, but have not attempted to attain any conception of distinguishable forces, and thus
of distinct substances in their causality.   Nor need
we now go into any very extended disquisition on
these topics, a very few considerations being sufficient
for all present purposes, while a more minute exami-

nation will be reserved to some favoring opportunity, when we may attempt a Classification of sciences in an apriori Universal System of all science.

We here need only to notice that different substances are forces differently modified. The living animal has a sensory which in its excitability to appetite is force for locomotion; the living plant has no sentient nature to be awakened in an appetite, and has no locomotive force, yet still an appetency to take in and incorporate with itself that nourishment which lies contiguous to its own organization, and thus a force of assimilation for its own development; the mineral gathers about a nucleus by super-position that which is homogeneous to itself, and thus a force of crystalization; many earths have their chemical affinities, and thus a force of cohesion; and fluids and gases their affinities which give a force of combination; magnetism, electricity, galvanism, perhaps also heat and light have their transmissions of influence through counter-currents and thus a bi-polar force; and gravity has every where an antagonism in its attraction and repulsion, and such counteraction in every point sent off from a central point, when fully apprehended, is seen to induce a force of revolution about that center. And here, let it be noted, that the higher force is always superinduced upon the lower forces and adapts itself to them, perhaps modifying but not destroying them. The higher holds all the lower in combination and subserviency to its own ends, but can neither exclude nor annihilate them. The force of animal life holds also that of assimilation in vegetable life; and vegetable life has the forces of crystalization, chemical cohesion, the bi-polar forces and gravitation, all retained in subservient combination; and so the crystal has its chemical bi-polar and gravitating forces, while the crystalizing force overrules all the others and holds them subordinate to its own end. We shall not here attempt to trace the apriori law through all these distinguishable forces. Past a doubt such a law exists, and determines how each distinguishable substance *must be;* and, determining how the substance in its causality must be will determine also how its modes of phenomenal manifestation in the sense must be, and thus what qualities and events must appear. But we are not here at all concerned with the tracing of nature in its substance downward, as it must develop itself in an experience in the sense; and only concerned in retracing its conception upward to a supernatural Author.

We will then, having made abstraction of the phenomenal, now make an abstraction of all the superimposed distinguishable forces, and retain only the most simple and that which is primary and present in all, viz: *the force of gravity.* In this we retain all that is essential to a space-filling and time-enduring force, and thus all that is essential in the notion of substance with its causality. Let there be the reason-conception of an every where antagonistic force, and we shall in this have substance with its causal laws of attraction, repulsion, and revolution; and thus, as it were, the frame-work or elementary rudiments of a nature of things, without regarding whatever other distinguishable forces and thus different substances and causes may be superinduced upon this. Whatever may be thus superinduced, we may know that it cannot exclude or extinguish this force of gravity. This must surely be as extensive as nature; for it is the primal force upon which all other superinduced forces must rest, and by which they must all be conditioned. We have in this all that is necessary for an apriori representation of a universal nature of things *in itself*, and not in phenomenal appearance.

We may then take any point in this primary space-filling force, and if it is not itself a center, it will be revolving about some center of gravity. When we approach that center of revolution, if it is not itself an ultimate central point, that point with all the sphere which turns upon it will be revolving around some higher point, and thus we might mount upward through worlds and systems indefinitely. Can the reason take its stand upon some central point, around which the universe shall revolve, and find an author and primal originating source for it, without needing any higher point of antagonism? Such ultimate point we now assume in conception, and the task of the reason is, to show how it is possible that that point

and thus all the universal sphere that revolves upon
it, may be originated and sustained. In the comprehension of that one central point of all antagonism,
we comprehend the universe of nature. And, here,
to prepare the way for attaining that pure ideal which
must be the compass for reason's comprehension of
nature, it is quite important that we attain to a clear
reason-conception of this *central force* upon which
universal nature must repose.

Conceive of two congealed pencils, such that when
their points are pressed in contact the pressure shall
equally liquify them both, then will this liquefaction
accumulate itself about the point of contact ; and if
no external disturbing force be present it will perfectly
ensphere itself there, the sphere enlarging as the pressure continues and the accumulation increases. If
now we will abstract all that is phenomenal in this,
and retain only that which is the space-filling as thing
in itself, we shall have the pure conception of force as
generated in antagonist action. The apriori substantial being is this force occupying space, and the phenomenal is only the mode in which it is given as appearance in sense. In our supposition above, for the
sake of more familiar illustration, we have assumed
pencils appearing as phenomena in consciousness ; but,
the purpose of the illustration being answered in
awakening the clear conception, we wish only to retain the conception of the pencils in two pure activities meeting in counteraction, and thereby engendering

and accumulating force about the point of their antagonism. This accumulated force is a perpetual protrusion, from the point of counteraction, of that which is truly a compound of each activity, and thus a going off of perpetual points of counter-agency, and these accumulating in space so that every point in the sphere is a point of antagonism and thus of force. This accumulation must manifestly be in proportion to the amount of antagonism or force of counteragency at the center; the force accumulating about the center constantly augmenting in reaction towards the center, the equilibrium is attained in a less or greater sphere proportioned to this central force. Let the antagonism at the center be adequate to fill the space the universe occupies, and the essential space-filling substance of the universe is a necessary conception. So, it is manifest, a universal space-filling substance may be. Other distinguishable forces may be superinduced upon this; and cohesive, crystaline, vegetable and animal bodies may have their distinctive substances; but whether filling only a few cubic inches of space, or whether they be revolving worlds and systems of worlds, they are all alike within the control of this central power.

It is very competent to the reason to find many principles of nature, wholly apriori, from this necessary conception of force as the central point in the substance of the universe. Such as the following—nature must be spherical; must have limits; must

revolve round a center; must have its poles in the line
of the antagonist action; must have repulsion in the
ratio of the radius to the circumference of the sphere,
and attraction in the ratio of the radius to the circumference of the circle made in the bisection of the
sphere, &c.—are at once seen to be conditioned in the
very conception of this central and accumulated force.
But these and other apriori principles belong to a
work which shall give a complete classification of
science. It is the course of reason here to follow out
this conception in the opposite direction; not down
into the principles of nature, but upward to the region
of the supernatural. This antagonist action is condition for all the development of nature below, but has
neither substance nor phenomena above. The central
force can hold and control the universe, and is to all
the causes and changes in nature the Unconditioned.
They originate in it, while it has no higher force; in
it force first began to be, and from it the accumulations have expanded.

But it is a fair and necessary inquiry of the reason—
while nature reposes upon this counter-agency, whence
is this antagonism? In what source may we find these
acts which counteract, to become identical? All force,
and thus all of nature is a genesis in a *duality;* in what
may this find a primordial and abiding *unity?* Nature
fills place in its own space, and its successions have
periods in its own time; how shall it be seen that its
space and time must be determined only in connection

with its own existence, and thus a station attained
where we may see both it and its space and time come
and depart together? How shall we find Him to whom
the conditions of nature, and of nature's space and time
are wholly impertinent? The reason must perpetually be propounding to itself these queries; and if no
answer come, we must per force stifle the interest of
reason in seeking for the supernatural as we may, for
we cannot even say whether there be any thing but
nature; or, if faith in reason should still hold that
there is a supernatural, it will be impossible for us to
find the way to it by any intelligible process in thinking in discursive judgments, and our highest conviction becomes mere opinion. Nature reposes on counteragency; what if one act be relaxed? the central
force collapses. What if one agency cease? nature is
at once extinguished.

In some way, reason must find an agent in his *simplicity*, in whom the *duality* of the space-filling force
and substance of nature may find an origin. While
he conditions all of nature, this very conditioning is
to rise within himself, self-originated. While substance in its causality is ground and source for nature
by virtue of its compound force, this agent must in his
own simplicity of being be author for that force which
fills the space of universal nature, and which is nature's substantial being. This author of nature must
thus stand free from all conditions imposed *ab extra;*
even from those of an internal force, which as action

and re-action would demand that he be a composite being. His only conditions must be such as are self-imposed in the dignity of his own transcendant unity. It is not, thus, an unconditioned which is given in abstraction—merely cutting off all occasion for changes and successions above, and assuming a source and cause for all below—this the space-filling force and substance of nature itself is. It must be a positive and intelligently affirmed unconditioned, whose only end of action is found by himself in his own being. Such alone can stand above nature, and condition nature, without the reciprocity of a conditioning back upon himself from nature. As thus positively unconditioned, we give to this conception of a supernatural being the high name, which must be his own preogative and incommunicable possession—THE ABSOLUTE.

The whole problem of the reason, therefore, is seen to be in this determination of the absolute. Nature can be comprehended by the reason in no other possible manner than as encompassed in the being of the absolute; and the determination of this, is the determination of the possibility of an operation of comprehension. In the pure ideal of the absolute we are to find our apriori position for overlooking nature, and thereby determining how its comprehension is possible; and in this we shall have the entire functions of a comprehending faculty, higher than that of the sense which only conjoins, and higher also than the understanding which only connects, even the faculty of the reason

36

which comprehends all that may be conjoined or connected. Such will be the Reason in its Idea.

It is quite important here to carry along with us, in this part of our work, the abiding conviction that we have passed completely out of the domain of the sense and of that of the understanding also. It will be wholly perposterous—when we have made abstraction of all that is phenomenal, and transcended all that the operations of conjunction and of connection have produced, and have taken upon us the task of an apriori examination of the comprehending faculty—if we shall any where unawares permit that there be a sliding away from this pure province of the supernatural, and we be found dealing again with the conceptions which are conditioned to nature and the modes of space and time. The absolute is not nature and possesses nothing in common with nature, and may neither be constructed in place and period nor connected in substance cause and reciprocal influence. The entire phenomenal and notional of nature is so wholly out of and beneath the absolute, that although originating in and depending upon the absolute, yet may it never be conceived as reacting and thereby throwing back any conditions upon the absolute. We may have nothing to do with any conditions here reaching back from nature, and putting us again to our old work of discursive connections.

SECTION II.

___

THE APRIORI DETERMINATION OF PERSONALITY TO THE ABSOLUTE.

THE reason-conception of the absolute, which the reason gives to itself, is above the notional; as the understanding-conception of the notion, which the reason gave to the understanding, is above the phenomenal. To distinguish this pure reason-conception from the pure understanding-conception of the notion we have termed it the Ideal. This ideal of the absolute is to be the compass for comprehending nature, as the notional was the medium for connecting phenomena in a nature of things. In this we are to determine how it may be known, as a synthetical proposition, that nature must have its author; as in that it was determined how it might be demonstrated, that phenomena must be inherent in substance, adherent in cause, and coherent in reciprocal influence. The phenomena were in distinct and definite places and periods, and could not be determined in one whole of space and of time, except through the media of such notions as gave universality to all spaces in one whole of space and all times in one whole of time. In this manner the phenomena in the sense and the things and events in the understanding came very well to be united, and the passage from the sense to the understanding was effected, and the synthetical propositions—all qualities must have substance; all events must have cause; all concomitant events must have reciprocity of influence—came to be readily demonstrated, when without such apriori demonstration they could only be used as assumptions. And now the same result of an apriori demonstration of a synthetical proposition is to be determined, but with this difference, the conceptions of the phenomena and the things were, the one in the sense and the other in the understanding; while here, the conceptions of a nature of things and of an author of nature are, the one in the understanding and the other in the reason. The passage from the sense to the understanding and from the understanding to the reason both demand a synthesis, and can neither possibly be effected by any analyses descending nor any generalizations ascending; and as we have found the passage for the first in the notional, so now we are to find the passage for the second in this pure ideal.

And yet still farther, as we found the very essence of substance in its causality to be a space-filling and time-enduring *force*, and that as counter-agency it filled its place in space from a permanent center and might thus determine all places in its own space, and also as enduring center it might thus determine all periods in its own time; so now we must find the very essence of the absolute to be a spaceless and timeless *personality*, who, as above all the modes of expansion in space and duration in time, may be not nature but supernatural ; not thing but person. If conditioned to the one whole of nature of space and of time then it must be of the substance and causality of nature, and can never be the Divinity above nature. No matter whether all of the phenomenal be abstracted from it or not; in naked substance and cause it is but pure force, space-occupying and time-abiding, and must re-act upon nature and nature upon it, and the compound thus effected must still be nature altogether. And no matter whether it be carried above all phenomena ; it is then pure force in its antagonism at the center, and as undeveloped must yet go out in development, and such is only nature in its rudimental germ, and not at all nature's author and God. Except as we determine the absolute to be personality wholly out of and beyond all the conditions and modes of space and time, we can by no possibility leave nature for the supernatural. The clear sighted and honest intel-lect, resting in this conclusion that the conditions of space and time cannot be transcended, will be Atheis-tic ; while the deluded intellect, which has put the false play of the discursive understanding in its ab-stract speculations for the decisions of an all-embra-cing reason, and deems itself so fortunate as to have found a deity within the modes of space and time, will be Pantheistic. The Pantheism will be ideal and transcendent, when it reaches its conclusions by a logical process in the abstract law of thought; and it

will be material and empiric when it concludes from
the fixed connections of cause and effect in the generalized law of nature; but in neither case is the Pantheism any other than Atheism, for the Deity, circumscribed in the conditions of space and time with nature, is but nature still, and whether in abstract
thought or generalized reality, is no God.

This determination of personality to the absolute,
and which takes it out from all the modes of space and
time, is the only possible way in which it may be demonstrated how nature may have an author, which author shall not be nature still and yet demanding for
itself an author.   In such a pure ideal as the absolute
in its personality, a compass is given by which the reason may comprehend nature, and the completed process of comprehension thus effected is a faculty of the
reason in idea.   This, therefore, is a necessary, and
our next work, to determine personality to the absolute.   This will give all the necessary elements in the
work of COMPREHENSION.   We termed unity, plurality
and totality the apriori Elements in the operation of
Conjunction; and also substance and accidence in
space or as the same thing source and event in time, and
cause and effect, and action and re-action, the apriori
Elements in the operation of Connection; we will now
term these when found, the apriori Elements in the
operation of Comprehension.

It will result here, as in each of the former operations, that the apriori elements will be three in num-

ber; and also as in each former case, that the first and second elements will stand to each other in an antithesis, while the third will be the synthesis or point of indifference between the first two.

1. Antagonism, by which is meant the point in which two agencies meet and counter-work, determines position in space. The accumulated and ensphered force determines place in space; and, as fixed in its center, the entire sphere though revolving occupies perpetually the same place in space. From this space-filling substance in its permanence the one whole of space is determined, inasmuch as its permanent place gives a datum for determining direction and distance from its center to all the places in space which it occupies. But if we were to conceive of its extinction, though it were impossible to conceive that space itself were extinguished yet it would be wholly impossible to determine sameness of place, and thus impossible to determine the same wholeness of all space. The conception of a new antagonism would give again new position, and the engendered force would give again new definite place, and thus a determined whole of all space; but whether this whole of all space were the same as the former whole of all space could no more be determined than whether the places in which the reflected moon and stars in two different lakes appeared were the same whole space. The first position and place and thus wholeness of space are lost to all determination so soon as the space-

filling force is extinct, inasmuch as there is then nothing by which permanency of position and place can be indicated. It thus follows, that the single pure agency which can have no antagonism, can have nothing to which the conditions of space have any significancy. It can never be determined in position, place, nor in the sameness of any one whole space.

So also this point of meeting in action from whence counter-agency takes its rise, determines instants in time. The successive counter-working and accumulating of force and continuance of changes determines period; and, as reckoned from the primal instant onward, gives a datum for determining all period in which the series of changes occur, and thus of determining the same one whole of time. But, were we to conceive this counter-agency to be extinguished, and another antagonism with its determined instants and successive periods and same whole of time to be determined; it would be impossible to determine that the two wholes of time were the same whole of time, equally as much so and for the same reason as to determine whether the successions and time inherently in two dreams were in the same whole time. There would be no perduring source which could indicate the periods of its own changes. It thus follows, that the single pure agency which can have no antagonism can have no fixed instant, no definite period, and no determined whole of time; and thus to it none of the conditions of time can be significant.

Moreover, in this antagonism the primal condition of a nature of things is determined. Its counter-agency engenders the space-filling substance in all its causality, and evolves the successive changes as cause and effect, all of which in their conditioned connections depend upon this primal condition; and thus all of nature is determined in this central counter-working; and if any other distinguishable forces be introduced, they must be superinduced upon this, for this primal force must condition all that shall come within it. It thus follows, that the simple pure agency can come within none of the conditions of a nature of things; inasmuch as within itself there can never be antagonism, and thus an engendered force which is causality and condition for all of nature, and, therefore to it the notions of substance cause and reciprocal influence are wholly impertinent and insignificant.

This reason-conception of simple pure activity is thus wholly unconditioned to space, time, and a nature of things; and is apriori conditional for all transcending of nature. It were wholly impossible to find any passage out from nature to the supernatural, except in this reason-conception of a pure agency which can come within none of the conditions that belong to nature, and has none of the necessitated connections of a discursive judgment. But such pure activity is the conception of *pure spontaneity;* and this must stand as our first element of Personality.

But this reason-conception of pure spontaneity must be most carefully distinguished from what sometimes takes the name of spontaneity in the understanding, and which belongs to nature. Thus, we speak of the spontaneous productions of nature; spontaneous growth; spontaneous combustion, &c. Spontaneity here is negative only of applied conditions. The earth produced its fruits without the application of human toil as a condition; the combustible took fire without the application of a spark or flame as a condition. But in neither case is it a negative of all condition and thus an exclusion of necessity. There is an inherent causality already in possession, and in virtue of which the product appears. The earth is already cause for the germination of the seeds in its own bosom; the combustible is cause for combustion in its own fermentation; there is no need for the application of any other causality than that already in possession. But this efficiency has been transmitted from a higher causality and is thus truly conditioned in its antecedent. The causation has itself been caused, and could not have been a *causa causans* had it not also been already a *causa causata*. It is wholly a discursive process that we here pursue, and the efficiency must be followed up from event to event, the subsequent always conditioned by what has already taken place in the antecedent. Nature has only conditioned causality, and though it may negative all applied conditions and call this spontaneity,

yet can it never negative all communicated or transmitted condition and be pure spontaneity.

There is also, sometimes, a passing up to the primal conditions, and by a negation of all antecedents
an assuming of a spontaneous beginning in this primal condition. But such attains no positive reason-
conception of spontaneity, and only an arbitrary negation of all higher conditioning. The only method
of a distinct conception of this assumed spontaneity
is, to figure to the mind the origin of force in a point
of counter-agency. This gives the genesis of a substance which fills definite place in space. The force
as substance in its causality, begins to be in this antagonism; and above this it is not properly substance
or cause, but pure act. Causality begins in this
counter-working, and develops itself in a perpetual
unfolding of new conditioned products. Here, therefore, is cause in its highest conception; unconditioned,
except in the inherent antagonism which is its own
being. And now, this is sometimes taken to be the
Unconditioned; the Absolute Cause; the Spontaneity
that begets nature; and that in which not only all
philosophy of nature, but all science must terminate.
It is the starting-point for thought, and nature must
be evolved from it. It must go out in effects, filling
space and evolving the universe from its own efficiency, and must ever work on in the interminable progressus of pushing new conditioned products from the
last; and is thereby the author of a perpetually un-

folding nature of things. The author of nature can
no more be without the universe, than the universe
can be without its author. The universe is but the
perpetual unfolding of the absolute cause.

But, in this there is no pure spontaneity. It is
bound in its own conditions, and is under a necessity
to develop itself. It is not nature's author as supernatural but only nature's germ including the rudiments of a universe, and is as much nature at the
first as in any successive step of its development.
Causality is ever counteraction; and thus inherently
conditioned action; and is notional for the understanding, not pure ideal for the reason. It can possibly
have no element of personality within it, and thus no
pure spontaneity may be analyzed from it. The supernatural is not absolute cause; this is an absurdity,
inasmuch as cause is ever inherently conditioned.

The reason-conception of a pure spontaneity must
be found in the simple activity, and not in any force
which is the product of counter activities. The substance in its causality originates in, and cannot itself
possess a pure spontaneity. The counter-working of
causation must be transcended, or we only mount to
where nature begins, but we do not go over at all
within the supernatural. Nature is connection through
dynamical conditions; the supernatural is uncompounded, uncounteracted self-activity. That an author of nature may be person independent of nature,
he must be pure activity, neither caused by, nor con-

ditioned to, any efficiency imparted or transmitted *ab extra*. If this activity stand conditioned to any thing *ab extra*, then does nature reach beyond its author; and he is comprehended and no compass for comprehending nature. The absolute must comprehend all counter-agency, and must therefore be pure spontaneous agency; and in this is found the first essential element, which transcends the agency that is compound and conditioned as *thing*, and is agency in its own unconditioned simplicity as person. The *first* Element in determining personality to the absolute, and thus the possibility of comprehension, is *pure Spontaneity*.

2. Pure spontaneity in itself is wholly blind and lawless. It cannot of itself be sufficient to determine personality to the absolute, nor give the compass for an operation of comprehension. There must be some end to which the action as spontaneity is directed, and such end must give the law to the action, and thus as antithesis to spontaneity give the conception of spontaneity controlled and determined. But the conception that such end is in nature, or that it is nature itself, will subject the spontaneity to nature, and at once condition the absolute in necessity. It is, only that nature may be. This controlling end must be other than nature, out of and independent of nature, or it can not possibly give us the apriori condition in what way nature itself must be, and thus comprehend nature in the eternal design and reason of its author. As above nature, that end which is to give law to the

agency creative of nature must be supernatural. It must determine how nature is to be, while yet nature is not brought into being; and must thus be controlling over the spontaneity, independent of any and all conditions to which it is to direct the spontaneous agency that it may give them their birth. The absolute itself as author of nature exists alone out of nature, and is the supernatural; and thus this end, controlling the creative agency as spontaneity must be in the absolute itself. This must be its own end, and thus also its own law; and thereby comes out the reason conception of personality in this, that the absolute is pure Will : He is self-active and self-directed. His end, and thus his law of action is not in nature; for that would degrade him at once to a means, and a thing to be used for a further end. He would be, only that nature as end might be. His end is in himself, and his law of action is self-imposed; and he thus makes nature to be for his own behoof. That spontaneity may become *personal* activity, and thus a will which may *behave*—i. e., have possession and control of its own agency—it must possess an end in itself, and thus impose law upon itself, and thereby be autonomic. But such a conception of end and law in the absolute itself, is *pure autonomy ;* and this must be a second element apriori in personality.

But this reason-conception of *pure* autonomy is not very readily attained in its complete discrimination from all the allusions which a discursive understand-

ing constantly obtrudes upon us. It is not by any
analogies with the dynamical connections in an understanding, much less any analysis of such conclusions
in judgments, or any abstractions of conceptions gained
in discursive processes of thinking, that will bring us
to any right and adequate apprehension of what a pure
will is, and in it the everlasting distinction in kind of
all person from thing. It is not in itself probable that
this knot in all dialectics and vexed problem in all ethical metaphysics—so intricate that the labor of centuries
has been here exhausted—is so easily to find its solution, as by a mere change of the discursive connection
from the conditioned series in *outward* nature to any
conditioned successions in *inward* experience, that we
are henceforth to have it free from all entanglement.
If we keep the discussion within the discursions of the
understanding, we shall have necessity and heteronomy; never spontaneity in autonomy. We may have
a sensibility awakened to appetite, but no such action
from awakened desire can be pure will, any more than
is the flowing stream when impelled by its own gravity and retained within the banks which its own action has constituted. The present has always its condition in a higher period than its own, and when it is
to go forth in action, that action has already its law
imposed upon it by another above and out of itself,
and it cannot thus become its own end, and arrest the
whole process, and throw itself out of its long and deep
worn channel, and originate some new product of its

own for which it shall be beholden solely in autonomy. Its perpetual flow of activity can in no way be discriminated from physical necessity, by any arbitrary terms that may be put upon it. It is important that we here distinctly apprehend how completely we must transcend the whole province within which work the functions of the understanding, or we can never find the compass for comprehending nature. For this it is apriori conditional that we have a will, in which only can there be personality; and a pure will is in its very conception self-action self-directed; spontaneity in autonomy. If, in any way, we put the end which is to condition the activity out of the absolute itself, we thereby bind the absolute in conditioned nature.

This will appear in the conclusion of the following considerations. *First*, let it be considered that in nature nothing is for itself. Through all her series, nature now is, not for what it is, but for something to be. It is not itself its own end, nor professing any thing which is its own end but is ever an unfolding to attain something not yet consummated. No portion nor aggregate of nature can be autonomic, but is and ever most be under conditions imposed upon it, and thus is ever a means to an end not itself nor its own. It is ever more used as a thing, and can never become a user of things for its own end as person.

But *secondly*; we will rise above the phenomenal in nature, and thus pass from the changes which give coming and departing events in a perpetual series of conditions, and take the space-filling force at the point of its antagonism on which all nature reposes ; and here we may find a sort of autonomy, but not pure, or such as elevates from thing to person.   This central antagonism is force ; and in its counter-working supplies force which enspheres itself in space, and thus has within itself its own law, and in its working diffuses its own law through all the sphere ; and thus the universe is in this view under a law self-imposed. The space-filling force diffuses its own law through all the space filled, and is ever thus working on under the conditions of its own laws self-perpetuated.   This is *mechanical* autonomy.   The central force developes itself, and carries its own conditions throughout all the space of its working.   But such substance in its causality becomes force in the meeting and counteracting of the two simple agencies, and has thus its law put into itself by agencies from above and out of itself, and it can only transmit this inherent but imposed law from condition to conditioned indefinitely.   It must ever work for some end not yet reached, and can not thus ever find its own origin or its consummation.   It cannot propose itself as its own end, and thus arrest or modify its agency for its own sake ; but must evermore work on blind to all other ends than that of filling space and evolving the conditioned from the antecedent condition, and be a thing used by others and not person to use others or itself for its own behoof. Its inhering law is yet imposed by a higher, and for an

37

end yet to be, and is, therefore, truly heteronomy and not pure autonomy.

And *thirdly;* there may be conceived any other distinguishable forces superinduced upon this space-filling force, and we may have the forces of magnetism or electricity over-ruling but not extinguishing the force of gravity; or chemical or crystalline forces successively over-ruling and modifying all on which each may be superinduced; and we shall have each higher distinguishable force possessing its own inherent law, and diffusing this law through all the sphere of its operation, and thus acting for another and higher end than that which lies within any distinguishable force beneath it; but this inherent law will have been still imposed upon it by some simple agencies above it, and conditioning its action to the attainment of ends not yet reached, and thus no more an end in itself, and autonomic, than the primal antagonistic force of gravity.

And *fourthly;* we may have the distinguishable force of vegetable life, and which may control all the forces of attraction and repulsion, and chemical affinities, and crystalization, and use them all as subservient to its own higher end in assimilation and growth; yet still will this *vegetative* autonomy be a law imposed from above itself, and necessitated to a perpetual working for an end beyond itself, and can never attain to the completed and final plant in its consummation for which all preceding generations of plants have germinated and died. The vital force works on evermore from parent plant to produced germ in the servile toil to get an end which is not its own, and under the compulsion to a task which will never be finished. Here is only a thing and not person in pure autonomy.

And this may also be extended to the superinducing of the distinguishable force of animal life in its sentient capacity, and its internal organism for receiving and masticating and digesting its food, and this including all the irratibility of nerve and muscle which induces appetite, and locomotion, and selection of food, or objects of appropriate gratification for any sense ; and we shall have here a *sentient* autonomy which seems to be a user of many things for its own end in its self-gratification, and which, as controlled by self-enjoyment may sometimes be called will (*brutum arbitrium*); but this entire *anima* is still nature altogether and wholly shut up within necessitated successions, and is thus utterly thing and not person. The entire animal force is conditioned in its primal constitution, and the sensory necessitated in its internal pathognomy, and must thus work on as the servant of the animal organization and made to do the work which the body wants and when it needs ; and it can never finish its toil, for it is perpetually kept in successive animal organizations from generation to generation which never cease their craving. It can never rise to the dignity of making itself its own end and satisfying itself in its own action, but is ever lashed on by a master who imposes the task, and reaps the products, and allows that there be occasional gratifications amid the toil only as necessary to keep the slave alive and in a working condition. A sensory is a thing under necessity, not a person in autonomy.

Nor, though we add a light above its own instinctive cravings, in which the sentient force may work, shall we thus give to it personality. Make it competent to generalize its own past experience and thereby come to the conclusion that some gratifications cost too much in their subsequent exactions or inflictions, and that there is a rule of prudence which lies in this generalization of consequences to be heeded, and let this rule be very accurately attained in its own well-weighed experience; still every present result is already conditioned in some past event, and whether a specific appetite shall be strongly excited and control the action, or whether a generic desire of self-love as prompted by prudence shall carry the movement, this is already settled in some previous period which has conditioned the sentient force then to go out in operation. The end of action is out of itself, and imposing its law upon itself, and the sensory with all its prudential considerations is conditioned force and not will, and acting under a law imposed upon it, and not in autonomy.

Yea, should we conceive that there was the capacity to generalize universal experience, and find the rule of prudential welfare for all sentient beings ; the force which should go out in beneficence towards all would have been already determined in that which has conditioned its amount of sentient kindness. That it is prudent to itself, and congenial to itself, to be kind to others, is a law imposed upon it by that which out of itself has conditioned its sentient force to be such and so great as it is. Its benevolence would as completely stand conditioned in its pathology as any other constitutional appetite. It would be the product of its physiology as truly as its hunger, and as much bound in the series of conditioned changes as its digestion or its growth. It is all nature ; wholly a thing and not a person.

By none of the distinguishable forces of nature, from the mere antagonism of the primal force to those of the most complicated in animal life and sentient gratification and function of judgment in generalized experience, do we find any passage to the supernatural, nor any approach to the clear discrimination of thing from person. All is wholly under law imposed and in no case itself an end in itself. All is a means to an end ; that which knows no indignity in being used for another ; a thing that may have a price ; and thus never rising to the dignity of personality, which has rights that it may not compromit, and can never consent that it should be bought and sold, nor that it should ever permit itself to be used by another regardless of its inherent autonomy. Just as little is there pure autonomy in nature, as there is pure spontaneity; and though one thing may over-ride and control another thing, yet is the highest still a thing and subjected to conditions above and out of itself.

We rise then, *fifthly*, to the absolute above nature as we must for determining pure autonomy to personality. And here an accurate and extensive discrimination is to be made, and which cannot be effected without care, or we shall possess this second element of personality but very confusedly and obscurely.

Let it be considered that in one aspect the spontaneous pure activity may be contemplated as simply *artistic*. It is to go out in the production or creation of distinguishable forces, and thus in the genesis of a nature of things. But in such going forth of the pure activity there must be some end to be attained, and some law must be given to the process by which the agency may go out the most directly and completely to its issue. This cannot be in the light of any copy or pattern already objectively existing, in which may be found the model of what is yet to be, for the creator of nature has not yet an objective universe after which he may fashion another. As artist, the absolute must possess the primary copies or patterns of what it is possible may be, in his own subjective apprehension, and the first creations are subjective in the absolute reason as universal genius. The pure ideals of all possible entities lie as pure reason-conceptions in the light of the divine intelligence, and in these must be found the rules after which the creative agency must go forth. That subjective pure conception of what is to have objective being in an actual space-filling force, is the law by which the pure spontaneity is to be controlled. The agency which has this subjective archetypal rule in its own light has artistic genius, and such directing genius may be termed wisdom. When nature is to be brought forth into space and time, the creator must possess this in the beginning of his way. Of the whole work, this artistic wisdom personified may say, " When he prepared the Heavens I was there; when he set a compass upon the face of the depth; when he established the clouds above; when he strengthened the fountains of the deep; when he gave to the sea his decree that the waters should not pass his commandments ; when he appointed the foundations of the earth ; then I was by him as one brought up with him, and I was daily his delight rejoicing ever before him." And now this artistic wisdom and rule is in one acceptation, autonomy; it is law and guide for the creative agency, and it is a possession in the absolute itself. It is like the architect who has his own rules in his own intellectual being. He is in an important sense a self-regulated agent, working after his own subjective archetypal pattern.

But this will not suffice for the attainment of a pure autonomy. This artistic skill is something to be used, and the personality using has not yet been found.

What is to determine that it shall work? and after what pattern it shall work? and whether at the expense of marring the product the workman shall not be induced to violate the artistic rule? If there be nothing but some want in a sensory to be satisfied, like a mechanic who builds his own dwelling for his own convenience, then will the end be found in the gratification of that craving; and no matter how skillful, how spacious nor how costly the building, it has all been conditioned to the want he found himself constrained to gratify, and for which the agency must go forth or his sentient nature must abide the unhappy consequences. The value of the work and of the workman is estimated solely by the sentient gratification as end.

When material worlds in all their distinguishable forces have been put into space, and gravitating and chemical and crystaline agencies have been made to develop themselves in perfect conformity to the archetypal rule; if then this material creation is to be clothed in the verdant beauty and luxuriance of vegetative life, and the sentient want in the maker and his artistic pattern be given, the work will go on to this higher consummation and the gratification be therein attained. And should, again, all this beauty and bounty seem to lie waste as the stream in a desert until some sentient created beings be introduced to partake and enjoy, and the great Architect find within himself a want that can only be satisfied by making

and seeing sentient beings happy ; then would the artistic energy again be put forth to gratify this craving
desire in his own sentient being, and the air and waters and earth o'er all its hills and plains will teem
with living happy millions. We might thus go on
through indefinitely higher grades of sentient desires,
and furnish our artist with higher patterns for created
products, and we should keep an artistic skill perpetually energizing for the gratification of sentient
wants, and which, if finally terminating in some highest wants and thus in some highest happiness, would
still be all of nature.   The want is found to be already
determined ; a conditioned nature conditioning all the
working, and all the products of the artistic workman ;
and which is thus mere automaton, not pure autonomy.

We may assay to elevate such artistic autonomy,
which merely governs its actions by the rules given
and for the end of gratifying some sentient wants, to
the place of supreme author of nature, and as if we
had found in this a personal Deity may call him the
divine Architect ; and his wisdom may be consummate
in adapting means to ends, and manifold in working ; but the end of all is already conditioned in his
necessary sentient cravings, and as truly in nature
when his own want can be satisfied only with the
happiness of other sentient beings as when the animal
hungers for its daily food. Whoever possess the
sensory with its craving want must seek for this artis-

tic skill, and use the artisan only for the gratification
to which he may minister; and he may thus be *good*
in the acceptation of *useful* beyond all else, inasmuch
as he alone may minister to the highest want. Such
an artist, to such highest sentient craving, would be
invaluable; above all price in exchange; worth more
than all else, because serving a want the highest of
all; and, brought in barter to the market, would buy
out all that in the universe could be put to sale; but
still this would be only a thing among other things as
goods in the market, and more valuable only as a more
profitable instrument for the gratification of a higher
sentient end. He is a workman who can guide his
hand by his own eye, and whose skill is worth so
much by the day or by the job to the employer who
wants him. He is only a means to be used for an end,
precisely as a master may want the higher faculties
of his slave to accomplish such ends as he can never
reach by the brute strength and instinct of his horse,
and on this account only the slave is worth just so
much more than the horse. When the absolute is
thus viewed as a means to some end in sense, and out
of and apart from his own intrinsic excellency as end,
he is at once degraded from a sovereign to a servant;
from a person to a thing; he exists for what he makes;
his price is fixed by his products; and he is worth so
much more than other workmen only as he can make
better wares. A sentient nature, somewhere secretly
wound up to an undeniable craving, is the spring

which sets the automaton in action; and he works for, and works out, the end for which he is already conditioned in his own constitution. The only autonomy that may be affirmed of such an artist is, that he carries his rules in his head, but the spring and end of his action are wholly from and in another who employs him. We have not thus attained to any Personality.

What we need is not merely a rule by which to direct *the process* in the attainment of any artistic end, but we must find the legislator who may determine *the end itself.* This question is not the ultimate—In what way shall an artist be furnished with rules for doing his work to the greatest perfection? When that is decided to be after his own pure subjective archetypes, the ultimate question is altogether this— Whence is the ultimate behest that is to determine the archetype and control the pure spontaneity in its action? Shall it go out in an antagonism as central force, in which shall be the genesis of an ensphered and revolving space-filling substance? and why thus? Shall we answer, it must be thus in order that a subsequent superinducing of distinguishable forces upon this mere space-filling substance, such as magnetic chemical and crystaline agencies, may all together work on and work out the complicated but exact machinery of a material universe through all its component systems and worlds? But why such a material universe in its perfect architecture? Shall we again answer, this is all thus in order that the beauty and bounty of a vegetative life may be spread over hill and valley ?—but why this exuberance of vegetative life ? In order, again shall we say, that glad sentient beings may people the material worlds, and find a home amid all these adaptations in the heavens above and the earth beneath to their animal wants ?—but again the inquiry is just as prompt and urgent—why this world of sentient beings ? And should we again, answer; all this is for this great end, that some sentient beings may possess the exalted faculty of generalizing their own and their fellows' experience and determining rules of utility and prudence and economy which must regulate the action of each for his own highest welfare, and the interaction of all for the highest happiness of the whole ; and that thus there may be a social organization and a political sovereignty, which may administer a government of penal sanctions, coercing each to act for the highest happiness of all ? But this social world, thus legislating for itself on the grand principle of its highest happiness in the aggregate, is still a created world ; a product of an artist after the rule of his own subjective archetypal perfection ;—why such a social world ?—whence the behest that set this artist to his work, and called out this artistic wisdom in the service ? And here shall we answer, as if it were to stop all farther questioning ; that this artist had a sensory the gratification of whose highest desire was the impartation of happiness to other sentient beings ;

and, that thus his own inner want put him to the work
of making other sentient beings, who in their own happiness might satisfy him and make him to attain his
maximum of gratification? But surely in this, we have
nothing but nature in its necessitated conditions. The
absolute is simply kind and good-natured, and acts
from constitutional cravings, as really as all other sentient natures. The susceptibility to happiness from
benevolent action is in this way as truly an appetite
in its awakened desire, and necessitated in all its cravings, as any animal want. Quetions like these still
necessarily return—Why such susceptibility to beneficence?—What if the want in the sensory had been
of an opposite kind? Must the artist work merely because there is an inner want to gratify, with no higher
end than the gratification of the highest constitutional
craving? Can we find nothing beyond a want, which
shall from its own behest demand, that this and not
its opposite shall be? Grant that the round worlds
and all their furniture are *good*—but why good? Certainly as a means to an end. Grant that this end, the
happiness of sentient beings, is *good*—but why good?
Because it supplies the want of the supreme Architect.
And is this the *supreme good*? Surely if it is, we are
altogether within nature's conditions, call our ultimate
attainment by what name we may. We have no origin for our legislation, only as the highest architect
finds such wants within himself, and the archetypal
rule for gratifying his wants in the most effectual man-

ner; and precisely as the ox goes to his fodder in the shortest way, so he goes to his work in making and peopling happy worlds in the most direct manner. Here is no will; no personality; no pure autonomy. The artist finds himself so constituted that he must work in this manner, or the craving of his own nature becomes intolerable to himself, and the gratifying of this craving is *the highest good.*

We must find that which shall itself be the reason and law for benevolence, and for the sake of which the artist shall be put to his beneficent agency above all considerations that he finds his nature craving it. It must be that for whose sake happiness, even that which as kind and benevolent craves on all sides the boon to bless others, itself should be. Not sentient nor artistic autonomy, but a pure ethic antonomy which knows that within itself there is an excellency which obliges for the sake of itself. This is never to be found, nor anything very analogous to it, in sentient nature and a dictate from some generalized experience. It lies within the rational spirit and is law in the heart, as an inward imperative in its own right, and must there be found. The pregnant illustration of the Apostle is explicit that spirit only may know what is in spirit : "What man knoweth the things of a man save the spirit of man which is in him? even so the things of God knoweth no man but the spirit of God. The spirit searcheth all things, yea, the deep things of God." This inward witness-

ing capacitates for self-legislating and self-rewarding.
It is inward consciousness of a worth imperative
above want; an end in itself, and not means to another end; a user of things but not itself to be used by
anything; and, on account of its intrinsic excellency,
an authoritative determiner for its own behoof of the
entire artistic agency with all its products, and thus a
conscience excusing or accusing.

This inward witnessing of the absolute in his own
worthiness, gives the ultimate estimate to nature,
which needs and can attain to nothing higher, than
that it should satisfy this worthiness as end; and
thereby in all his works, he fixes, in his own light, upon
the subjective archetype, and attains to the objective
result, of that which is befitting his own dignity. It
is, therefore, in no craving want which must be gratified, but from the interest of an inner behest, which
should be executed for his own worthiness' sake, that
" God has created all things, and for his pleasure they
are and were created."

It is not sufficient that a product is attained which
is good only as a means to some further end; nor yet
that a personality is assumed who is only artistic skill
and wisdom, for this is only means to an end, and
wholly a servant for an other's using; nor yet that
this servant have wants, even that he should make
others happy for the sake of his own happiness, for
this keeps him in servitude still, inasmuch as the want
can only be as a means to the creation of a happy

race, and the creation of such a race a means only to
satisfy such a want ; but above all the artistic skill
and the imparted happiness, we must come into the
light and purity and majesty ineffable of an uncreated
personality, before whose presence all this sublimity
of architecture and all this exuberance of bounty and
of gladness may be laid as an offering, whose only estimate can be that it is worthy to be accepted of him,
and whose only end can be that it has been created
for him. The SUMMUM BONUM is in his dignity and
excellence, and in this the great Eternal read the law
how created nature should be, and under such behest
the fiat went forth, and such Nature is.

It is precisely in this light, and solely in this presence, that we wake to the consciousness of what reverence is, and know that we stand before an awful
Majesty where we must bow and adore. We may
stand amid all the sublimities of that wonder-working
power which is fashioning the material mechanism of
the heavens and the earth, and we shall admire and
praise in profound astonishment; we may look upon
all the arrangements which, in the bounty of an ever
working *wisdom and kindness*, is diffusing sentient joy
and gladness over millions of happy beings ; and we
may go with such as are competent to recognize their
kind benefactor into his presence, and hear the ten
thousand times ten thousand voices, in different ways
proclaiming their *gladsome gratitude* as the sound of
many waters, and we shall sympathize in their joys

and praises with a rapturous delight; but it is only
when I see all these standing in the presence of that
absolute sovereignty and pure moral personality, who
searches them all in the light of his own *dignity*,
and judges them by the claims of his own *excellency*,
and estimates their worth solely in reference to his *worthiness*; and when also I see that thus it behoved they
should have been made, to be fit creatures of his ordering and accepting, and that he made them thus after the behest of his own uncreated reason, and in the
light of his ethical truth and righteousness, and governs them and holds them ever subordinate to his own
moral glory and authority; it is in such a presence
only, that I reverently cover my face, and fall pros-
trate, and cry from my inward spirit, "Holy, Holy,
Holy, Lord God almighty;" "Heaven and earth are
full of thy glory." "Thou art worthy O Lord, to receive glory, and honor, and power, for thou hast created all things, and for thy pleasure they are, and were
created."

In this is the very essence of personality, that it may
assume in its own right the authority to control its own
agency; and may lay claim to the high prerogative of
being an end, and must resist whatsoever would degrade it to be used as a means to any other than its
own end. In this is Conscience; which must forbid
all intrusion from any possible source within its own
domain, and in violation of its own end as moral character. And in this also is Will; that the act is not

38

nature necessitated in its conditions, nor alone pure spontaneity in its blindness, but held in control by that witness of what is due to itself as personality; and thus possessing that inward spring in the interest of its own worthiness, which may resist and shut out and beat down all that would seduce or force it from allegiance to the claims of its own dignity. Nor except in the possession of such intrinsic excellence and dignity of being, and for the behest of which every thing else must be trodden under foot, can there be an agency, however mighty, or skillful, or beneficent, that may be permitted to take rank among personalities; but at the highest must be put among utilities, which may command its own price, but can never claim a reverence for its own dignity. We thus come to the safe conclusion, that in order to personality the absolute must have, not only the element apriori of pure spontaneity, which would give autocracy, but moreover that inward witness of its own worth and dignity which makes itself end and not means, and which gives *pure Autonomy.*

3. Pure spontaneity in the absolute is simple act, standing above all the conditions of force, and thus under a necessity as nature. But mere spontaneity is blind action, aimless and lawless, and though essential to personality is not itself sufficient for it. Pure autonomy is end above nature, and in its own intrinsic excellency worthy to be end itself and thus a law to its own action. It gives the inward witness of a right

to hold on to its own worthiness as end in every action ; and that it behoves itself, never to let its action
become subservient to any end that collides with its
own dignity ; and thus affords the spring within itself,
in the interest of its own excellency, to control and direct its own agency. The intrinsic excellency and
dignity of the being gives its own law to the action of
the being, and hence it is no longer pure spontaneity
merely, but spontaneity under law, viz : the behest of
its own intrinsic worthiness. This antithesis of pure
spontaneity and pure autonomy has its point of indifference—i. e. a point in which pure spontaneity combines with or comes under the autonomy, and is no
longer mere spontaneity but spontaneous act governed; and also in which the pure autonomy combines
with the spontaneity, and is no longer mere autonomy
but self-law governing. We have, thus, not the two
elements in their separate singularity, as set over the
one against the other ; but in their interaction as in
synthesis one with the other, so that we may say that
neither is extinct and that neither in itself is, but a
tertium quid is, which may be called indifferently a
self-act governed, or a self-law governing. In this synthesis of self-action and self-law a will first emerges,
and the very essence of person as distinct from thing
is in the possession of will. In this only can the being have possession of his own action, and in this *having* of his action comes his capacity *to behave*. Responsibility to his inner self calls for perpetual allegi-

ance to the authority of this inner sovereignty. Here is the holy of holies with its Shekina in the temple of each personality. In the absolute underived I AM, this self agency and self-law is ever in perfect synthesis, undisturbed by any intruding act or colliding law from any possible quarter, and thus ever a pure will in the the tranquility of its perfect holiness.

When, therefore, we have the element of pure spontaneity and pure autonomy in synthesis, we have a *third* reason conception in a completed personality, which is *pure liberty.* Without spontaneity the absolute must be linked in the necessitated successions of nature; without autonomy it must be mere blind and lawless action; but in the synthesis of these there is a will, which may make its alternative to any foreign end or agency or law that can obtrude itself, and thus a liberty. A will in liberty is completed personality.

It is important that we come accurately to discriminate this reason-conception of pure liberty from all the false and spurious understanding-conceptions of freedom with which it is often confounded; or, rather, above which it has very generally been denied that it is possible for the intellect to reach; and thus, by denying the possible conception of pure liberty, the entire province of the supernatural has really been discarded. The Deity, proposed to the faith of many an assumed Theist, has been in this way a mere *Naturatus;* a deity bound utterly in the discursive connections of substance and cause. In vain will any assumed terms, borrowed from the supernatural, be brought in to assist us; without a pure liberty we cannot rise above nature.

In the operations of cause and effect, when the work is unhindered by any opposition, it is often said that nature is *free*. But all application of the term *freedom* to nature must be with a different acceptation than that it is pure liberty. Nature can in none of its operations be found as an agent controlling its action for itself as end, but is every where going out into effects in which there can be no resting as end, but which always exist only as means to a further end. Nature is wholly a means, and can never cease its action as if it had found its consummation in itself, and had thereby satisfied itself; but must work on interminably, and ever in the line that a previous condition has made already to be necessity. It may be free in this acceptation, that its development has nothing in advance to condition it, and thus its work goes on unhindered. The progressus of cause and effect finds ever an open and unobstructed pathway. But in all cases the working of nature must be conditioned by something from behind, and urged forward by a force *a tergo*, both that it must be, and be just what it becomes. In no one step of nature is there any alternative; from what already is, that step which is now proximately future must be taken, and must be so taken as has already been conditioned. There is no autonomy, no will, no personality, consequently no liberty.

Again, the animal is often said to *choose*, and that choice is freedom. But the word choice is very ambiguous; and the freedom of choice may be equivocal, with very different meanings in different applications. The *anima* is a sensitive nature superinduced upon a *vegeta;* and animal life is as truly nature as vegetable life. The force of vegetative life is, also, superinduced upon material being; but all the distinguishable forces in material being, and that of vegetation, are alike nature. And now of all, we may say that they have their affinities or congenialities, and that they thus make selections, and in all cases this selecting may be a force which works unhindered; but by whatever name we call it, we shall be able to see that so far as its freedom is concerned it is in all cases alike, and is simply that of unhindered causation; not at all, that which from the end of its own worthiness can bring in an ethical spring as alternative to nature's conditions, and thus in liberty. Chemical combinations select according to conditioning elective affinities; crystaline formations select the homogeneous from the heterogeneous; the magnet selects the steel-filings from saw-dust; the fire selects the stubble from the stones; the plant selects its own congenial nourishment; the ox selects grass, and the tiger selects flesh; but all these varieties of selection are alike in nature, and necessitated by their conditions. We may give the name of *choice* to the animal selection; but it is not because there is any approach towards a will in liberty, that may supply an alternative to nature's conditions; and if it seem less appropriate to say the fire chooses than that the animal chooses, it is only as we permit ourselves to be deluded with the false play of the understanding, which would assume to rise from thing and approach to person, by merely modifying discursive conditions. The "half-reasoning elephant," and the "architectural beaver;" the "cunning fox," and the "sagacious dog;" all rise to the exercise of a force, which concludes in a judgment according to conditions in the sense, and thus come quite within the province of an understanding, and we may thus be less offended by applying to them the attributes of personality than to inanimate, insensate matter; but the one is no more removed from the fixed chain of conditions in nature than the other, and the action of the most intelligent animal is as little in liberty, and as truly necessitated by previous conditions, as the fire or the magnet. All is controlled by the sentient nature, which in every act has its condition in some already conditioned events, and which no amount of sagacity can lift out of the bondage of necessity. That its action in a change of perceived circumstances changes is no more an index of choice in liberty, than that the current of the stream changes its direction when it meets the obstacle thrust in the way of its progress. The conditions at the time are the events which have come out from a previous period, and are themselves the conditioning facts of what is next to arise; and amid such conditions, neither the magnet, the stream, the vegetable, nor the animal, can bring in the interest of a dignity in its own personality, as spring to carry itself against, or to throw itself out of the necessitated successions of nature. All its freedom is this, an unhindered progression in following down the current of nature's conditions. The choices of animal nature are component links in this iron chain as truly as the effects of gravity. It is controlled by appetite and thus by nature, not by its own behest in reason and thus in liberty. Hence the animal is ever thing, and never person ; it has a price, but not a dignity.

Man, also, by so much as he is sentient, is animal only. All the cravings of his sensory are constitutional and thus conditioned, and the action in an appetite and in its gratification is wholly of nature. As animal alone, man has no will in liberty, and thus no more a personality than the brute which perisheth. Except as man has a higher endowment than a sentient nature, and in which he may find an inner witness of an intrinsic excellency and dignity, that forbids all prostitution of itself to be used as means to gain any end of the sensory, but which is imperative that all possible gratification of sentient nature shall be wholly controlled and even thrust aside and beat down for the higher end of its own worthiness, and which may thus take hold upon an interest in its own excellency of being and resist and subjugate all the clamorous appetites of sense, and hold them in perpetual servi-

tute to its own ethical end, he neither has nor can
have any personality nor responsibility, inasmuch as
otherwise he can possess no will in liberty. He may
bow his personality to the ends of animal gratification
and in his depravity make the ethical to serve the sensual; but it is because of this inner witness of intrinsic excellency and dignity degraded and debased, that
he has remorse as a gnawing worm.

His personality in his will is thus enslaved to sense
and subjected to nature, but it can never lay aside its
high prerogatives and become nature. In its lowest
degradation and debasement in guilt, the inner witness of its own intrinsic rights disregarded and sacri-
ficed will give a perpetual self-condemnation, and
urge the behest to reassert and regain its rightful supremacy and authority. Man can only thus sell his
liberty to the sense against the constant claims of his
own personality, and stand every moment self-con-
demned in his self-degradation. Were he only animal
he would ruminate in quiet enjoyment upon the past
croppings of sense; it is the recoil of the accusing
spirit back upon itself in conscious guilt and debasement, that gives the sting to all man's reflections upon
his sensuality. Deprive him of this higher endowment and you leave him wholly to nature, and no
matter how extensive his force of understanding in
generalizing his own and his fellow's experience, and
attaining the rules of prudence and benevolence; he
can make neither an end, except as he finds the want
already in the sensory, and that want as conditioned

in nature will condition the act, and link that also in the necessities of nature.

But, in determining to the Absolute his own right to be himself his end of action, in the dignity of his own excellency, and thus to control his pure activity by his own worthiness as ethical law, and that whatever may be the ends proposed out of himself he may fix upon them or utterly exclude them according to this behest in the inner witnessing of the rights of his own being, we have that self-agency and self-law which is spring for alternative action to any ends possible to be presented, and thus is ever pure will in the sovereignty of its perfect law of liberty. He is a personality above nature, who may steady himself against the obtrusion of all ends in a real nature of things or all archetypes in a possible nature of things, and stand utterly unconditioned by an actual or a possible series of condition and conditioned, and answer only to the supreme, all-controlling ethical claims of his inner being, viz: that he magnify his own worthiness as his highest good, and the absolute end and right. This is quite other than the freedom of unhindered causality; or, the choices of sentient nature that go out in gratification for conditioned wants; even the acts of a Rational Personality in a will, which, though not lawless, has only an ethical law in liberty.

That may be said to be the *good will*, in the acceptation of the *holy will*, which is pure spontaneous act under the ethical law of its own dignity as person;

which knows no colliding end with the ethical law:
which preserves the perfect tranquility of finding
every end in his own interest perfectly conformed to
the ethical end of his own worthiness; and thus never
subjected to the conflict of a law in himself with a
law out of himself. That would be the *good will* in
the sense of the *virtuous will*, which has the colliding
of sensual end with ethical end, but which in the conflict ever valorously beats back and subordinates the
sensual end. Such may ever have the peace of a
strong and watchful government, but never the tranquility of perfect love. One is self-regnant, the other
self-complacent.

The Divine will must ever be the purely Holy will
in its tranquility. The Absolute, as pure Uncreated
Reason, can have no ends appealing to any interest in
collision with that which is the highest ethical law of
Reason ; ever to act according to his own rationality,
or, as the same thing, worthy of himself. It is thus
in the same sense "impossible that God should lie."
as it is that "he cannot deny himself." He "ever
abideth faithful," inasmuch as within the personality
of the absolute reason, it would be absurd that there
should be an interest that should collide with the
highest rationality. All possible ends must, to the
absolute reason, be held in subordination to its own
end, and this is the control of pure spontaneity by a
pure autonomy, and which, as furnishing an alternative to all possible ends as interest, is *pure Liberty*.

These three, Spontaneity, Autonomy, and Liberty
are all the elements which determine Personality;
and, as in the Ideal of the Absolute, determined in his
personality, we are to comprehend universal nature,
so in these, we have the apriori Elements of an operation of Comprehension.

SECTION III.

THE APRIORI COMPREHENSION OF NATURE IN THE PURE PERSONALITY OF THE ABSOLUTE.

PERSONALITY involves pure spontaneity under a pure
autonomy, and this is the sole condition of pure liberty.   It is a capacity of action in will, and possesses
within itself the spring of an alternative to any possible external end which may be proposed to it.   This
is pure self-determination; not as arbitrament with no
end, for this would be the absurdity of a determination undetermined; but an arbitrament from the ethical end of its own worthiness. The supreme intrinsic
excellency of the absolute, as person, is itself the reason and the ethical behest that he should not be a means
to any end out of himself.   It behooves that he be the
user of all possible things, and that he be used by
nothing possible.   His own agency should be directed
by those rights which are inseparable from his own
excellency.
    All right as ethical exists in personality, and is foun-

dation for the peremptory demand that nature as servant shall find its end in the person, and that no possible end in nature shall be permitted by the person to hold himself in bondage to it. Finite personalities must in this respect be in the likeness of the absolute person, and each be an end in himself which he may never subordinate to any end in nature without violating the rights of personality and making himself guilty of self-degradation. It would thus involve an ethical absurdity that the absolute person, for whose use is all possible nature, might use the finite personality as he may use nature. Nature is not end in itself, and can have no rights, and can therefore never rise above the instrumental; personality, even finite, has rights which it would be an unworthiness in the absolute to disregard or invade. The ultimate end and supreme good of the Divine dignity will give an ethical behest that all of material and sentient nature be *used as thing*, and that all of moral being be *treated as person*. A sovereignty supreme and universal, legislating and governing in the right and for the end of his own dignity with a purely holy will, must control the material and moral worlds, by widely different laws; conditioning all of the former in the necessitated connections of nature, and holding all of the latter to the responsibilities of "the witness within" as the perfect law of liberty. Nature must glorify its maker as thing to be used for an end not its own; finite personality, as offspring of the Deity, must glorify God in the joyful service which it is its own ethical end lovingly to render.

But such conception of personality, which may originate action from a spring within itself and control a consummation that shall be wholly for itself, is exclusively a reason-conception. To the understanding, all that is personality, or a will in liberty, must be wholly without signification. Its functions can only connect discursively and never contemplate existence comprehensively; and that there should be action, from a being who may originate and consummate within himself, must to it be utterly unintelligible. But if we will keep our philosophy here wholly within the province of the supernatural, and not permit the illusions of discursive connections in an understanding to obtrude themselves upon us, we may surely and soundly attain to an apriori demonstration. In order to this it is now quite necessary to guard against any deceptive ambiguities in the terms which it may be convenient we should here use. We have transcended the whole region of phenomena as the qualities and events constructed in place and period, and our use of the word *attribute*, as applied to the elements of personality, must not be considered at all the phenomenal *quality* which inheres in a space-filling substance, and may be given in sensation and constructed in a definite quantity.

And so, moreover, have we transcended all the region of the notional, which as substances and causes connect nature in a universe; and when we now use the terms *influence, power, essence,* or *source* as referable to person, we must not at all consider these as the physical forces, which in nature may be made to push or pull and thereby modify and displace existing things. Even when it is convenient to borrow words from the understanding, and thus bring up the terms from the natural to the supernatural, and call the absolute a *First Cause,* and speak of the behest of his own dignity as *causative determiner* of his acts, or of the will as *causality* of the personal agency, we are by no means to allow ourselves to come under the delusion, as if with the terms there had come up the things of nature, and that such supernatural causation had any connection with nature's causes in their necessitated conditions. If the words are sometimes borrowed, the meanings must never be confounded. The attributes and causalities of the supernatural both transcend and comprehend the qualities and causalities of the natural. All the substantiality and causality of nature originate in, and are used by, the absolute will in liberty. Thus carefully discriminating our reason-conceptions of personality from all understanding-conceptions of things in nature, we now proceed to the consideration of a possible comprehension of universal nature in the absolute personality.

As incorporeal and uncreated reason and will, the absolute has his own spring of action within himself, and in this a power in liberty which is wholly above and separate from all force in nature, and which may be creative of force. He may originate simple acts which, in their own simplicity, have no counter-agency and can therefore never be brought under any of the conditions of space and time and nature.

From his own inner capacity of self-determination he may designedly put simple acts in counteraction and at their point of counter-agency a force begins which takes a position in space and occupies an instant in time. There is a beginning in something where nothing was; and this has position, instant, and permanence. The perpetuated energizing in counteraction is creation in progress, inasmuch as force accumulates about that point of antagonism, and enspheres itself upon it as a centre; and a space is thereby filled, which may be conjoined in a definite figure; a time is thus occupied which may be conjoined in a definite period; and an impenetrable substance is made, which may give content in a sensibility, and be conjoined in a definite phenomenon. Above that point of counter-agency all is simple activity—unphenomenal and unsubstantial, and having all its essentiality in the power of the supernatural as will in liberty; in, and below that point all is force—phenomenal in the perception of the sense, and substantial and causal from its antagonism in the judgment of the understanding, and existing as physical nature in its necessitated conditions. In this substance, place in its own one whole of space is determinable; and in this also as source

or successive events, period in one whole of time may
be determined; and thus an existence is given in a
space and time, which cannot come and depart as in a
mirror or a dream. The energizing of the absolute will
may fill so much of this one whole of space, and in so
much of this one whole of time, as shall be directed by
the archetypal rule of his artistic wisdom; and may
give the modifications of distinguishable forces, also,
in accordance with such rule; and all for the end of
his own excellency: and thus, at the fiat of the absolute will, nature is, with all her substances, causes and
reciprocal forces, and with all the tribes of vegetable,
animal, and human beings. God need only to will it,
" and for his pleasure they are." Nature henceforth
goes on in her development according to the law of
physical forces, and is perpetually a *natura naturans;*
but, at the great central point of all counter-working,
and in all the points of a superposition of distinguishable forces, a conditioning of nature is determined by
the absolute in his own liberty, and thus all nature is
still *natura naturata.* Physical causes perpetually
work on, and all is thus *causa causans;* but all these
causes are conditioned in their sources by the self-de-
determining will of the absolute, and are thus *causa
causata.* The power which imposes conditions upon
nature, and gives causality to causes, is wholly above
all the conditions and causes of nature, and with nothing of the necessities of physical force, has no other
controller than the supreme artistic wisdom under the
39

behest of the absolute in liberty. And still further, while this space-filling force takes its place in space, and is impenetrable, inasmuch as it can admit the substance of no other space-filling force into its locality except in its own displacement, so also is all the reflex action of this engendered and ensphered force sustained upon the central point of the primal antagonism. Action and reaction, attraction and repulsion, centripetal and centrifugal agency fill the whole sphere of universal nature; but no working of physical forces can press back of the central point in which they have their genesis, and invade the world of the supernatural. The Deity needs but to will the counteraction in its perpetuated force, and universal nature finds its equilibrium in the repulsion from the center and the reflex pressure to the center, and holds itself suspended on its own conditioned forces, without the possibility of any weariness or exhaustion to its maker. It is wholly the product of the Divine will; and wholly external to the absolute; and while utterly dependent for its being upon the Divine will, can yet never react upon or in any way condition the being and agency of the omnipotent producer. It is thereby a veritable creation distinct from its creator, of which it may intelligently be affirmed, that the creator is conditional for it, but it in no wise conditions the creator. Within it are contained all the series of conditioned and thus of necessitated successions; and from the rudimental germs in their primal creation as distinguishable forces, is already determined the fact and the order of development. The conditions for ensphering worlds; for centripetal and centrifugal forces, and the ratios of their action both as to quantity and distance from the center; their revolutions upon their axes, and their orbits about their primaries; and the relative inclination of the planes of these orbits, and of the axes of the spheres to them, and of the proportions of the axes of each to their equatorial diameters; and, in short, the whole formal arrangements of the universe are given in the very points where the primordial forces have their genesis; as is also the whole science of nature in its original bi-polar, chemical, crystaline, vegetable and animal forces. An apriori philosophy may long be detained in this broad field, before it shall be competent to detect all these forces in their distinguishable rudiments, but their laws, and thus all their possible conditioned changes, have already been settled in their creation, and may be determined.

All this context of conditions, constituting universal nature, is dependent, while the absolute maker is wholly independent; it is his creature and subjected to his use. He is its Lord, and has the right of sovereignty over it to make it subservient to the end of his own dignity. It is, only because He is; and the ethical behest of his own worthiness has summoned it to fill its place, and endure its time, and subserve his purpose. God made it, and is wholly independent of it; and thus both Atheism and Pantheism are utterly excluded, in this reason-conception of the absolute as person. This determination of an origin to nature, in its own space and time, is a complete comprehension of nature on the side of nature's beginning.

And now, that on the other side we may comprehend nature in its *consummation*, we have the same compass of an all-embracing reason in the absolute as personality, and who as having the final end of all his agency in himself, must govern and direct all of nature to the end for which it has been created by him. The Supreme Architect must have the archetypes of all possible nature in his own subjective apprehension. There is no inward craving want of a sensory, which may subject the will to the bondage of a blind necessity in going out to gratify it, nor put the will in a perpetually militant attitude in resisting it; but there is the one high and controlling behest of his own excellency, that every possible end shall be determined in subserviency to the right of his own worthiness. It is the highest rationality, that the absolute reason be himself the end of all ends. This inward ethical spring to all action finds no possible collision in the Divine bosom, and nothing hinders his will in the sweet and loving execution of an eternally steady and tranquil disposing of itself to the ultimate end of his own glory. In this is pure and perfect holiness; and it will control the artistic selection and execution, from amid all possible archetypal creations, to that which will be most worthy of his own making and accepting. There is a measuring of things by things, but no thing can be an absolute good. The measure of all things is in the personality of reason; and the absolute reason is the perfection and glory of all possible persons; and whatever magnifies *His* dignity will include the exaltation of finite personality. The supreme good for all moral personality is this unbroken reign of the Divine Holiness. And this grand end in all the works of God must secure an optimism in nature, as the product of his creative power. His will must be on that archetype which in the end of his reason is the most reasonable; in the end of supreme loveliness, is the most lovely; in the end of an excellency above all price, is the most excellent; and in the presence of a dignity where all finite worth fades, is the most worthy.

In this autocracy and autonomy of the Deity, we have the ultimate and complete measure of his creation. In the tranquil self-possession of a perfectly holy will lies his eternal purpose; and the steady agency moves on in artistic wisdom, to the fullfilment of his settled counsel. Material worlds and systems, with their distinguishable forces as substances in their causality, are made and arranged in their order and perfection of mechanical adaptation, action and movement; and the rich abundance and beauty, which vegetative life throws over the surface of the green earth, are brought out; and the changing seasons with the changing years roll on, and day and night and "sweet return of morn and eve" are in perpetual alternations.

But not in this perfection of arranged forces, though worthy of the power and manifold wisdom of the absolute maker, shall we find the ultimate end for which the Almighty works. He is more than artistic perfection, and may not permit his action to be exhausted in the satisfaction of the artist. He is architect only in subserviency to a higher end in a higher excellency, and material worlds with all their furniture exist only as instruments to be used for a higher behest. Sentient tribes of living beings people these wide fields, and gather the good harvest of nature, and live in gladness and joy on this bounty, and thus in addition to the wider action of artistic skill in the adaptations of material, vegetable and animal nature, we have the much higher product of animal enjoyment and happiness. But God is good, in the acceptation of bountiful and beneficent, only that it may subserve a much higher intrinsic excellency in his being, than that he should be benevolent. Human beings, to whom may be given an intelligent apprehension of that which is rule for their highest happiness, and an immortality, that they might endlessly obey and enjoy, would so far be only of nature; and their rule of life, a generalization of experience as they found it to be; and their obligation to obey, not any thing of ethical worth and dignity, but solely as slaves to a nature that can pay in pleasure or in pain. Their ultimate master would be the power of the leviathan who may caress or torture; and their only virtue would be that they work on with the eye on the greatest wages before them, and the consciousness of the lash behind. But God is author of the nature which rewards and punishes, for a much higher end in himself than that so he must do if he would satisfy a want he finds in himself to be made happy by making others happy. This would leave him the slave to a necessity as tyrannical as that of the animal, and stretch the iron chain of nature completely around him. There is here nowhere a will in liberty but the mere brute *arbitrium* of nature's strongest craving. The Deity should not thus exhaust his action in giving laws to nature, from which the rules of prudence in attaining the greatest happiness on the whole may be derived, and this only to sit by and enjoy himself the happiness, which this on-going of nature may work out for him in the perceived happiness of his creatures.

It is no possible craving want to be gratified that can be the ultimate end and law of the absolute power, and which must at once condition the absolute, and exclude from the prerogative of personality with a will in liberty; but it is an ethical interest in reason alone, which in its own right demands when and how and what the happiness shall be, and what artistic arrangements shall be given to nature, conditioning the happiness it shall work out. God will keep his benevolence subservient to his holiness, and make it to find its end in his own worthiness, and impart happiness in no way that shall be derogatory to his essential excellency and dignity. And this discloses at once the crowning end of the whole physical creation, with all its sentient happiness, viz : that it may subserve a personal and moral creation, in its advancement of virtue and holiness to such a degree of dignity and moral worth, as the ethical behest of his own person will admit that the absolute Author should secure.

The absolute fully comprehends himself, and fathoms all the depths of his own being, and has other and far higher capabilities than any material or sentient organizations can exhaust. To create and superintend the development of only such forces could not reach the ultimate end of his own worthiness, inasmuch as it would be a termination in the less while he held within himself the archetypes of the greater, and involve the absurdity that the absolute reason should satisfy itself with something other than reason. Its behest must be the maximum of archetype, and the consummation of working. A moral world—a system made up of varied orders and ranks of persons in liberty—will be brought into existence ; and thus, the congeniality of accordant being in reciprocal communion and affection, will be disclosed. There may then be an ethical society, governed by the spring which the "inward witness" of what is due to each in the worthiness of his own personality shall give; and the whole rewarding itself, in the blessedness which accrues to each in the holiness and blessedness of all, and God and his moral creation come together in a reciprocity of holy love. Somewhere, this moral world will be brought in connection with the conditions of the physical world; and all the adaptations of material, vegetable, and sentient being be found to have their end in the interests of the moral system. A race of beings, compounded of the material, sentient and moral, may be created; and thus, that which is personal becomes incarnate, and the free is subjected to the colliding action of the necessitated, and personal liberty is put upon its probation in conflict with the conditioned force of nature, and through this one point of connection with nature a modifying influence is consequentially carried over all the sphere of moral being. God will use the natural for the ends of the moral; and he will govern the moral, by ethical laws and influences which originate in the behest of his own intrinsic excellency and dignity. When the ends of nature are kept wholly subordinate to the ethical end of personality, then are the physical and the moral worlds in harmony, and the entire creation of God is good, and " the morning stars sing together."

Sin may enter by any prostitution of an ethical claim to a physical want; but this must be somewhere below the creator, and from the creature-personality; inasmuch as no colliding want can reach to the absolute, and sin enter through him; and no moral responsibility to an " inner witness " can be found in physical nature, and sin inhere in it. Through any finite personality sin may come in; and that it should come in somewhere, in any possible modification of a moral system in its necessary subjection to a conditioned nature, may be a certainty to the omniscience of the absolute, except in such interposition for prevention as would compromit the higher ultimate end in the behest of his own dignity. God may not lay aside his own dignity, and act unworthy of his own excellency, to save a moral creation from ruin. He may not leave the throne of sovereignty, ethically his in his own intrinsic excellency, and permit himself to be used as servant and instrument for some other end that then takes the throne; even though it be the holiness and blessedness of a moral universe. What he may do, he will do to exclude sin; both in the use of sentient nature as a penalty, and when sin has entered, in its use as a tabernacle for divinity to " set forth a propitiation, to declare his righteousness; " but not for the prevention of, nor the redemption from sin will God " deny himself." He will so create natural and moral worlds, and so arrange them in their connections, and so act upon them in all his agency, as shall completely meet the end of his own worthiness; and give that archetype as the pattern for artistic wisdom, which, of all possible ways for creating energy and governmental influence to go forth, shall be most reasonable, most lovely, most righteous and holy, when tried in his presence, and by the ethical rights and claims of his own personality. This must comprehend every event in nature, every act in the moral world, and conclude the entire creation in that final consummation of the whole plan and work, when it shall be worthy to be presented to, and accepted by the God and Judge of all. Then shall come the full and eternal chorus, "and every creature which is in heaven, and on the earth, and under the earth, and such as are in the sea, and all that are in them, shall be heard saying, Blessing and honor and glory and power be unto him that sitteth upon the throne, and unto the Lamb forever and ever."

Here, therefore, in the complete ideal of the absolute in personality, it is possible that we may attain to a perfect and entire comprehension of nature, and indeed of all creation physical and moral. A nature of things may originate in the Deity as personal creator in liberty, and stand out distinct from, and wholly excluded from all conditioning reaction upon, the Deity; while itself is wholly dependent upon, and subjected to, his supreme will. We no longer seek a resting place through the discursions of the understanding, where we must ever be hastening the footstep from the conditioned to a higher condition; but we have found a conception for a safe and permanent source of all things, in the self-sufficiency of an absolute, personal Deity. Nor do we run on the interminable line of final causes, and find one thing to end only in that which must yet run on to some further end; bnt we have a summum bonum, and ultimate end, in the intrinsic worth and reverence due to the absolute personal God, before whom all his creation should stand uncovered. The chain of nature's conditioned events may lengthen down the depths of the void below, but the hand out of which it comes forbids all anxiety lest unsupported it should fail, and nature be extinguished; or, lest it should go on downward with no aim but to lose itself in unfathomed emptiness. Nature has a beginning; a guide; a consummation; and in this, nature is completely comprehended; nor is it possible that in any other manner, it should find its comprehension.

The complete Idea of the Reason, as faculty for an operation of Comprehension, is thus given in the compass of the Absolute in personality. *Nature may be comprehended in a pure Spontaneity, Autonomy, and Liberty: or, which is the same thing—Reason may comprehend Nature in the compass of an Absolute Person.*

CHAPTER II.

THE REASON IN ITS OBJECTIVE LAW.

FINITE AND ABSOLUTE PERSONALITY.

COMPREHENSION determines things in their origin and their consummation, and which we have already seen is only to be effected through a free personality. Sense can merely *conjoin* in definite place and period, and thereby give in consciousness the arising and departing phenomenon; but cannot tell whence it cometh, nor whither it goeth. An understanding can merely *connect* the phenomena in their substances and causes, and thereby give to the flowing events in nature a perduring substratum of existence which ever is, and only changes its modes of being and manifestation; but cannot say, what is origin for this substance in its causality, nor to what consummation these changes in nature are tending. It may go up and down the interminable series of changing events, but can by no means overleap the linked conditions and determine from whence the whole have come, nor whither the whole will find their end; and in such perpetual running from link to link there can never be effected a comprehension of the entire chain. The reason is the only faculty for *comprehending*, and this by encompassing both origin and end in a personal author.

We have determined the apriori possibility of such comprehending operation, in the compass of a personality in liberty, and in this have attained to the complete idea of an all-embracing reason. But thus, far the all-comprehending reason is only a void conception. We have not yet found such a comprehending faculty in actual being and operation. So it *may* be; so, if at all, it *must* be; but that so it *is*, we have yet to find. Our remaining task is this, that we take any facts which may present themselves in the whole field of a comprehending agency and find whether they come at once within the actual colligation of this law of free personality. It is incumbent, that from these various facts, we should show that a comprehension of things reaches so far as, and no farther than, an applied law of personality in liberty reaches. This will give the accordance of Idea and Law which has all along been our criterion of true science. This will perfect our entire Psychological System; but as in the sense and the understanding we gave an outline of the Ontological Demonstration of their objects, we will here do the same for the reason—The Soul, God and Immortality.

We shall find an occasion for distinguishing these

facts of a comprehending agency and putting them into two separate classes, accordingly as they belong to the world of a *finite* or of an *absolute* personality

We shall find that a finite personality is the compass by which we comprehend one class of these facts, and the absolute personality the compass by which we comprehend the other ; and to mark the distinction between these, it is important that we familiarize ourselves to the following considerations.

We may speak of a *sensorium*, reached by any content as quality given in an organ of sense, and thus excited, becoming capacity for sensation ; and all this will lie wholly within the fixed conditions of nature ; and the phenomena which it will give occasion for constructing in consciousness, and thus all perceptions, will stand wholly within necessitated conditions. We may also speak of a *sensory* as more deeply subjective, reached by the perceived objects and thus excited becoming capacity for appetite in any way of a constitutional craving or want, and all this will be within the linked conditions of nature; and the desires, as well as perceptions, will be necessitated. The entire sensibility, call it sensorium or sensory, capacity for perceiving or wanting, is wholly within nature.

The perceptions of objects may vary, and remembered consequences of former gratifications may modify desires, and changed circumstances may demand a changed course of action to secure the object wanted, and all this will induce a judgment relative to the ends of a sentient nature according to what is actually given in the sense, and which must thus change as the perceived circumstances and wants have changed; but all this will still be controlled wholly by the conditions of nature, and an animal understanding will be mere instinctive subtlety or brute sagacity, and held completely in servitude to the conditions imposed upon it. Even should we admit a generalizing of all experience, and thereby a rule of highest gratification in the aggregate, and in this the dictate of prudence; the whole would still be within the bondage of necessity, and the perception and the appetite and the judgment all conditioned in nature, and no other prerogative would be gained than a mere expansion of an animal understanding necessitated in all its judgments, its wants, and its gratifications. Its aggregate want in its prudential judgment would be conditioned and would itself condition the act to gratify, as truly as in the craving of particular appetites. In no way can the merely sentient force rise above nature.

Man has within him, all the distinguishable forces of *material* being; and, as material, is conditioned in nature as truly as the clods on which he treads. He has also *animal* life; yet this, in the farthest extension of sentient wants and sentient gratifications, and in the highest generalizations of consequences in an attained experience, gives to him no prerogatives above his fellows of the stall or of the stye; but he, equally with all animal nature, is wrapped about by the iron chain of necessitated successions. The *degree* is nothing but a consideration of a longer or a shorter chain; the *kind* of connections, as animal, in man and in brute is the same. We have in nature, throughout, a superinducing of distinguishable forces one upon another, the last using the former for its own ends, yet itself still held in all the conditions of the former but as it overrules without extinguishing them; and in this, different grades of space-filling substances are given, while all are ensphered about a common center, the whole of which is the *physical universe*, bound every where in conditions which make it a fixed nature of things through its perpetual development.

And, again, in contradistinction to the *physical* we have the *ethical world.* The intrinsic excellency of the absolute is the central law of the moral universe. The spirit of God knoweth perfectly what is in God, and this inner witness of his own excellency and dignity is the consciousness of his own right, and what alone is worthy of him, and is thus inner law as a divine conscience in the autonomy of his own being. In this is also an ethical spring for the direction of his own agency, and in this self-determining capacity lies the Divine will. And as, moreover, there is in this will, self-determined in the right of his own excellency, an alternative to any other end than his own dignity which can be presented, so there is here a will in liberty. This determines personality to the Deity; and as

40

ever self-determined in self-complacency, with no colliding ends to disturb the perpetual tranquility, we have in this, properly, the HOLY and the EVER BLESSED GOD.

Man, as spiritual, is the offspring of the Deity, and although only finite rationality is yet in the very likeness of the absolute reason. To every finite spirit there is the inward witness of its own intrinsic dignity and excellence, and thus a knowledge of what is worthy of itself in its own righteous claim, and thereby a conscience as law within written on the heart. In this is spring for an alternative to any colliding end that may come before the man, and thus a will in liberty is his endowment. The yielding of the good will to any colliding end whatever is a degrading servitude, and makes it to be a depraved will; and the valorous beating back and holding in subjection every want of nature to the worthiness of the spiritual, becomes the virtuous will. The will of the holy God and of the virtuous man are directed by the same principle, the intrinsic excellency and dignity of the spiritual; and the inner witness differs only in this, that in God it is an absolute reason and in man it is a finite rationality, which in its excellence gives energy to conscience. The will of God, in whatever way made known to man, will thus come to his conscience as the right of the absolute, and which it will be imperative that he should obey on the ground that the finite excellency cannot otherwise maintain its own excellency, but must really debase itself by any rebellion against the abso-

lute, and bring the conviction of degradation and guilt
to its own conscience; and where there is this disobedience of the finite, it will behoove that the absolute in-
flict penalty on the ground that thus he should vindicate his own dignity, and sustain a worthiness that
must be reverenced.

The intrinsic excellence of rational spirit is every
where end and law, and the inward witness of what
is its right is the ULTIMATE RIGHT; and every where
holds all personality responsible each to his own conscience. The absolute right includes the finite, and
in this harmonizes all possible ethical claim through
all possible persons, and makes of all possible grades
of spiritual being an ensphered moral universe. Any
part acts unworthy of itself and in violation of the right
of the whole, when any colliding want carries the will
in servitude to it; and the vindictive penalty for such
violation must be made to meet every sinner, through
his own conscience. In this, we have an ensphered
moral world, held together by the law of liberty, as
the ensphered physical world is held together by the
law of conditioning forces; and these two spheres
meeting and intersecting in man. So far as man is
only material or animal he is wholly nature, so far as
he is purely spiritual he is wholly supernatural; but
as the two spheres of nature and of rational spirit come
together in man, and thus make him to be neither mere
animal nor pure spirit, we have that complex existence
which we call a *human being.* So much of the natu-

ral as is thus put in combination with the rational, constitutes that which, as entire, we properly term the *world of humanity.* The law of the sentient in this world of humanity is wholly of nature, and may be called *appetitive;* the law of the spiritual is wholly of reason, and may be known as *imperative.*

And now, our object is to gather these facts where there is any comprehension of things in their origin and end, and see whether they may all be held in colligation by this hypothesis of a free personality. In nature we shall not expect to find such facts of a comprehending agency on this hypothesis, inasmuch as in nature there can be no free personality. Within the field of humanity, inasmuch as we now assume that it is not all nature, we may expect to find some facts to be comprehended in the free though finite personality with which humanity is endowed. But in the broad field encompassed by Divinity, we must anticipate the most satisfactory instances of an all-embracing reason, as practicable and actual only through a manifest application of the law of an absolute personality in liberty. If we find the comprehension to be only as we apply the free personality, and always when we do so, and precisely to the degree in which we are able to do so, it will prove itself to be the actual law, holding all facts of a comprehending reason in colligation by virtue of its own universality. We thall thus need two Sections for the classification of facts under the *finite,* and under the *absolute* personality in liberty.

SECTION I.

—

THE FACTS OF A COMPREHENDING REASON WHICH COME WITHIN THE COMPASS OF A FINITE PERSONALITY.

HUMANITY in its sentient nature comprehends noth-ing, and only as it rises within the sphere of the ra-tional, and stands out in the prerogatives of its free personality, can it possess the conditioning law for all comprehension. The perceptions and wants and judgments are wholly enchained in the prison-house of nature, and all intelligence circumscribed and con-cluded with no comprehensive capacity ; and only as man awakes in the higher consciousness of rationality and freedom does he know, or even dream of or care for, any existence beyond his dungeon, nor have any impulse to inquire what he or his prison of nature is. But we have assumed for man the prerogative of a spiritual being, and in virtue of a free personality habi-tant in humanity, we are now to induce a variety of facts in this field, which will evince for themselves the actual law of freedom as the only hypothesis by which they may be brought in colligation. These facts of a comprehending capacity will, indeed, include all that distinguishes man from brute, inasmuch as it is only in that which is elementary in his personality that any discrimination of an order of being can be made.

In virtue of this only is it that he can rise above nature and comprehend his own operations and products, while the brute is all nature and can comprehend nothing.

But, for the clear apprehension of the degrees of freedom, and the peculiar springs which may give an alternative to sentient wants, in the finite personality which inhabits every human breast, it is important that we attain the peculiarities of the world of humanity, as lying solely in that region which is formed by the mutual intersection of the two spheres of the physical and the ethical systems. This intersection, and consequent mutual interaction and composition of the two, modifies each; and thus, neither the physical nor the ethical is as it would be in its separate existence. The sentient force does not act alone, but has the influence upon it of the rational power; the rational spirit is not incorporeal, but is subjected to the colliding desires of the sense. There may thus be modifications, and mediate degrees of freedom, between the utterly conditioned in the merely sentient nature, and the unruffled calm in a purely holy ethical agency. How this may be, it is not difficult to trace; and it is directly in the way of preparation for the attaining and classifying of our contemplated facts of a comprehending agency, that we show the discriminating points in the different springs, which in its rational interest may give to humanity a freedom from the bondage of its sentient wants.

The craving in the wants of sentient life, solely considered, we have termed *appetite ;* and under this we include all the constitutional sentient cravings though sometimes called by softer names, as sympathies, affections, &c. When the force of excited appetite is towards gratification, it is known as *desire ;* when it is turned away from its object in disgust it is known as *aversion.* But without further discrimination, it may be sufficient to let the whole of conditioned sentient nature be known as *appetitive.* On the other hand in the ethical world, the claims which an inner witness of the intrinsic dignity of rational personality possesses in its own right, we have termed *behests ;* and as inclusive of all pure personality, whether of the absolute or the finite, it may be sufficient here that we speak of all purely ethical being as in its own right *imperative.*

In the sentient nature, every thing *works for wages.* It is conditioned in the happiness it wants, and in the way to attain it; and it must work, and work in such a manner, or starve. Its highest law is gratification of want, called love of happiness, and is wholly of physical necessity. On the other hand in the rational personality, all *acts in complacency.* It is pleased with the behest, for it is its own, and in right of its own worthiness ; it is tranquil in its action, for no colliding end disturbs it. Its highest law of action is the inward witness of its own worthiness, called love of right, and is wholly liberty in its own lawfulness. The sentient works as means to an end imposed upon it, and is worth so much as nature pays for it in gratification ; the personal acts in its own right and blesses itself in its own worthiness, and has no price in barter but a dignity to which it were the highest affront to offer any thing in exchange. The sentient satiates itself and rests in a surfeit; the rational maintains its dignity, and has the tranquil bliss of unwearied holiness.

When, now, we have the two spheres in mutual intersection, and spirituality given incarnate as in humanity, to the full extent of this intersection must we have reciprocal modification, and by so much must the experience of humanity differ from mere sense or from pure reason. It will not be all animal and thus wholly the brute, nor will it be all spiritual and thus wholly the divine. It will have both a price and a dignity ; a law of happiness and a law of righteousness ; an appetitive nature and an imperative personality. And here, between the solely appetitive in the animal and the purely imperative in the spiritual, is the region of humanity compounded of both. Such a complex existence may well give rise to that in an. experience which is neither a craving want nor an ethical behest ; but which may be spring for action alternative to any thing of the sentient, and thus give a modification of freedom, though it be not in the claim of a moral right. And such a spring may vary in successive modifications, according as the rational makes use of th e lower

or the higher elements in the sentient for its own ends.
To just such an extent may humanity become creative,
and make and enjoy its own products in it own sphere,
and thus so far be comprehending agency because so
far it may originate and consumate as author and designer.   In such creations there will not be *work* as in
the service of the sense, nor will there be the *holy tranquility* as in the pure ethical activity of the spirit ; but
in proportion as it is spirit using sense for the ends of
its own rationality, and thus controlling and not controlled, there may be a *serene interest* that rises as the
product rises in the ends of the reason, and carrying
humanity from the very confines of the animal in savage life upwards in culture to the border of the ethical,
which controls every faculty in duty and for the dignity of the rational personality.   This impulse in humanity which is neither that of craving appetite in the
sense nor of sovereign behest in the spirit, but a serene
interest in some end in the reason, has been termed
the *play-impulse ;* inasmuch as on one side there is no
servility, and on the other there is no reverence.   The
reason uses its connection with the sense, not for any
end of the sense ; not in the ethical behest of its own
dignity ; but simply in the interest of its own cheerfulness.   It plays with nature, not in frivolity as a sense-
play ; but with the elevating and invigorating exercise
of a sportive rationality.   It is this impulse, which
takes us from sensuality, and raises us, through the
beauty of art, and the truth of science, up to the duties

of morality and the sanctities of religion. We play with beauty, and cheer ourselves with the pursuit of truth, and thus lift ourselves above the slavery of appetite, and are prepared for the ethical claims upon our personality, either in duty or in adoration. The free personality is present in art and science, as truly as in morality.

Having thus indicated the region in humanity from which we are to gather the facts which have their comprehension in its free personality, we shall now, at once, enter on the work of induction, and having reference only to such as come within the compass of a finite personality, we will make it sufficiently broad to show that we have the operations of a comprehending reason in humanity, and that it is every where, and only, through the freedom of that which is rational and personal. We shall classify them under the several heads indicated by the different interests which give their spring to the producing agency.

1. *Æsthetic facts.*—The merely animal sentient nature finds that which is *agreeable* in all the five senses. There is the appetitive force inducing a craving for its object of gratification in them all. The agreeable sensations from temperature, odors, and viands, as merely animal, will be more intensely appetitive than colors and sounds; and thus the senses of feeling, smelling and tasting are more important, as sources of gratification, to the animal than seeing and hearing. Doubtless, also, the mere animal may re-produce, in

a dreaming fancy other than distinct memory, the fictions of past sensations, and so far live in the enjoyment of fancied happiness; and in such a world of the animal fancy, it is just as little to be doubted that feelings, smells and tastes will have an ascendency, as fictions, quite as decidedly over sounds and sights, as they have in actual animal gratification. Let the animal nature do what it may, in actual gratification or fancy, and it will obey the conditions of appetite.

But, we find this remarkable fact in humanity, that the two senses least intensely appetitive are the sole media through which the play-impulse can be at all reached. Sights and sounds have ever their definite outlines, and we can give shape to the color and form in tune to the sound. It is not so much the object seen and heard, as the form in which it appears that interests us. Our pleasure is not in the *matter*, but in the *shape* in which the matter comes to us. Nor is it every shape that pleases, much less that it is mere shape; it must be such shape as may blend with life, and figure to the mind some in-dwelling emotion. The murmur of the waterfall, the sighing of the wind, the very silence of the night, must all put on a living form; and the landscape, the fountain, the sky, the rosy dawn or crimson eve, must all glow with an inner life, and the form be vitalized and not some dry and dead husk, which life has thrown aside as its mere exuviæ. Not that there is life; not that there is form; but that there is life *in* form, that there is *living shape*, is there *beauty*. This is every where in nature, coming to man as a perpetual visitant through the eye and ear, yea as a constant presence where we have but to awake in consciousness and find ourselves ever gladdened by it.

" There's beauty all around our paths,
If but our watchful eyes,
Can trace it midst familiar things,
And through their lowly guise."

All this, though in nature, is as nothing to the mere animal. Humanity finds it, separates the mere matter from it, and has the beauty of nature in its pure living forms as objective to daily contemplation. But much more than this. Humanity is not restricted to beauty as nature gives it; the whole world of art belongs to man, and he may fill it with his own living forms of beauty. Here lies his æsthetic power. He may not only find what beauty nature has, and take it purified from nature and make it his own; but he can create for himself a beauty more perfect than nature any where can give to him, and put his own Apollos into nature, and from his own perfect ideal beauty criticise the beauty of both nature and art. He plays with nature, with his own productions of the pencil and the chisel, and sports in a subjective ideal world of beauty more rich and glowing in its living forms than matter can any where take upon itself, and his inner ear hears music, and his inner eye sees blended color and shape in living expression, which no combinations or sublimations of matter may convey to outer hearing or sight. How completely can he include all that is or may be, in any general class of beauty "in earth or sky or human form or face divine," within his more complete ideal archetype! How effectually comprehend both nature and art, as made objective, in his all-encompassing subjective creations! Here are all the facts of an æsthetic comprehension, on which we need not longer dwell, and whose particulars we need not minutely recapitulate, and the only inquiry important for us now, though in the mist of so much to interest, is simply for the law which holds all these facts in colligation. Whence the spring and interest in this play-impulse? and how does humanity comprehend its own apart from nature, and draw the encompassing line around the world of art? And how say that nature, in all her forms of beauty, is yet included in the more complete æsthetic world? All this it is not difficult to answer, and the answer reveals the law which holds in colligation all the facts of an æsthetic comprehension.

Take from humanity its free personality, and leave all that is animal unweakened and unrestrained in its sentient force, and you will have simply *the agreeable* —the appetitive want and the conforming gratification. Put the rational into humanity, that is may separate the living form from the material in nature, and you will have *the beautiful*—the serene interest in and the cheering contemplation of reason upon, its rational forms. Shut this rational up so completely within nature, that it must go only to the forms in nature for its beauty, and take what nature has, and satisfy itself with what nature gives, and you have imprisoned it within nature and bound it in servitude to nature; and now, although you cannot quench its interest in beauty above all appetite, yet you compel it to drudge in nature and work on nature's conditions for nature's wages, and it is cheerful play-impulse no longer. But, merely let the sphere of the rational intersect the sphere of the physical, and while the rational and the animal are compounded in humanity, let the rational have its own pure sphere stretching away beyond all intersection with the physical; and thus, that the rational can both act within nature and elevate itself above nature; and either find nature's own beautiful form or put its own, impressed upon the material as art, within nature; or, in the productive imagination, blend its own forms amid the colors and sounds of nature; or, quite away from nature create its own pure ideals in its own subjective being; and in all this, you have a free personality, which comes within and excludes itself from nature at its pleasure, and may make nature its play-ground and not its work-shop.

And such is manifestly the æsthetic law of humanity —a law of liberty in personality. Beauty must dwell in living shapes; and must be contemplated to be known; and so far the world of beauty is conditioned

to space and time, and there cannot be an absolute
beauty. But humanity is not shut up to nature for
its beauty. It can create its own ; and judge nature's
beauty by its own ; and put its own, as art, into nature, or keep it as subjective ideal out of nature ; and
separate its own from nature, and comprehend its own
as originated and consummated in its own action; and
can encompass nature's beauty by the greater completeness of its own. Humanity is thus æsthetic comprehension, solely from the prerogative of its free personality.

2. *Mathematical Facts.*—Humanity is competent to
fulfill all the claims of a pure mathematical science.
Man constructs particular diagrams, and in a process
of intuition attains universal demonstrations. That
this cannot be in virtue of the animal element of his
being is sufficiently manifest from the fact that no animal, however sagacious in concluding from experience,
ever rises to the most simple intuitions in the region
of pure mathematical science. We may soon determine why this must be so; inasmuch as nothing of the
sphere of the rational comes within the sentient nature
of the sphere, and no free personality capacitates for apriori constructions in which may be found universal demonstrations.

The brute constructs the content in the sensibility
into a phenomenon as perfectly as man, and in some
cases of animal vision the perception is more acute and
minutely exact than through the human organ. To

the mere animal, there may thus be all the empirical intuitions of greater and less, container and contained, like and unlike; &c, and the capacity to change the outward action, from a change in the perceptions, may be within the endowment of mere brute nature. There may be widely different degrees of brute sagacity, from a less or more restricted capacity to judge according to sense, but in the highest exhibitions of it, the whole will stop within the empirical intuition, and can never reach the region of pure intuition. The animal judgment controls no further than taught by sense in experience, and can use only what it perceives or remembers; but can construct no pure diagrams in which an apriori necessity and universality is attained, and from which alone pure mathematical demonstration can be educed.

Man, on the other hand, constructs his pure forms, not at all as the copies from perceived or remembered phenomena, but perfect and complete beyond what any experience can attain; and these pure figures he combines in varied diagrams according to the purposes of the demonstration, and in these combined pure figures he carries his intuition onward step by step, till he attains his conclusion. Nor is it at all necessary that he should construct new diagrams and attain new conclusions for every particular of a class, nor even to so multiply them as to deduce a general rule from the many examples; his one demonstration is as conclusive for the universal as for the particular.

When he has constructed three points in the same plane in pure space, he has not only this intuition that these three points *are* in the same plane, but his diagram is quite sufficient also for the intuition in a universal axiom, that any three points in space *must ever lie* in the same plane. Once, to demonstrate the three angles of a triangle to be together equal to two right angles, is a demonstration in the particular conclusive for the universal. And here man may multiply his diagrams and enlarge the field of his mathematical demonstrations, and his mathematical science will be comprehended within his constructions and the intuitive processes through which he passes to his conclusions. Men may widely differ as mathematicians, but in all cases their mathematical science is as their constructed diagrams and their completed process of intuition. And so of humanity entire, we can say, that it is mathematician in so far as it constructs pure diagrams and completes the processes of distinct intuitions. We have the facts of a comprehending agency in this field of mathematical science, but the comprehension is only in this, that an intellectual agency constructs the particular diagram, and a process of intuition attains the conclusion which, in that class, is universal demonstration. Humanity comprehends itself as mathematician in its capacity for pure construction and intuition.

And now, this whole law of mathematical comprehension is manifestly nothing other than that of free

41

personality in humanity. An interest of reason for
mathematical truth is adequate spring for all mathematical construction and completing of the process of
intuition, without any interference from any want in
a sensory, and even against, and above, and in opposition to all such wants. The mathematician may
regard wholly the ends of sense, and make his science
wholly subservient to the agreeable in human wants ;
but he is then a servant to his sentient nature, and is
working for wages. He may have an ethical claim,
which involves the worthiness of his moral character ;
and his mathematical study will then be loyalty to the
claims of duty. But he may also have only the end
of mathematical truth, and his whole action be
prompted and directed, purely in the interest of reason, for science ; and in such case, the spring though
not an imperative is manifestly also not appetitive.
It is a love of mathematical truth, and prompts to action in mathematical demonstration solely for the
truth's sake. It is of the same class as in art, though
a more serious and grave employment than in the
reason's play with the beautiful. There is not the
servile drudgery as in working for the wages of sense,
though the activity does not rise to the dignity and
holiness of an ethical imperative in its own right. It
gives freedom from the necessity of nature. It has
the spring of the serene interest in the play-impulse,
and can take an alternative to all the ends of a senti
ent nature, and in its own freedom originate its pure

diagrams from itself, and go through the processes of its intuitions in the rational love to science as the end of its demonstrations; and in this freedom of the rational is found the only compass by which to determine to each person, and to all humanity, the comprehending of its mathematical science. The diagram must be in some diversity of the pure space and time, but it is wholly indifferent what diversity in the pure space and time; it may be in the one whole of space and time with nature, or in any mirrored space, or in any purely subjective space in the primitive intuition; but in all cases the person's own free constructions and intuitions will be comprehensive of all his mathematics. He neither measures nor copies nature as his pattern, but makes his own perfect lines and angles and circles, and asks no want in the sense to condition his action and hire or drive him to his work; but he free ly engages in it, in the cheerfulness of its own interest.

3. *Philosophical Facts.*—The animal may be philosopher to this extent, that in the experience of antecedent and consequent in the flowing events of time there may be apprehended a successive connection and orderly ongoing of nature. A generalization of this experience may give the rule for anticipating what is coming, and the dictate to shape the conduct accordingly, in proportion to the number of facts which may be gathered within the induction. But to whatever extent of sagacity such a force might reach, it would be bound in nature and subjected utterly to the con-

ditions of a necessitated experience. Pure philosophy reaches much higher than this, and determines the physical forces which must condition all sequences, and bind nature together in one universe and one orderly and already conditioned method of development. It apprehends nature not merely as from experience that so it is, but from the higher point of its apriori conditions that so it must be. Nature is apprehended in its physical laws; and that these condition each event in its own place in the flowing sequences, and fix it to both its place in space and its period in time; and thereby determine a whole of space and of time, and not mere appearance in coming and departing phenomena, each in its separate place and period. It takes force, as in any possible substances and causes, and determines what is truth in reference to any possible nature of things. All possible nature must be determinable in its place in a whole of space, and in its period in a whole of time; and in order to this the phenomenal qualities and events must stand in a permanent substance, come out of a perduring source, and connect themselves through successive causes and concomitant reciprocal influences. This is not only what a particularly existing nature is, but what all possible nature, as determinable in space and time, must be. A pure philosophy is thus as comprehensive as pure mathematics. The mathematician comprehends in one intuition, all that may any way have place and period; the philosopher comprehends in

one discursion, all that may in any way have determinable place and period in a whole of space and of
time. All sensation, that is to be phenomenon in
place and period, must be definitely conjoined; and
all phenomenon, that is to be nature in a whole of
space and time, must be connected in substances and
causes. Humanity has thus the comprehension of
nature in a philosophy, as truly as the comprehension
of forms in a mathematical science. We have a universal truth of physical principles, as completely as a
universal truth of mathematical demonstrations. We
know what physical force is, as comprehensively as
we know what mathematical form is; viz. that what
is demonstrated in each, to be true in the particular,
is therein a demonstrated truth for the universal; so
that we may as conclusively affirm—like causes must
universally produce like effects, and that action and
reaction must universally be equal; as that any three
points must be universally in the same plane, or that
the three angles of any triangle must universally be
together equal to two right angles. Humanity as
philosopher concludes with equal necessity and universality that humanity as mathematician does.

And, here, precisely the same principles apply, as
above in the case of mathematical comprehensiveness.
There is the serene interest of the play-impulse, as
spring in philosophy, as really as in mathematical science. The philosopher may be slave to sense, and
work for pay; or loyal subject to an ethical sovereign,

and act from duty; but, he may also from pure love
of philosophical truth push on his investigations, and
live and act indifferent to all the ends of sense, and
solely in the serene interest of philosophizing freely
for the science's sake. And here, it is only in the capacity to rise into this region of the free personality,
that humanity is competent to comprehend its own
philosophy. Just so far as it attains the conception
of physical forces, and makes its discursions from phenomenon to phenomenon through them, as the substances and causes which connect all together, it has
a demonstrated natural philosophy; and only so far
as this reaches, can it conclude in any judgments beyond its own experience. Each man builds his own
philosophy, by his own notional conceptions of the
substances. and causes he uses for connecting events ;
and we can comprehend each man's philosophy, or
each man can comprehend his own philosophy, or any
comprehension can be made of the philosophy of humanity generally, only as the free personality, in every
case, is made the compass for originating and consum-
mating the entire connections of the philosophical system. If he only takes nature, as experience gives it
to him; he has it just as the animal has it, and is simply an empiric: if he has his own conception of substances and causes as primitive forces, and makes his
own discursions through these to his conclusions in
a systematic judgment; then has he a philosophy
which is his own, and is comprehended only as his in

these free conceptions and discursions of his own rational being. All philosophy is mere particular *fact* and not universal *truth*, except in the free personality.

4. *Psychological Facts.*—In our animal sentient nature, we may have a psychology which reaches over the whole field of our conscious experience. The phenomena of the internal sense may be singly apprehended, and even a broad induction of such remembered experiences may be made and generalized and classified, by an understanding judging only by sense. But if all experience could be thus generalized, it would simply give us a psychology as a fact, and capacitate us to affirm that so experience in consciousness is; but we could not thus attain any apriori conditions for these mental facts, and determine that so universally human consciousness must be. We should have no universal truth in the operations of mind, and thus no rational psychological science.

But, humanity is competent to reach an apriori field, quite above and conditional for all consciousness. The pure diversity in space and time can be taken in the reason, and the whole operation of conjunction in all possible definite form be determined. And also the conditional space-filling and time-abiding force, as substance and cause, can be taken in the reason, and all possible operation of connecting events in a nature of things be determined. And once more, the ideal of the absolute may be attained in the reason, and all possible operation of comprehending nature thereby determined. The entire world of intellectual action is thus brought within its apriori conditions, and we have a psychology, not from experience merely, but rationally demonstrated and determining how experience itself is possible. Each man has thus his psychology so far forth, and only so far forth, as he has attained the primitive elements of these intellectual operations of conjunction, connection, and comprehension, and determined their ideal possibility ; and humanity in general comprehends just so much of psychological science, as has been apriori determined in these operations conditional for all intellectual cognition. The entire field of all possible intellectual apprehension lies before humanity, and in so much as human investigation has already reached, has humanity acquired a true science of mind.

We have, therefore, the same law for the facts of comprehension in psychological science, that we have before found for comprehension in philosophy, mathematics, and æsthetics. Only in the free personality, above and quite independent of a sentient nature, do we originate and consummate all our psychological demonstrations. We find humanity to have a comprehension of its psychology only as it may move in rational freedom.

5. *Ethical Facts.*—In all the foregoing facts of a comprehending reason in humanity, we have been wholly confined to that region where the physical and rational spheres intersect each other, and have found

the free personality only in the rational as it could make its spring in its own interest, and thus always originate action alternative to the gratifications of sentient nature ; and yet never rising to the purely spiritual, as wholly independent of a possible or ideal nature. Æsthetic personality stands the lowest in this complex region; above the animal, inasmuch as it may contemplate beauty and create in the productive imagination its own world of living forms, without any aids or promptings of sense, and solely from its love of the beautiful; but still below the purely spiritual, inasmuch as all the pure ideals of art must take some form, and be conditioned within a possible nature of things. Scientific personality, whether in mathematics philosophy or psychology, stands higher but still within this complex region; above the animal, for the same reason, that it may pursue science for its own sake, and make for itself its own subjective system, which shall have strict universality beyond all the generalizations of experience; but yet below the purely spiritual, inasmuch as all its scientific systems, even in their ideal creations, must be conditioned in possible nature. The world of taste, though of the free originations of the productive reason, must still have its artistic product put objective in nature, and holding some matter within its living forms of beauty ; and the world of scientific truth, though a free origination of reason like art, and higher than art in that it is not conditioned to em-

brace any content of matter, must still be restricted to
what is possible to be given in nature, and conditioned
within the determinations of space and time; and
thus both beauty and truth, art and science, while
possible to be given only in the comprehension of a
free personality, are yet incompetent to rise into the
region of the purely spiritual divorced from all the
conditions of a possible nature, and attain to the dignity of an ethical imperative, which does not merely
cheer in its own interest but obliges in its own right.
There is a comprehension of nature as below humanity, but not a comprehension of humanity itself as
both natural and supernatural; sense and spirit.
For this purpose it is necessary that we be able to
rise above the intersection of the two spheres and
stand wholly and purely within the spiritual. In the
play-impulse we rise above the animal; we attain
the interests by which we may cultivate refine and
enlighten savage humanity, and thus effectually lift
man above his brutal instincts and appetites, and this
is surely a great achievement and most auspicious beginning; but we do not thus introduce him to the
claims of an ethical life, and the communings of a
spiritual society. Neither the beauty of art, nor the
truth of science, while they elevate him above the
physical and the animal, can possibly place man
among the moral and the immortal.

But humanity has the facts of an ethical comprehension, and which give to it that which is its own

as solely the obligated and the responsible; and as higher and more important than any yet considered, it is now especially incumbent that we attain a clear view of these facts of an ethical comprehension, and see whether they all come ultimately within the colligation of the same law of a free personality; the freedom only so much the higher, as the personality by which we encompass the facts is the more exalted. We here need, not merely the æsthetic and the scientific freeman, and thus the artist and philosopher as person; but the ethic freeman, and thus the sage in his wisdom and virtue. We do not here reach to the sanctions of religion, natural or revealed, because we are not now in the recognition of the absolute, but only the finite personality; we have a morality in the right of humanity, and we here seek for the law of its comprehension. In order to this, our hypothesis demands in the facts a spiritual or ethical personality; and we need under this last division, this important sub-division in our induction—*First*, the facts which indicate our recognition of an ethical personality in humanity; and, *Secondly*, the facts which evince that we make this ethical free personality the perpetual and only law of all ethical comprehension.

First, the facts, which indicate the universal recognition of an ethical personality in humanity.—By this is meant the recognition that the human may always figure himself not merely as material or animal, nor yet merely as artistic or scientific, but altogether

as spiritual in an ethical and immortal being; **and**
thus possessing an end which is imperative in its own
right, and for its own sake. This is seldom explicable even to him who yet manifestly recognizes such
ethical personality. Very often, from the delusive
false play of an understanding which may connect and
never comprehend, the very conception of such an
ethical personality is affirmed to be an impossibility,
inasmuch as it involves an absurdity. And so indeed
it would be, were the connections in nature's conditioned substances and causes our only method of judging, inasmuch as all judgments of existence must thus
be discursive and never comprehensive; yet we now
undertake to adduce some of many facts, which indicate the universal recognition of such ethical personality in humanity, though quite inexplicable or even
speculatively denied by him, who, notwithstanding,
does most unequivocally evince his full recognition
of it.

(1.) *An ethical end controlling by an imperative all
other ends.*—A sentient nature with its animal appetite must have one particular course in which its
highest gratifications in the aggregate will be attainable. This may be found from a generalization of experience in a calculation of consequences, or be given
as a revelation from some higher source of knowledge.
In whatever way attained it is a dictate of *prudence*,
resting upon the consideration of the greatest happiness. Moreover, a sentient nature in the midst of

other sentient beings, must have one particular course for its action in which it will render itself the most useful to all others, and so to every being in that community of sentient natures, there is the course for each to be the most useful for all. And whether such a line of action be attained by an accurate calculation of general consequences or by revelation from a higher experience, its course is the dictate of *benevolence* or *public utility*, and rests upon the greatest happiness of the greatest number. These rules of action are conditioned in the sentient system, and are as truly facts (*res gestæ*) as the sentient beings themselves. The dictates are *made* in making the sentient beings, and would be *changed* in any change in the constitutional nature of these beings. The sentient being and his system of fellow beings, existing as they do, must of necessity enforce such *dicta*.

When, then, we put the inquiry—Why be prudent? the answer at once comes from the sentient craving of nature; there is thus the higher wages, in the greater sum total in individual happiness. Better make the present or the partial sacrifice, for the future and the greater gratification. And why be benevolent? The answer of a sentient nature must be, either that the result of obeying the dictate of benevolence will be a fuller stream of gratification, poured back from the many upon the one; or that it finds within itself an appetitive want, which is gratified in seeing others happy. The first is merely prudence in the form of beneficence, lending to get more in return; the last is mere kindness, the gratification of a sympathy which craves like any other appetite; and both are conditioned in the necessities of a nature of things, on all sides. Nature wholly works in and controls the sentient subject; and nature is also the lawgiver, the judge, and the executioner. It is in vain to rise above nature by any attempt and question any part of the procedure; either the obedience or disobedience of the subject, for a conditioned nature controlled him; or, the legislative, judicial, and executive departments of the government, for these are all conditioned in nature. The animal is in his action conditioned to the craving of his sentient nature, whether of any particular appetite or the highest gratification on the whole, and all such craving is necessitated by the antecedent conditions, and then the ponderous iron wheel as executive in nature rolls on, crushing the imprudent and the unkind. The omnipotence of nature is all that can be regarded; whether in the good or bad fortune of the sentient being; the dictates given; or, the consequences accruing to each and to the whole. Humanity, in its sentient nature, can never rise to any end other than the appetitive, and that is throughout necessitated in the conditions of nature.

But, as æsthetic or scientific, humanity has ends which may entirely control those of sentient nature. Merely as artist, man may so recognize the baseness

of sacrificing taste to appetite, and selling beauty
for bread; that he shall thereby hold in check any
craving of sense, and refuse to prostitute his genius
to any mercenary consideration. And merely as
philosopher, also, he may so regard scientific truth,
that he shall hold all the ends of animal nature wholly
subservient to its attainment; and be so in love with
it, that no consideration of sensual gratification or sacrifice can draw him from it. Without regard to the
ethical claim for veracity, and solely from the stedfast
inner adhesion to scientific truth, Gallileo departs
from the bigots who had forced him to recant his
doctrine of the earth's revolution, still repeating to
himself "but it does turn." There may very well be
so lofty a deference to the interest of reason, that the
man shall be a willing martyr to the beauty of art,
or to the truths of science. This is not the sacrificing
of one gratified want for a greater; it is a sacrifice of
all gratified wants, in order not to debase the ends of
reason to sense, and sell its beauty at a price, and
barter its truth for a hireling's wages. Few, perhaps, may possess so deep and absorbing an æsthetic
or scientific interest; but to every thinking mind, it is
quite manifest how humanity may be brought up to
such an elevation of rational culture, that all of sense
shall be made to succumb to the rules of taste, or defer to the truths of science. Here, then, is a field for
freedom; and the savage, in whom the sentient completely reigns, may be brought up into it from his

state of brutality, and attain to a personality in liberty. But his spring, alternative to the appetites of nature, will be simply the love of the beautiful and the true restraining the gratification of the agreeable, while he still may know nothing of the ethical in its imperatives and responsibilities; and thôugh elevated quite out from the animal, he does not thus attain to a moral and immortal existence.

But we now turn to a fact which every mind may recognize, viz: an end in moral character; or worthiness in the ethical personality; which wholly subordinates all other ends of the sentient, or the human being, and makes every want of the animal nature, and every interest in art and science, amenable to its behests. It over-rules both prudence and benevolence, and commands by a higher imperative than for the sake of happiness or of kindness, even from personal worthiness, and thus that the action ought to be prudent and kind. And this higher end has also rightful sway over the whole world of art and science; and is imperative that neither beauty in taste, nor truth in philosophy, shall be pursued, otherwise than in full accordance with the worthiness of the ethical personality. As "the life is more than meat," so is the integrity of moral character more than appetite or art or science. If any want whatever, or any happiness in any degree or duration, or any interest in beauty or truth, induce the will into its service as end, so that it shall cease to hold the intrinsic worthiness of the ethical personality as supreme end; then is the moral character degraded and debased; the spiritual birth-right is sold for " a mess of pottage; " and the soul is forced to blush in conscious shame, in the inner witnessing of its own vileness.   " The spirit of a man will sustain his infirmity, but a wounded spirit who can bear ?"   Whoso thus saveth his animal life shall lose the life of his spirit.   This every where recognized fact, of an imperative to curb every appetite, and all æsthetic and scientific interest, by the higher end of an ethical worthiness; and to have no happiness nor beauty nor science in the subversion of this ultimate end and right, evinces the universal recognition of an ethical personality in humanity.

(2.) *Ethical affections above all others.*—That which ministers to the gratification of sentient want is agreeable, and that which offends the appetite is disagreeable.   Hence we often term one affection or love, and the other hatred.   In the various ways in which the agreeable and the disagreeable apply to our sentient natures, there may be the emotions of joy or sorrow, gladness or grief, hope or fear, &c.; and in this manner may arise all the constitutional affections which are found in a sentient nature.   They are wholly natural affections, inasmuch as they are wholly necessitated in the conditions of the sensory, and are thus wholly bound in a nature of things.   Were there nothing in humanity but the wants of a sentient nature, all our affections must be strictly nature, and

42

stand in their conditioned connections like all the successions in the physical world. And, moreover, we may apply the beautiful and the true to the play-impulse, and awaken the cheerful interest which gives the rational pleasures of taste and science. And we shall have those affections in humanity in which the artist and the philosopher may participate; but though these affections are awakened in freedom, yet are they all circumscribed within nature and conditioned to space and time; inasmuch as these pure objects which awaken the affections, though destitute of matter, must yet have form, and though above the sentient must yet abide in the region of the human. To possess such affections, in the full perfection of art and science capacitates for no participation in the ethical affections of the purely spiritual and immortal.

But we may bring in here, from the experience of humanity, an array of facts which evince the full recognition of affections that can come from no such parentage. They evince their pedigree from an ethical personality, and in their own right take precedence over all other affections. They are no result of any application of the agreeable to a sentient want, nor of the beautiful to an æsthetic or of the true to a scientific interest.

An occasion for a high degree of sentient gratification presents itself, but with the clear conviction that indulgence will be followed by a more than counterbalancing sentient suffering; and the gratification is forborne from the dictate of prudence. When this is all that restrains, the only possible affection induced in the experience is the gladness that so much sentient evil has been excluded, blended with a certain measure of self-esteem for the prudential fore-sight. But when, in externally similar circumstances, such affections as the following are experienced, we surely have something higher than any dictate of prudence on the ground of greatest happiness. A conscious self-approbation in an act of self-denial and a complacency in the review of the act as worthy of my spiritual and immortal being; and that I must have forfeited my self-respect and found occasion to hide my face in shame at my degradation, if I had done otherwise. Not the price of happiness in greater gratification, but the intrinsic dignity and worth of my ethical personality; and the affection is wholly that of complacency in character, not of gladness in so cleverly excluding sentient suffering. And moreover, when in some period of intense suffering I endure it, and refuse to escape from it in the prudential conviction that greater suffering would be otherwise unavoidably incurred; the only affection which this can induce is the patience, which comforts itself in the wretchedness to which nature dooms me by reflecting that it is better so than to change; I could only throw off this burden to take a greater; I could not make myself more happy by escaping, I am the less miserable by enduring. But if now such considerations

and affections as the following come up ; it is manly to
endure; it is an honor to humanity, and an ennobling
of character to stand firmly amid the severity of these
sufferings; then is it necessary to recognize a free
personality altogether above any appetitive want. All
the considerations of happiness in greater gratification
or less suffering are forever banished as mean and
mercenary ; and the sole question is the end of my
own worthiness—What in the right of the spiritual in
my humanity is my duty ?—and whether for a day, for
life, or forever, I shall as I ought stand by my duty
to the rights of my ethical personality, and bide the
blow that any force in conditioned nature can bring
upon me.

And so, also, when from the dictate of kindness I
have made great sacrifices to increase the happiness
and relieve the misery of man, and in which has also
been included the dictate of prudence in that thus my
own greatest happiness is promoted; I shall doubtless have a refined gratification of sympathetic want
in witnessing the fruits of my kindness, and receiving
the pledges of their grateful return ; and while they
enjoy the happiness I have imparted, I also enjoy
with a sweeter relish the happiness that flows back
upon me; and I find it thus true even in my constitutional nature, that " it is more blessed to give than to
receive."   But if, on the other hand, I have contemplated humanity as spiritual and not merely as sentient, and have had the worthiness and not merely

the happiness of my race in view; and my labor and sacrifice has been to win them to virtue, and that the rights and claims of the spiritual, and not the appetitive wants of the sentient have been my end; and that I can hold on my course amid discouragements, and hatred, and persecution; and, if at all successful, I rejoice for virtue's sake in their recovered dignity, but if without success, and only from the imperative of my personality, I can still persevere in my duty, and find my reward solely in the end of my worthiness without one sentient want gratified. In all this I recognize a spring to action which cannot lie in the dictates of prudence and benevolence, and can never stand in a generalized self-love nor a kind sensibility; but must originate solely in the inner witnessing of the spirit, as imperative for its own worthiness' sake.

If an emotion of *reverence* ever arises, it has not been in the presence of any thing which nature, material or sentient, can set forth. I may fear, wonder, and be terrified before the working forces in nature; but I can never revere, except as I find a personality, which in his own right can hold every appetite and affection that nature can awaken subject to his own behest, and will not go at their bidding though nature do its worst. So if I am affected in *remorse*, I at once distinguish it from regret for some imprudence or unkindness, and feel that it bespeaks something more than happiness lost, even ethical dignity debased and worthiness of moral character degraded. I may experience *shame* in my sentient being, if some conditions in nature have made me to appear ludicrous; or, when through mere imprudence I have exposed myself to ridicule; but I well know the difference between all such shame, and that ethical debasement, which blushes even before its own consciousness that it has been guilty of subjecting the spirit to the flesh. I can *grieve* under nature's bereaving calamities, and weep in sorrow that I have been imprudent; but I shall distinguish all this from the tears of contrition and penitential sorrow that duty has been neglected, and my virtuous character tarnished. I know in all cases, the mighty difference between wounded sensibility, and violated authority; a want made empty, and a right wronged. And in all such distinctions of affection, every man recognizes the existence of an ethical personality, which alone can give to such experiences in humanity any exposition, and to such distinctions of affection any consistency.

(3.) *Reciprocal complacency in communion.*—Different animals herd together, induced by kindred appetites. A constitutional want brings man into society, and the cravings of nature would be sufficient force for collecting human beings into communities. Congenial temperament, the instincts of consanguinity, common pursuits and reciprocal advantages bring different persons together and hold them in companionship, and often with much mutual satisfaction. Very much of what is termed friendship and love among

men reposes upon such conditions in nature. But all
this, operating in its fullest measure, can produce no
reciprocal complacency. Here are the strongest bonds
which the sensibility may give to social communion;
and still all is appetitive and conditioned by the cravings of nature.

A higher communion may be cherished in the cultivation of similar tastes, and the study and contemplation of the same truths. Art and science, insomuch
as they rise above sentient wants, give purer interests; and a communion of such pure interest in the
same living forms of beauty and conceptions of eternal
truth, will constitute rational attachment far superior
to any mutual gratifications of animal want. And
yet, such a community would be utterly destitute of
mutual ethical complacency. No one would have the
inner witness of his worth, and the imperatives which
this imposed; nor could any thing be known of self-
approbation, or the approbation of others. All communion in spiritual personality would be impracticable, for they have not as yet waked to the consciousness of such an existence.

But wholly above all such attachments, we have examples of a communion in common rights and mutual
claims and the fulfillment of reciprocal imperatives, and
thus attachments which strike their root in virtue, and
repose upon confidence in mortal worth and integrity.
All men may witness acts of virtue, and approve; but
the virtuous will be conscious of more than approba-

tion; there will be a complacency and sweet communion of spirit in the whole transaction. Every
mind reveres the steadfast good will which holds firm
to righteousness, and bears up in duty against all in-
ducement and danger; but a vicious mind, though
compelled to respect, will not be pleased with such
stern and inflexible consistency of character. The example throws back upon him the consciousness of his
own debasement, and awakens self-condemnation;
and he will never hold communion with the rigidly
virtuous for virtue's sake. Such moral repellency,
between the virtuous and the vicious, evinces in both
an ethical personality; on one side, a will enslaved
to the gratification of sense, and on the other, a will
free in its loyalty to right; but in both a character
which is estimated by each, and between which there
can be no reciprocal complacency.

The virtuous man on the other hand, knows that
his virtue lies in the valor with which he beats down
all the contending appetites of the sense, and subjects
every end to the ultimate claim of his own true dignity. In the society of the virtuous, there is a reve-
rential respect of each for all; and, while each possesses an inward self-approbation, there is also mutual complacency which can be found in nothing but
the possession of a virtuous ethical character and the
recognition of the same character in others. No other
than a free ethical person can love the virtuous for his
worthiness' sake; and none but the ethically good, in

their free personality can be loved by the virtuous. I
may value as of such a *price*, that which I may use
for my happiness or interest; but there is no attaining
to the complacency of personal communion in this, for
the means I use is in that very use made thing and
not person. A good, as a means to an end, is wholly
a different good in kind from that which, as ultimate
end, must be the supreme good. If another person is
good only as means to end; if the absolute Deity is so
held as good, only that he makes a heaven of happiness
for me; then to me he is at once made a thing and
has a price, and not a *dignity* which is above and beyond all bartering. When the reciprocity is only that
of happiness, and men regard each other only as each
is subservient to the others' happiness; or man regards
God as only the maker and dispenser of happiness, and
God regards his creatures only as they minister to him
in happiness; then is it impossible that the ethical
love of complacency should subsist between them. A
want and not a worthiness is thus put as end; and that
each were reciprocally *useful* to each, as joint stock
co-partners in happiness to be distributed among them
all, and valued by each only in proportion to his own
share, would be the only point of congeniality between
them; and each would be to others, a thing to be used;
a means to be valued for what it could get; and not a
person, who had rights in his own intrinsic worthiness,
which must be ethically respected by all. Reciprocal
complacency requires the communion of free person-

ality—like with like ethically—their rights mutually respected, and their imperatives individually fulfilled; not each a means to the others' happiness, but each complacent in the others' worthiness.

That we have such facts of complacent communion, and that every man is conscious of a capacity for and an imperative to such communion, is the clear recognition of his own and others' free ethical personality.

(4.) *Capacity to resist all the conditions of nature.* The cravings of a sensory are wholly conditioned in nature. The cravings must be as nature develops, and there is no alternative to what nature imposes. The whole sentient life, constitutional temperament, physiological propensity, native susceptibility, is bound in cause and effect, and were there nothing but desire for happiness, there would be no alternative to nature's conditions in the experience. A dictate of prudence, settled by the most comprehensive generalization, is as truly appetitive as any single want in its sudden excitement. The conditions of nature will determine that the prudent judgment shall or shall not be concluded, and gratification is sought accordingly. All action from a want is as completely one with nature as the flowing and ebbing of the tides or the revolving of the planets. Sentient life must ever more flow in the current of nature's conditions, and can possibly find or admit within it no spring to action as alternative to nature.

When, therefore, we recognize any facts which evince a capacity to turn and stem the stream of nature's conditioned sequences, it is quite manifest that in them we recognize an ethical personality in liberty. It is no more manifest, when the tempest-tost ship rides out the storm and maintains her steady and safe position against the elements, that her anchor holds on to that which stands beyond the contending billows; than that when the good will holds firm against all the cravings of appetite, it has its end above all that a sensory may contain. To play off one appetite against another, to stifle one want in the stronger craving of another, to hold each clamorous passion in subjection by the prudential consideration of the greatest gratification of all, is still to be only in nature. It is merely using one part of nature as a defense against another part, or the whole of nature against any particular interference. But, when all of sentient nature is setting in one direction, and an inner witness of what is due to the worthiness of an ethical character puts its imperative prohibition to the attainment of any such end; then, is the ethical end wholly out from the sentient end, and the ethical right gives a spring to control the sentient want, and an alternative is afforded to nature's conditions by putting a sovereignty over nature, and giving to sentient want a master that in his own right may subject and control it as a whole and forever. Should it be said, after all the fair appearance there may still

be some secret want or prudential consideration, that
is controlling the whole sentient nature beside, as
an o'ermastering craving; we should then at once
appeal to any man's own consciousness of either what
is, or of what *ought* to be, in his own case; and such
facts of consciousness are at once the recognition of
the ethical personality.

Thus, you have yourself been thrown into circumstances, where all the inclinations and tendencies of
sentient nature were in one direction, and appetite
and example and opportunity were all in combined
impulse towards gratification. But there sprang up
the irrepressible witnessing within—I *ought* to resist,
and turn back this whole tide of appetitive desire,
and stand firmly uncompliant. And here the question is—Whence this *ought?* Surely not from any
portion of the sentient nature; not from any æsthetic
or scientific interest; it is the claim of some ethical
sovereignty, as imperative over appetite and taste and
philosophy, and holds the agreeable the beautiful and
the true in science subordinate to the good and the
right in morals. Nothing can possibly awaken this
conviction of obligation but the inner witnessing of a
right, and never the mere craving of a want. All of
appetitive want may thus be combined, and yet the
counter conviction may come that *I ought*, and therefore that *I am able* even when I do not, to resist every
impulse of the sense, and stand unswayed by all the
promptings of constitutional desire. The considera-

tion of time, how long such subjection of gratification shall be maintained, has no possible relevancy; the end of ethical worthiness is supreme for all possible period. Nor, has the consideration of the degree of trial and sacrifice any pertinence; the highest possible susceptibility of a sentient nature is still to succumb to the worth of ethical character. All that a sensory in its keenest craving and most passionate want can sacrifice may be demanded in the right and for the rational end of the spiritual excellency ; and thus an imperative may fix an obligation to resist nature, great as the trial may be and long as it may endure. The firm will, in its ethical integrity, is thus capacity for standing against nature in all her force. Let her do her utmost, and I may still be firm and unyielding ; let me be crushed beneath her iron conditions through all my sentient being, and I may still say, in obedience to the end of my own worthiness, that I will go down to death in the integrity and loyalty of my good will and pure conscience.

Even in the degradation of the spirit to the lowest depravity, and the submerging of all imperative beneath the raging tide of passionate gratification, the man is still compelled to the conviction, that he has put himself under the domination of nature in the flesh by his own consent, and that this degradation is not misfortune but guilt, and that he ought to break the chain of his sensuality at once, and come out from his foul and noisome prison-house, and stand up in man-

ly valor and virtue, with the free and the good. He is
conscious that while his appetites are of nature, there
is a nobler part of his being which is not bound in the
conditions of nature. He can take hold of what is beyond all of nature's conditions, and stand thereby in
steadfast resistance to every thing which would degrade and enslave him, and for the sake of his dignity trample on all of happiness which collides with
duty. This the virtuous man knows as achieved in his
righteous integrity; this the vicious man knows as
claimed in his conscious responsibility; and in this is
the full recognition of a free ethical personality, whose
right is above all the ends which any conditions in
nature may propose.

Here are now sufficient facts for the evincing of a
universal recognition of an ethical personality in humanity, and this prepares us for the remaining consideration in the induction of ethical facts, viz:

Secondly—That we make this ethical personality
the only compass, by which to comprehend all the
facts that are moral in humanity. The successive
events in the flowing stream of nature around us, as
the seasons, the weather, the alternations of day and
night, the growth and decay of vegetation, &c., how
much soever they may affect us favorably or unfavor-
ably, we never call ours as if we had any responsibility in originating them. We always refer them to
an agency quite above and beyond all that is human.
The changing events in the physical world affect

mankind, but are never brought within the compass
of humanity, as if they belonged to it, or were at all
comprehended in it.

So also with the changing wants and craving appetites of our sensitive nature. We may call these ours
inasmuch as they come within the unity of self-consciousness, and take place on the field of our experience; yet we never appropriate them to our personality and consider them as comprehended within our
agency. They are the affections which nature within
and around us works upon us, in which we are passive, and not that we in any sense originate them.
That I am cold, or hungry, or sleepy, and desire to
gratify or relieve these craving wants is nature's
work on the field of my sensibility, and not my work,
as originating in my purpose, and carried out according to my intention. I hold myself to be wholly ir-
responsible therefor, except as in some act of liberty,
I excite or control the executive acts which gratify
them. The promptings of self-love, though generalized to the broadest dictates of prudence or kindness,
are wholly pathological and bound in the necessity of
nature's conditions. The brute and the man, as animal solely, move in the same lines of conditioned appetite, and take or leave the objects of gratification
according to the craving want, or as controlled by
the teachings of experience. We never comprehend
such facts in the compass of any responsible personality.

Moreover, we create our own forms of beauty, or construct our own pure diagrams in geometry, or connect our primitive conceptions in a philosophical system, and we may call these productions of art and science ours, in the acceptation that they are the works of our rational genius. We comprehend them within the compass of an æsthetic or scientific personality in humanity; but inasmuch as all such products are not within the region of spiritual rights and behests, we shall never here recognize the claims and imperatives of moral obligation and responsibility, nor attempt to comprehend the beauty of art nor the truth of science in an ethical personality.

But, there are facts, which evince that man is in himself an ethical whole; a moral world; self-separated from all other things and persons. As each man has his own, so humanity in the aggregate becomes a comprehensive total as human responsibility and obligation. Here is excluded all the facts of a merely sentient existence, and all of taste and science, inasmuch as none of these are bound up in the imperatives which originate in what is due to the spiritual and immortal in humanity.

Every man's virtues and vices are his own, in a meaning wholly other than that his appetites are his own; and wholly other than that his productions in the fine arts, or his attainments in science, are his own. They are his, in that they are wholly comprehended in himself; and their origination, and final intent are compassed in his ethical personality. That voluptuous indulgence, which has not merely brought pain and loss from its imprudence, but far more has induced conscious debasement and remorse, must the guilty man say, is all my own in its entire moral and responsible being. That selfish counsel given to another; that deceptive and ensnaring influence; that tempting solicitation; that dishonest intention and matured plan of wrong-doing; that perverse and perpetuated immoral habit; that malicious slander, or profane speech, or licentious publication; that unholy deed, and that wicked lie; all are in my own consciousness confined to my personality; and it were quite vain for me to attempt to shrink from a full and final account.

So also, on the other hand, that firm purpose and decided adherence to principle; that disregard of all allurement and threatening in the line of duty; that good counsel on virtue's side; that cheerful sacrifice of pleasure for the right; all have had their origin in my personality; and are deeds, for which none but myself can be conscious of a complacent self-approbation. They have dignified and adorned my character, and in them no other personality can participate. These deeds of vice or of virtue have gone out and mingled with the facts of nature, and become linked into the conditioned series of physical causes and effects, and spread abroad their baneful or beneficial influences; but they did not come of nature, and cannot

43

be transferred from myself to any of the necessities in
nature.   They must forever stand to my account, and
come back to me for their origin and final design.   And
thus with every man ; he separates all that is his from
all that is nature's or another person's, and thus comprehends his own in himself, and as proper person
with his own deeds stands self-isolated from all else ;
and neither nature, nor his fellows, can be made to
share in his responsibilities.   What nature has
wrought within him or thrown upon him, and what
another person as mentor or tempter has done, he
puts entirely distinct from his own agency, and thus
takes his own, and stands forever and completely ab-
solved from all that is not his own.

In this, and in this only, is the comprehension of
human morality.   Every man owns as his, and at his
responsibility, that which has origin and direction
from his ethical personality ; and he can be made to
own as his no other events beside.   His personality
in liberty is the only compass by which to include his
responsibility ; and the morality of the human race
can only be comprehended in that which is ethical
personality as habitant in humanity.   Sentient craving is nothing but conditioned nature working in man ;
beauty and truth have an interest above appetite, but
cannot give imperatives nor awaken responsibilities ;
the end of his own worthiness and dignity, as moral
character, gives the inward witness by which he knows
himself and his own.

And now, in conclusion we say, that all the facts under all the foregoing heads are fully held in colligation by this invariable law of comprehension. On the whole field of humanity, we never comprehend any portion of its facts in their origination and consummation, except as we bring them completely within the compass of a free personality. Whatever in human experience is conditioned in material nature, or in sentient nature, we never attempt to comprehend, except as we ascend to the comprehension of nature itself. It is found in human experience, only as this is subjected to necessity; and hence its comprehension if attained at all, must be brought within the compass of a personality, which is sovereign author of humanity itself. In this section of comprehend facts in *human experience*, we have our invariable hypothetical law; that we comprehend nothing, which we may not bring within the compass of a personality in liberty. We have yet to carry out the same hypothesis over the facts in a comprehension of nature itself, and this we will effect in the next section.

SECTION II.

THE FACTS OF A COMPREHENDING REASON WHICH COME WITHIN THE COMPASS OF AN ABSOLUTE PERSONALITY.

In the previous section we determined the fact of a universal recognition of a free personality in humanity, and that all comprehension of the products of hu-

manity was wholly by the compass of this free personality.   We rise from nature, and find that which
is not conditioned in nature, and comprehend this in
an author and designer.   The artist is rational and
free person, in that the love of the beautiful is spring
for an alternative agency against all the appetitive
wants of sentient nature, and thereby all the productions of an artistic taste are comprehended in the
compass of the æsthetic personality in humanity.
The philosopher is rational and free person, in that
the love of the true is spring for an alternative agency
against all craving want, and thereby all the attainments in science are comprehended in the compass of
the philosophic personality in humanity.   The moral
agent is rational and free person, in that an ethical
imperative is spring for an alternative action to all
sentient want and all æsthetic and scientific interest,
and thereby all moral character and responsibility are
comprehended in the compass of the ethical personality in humanity.   A comprehending reason thus actually comprehends all the products of humanity,
æsthetic, scientific and moral, as facts in human experience, solely by the compass of a recognized free
personality.

It is much to have thus found that the facts of comprehension, so far as they lie among the products of
humanity, are all in complete and perpetual colligation by this law of a personality in liberty.   We never
comprehend within the products of humanity any

events, which we do not at the same time recognize
as within the compass of a free human personality.
Whatever is bound in the conditions of nature, though
appearing on the ground of human experience and
coming within the field of human consciousness, is at
once attributed to nature and not comprehended as
within that world of events which humanity originates, and for which it must stand accountable.

But, therefore, we have the facts of comprehension
only amid the products of humanity. Each person is
compass by which we comprehend all that is his ;
and all persons constitute all of humanity, and in the
aggregate give compass by which we comprehend all
the creations of man ; and if any facts should disclose
themselves as the product of angelic agency, such
events would in the same manner be comprehended
within the compass of angelic personality. In this
way, however, we could attain to but a very partial
induction of the facts of a comprehending agency.
Very few of the events in nature can be considered as
the product of either human or angelic personalities.
Take away from the series of conditioned causes and
effects in nature all the events which have found their
origin in humanity and may be comprehended within
the compass of human personalities, and though such
substraction would give abundant manifestation that
nature had been much modified and indeed augmented
in the stream of her flowing sequences by man yet
would that which was taken bear but a very small pro-

portion to that which would still remain. These modifications of material nature would not at all reach
to its primitive substantial space-filling force. The
essence of nature would be found to be neither increased nor diminished, inasmuch as the products of
man's creation are never any distinguishable physical
forces, which may fill space with new substances or
superinduce upon existing matter new organizations.

We have, therefore, occasion for many facts of a
comprehending agency in the origination and consummation of events in nature, which can by no means
be brought within the compass of any human personality. Indeed, our grand object is to determine the
law of a comprehending reason in reference to nature
herself, and we have only dwelt upon the facts of a
comprehending reason within the products of humanity, in order to show that as the actual law is here also the same, we might thereby have the more abundant confirmation, that this one hypothesis of a personality in liberty holds all facts of a comprehending
agency every where within its colligation. We shall
make it our object in this section to show that all
comprehension of nature has this one law, the recognized compass of a free personality, as the author and
finisher of all that is thus comprehended; and where-
ever such encompassing personality is recognized,
there do we at once comprehend all the events in him.
Since the events are of nature, and not the product of
any finite personality, it follows that we must take it

for our hypothesis that all such comprehension of events must stand within the compass of an absolute personality. We shall, therefore, find it convenient to pursue this order of induction—*First*, to induce such facts as show a universal recognition of an absolute personality above nature; and *Secondly*, to induce such facts of a comprehending reason for nature, as shall evince that all operation of comprehending nature is by the law of this absolute personality. In this last division, inasmuch as we have both a physical and an ethical system as universal, it will be necessary to have this sub-division of facts for the law of comprehension, *first* in the physical, and *secondly* in the ethical universal system.

1. *Facts evincive of a universal recognition of an Absolute Personality.*—There are many facts which show that the human mind readily recognizes a personal author and governor of nature, and it is only from the influence of perverted speculation that such recognition comes to be discarded. Humanity is not Atheistic except as deluded. The conviction that there is a personal God above and Lord of nature, would be perpetual and universal except for the paralogism induced in the antinomy of the connections of the understanding and the comprehension of the reason, of which more notice will soon be taken. This is not the place for an ontological argument demonstrative of the actual existence of a personal Deity ; we seek now only to establish this conclusion, that the hnman mind

readily recognizes such a being, and that the conviction is not discarded except through a process of speculation which may be easily exposed in the very
sources of its fallacy.

(1.) *The ready assent to the fact of final causes in
Nature.*—The common and most satisfactory basis of
Natural Theology is the universal conviction of final
causes in nature.   The evidences of adaptation to ends
are so numerous and so prominent, that no observing
mind fails to be impressed with the conviction, that
there has been an intelligent design in such adaptations.   The argument, accumulative with every fact
of adaptation, is at first satisfactory and convincing to
every apprehending mind.   It is when we begin to
speculate upon the process of proof, and examine the
conclusiveness of such argumentation, that we lose the
force of this first conviction and may pass through all
grades of skepticism to a confirmed infidelity.   The
speculation does not at all weaken the evidence of
adaptation to ends in nature, but it obscures the conviction that such facts may be made demonstrative of
a personal Deity.   When we examine these connected
adaptations more closely, we find them all conditioned
in their sequences, and the succeeding to be necessitated by the preceding and the on-going of nature a perpetual series of link in link without alternative.   The
means to an end now future were themselves end to
be reached by former means, and how are we to leap
in our conclusions, from this linked necessity every

way shutting us within its fixed connections, to some
independent and free personality as an original designer?

Instead of the phenomenal adaptations connected in
their conditioning causes, we may assume that an intellectual attribute which we call *intent* or *design*, appears as element in this combination; and we may
then take that intellectual element as the fact from
which to conclude upon an absolute and free maker
and designer of all things. But we shall still have the
same endless chain of conditioned sequences. There
is design, as intellectual element, in the arranged wires
of the carding-machine, and this may be deemed sufficient proof for an intelligent designer. But when I
see that busy little iron hand, with astonishing precision, bending and cutting the wire and puncturing the
leather and exactly inserting the card-teeth, I find here
the intellectual element higher up in the development
of sequences and conditioning in necessity what is below it. How shall I leap from the conditioned mechanism to the free personality. The man makes the
iron hand that makes the card; but that man again
is an adaptation as means to such an end, and in his
wants and interests and circumstances as much conditioned, it may be, to make card-teeth machines, as
such machines are to make cards. In the man then
is now found the intellectual element conditioning all
that follows. But I need a designer adapting the man
to his sequences, as much as in the former case I

needed the man adapting the machine to set card-teeth ; and then, when I find the designer of the man in his adaptations, I shall find the intellectual element there, and yet shall be no nearer to a demonstration of an origin of all design in a free personality than when I began with this design in the arranged wires of the carding-machine. It is ever design apprehended only in some already conditioned connection, and I cannot leap from conditioned result to a free originating personality.

It is thus with every form of argumentation on the basis of final causes. That which seemed so conclusive at first, when speculatively examined fails utterly to reach to any conclusion. The regressus is ever with an open backward way, and when pushed, the understanding must perpetually tread back from one conditioned to a higher condition, and never reach its origin in an unconditioned. It is thus that all teleological proof of the existence of a personal Deity must fail of a demonstration, because it is impossible that the process should rest in other than an arbitrary conclusion. The personal designer is surreptitiously assumed because we rationally need him, but not at all because we logically find him. But, when we now know the clear distinction between a connecting understanding and a comprehending reason, we can at once free ourselves from all the delusion and paralogism of such speculation. Reason demands an absolute and can rest in nothing else, for it can possibly comprehend nothing except in this *compass* of a free personality; but an understanding forbids all such origination, and can possibly conclude in connected judgments only through the *medium* of perpetually underlying and interlinking conditions. The very idea of a personality in liberty is an absurdity to the discursive faculty, and to which the conception of a deity can possibly be none other than the notion of a substance filling all space, and in its casuality working through all time, and connecting within itself all the conditioned phenomenal changes in nature. The reaching forth of the comprehending reason, and the short-coming of the connecting understanding utterly forbid that we should put the two faculties at work together, or one for the other, and suppose that their results may be brought concentric with each other in the same sphere. If we would attain to the personal Deity of a comprehending reason, we must not delude ourselves with the folly, that such can be measured in the connections of a discursive understanding. The discursive faculty cannot move at all without its media of substance and cause, and when it thus moves it must be from condition to conditioned; how then may it assume to determine any thing about the originating of space-filling substances and time-abiding causes? It is quite as incompetent to *deny* any thing about free personalities as to *prove* any thing. It cannot say how substance and cause may begin to be, but as little can it say that they may not begin, and have their origin a free personality. It is wholly impertinent to this faculty, that it should meddle at all in the questions of final causes and free originations, and ethical personalities. The sense might as well attempt to perceive the essential force which connects the phenomenal universe. Neither is competent to affirm or deny beyond its own legitimate province.

We may at once therefore, utterly disregard all these delusive speculations of a discursive judgment; and if they are found wholly incompetent to comprehend the adaptations in nature, by the compass of a personal Deity, so also are they wholly incompetent to exclude the possibility of such comprehension, and deny the actual being of a personal God of nature. The ontological demonstration may hereafter come in its proper place, but enough is here given to show that the conviction of final causes in nature should not be at all weakened or modified from any speculations which are manifestly so preposterous. And yet, all such recognition of final causes is, in the fact itself, the recognition of a free personality above nature. A final end to be attained in and by nature involves an overruling and a using of nature for some personal intent, and is, in that mind, the recognition of a personality independent of and absolute over nature. To such a mind " the heaven's declare the glory of God and the firmament showeth forth his power." " The invisible things of him from the creation of the world are clearly seen, being understood by the things that are made, even his eternal power and Godhead."

(2.) *The recognition of miraculous interpositions in nature.*—It is not contrary to, but quite in accordance with the convictions of mankind generally, that there should be miraculous interpositions. All skepticism in reference to the competency of human testimony for the proof of miracles is, as in the case of final causes, a result of delusive speculations. Deny that philosophy can reach beyond experience and generalizations from experience, and we shall then have nothing but the connections of an understanding, and cannot conceive where a miracle should come from. No amount of human testimony can rise to as high a source of conviction against the uniformity of nature and for the miraculous interposition, as is given in universal experience against the miracle and for the uniformity of nature. The very basis of all philosophical conviction underlies the belief of the uniformity of nature ; but the credibility of a miracle has only testimony, which all experience shows may be fallible. An assent to the fact of a miracle, therefore, on any amount of testimony is credulity, and a philosopher should be wholly above it. And, surely, if we keep this philosophy, there is no alternative to this skepticism in reference to all testimony for a miracle. That a Deity is assumed, who may control nature miraculously, can be only through the same credulity ; for all science is wholly within the generalizations of experience, and no experience, however generalized, can reach beyond nature, but must ever run up and down the interminable sequences of her conditioned connections.

But we may readily pass by all this when we have learned the antinomy of the two operations of a connecting understanding and a comprehending reason. If we will admit nothing but the logical conclusions of a discursive connection, then verily are we shut up within nature, and the testimony of such as might rise from the dead could not avail to carry us beyond nature's linked successions. But if we have attained the complete idea of a comprehending reason, then nothing forbids that we should readily cherish the common conviction of miraculous interpositions.

Without canvassing the testimony for the validity of any specific miracle, in this place, it is sufficient that we show a ground in philosophy for such conviction when properly substantiated by testimony, and we may then take such common recognition of the fact of miraculous interpositions as involving the recognition of an absolute personality above nature. I do not at all apprehend, in any recognized miracle, that nature has violated her own laws of connection, and that any distinguishable forces in nature have of themselves broken away from their fixed order of development; for this would not merely transcend, but contradict the laws of an understanding. I conceive of a new event put into nature, which did not come from any previous conditions in nature, but from wholly a supernatural source. Nor is this new event

such as might originate in a finite personality, as when
by human volition changes are made in nature, which
do not come of nature but of our free personality. The
new event has its source *ab extra* from all nature's
conditions, and is also such a counteraction of nature,
as evinces a power superhuman over nature. Opening blind eyes, and unstopping deaf ears, and healing
the sick, and raising the dead, and controlling the elements, and thus directly overpowering nature in her
own causal operations by a direct counteracting of her
flowing conditions; these and such like events alone
rise to what we mean by miraculous interpositions.
Nature may then receive these new events and incorporate them within her own conditions, but they began to be in nature from no paternity of nature, and
had their genesis wholly from a superhuman source.

And now we affirm the fact, that the human mind
readily admits that such interpositions have occurred
in nature, and it is only from a delusive speculation
that skepticism arises while a complete philosophy
sustains such conviction; and such conviction involves
the recognition of an absolute personality; a will in
liberty; unconditioned by nature and having a sovereign control over nature, and which may make new
things or annihilate old things in nature at his pleasure. It is not nature at work upon herself, nor anomolous and monstrous originations in nature; but it is
a hand from without thrust in sovereignty within, and
modifying and making and extinguishing the forces of

nature as it pleases. Such conviction cannot be, but in the recognition of an absolute and free personality.

(.3) *The order of nature's formation, as given in Geological Facts.*—Here we meet with no speculations of a delusive philosophy to obscure or deny the facts themselves, but we take them as nature has left her own record of what has been done within her upon her own successive pages, and in legible characters and a meaning unmistakable. The facts to which we here refer, and would present in the most comprehensive manner, are as follows. Repeated convulsions from deep subterranean forces have in frequent instances broken through the solid crust of the earth's surface, and turned out the edges of these upheaved strata to our view, which have their dip of a greater or less inclination to the horizon, according to circumstances. These exposed strata are the leaves of nature as a book, and contain the memorials of past historical occurrences through a long series of many and diversified geological epochs.

In the reading of this record backward from the present, all traces of man's existence on the earth cease to appear, when we pass the accumulations of a few feet of soil upon the surface. Comparatively slight modifications of the alluvial deposits, or more violent and extensive changes of alluvial action which yet do not mark any deep convulsion, are alone contemporaneous with the history of man's abode upon the earth.

Passing these we come to the TERTIARY formation, and have commingled strata of *sand, clay* and *lime* of a thousand feet in thickness. The remains of animals of existing species are here found in large numbers, and yet such are constantly diminishing as we go down, until in the lowest formation of this series, very few traces of the existing forms of animal life now on the earth there appear, while their places are filled by strange fossils of many different and now wholly extinct species.

The SECONDARY formation succeeds, and we have the *chalk beds* of a thousand feet depth in which no fossil shell-fish and only one animal is found of the present existing types of sentient being. We find next the *oolite* formation of half a mile in thickness, deposited by subsidence from rivers and seas alternately, and in this we lose utterly all traces of any existing species of animated nature, and among other new forms we encounter here the strange and monstrous saurian remains. The *new red sandstone* of two thousand feet comes next; and this followed by the *coal* formations of many thousand feet in depth, the carbonized remains of the immense vegetable productions of an older world, and in which no plant of present forms appears, nor is there any indication that any fowl then existed or any animal roamed through these primeval forests. Here are interposed, between the coal-strata, *lime stone* formations of great thickness, not as the sepulchers of fossil shell-fish, but the

44

remains in mass of myriads of testaceos or coralline animals. We came next to the *old red sandstone* formations many thousand feet in depth, and which are an aggregate of older rocks fractured and decomposed and promiscuously put together by successive depositions, and containing such organic remains as there lived and died, but which have left no successors among the latter fossil species.

Deeper and earlier than all these, come the PRIMARY formations. The *Silurian* system here has place for a mile and an half in depth, with its hundreds of animal species utterly extinguished in its own stratifying process, and their petrified remains testifying to the long cycles in which successive species one after another came, and ran through their respective generations, and then utterly ran out of being for later types of new organizations. Then we reach the *Cambrian* system of nearly equal thickness of old slate rock, and in which the fossil remains of animal life are much diminished, and admonish us that we are coming to an age more solitary than the places of death and of graves, even to periods when sentient life had not yet a beginning.

The *Cumbrian* formation receives us still lower down, and here we stand with all the generations of life above us, worlds on worlds which have for countless ages slept in death, and read around us only the records of material nature ere life was given or death began its reign. *Mica schist*, in stratifications of many

thousand feet, are given; and then *gneiss* formations
bring us down below the records of all stratifications;
and the crystalizations of the solid *granite*, deeper
than we can penetrate, tell us only of the *fusing fires*
beneath; and the leaves of nature's book are all sealed
up from mortal eyes beyond. A region of ten miles
in depth below the surface has thus been explored,
and we can here deliberately trace the history of nature's operations, and the interpositions occurring in
its own successions with unmistaken certainty and
precision; through every foot of which there must
have been the passing away of geological ages, to have
sufficed for their accumulations.

Whatever the geological epochs, there is the evidence that antecedently to all accumulation in regular
strata by any subsidence, there was in action the antagonistic force of attraction and repulsion, ensphering
the mass about a common center; and also that the
distinguishable forces of heat, and electrical and chemical agencies were superinduced, without at all sub-
verting the original space-filling substance in its causality. Matter had thus chemical combinations as
the development of such forces, and above these the
crystaline force is superinduced, and thus as preparatory to organic productions material existence is
brought into form, and its conditioned changes run on
in the development of causes and effects, and nature
works itself out in the action of its intrinsic forces.
Attraction and repulsion, bipolar forces, chemical af-

finities and crystaline agencies have their inner conditions, and their inter-working necessitates their resulting products. But neither of these distinguishable forces can carry their action beyond their own inner conditions. Gravitation cannot act as caloric or electricity, nor can they act as chemical affinity and crystalization. By so much as the higher force conditions the working of the lower is there a superinducing of the higher upon the lower, and it were no more absurd to say that the lower originated in an utter void, than that the higher originated from the lower. By so much as it is higher and controlling it is a superinduction, and the excess to have come from the lower must have originated from utter emptiness. No distinguishable force can do more than develop its own rudimental being, and thus nature can never go out of herself as she is and bring into herself new and higher forces. All superinduction can be no development from inherent endowment, but must be causation imparted by an *ab extra* interposition. Crystalization overacts chemical affinities and gravitating agencies without extinguishing them, and could not thus have found its genesis from them, but must have been superinduced by some agency beyond them ; and so in turn with all distinguishable forces, which shall overact crystalization, or any succession of such forces as shall one overact the other.

We may not, yet at least, be able to read from this book of geological records the fact that nature in her distinguishable forces was successively brought into being, and that the superinduction of one force upon another, in simply physical organizations, was with interventions of long geological periods. We may confidently affirm that the lower could not beget the higher, but we cannot affirm that they were successively superinduced, nor deny that nature began with the combination of the gravitating, chemical and crystalizing forces. As yet we have nothing but probabilities from analogy, to guide us in our conclusions higher up in geological periods than the originations of vegetable organizations. Though the probabilities are all the other way, yet we will not here decide that the crystalization of the granite mass, and the action of heat and electricity, and magnetism, may not all have been coeval with the force of attraction and repulsion in the space-filling substance. But whether contemporaneous or successive, their combination is no identification of these forces. They are as readily distinguishable from each other as if we had them in isolated action, and we can distinctly determine the parts which each perform in the formation of the physical structure of our globe. In this combination of agency, distinguishable through all its superinduced elements, we may now leave the consideration of the *times* of superinduction to some farther study of the record, and merely apprehend, in the causality induced by the overacting and controlling of the higher with the still perpetual operation of the lower forces, that the subterranean fires, and the crystalline rocks, and the half fused gneiss formations, and superimposed depositions of mica-schist, would be a necessary result of the conditioned development. Nature would put on her conditioned forms, and take her conditioned positions, and pass along in conditioned loco-motion, and have her conditioned changes, from the action of her own forces.

But, after all this, we have a sure and clear record of successive interpositions. We can very legibly read what has been done since such forces had brought the merely material development through its preliminary stages, and it is to these results, as far more important now for our purpose, that we give a more special attention. Indefinite geological cycles passed round in the inward action and onward development of physical forces, and the onward series of cause and effect induced their combinations and cohesions, and the heat gave its molten masses, and the crystaline forces arranged the firm and deep granite beds, on which the entire geological superstructure through all its varied strata reposes; and yet periods of incalculable duration passed by, while the primitive gneiss rocks were attaining their consolidation and position, and while still later the mica-schist was being deposited; but at length a point in the ongoing of nature's conditioned changes is reached, where we have her record that what had never yet appeared, and what could not be begotten from all that nature was—a new and higher force than any yet in action—began its being and its manifest control, over the other forces on which it had been superinduced. In some shallow of the primitive ocean, where the broken and triturated particles of this primeval world had been accumulated by the forces then in action, wholly a new force is at work; and, overruling other forces for its own uses, it is building up forms and combinations of phenomena unlike all that nature has before known. A field of marine *algae*, the product of a *vital* force, which organizes, and energizes through all the organization of root, stock, branches and leaves, is in its first existence. The germinating life begins while yet through nature no parent stock or seed is found; and the plant expands and matures, and while the primitive organization falls and is utterly decomposed, this vital force still lives on in the ripened germ, and propagates itself in its undecayed energy in the newly shooting plant. Thus vegetative life begins, and runs on its course through all the following generations of that species of the seaweed.

Whence, now, is this new force in such controlling action? It has just come into nature, and over-rides the other material forces, and is itself source for all these new phenomena, but whence is *it*? Gravitation, chemical and crystalizing forces, all say it is not *in us*, and cannot have been brought out *from us*. It is their superior, and uses them and modifies them for its own ends. That it should be deemed some genesis of na-

ture is absurd, for nature has till now known no causality which could reach so high and control so far, and
by so much as it exceeds all former force in nature, it
must thus have originated from an utter void; and
which is just the same impossible supposition, as if all
nature were deemed the offspring of an utter negation
of all being. It has been superinduced upon nature,
and has thus become an addition to nature, and can
therefore only be a creation from some being supernatural. And yet so perfectly is this new force superinduced upon all the other forces which it uses, in the
harmony of its conditioned and conditioning operation,
that it is quite manifest this hand, which interposed
and put it into nature, is the same hand which intelligently holds and guides all nature. We have not before been able to open the book to the record of nature's
beginning, but all has been developed nature, stretching back to a beginning we have striven to find, but
could not reach. Here we find so much of nature as
vegetable life begins to be, and so in harmony with all
else of nature that it uses without extinguishing its
other forces; and we recognize in it a supernatural
personality, who is absolute for it, and for all of nature.
And here also, we may see that the evidence for this recognition of an absolute personality accumulates through
all the succeeding epochs of geological formations.
The primitive forces of gravitation, cohesion and crystalization act on, and the new vital force controls them
and perpetually reproduces itself in harmony with them

through all its propagations ; but, with the vital force
as essential being for one marine plant, we can have in
nature only its generations and in its own kind.   This
vegetative force is conditioned to its own organizations and can build up only its own phenomenal struc-
tures, and can never go out and originate a new species of organic life.   Each new species of vegetable
life is a new force in nature, more emphatically so for
animal life, and onward from the lowest orders of tes-
tacea or corralline existence up to the highest species of
the mammalia.   A new superinducing of beings, upon
that which nature before possessed, is effected in each
case ; and as it did not come out of previous forces of
nature in their conditioned development, so in each
case, we have a new recognition of that same personal
and supernatural interference which, out of nature,
puts into nature what he pleases.

We come along up from this great depth to which
we have descended and reach the lower sepulchers in
which the earliest dead lie entombed, and from thence
we pass along by the myriads of once living beings
preserved in their forms beyond the skill of all em-
balming, while at every step of our ascent we pass
above entire species of animals, which had run on
through many generations and then died out utterly
in the extinction of the race, and another put anew
within nature as its successor in time but without
any geneological connection.   One form of sentient
nature has thus been built up by a distinguishable vi-

tal force, which has propagated itself through all its generations and occupied its geological era, and that entire organic energy has ceased to act and its kind become extinct; and other species have in like manner been successively put anew within nature, and each has recorded its type of being in form and locality and habitude on the spot where its generations came and went, and we can as readily determine the originations and extinctions of the species as of the individuals themselves. New forms of life begin and end, sometimes in the same geological formations and sometimes perpetuated through successive strata, and these followed by others to become themselves in turn extinct, and thus nature has from the beginning of animal and vegetable life, been replenished by repeated and successive creations. Among the last products of his forming hand we find the book of nature like the record of Moses, to teach that man was made by God in his own likeness, and that his origin is of very recent date compared with the geolocial cycles since other and lower types of sentient beings began. What, in all cases of these superinduced forces of vegetable upon material, and of animal upon vegetable being, was there in the lower which should beget the higher? What, when one species become extinct, that should be the genesis of another widely different species? What, in all that existed through nature, could rise so high as to give birth to man, when there was yet no human progenitor? As well might all nature rise into being from an utter void of all being at once, as to rise by progressive steps, with each addition an origination from a void of all being beyond what nature then contained. Over and over again we here recognize in these legible records of a supernatural interposition, which has put into nature that which nature yet had not, the existence of a free personality wholly unconditioned by nature.

(4.) *The recognition of a free personality in humanity.*—We have before found that this is a universal conviction, and that the personality comprehends all that is moral in humanity and for which man is held by himself to be responsible. This we are convinced did not come of nature, inasmuch as it is competent to resist nature, and to distinguish its own originations from the conditioned successions of nature, and thus stand forth with its own in separate unity. Still this free finite personality is recognized as in combination with nature. The free force of the reason as spring of action in the right of its own dignity, is the power of will ; and yet, while this may ever stand in resistance to all the wants of its sentient nature, it may never wholly separate itself from it nor prevent the appetitive wants from coming frequently in collision with it, and can maintain its sovereignty only by perpetual vigilance and valor. The personality is habitant in sentient nature, and has the prerogative of an end above nature, and thereby an imperative to maintain its dominion over nature ; but with all this prerogative above nature, it cannot break up its combination and stand forth wholly pure from nature. Humanity is ever animal as well as rational, and it cannot exclude nature's wants from colliding often with its own ethical end, but only prevent such colliding wants, when they do and will intrude, from attaining the mastery. Nature, both without and within the human sensory, keeps on in her own unbroken succession's of cause and effect, and the human will cannot stop this, but only exclude her dominion within its own sphere.

Thus is it manifest that the human personality did not come of nature, since it may wholly exclude all domination of nature's conditions over it ; and as manifest is it that nature did not come of it, for it can no otherwise free itself from nature than by excluding not by annihilating nature. It is a distinguishable energy superinduced upon nature, and as controlling nature in its own right is a power above force, competent to hold itself free from all external force and to hold in subjection all the inner forces of its own sentient nature.

Personality in humanity is not, therefore, deemed to be a higher force in nature superinduced upon existing lower distinguishable forces, as when the force of heat overrules gravity without extinguishing ; but this personality as power of will is itself supernatural even in its superinduction upon nature. We recognize in this, not a new physical force, but an *ethical* personality as absolute above nature, who not only originated nature through all its superinduced forces in succession one above another, that the highest might *physically* control and use all the lower, but also crowned the whole with a supernatural in his own image, that this finite personality might *ethically* control and use all of nature for its own worthiness' sake, while itself should be subject only to the absolute dignity in the personality of its author. In this author of human personality is universally recognized the absolute ethical personality of a Deity, who may originate not merely distinguishable forces superinduced upon some grand central antagonist force, but who must be of right the grand center of the whole ethical sphere, and have made both the physical and the ethical systems for his own worthiness' sake.

2. *The fact of a comprehending operation for universal nature is only by the compass of this Absolute Personality.*—Taking the universe of being, we have the material vegetable and animal worlds as purely physical existence, and wholly bound in the conditions of a nature of things. Their entire onward development is wholly necessitated from their primitive rudimental being, and all in combination as one universe had one fixed series without an alternative. We have in this universe of being, also, the complex existence of the sentient and the rational in humanity, and thus the human race so involved in the conditions of a nature of things, that in their constitutional being they belong

to the same physical system, and must be comprehended within the compass of the same author and designer. We need thus here to see the fact of a comprehending operation of reason for the entire universe of being, material, vegetable, animal and human. This human has moreover its personality in liberty, and is thus ethical being; and in the end of its own intrinsic dignity and worth, the human personality must stand in moral alliance with all ethical beings in their personality; and we shall thus have an ethical universal system, including all free personality. We need, therefore, to see the fact of a comprehending reason for an entire ethical system, in all its separate and comprehensive imperatives. We have, then, to attain the facts for a comprehension of both a physical and an ethical universe. And here, in each case, the hypothesis is, that we never effect such comprehension except by the compass of this absolute personality which we have found to be universally recognized, and never even speculatively discarded but by a delusive paralogism which is now readily exposed. We will here take them up in their order.

(1.) *The comprehension of the Physical Universe.*— The comprehensive agency performs its operations only by the compass of an author and finisher. If a true and proper beginning be not reached, then no act of a comprehending agency can commence. All is left to the conditioned series of cause and effect, evermore reproducing itself in every repetition. And when a

proper origination is attained, a designed comsumma-
tion must also be apprehended, or the work of comprehension cannot be completed. It is beginning and
progress with no aim, having no end to be reached,
and no goal of perfection to be attained; "a mighty
maze and all without a plan." Such encompassing
author and finisher is found only in this recognition
of an absolute person, as the God and guide of nature
and the sovereign of the moral universe.

This is manifest abundantly, from the facts given
in any direction where this conviction of the human
mind, that there is such an absolute personal Deity has
not been discarded or in any way lost. If the rational
in man has, among any savage people, been as yet so
little developed that the recognition of an absolute
personality has not yet been reached, then has there
to such a rude and barbarous tribe been no comprehension of any thing in nature; of nature as a universe; or of any ethical system. If through a delusive speculation, such original conviction has been discarded, there has at once been lost all rational comprehension of the universe. Whence it came? and
whither it tends? have been questions not only unanswerable to such, but in the discarding of all encompassing in a beginning and consummation, such
questions are without significancy. We might as well
ask whence come and whither tend the passing periods of time, for nature's connections are thus made as
aimless and endless as the conditioned successions

of indeterminate durations. No *Atheistical* system
ever attempts to comprehend the universe. Nature
comes, it knows not whence; and moves onward, it
knows not whither. If it talk of laws and principles
in nature, its talk is all absurdity; for its laws have
no law-giver and its principles no *principium*. If it
seek to generalize these laws and principles and make
its God of the aggregate, and thus atheism change to
pantheism; it is only to change the absurdity of its
language, for such an aggregate is still evermore but
a part, and the law and principle are yet ever more
contained in some higher law and principle. No
Polytheistic scheme can give an encompassing author;
for each god is tutelar deity for but his own region,
and all are in perpetual contention, until some recognized God of all gods harmonizes the whole, by encompassing the whole in his originating and consum-
mating control. A *Manichean* theory, of two original
sources of all being, is but just so far comprehensive
as its assumed personality encompasses; and light
and darkness, the good and the bad dœmon, divide
the universe between them, and all is eternal conflict,
except one be expelled in the supremacy of the other.
No intellectual comprehension of universal nature has
in fact ever been made, where the comprehending reason
did not encompass all from beginning to final end in one
absolute personal Jehovah; and wherever such recognition of absolute personality has been attained, there,
as a matter of fact, has universal nature ever been com-

prehended in him as sole author and finisher thereof. The law in the facts of all comprehension of nature is the recognition of an absolute and free being, and the process of all comprehension in the fact is in precise correlation to all such comprehension in the apriori idea.

(2.) *The comprehension of the Ethical System.*—Man is conscious of perpetual imperatives, and that there are perpetual moral obligations that must rest upon the race. It is not difficult to take the convictions of obligation, growing directly out of the inward witness of what is due to the dignity of man's rational and spiritual being, and find a perfect ethical system every way complete and comprehensive in its own autonomy. The existence of the ethical persons will itself originate the imperatives as universal moral law, and the control of the law universally will be the consummation of the moral government. This will include only such imperatives as may be made universally binding, and in which we may readily come to see that which *should be*, without regard at all to the enquiry, now, whether that which should be actually *is*. It is for the facts as imperative that we here seek, and not for the facts as they may be existing in real life.

Humanity in its ethical personality, is spring for controlling all the appetites of its sentient nature. They *should* in all cases be held so subject and the *good will* in each person should ever reign sovereign over *desire*. As separate persons the highest imperative would be,

45

the preservation of the integrity of moral character, which is found in making and keeping the ends of the sentient subservient to the end of the rational. The maxim for each person must be—do that which is due to the dignity of the person, in the complete subordination to it of the wants of the animal. This is the duty of each person, and hence it is due as a *right* in each person, that no other person be allowed to interfere, and endanger its continuance. As social beings, therefore, each having imperatives in the right of his own personality, and thereby the right to an unhindered compliance with such imperatives, the maxim for each must be—do nothing that shall infringe upon the freedom of another in his compliance with the imperatives of his own personality. Such individual maxims thus made into law universal would be thus expressed—respect thy own rights and regard the liberty of thy neighbor in his rights. All rights originate in the intrinsic dignity of personality, and all imperatives originate in rights; and thus all rights and all duties at once exist in the existence of human society, and the sum of all law for such society is found in the above maxim made into law universal. From this, by analysis, may be derived every private and social duty, but which it is not necessary should be here formally drawn out. The entire community in the aggregate would attain the consummation of a human society, by the control of such universal law. The aggregate would become an organic whole in systematic unity thereby. Each person, as component element in such a society, would be both end in himself, and auxiliary to the end of all, sustaining his own worthiness and contributing to the universal dignity. The social body would be altogether without schism, and the functions of a healthy life going on in every part. In the social system of humanity this *ought* so to be; and then the whole stands out in its completeness under the directory of its own law and blessing itself in every part through the perpetual results of its own action.

Such a consummation is no mere conception arbitrarily created. That humanity is in social being, is ground sufficient to induce the universal conviction, that such a consummation *ought to be*. The imperatives originating in its own being give the claim for such an ethical system in its origin and consummation. All should thus act from the maxim which is imperative as law universal; and all so acting, the aggregate worthiness and blessedness is attained, and virtue and moral self-complacency reign in every part. It is righteousness rewarding itself according to its merit in its own results.

But that which *ought* to be, *will not* be, when any one person has violated a right and introduced sin into the system. This one violation reaches through and breaks in upon the rights and the complacency of the whole. All have a righteous claim upon every other that they each fulfill the law universal, and that no one

shall be as "a broken tooth or a foot out of joint."
And when such offending member introduces his disturbing and colliding moral action, it is the equitable
claim of the whole, that the delinquent and all his de-
ranging action be at once excluded. But it *ought* not to
be that his exclusion be merely topical displacement,
as the removal from a material machine of some part
broken or become rotten. Remorse and shame is the
sinner's due, and the moral disapprobation of all the
holy, perpetually made manifest towards him, is the
righteous demerit of the guilty. The light, in which
he ought to regard himself as lost in dignity, is precisely the light in which all others ought to regard
him; and his retribution of shame, self-reproach, and
public abhorrence is as imperative, as the approbation and complacency for the virtuous.

And still further, the sin and colliding agency of
one does by no means release any other from the imperative of the law universal, but each is bound to
the same integrity of character personally as before
the unworthiness of one had been introduced. And
here then begins an evil which the action of the system cannot in itself remedy. The imperatives remain, but the bliss of all is marred. Even such as
are firmly loyal to the right rule feel the colliding influences of the sinner, and their freedom and rights
and blessedness are impaired. The system cannot
repair itself in its own action. An intruding evil has
come in which it cannot eject. The system must still

work on under its imperatives, but it will now perpetually and forever work wrong.

And so, precisely, we find the facts to be. They
are not in human society as they *should* be. What
ought to be is not, and the ethical system is perpetually contravening its own imperatives, and perpetua-
ting moral inconsistencies which it cannot itself re-
dress. The retribution of the wicked, and the exclusion of their colliding influence is not as from its own
imperative it ought to be. That which is differs far
from that which should be, and the perpetual on-going is a perpetuation of wrong-doing. In such a state
of facts all comprehension of an ethical system were
impossible. That has come in which should not
have originated, and that consummation which should
be is unattainable. The fact as it is has no satisfactory
origin or end, as ethical system. It stands itself, in
its own working, abhorrent to the moral reason and
conscience it embodies ; and is an ethical blot, eternal
and irremediable in its own helplessness of all self-
cleansing.

And here, the question is, how comprehend the
ethical system in humanity as we find it, marred, perverted and incorrigible from its own action ? We
can comprehend an ethical system as it *should* be very
readily ; since the existence of the human society
would itself originate the rights and the imperatives ;
and the fullfillment of the law universal would be its
consummation ; but it is a very different fact of com-

prehension when the ethical system is already perverted, and in itself helpless and hopeless of all restoration in its own movement. How such perverted
ethical system originated? how be consummated? is
now the problem. In what way is the operation for
comprehending an ethical system effected, as the system *is* in its depravity? And to this, the answer is
universal, both as negative and positive. No Atheistic or Pantheistic system ever did or ever can comprehend an ethical government over human beings in
their depravity, by accounting either for the origin of
sin, or for the recovery of the race from it. All Theistic systems ever have made such a comprehension, by
encompassing all with the hand of an absolute moral
governor from the inception to the consummation;
and in some way referred to Him, in the perfection of
his wisdom, the sovereign disposal of all that the moral government involved. Under the administration
of a Divine Sovereign, has the human race been created, and the ethical relations and responsibilities established, and the sin and disorder have come in and
will be so controlled as at last to work out a consummation worthy of his dignity, and corresponding
to every claim that his subjects may righteously lay
before his throne. Whatever may now be hid, in the
darkness of his inscrutible dealings, is only mystery
to the finite subject; "God is his own interpreter,
and He will make it plain." Thus, and thus only,

has there ever been effected any comprehension of an ethical system in depraved humanity.

It might be very easy to show here, that the provisions of the Gospel scheme of Redemption are precisely adapted to the interests of reason in effecting such an ethical comprehension, and that the divine interpositions have been wholly regulated by the behests of God's own worthiness and dignity. It behoved him so to interfere and no otherwise in the permission, the overwhelming and restraining, the expiation pardoning and punishing of sin. On the christian ground of a moral government, its comprehension is in complete conformity with every fact of man's ethical responsibility and God's righteous sovereignty. Man in his freedom *should* have been no otherwise restrained; God in his holiness *should* have no otherwise interposed. But our whole work in determining the fact and the law of a comprehending reason, for an ethical system as it *is* in fallen humanity, is completed in this, that we now see that it has never been attempted except upon Theistic grounds; and that in the recognition of an absolute personality as moral governor, whether without or with the light of a divine revelation, the moral system with the sin and evil in it has ever been held, as in some way having a rational origination and ultimate consummation.

Putting thus together all the facts of a comprehending agency, whether on the limited field of humanity, or of a divine operation in nature, or of a di-

vine government over au ethical system of fallen beings, and finding in all that the only law is that of a
free personality, and that without such compass of a
personality in liberty no comprehending as fact is any
where given, we have an induction sufficiently broad
for deducing the general law of all comprehension;
and this law in the facts is the precise correlate of
the apriori idea of all comprehension, and thus gives
science to the operation of reason. We have as demonstrative a science, for an intelligent *comprehension*
of universal humanity and universal nature, as for
the *conjunction* of phenomena into a nature of things,
and for the *conjunction* of the diverse in quality into
definite phenomena. We have thus the science of
our entire intellectual being, including the functions of
the Sense, the Understanding, and the Reason. This
is all that we have proposed to ourselves, and in this
we have a complete philosophy of the human mind—
a *Rational Psychology.*

We comprehend the Universe, and may give an ontological demonstration of the being of a personal Deity, but we leave this Deity himself uncomprehended
and incomprehensible by any finite intellect. God is
no subject for human science. If we may demonstrate *that* he is, we can still attain to no such law of
being which shall give to us an adequate apprehension of *what* he is. "Canst thou by searching find
out God? canst thou find out the Almighty to perfection? It is as high as heaven, what canst thou-

do? deeper than hell, what canst thou know? The measure thereof is longer than the earth and broader than the sea." "There is no searching of his understanding."

APPENDIX TO THE REASON.

AN ONTOLOGICAL DEMONSTRATION OF THE VALID BEING OF THE SUPERNATURAL.

A COMPREHENDING Reason in its process of operation has now been fully obtained both as subjective idea and objective fact, and in this is a complete science of the reason as faculty for comprehension and in which we conclude our examination of the whole field of Rational Psychology. As in our completed science of the sense which is faculty for conjunction, and also of the understanding which is faculty for connection, we found the data for an ontological demonstration of the valid being of the objects given in each faculty, so here it may be expected, that the science of the reason will furnish the data for an ontological demonstration of the objects cognized by it in its functions of a comprehending agency. These are, the finite personality in humanity; the absolute person as author and governor of nature; and the consummation of his final end of a universal system in some future state of moral existence. Our whole work will thus be concluded in this outline of a demonstration for the valid being of the supernatural, in the several respects of THE SOUL, GOD and IMMORTALITY. From what has preceded, a bare statement is sufficient.

1. *The valid being of the Soul.*—The conception of the soul as an existence which is supernatural includes more than living and sentient being, and a higher capacity of action than from any promptings of appetite or general judgments of greatest gratification deduced from experience. All this is conditioned and held in necessity by somewhat that has gone before, and is thus bound in the linked connections of nature, and through its most subtle analysis or in its highest generalization can be but nature still, making no possible approximation towards the supernatural. There must be an existence which is ethical, and which in the right of its own personality may act independently, and in liberty, and feel a conscious responsibility for such action. Is there a process of demonstration for such valid being as a Soul?

Two sources of argumentation may be taken.

(1.) *The fact of a comprehending agency.*—Neither a conjoining nor a connecting agency could attain the conception of an operation of comprehension, much less that either could actually comprehend. An acting liberty, as rational personality, can alone comprehend any thing as having a proper origin and consummation. The fact therefore, that man comprehends nature in the compass of an absolute personality is demonstration that he is Soul.

(2.) *The facts as given in an ethical experience.*—Were there the conception of an ethical personality, as soul somehow attained, still no mere conception of soul could give the actual facts of its rational agency. The following, among other facts, are in actual being —imperatives controlling all appetites ; affections above all sentient emotions ; reciprocal complacency between moral personalities ; and more especially a capacity to resist all the conditions of nature and stand firm on the ground of duty—and the fact that man has such experience is proof that he is Soul.

2. *The valid existence of God.*—There are three lines of demonstration.

(1.) *The fact that all atheistic speculations are from the antinomy of the discursive faculty as understanding, and which have been shown to be delusive.*—This delusion removed, the teleological argument for an author and governor of nature, derived from the traces of design in nature, remains irrefragible.

(2.) *The fact of new forces originating in nature.*—Such facts have been before given, and could not come of nature. No mere conception of a God could give such facts. The facts are, and they demonstrate that a God is.

(3.) *The fact that an ethical system is in being.*—This has beforehand been made manifest. Such ethical system can neither originate from nor be controlled by any thing in nature. That it is, is demonstration that an absolute ethical person as moral Lord and Judge exists.

3. *The validity of the Soul's Immortality.*—The existence of humanity is itself origin for the rights and imperatives in an ethical human system. Obedience universally to these imperatives is a consummation of the system in its perfection. But as fact, the law universal is not kept. The moral system is thus in its depravity, and if left to its own action its consummation in its moral perfection is quite hopeless. What *ought* to be certainly will *not* be, from the system's own action. Is there then any way of demonstrating the consummation of a moral system, and in this, demonstrating that the soul shall be immortal?

The process is as follows. The truly virtuous man has a righteous expectation of happiness; and his hope rests upon an imperative that his blessedness be equal to his merit. The vicious ought to anticipate misery equal to his demerit. The virtuous and vicious ought so to be placed, that the wickedness of the one shall not interfere with the liberty, endanger the virtue, nor diminish the bliss, of the other. The virtuous have not, however, what they might hope for; the vicious have not what they should fear; and the action of the bad perpetually annoys the good. If what ought to be is to be, an ethical sovereign must make it so to be. And unless morality is a figment, and all our ethical experience a chimera, such a consummation must some way be effected; hence, on this ground alone a strong *faith* in the being of God, and of a future state, might be cultivated. But at the most it would be faith, and not science. There would be facts in our conscious imperatives showing what *ought* to be, but we could not thus reach the facts for demonstrating, that what ought to be in fact *will be*. But if now we add what has already been attained, in the ontological demonstration of the actual being of a God, then we have sufficient for a conclusive proof. God *is ;* a future state of rewards and punishments *ought to be ;* the existence of God is a guarantee that what ought to be surely will be. God is ethical goodness, and it is impossible that he should deny himself. It is thus infallible that the soul shall live on in its obedience and bliss, or in its disobedience and misery, forever ; and also, that the time must come, when the separation of the righteous from the wicked shall effect the designed and demanded consummation of the moral system.